Dolce Vita
Confidential

ALSO BY SHAWN LEVY

King of Comedy: The Life and Art of Jerry Lewis

*Rat Pack Confidential: Frank, Dean, Sammy, Peter, Joey, and the
Last Great Showbiz Party*

*Ready, Steady, Go! The Smashing Rise and Giddy Fall of
Swinging London*

The Last Playboy: The High Life of Porfirio Rubirosa

Paul Newman: A Life

The Rat Pack

De Niro: A Life

Dolce Vita

Confidential

Fellini, Loren, Pucci,
Paparazzi, and the
Swinging High Life of
1950s Rome

SHAWN LEVY

W. W. NORTON & COMPANY

Independent Publishers Since 1923

New York • London

√ For information about permission to reproduce selections from this book,
write to Permissions, W. W. Norton & Company, Inc.,
500 Fifth Avenue, New York, NY 10110

For information about special discounts for bulk purchases, please contact
W. W. Norton Special Sales at specialsales@wwnorton.com or 800-233-4830

Manufacturing by Quad Graphics Fairfield
Book design by Chris Welch
Production manager: Louise Mattarelliano

Library of Congress Cataloging-in-Publication Data

Names: Levy, Shawn, author.
Title: Dolce vita confidential : Fellini, Loren, Pucci, paparazzi, and the
    swinging high life of 1950s Rome / Shawn Levy.
Description: First edition. | New York : W.W. Norton & Company, [2016] |
    Includes bibliographical references and index.
Identifiers: LCCN 2016023023 | ISBN 9780393247589 (hardcover)
Subjects: LCSH: Rome (Italy)—Social life and customs—20th century. | Rome
    (Italy)—Intellectual life—20th century. | Celebrities—Italy—Rome—
    Biography. | Motion picture actors and actresses—Italy—Rome—Biography. |
    Artists—Italy—Rome—Biography. | Rome (Italy)—Biography.
Classification: LCC DG807.6 .L47 2016 | DDC 945.6/320925—dc23
LC record available at https://lccn.loc.gov/2016023023

W. W. Norton & Company, Inc.
500 Fifth Avenue, New York, N.Y. 10110
www.wwnorton.com

W. W. Norton & Company Ltd.
15 Carlisle Street, London W1D 3BS

1 2 3 4 5 6 7 8 9 0

For Shannon

Contents

Prologue

I t's a hot night, and the Eternal City is dead.

The Roman summer can feel like that. The concrete and marble and asphalt turn the streets into an oven, and any place you might think to go for relief is closed. The air is so thick it can stick in your throat—and good luck finding a doctor if it does.

It's *Ferragosto*, the end-of-summer holiday, 1958, and anyone who can afford to escape town has, leaving only tourists, priests, politicians, and the unlucky ones who work for them.

Tazio Secchiaroli doesn't exactly work for big shots, but he depends on them for a living. Slight, spry, starting to bald in his early thirties, he grew up about five miles from central Rome, where he now works photographing the comings and goings and lingerings and dallyings of celebrities and then selling the shots to newspapers and magazines—the more candid and sensational, the more lucrative. It's his business to know who's in town and, more important, who's out *on* the town. And so, as almost every night, he heads to a small stretch of road near the Villa Borghese, a hot spot that pulses, twitches, and seethes with enough energy to make it seem as if the whole city is crammed full and awake.

Few Romans visit Via Veneto. But for foreigners with money, especially those in the movie business, the north end of this wide boulevard, with its posh hotels and cafés and nightclubs, just up the hill from the Capuchin Catacombs, is the heart of modern Rome—which makes it important to some Romans as well.

Secchiaroli is among a throng of a dozen or so photographers who haunt the street seeking famous faces. Most nights, no matter if the rest of town is quiet, Via Veneto hums with movie stars, jet-setters, chancers, gigolos, noblemen, poets, dreamers. Just by being on the right corner and keeping alert, a guy with a sharp eye, a steady hand, and a Rolleiflex can make a month's expenses in a single fortunate second.

This particular night, though, Secchiaroli and his chums scour sidewalk tables, barstools, taxi queues, and back alleys and come up empty. The movie people and their claques of hangers-on have fled the city. There's not even a pretty girl newly come to Rome from the provinces to seek her fortune: *È morto.*

At midnight, the hunt bootless, their cameras unused, a few decide to go for dinner—and *not* in some overpriced Via Veneto tourist trap. They drive off in Pierluigi Praturlon's Fiat, and then, a few hours later, return to make one last sweep of the strip before calling it a night.

They're cruising slowly, looking for anybody worth spending a flashbulb on, when the pinch-faced Praturlon shouts, "There's Farouk!" and hits the brakes.

And, in fact, there Farouk is, all three hundred pounds of him, the exiled Egyptian king who has made Rome his home and the tables of the Café de Paris, where he is now stationed, his court.

Inscrutable, gluttonous, distrustful of the press, Farouk passes time, between epic meals and trysts with prostitutes, staring out at the Via Veneto parade. He's such a fixture on the street that nobody bothers to take his picture anymore. But on a night like this. . . .

Without a word, like a seasoned wolf pack, the photographers spill into the night. Praturlon parks in the middle of the street and strides toward Farouk, camera and flash firing; Umberto Guidotti gets close to the sidewalk terrace, which is bordered by boxes of potted flowers, and shoots; and Secchiaroli, the one they call *Il Mitragliatrice Umana* ("The Human Machine Gun") in honor of his rapid-fire technique, leaps over the flower beds and gets one off from close-in: a full-on assault.

From out of the dark and quiet, Farouk and company are beset by blinding bursts of light, mechanical pops and hisses, darting figures. The king's Albanian bodyguards react instinctively to what looks like an assassination attempt. They grab Secchiaroli but are immediately surprised by their boss, who has leapt from the table with impressive alacrity and is trying to get his hands on the camera. Giving Farouk room to move, the bodyguards loosen their grip on the photographer, who scoots free.

(Later, Secchiaroli will have a fine shot of the king seated against a stone wall, caught by surprise, staring right at the lens, just about to rouse to fury. But Guidotti will have the real prize: a blurry, shadowy photo of Farouk trying to wrestle Secchiaroli's equipment away from him.)

A few cops show up, but by then the photographers have scattered. Not randomly, though: word has come that another Via Veneto stalwart, actress Ava Gardner, is arriving at Bricktop's, a nearby nightclub, in the company of her current costar (and, it is whispered, inevitably, her lover), Tony Franciosa. As Franciosa is married, to another actress, Shelley Winters, this is potential gold.

Somehow, once again, Secchiaroli is first to arrive on the scene and gets closest to the center. He moves right in on Franciosa and *bam*! Again, flashes and crackles blind and startle the target, who clutches the nearest photographer, not Secchiaroli but Giancarlo Bonora. But Franciosa has no bodyguards, no chance: Bonora wriggles away, and the lot of them skitter off.

Now, though, there's blood in the water, so presently they're back, camped outside the nightclub, waiting to see who'll emerge with whom. At about 4:30 in the morning, they're disappointed: Ava comes out of Bricktop's on the arm of her press agent; Franciosa follows some minutes later, all little smiles and waves of his hand: *Bastardo*.

Still, it's not yet dawn, which means that there may yet be something going on. And what should fate serve up as the dessert of this impromptu three-course meal but Anthony Steel, the big-jawed, barrel-chested English action movie star as famous for his wife, Swedish sexpot Anita Ekberg, as for enjoying his drink and blowing his stack.

When Secchiaroli and company find him, Steel is already revved up, quarreling with Ekberg in a car idling at the valet station outside the Vecchia Roma restaurant. Again, flashes and pops, and, again, fury: Steel staggers from the car, fists clenched, lips pursed, gaze watery, knees buckled as if he's just been socked on the snout. He lunges toward a nearby photographer, it doesn't matter which, only to give up after a few uncertain strides, too drunk, simply, to do anything else.

The couple's driver stares, stock-still, at a loss for protocol. Ekberg stays discreetly in the car. And Secchiaroli captures a perfect series of shots of Steel's impotent rampage, easily the best stuff of the night. You could animate them with a Dixieland sound track and have a comedy hit; for sure they'll make for a big sale.

The photographers call time on their work, their vigilance, instincts, and cheek well rewarded, the rising sun gilding them as they drive to their darkrooms and their beds.

Within days, word—and *pictures*—of their wild night makes their way all over Rome; then, via the tabloid media, throughout Italy; and then to France, England, Germany, even the U.S.A., where nothing quite like this spree has ever been heard of.

Rome is supposed to be dead in August; everyone says so.

But in August 1958 something is definitely happening in Rome.

Introduction

What can you possibly say about Rome?

That it's eternal? That all roads lead to it? That it wasn't built in a day? That when there you should do as the locals do?

Please.

For millennia, Rome has embodied and repelled every cliché, description, and act of comprehension or explanation applied to it.

As a city, it has been built and destroyed and rebuilt by—and has celebrated and signified and outlasted—caesars and barbarians and popes and Fascists and prophets and artists and pilgrims and schemers and migrants and lovers and fools.

As a symbol, it has contained almost infinite meaning, allure, and resonance, a vessel that appears entirely full and that nonetheless can absorb virtually anything poured into it. The concept of infinity may have been conceived in ancient Greece, but it arguably finds, like so many Greek inventions, its most apt instance in Rome. "How many Romes there are," sighed the English travel writer H. V. Morton in 1957, citing, among other Romes, the ecclesiatical, the diplomatic, the archaeological, the artistic, and the everyday. But, truly, he could have expressed the same sentiment any time during the previous two thousand years and been just as correct. Rome *is* eternal, all roads *do* lead to it, and the locals, with their daily acquaintance with depths of history, art, culture, religion, and eccentricity, really *do* offer a model for living, whether you are in Rome or not.

Rome has been a lodestar in the constellation of Western culture for thousands of years, partly because a certain nexus of lifestyle, manners, ethos, fashion, sensation, and art has coalesced in the city again and again, like a crystal or a reef, drawing and captivating the world's attention. To live life *alla Romana* has meant different things at different times, but among those meanings has always been, surely, to live fully and sweetly, in beautiful form and happy company, with an attitude of knowing-but-not-entirely-caring, at a high rate, in plain view, steeped in confidence and élan and flair, and liable to cause jealous pangs everywhere else.

It was true in the time of Cicero; it was true in the time of Michelangelo; it was true in the time of Keats. And it was, improbably, true once again not long after World War II, when, the capital city of a nation that had just been defeated and disgraced in a conflict in which it had inarguably been one of the villains, Rome stood as a shining light of style, culture, and ways of living for the outside world.

In the immediate aftermath of the war, huge swaths of Rome were little more than strata of new ruins atop all the ruins that had come before: the Americans, the British, and the Germans had all bombed the city, completely devastating the San Lorenzo district, just north of the main train station, and even striking Vatican City. Sizable portions of the population were homeless, jobless, hungry, or idle. The glories of the past were still intact—Rome was largely spared the far more devastating bombardment that was suffered by such industrial centers as Milan and Turin, partly because Pope Pius XII begged the world not to destroy the city. But to all eyes it appeared in most every way exactly what it was: a defeated capital, the seat of a vanquished empire, staggered, battered, bloodied.

And yet there were signs of vitality and even sparks of brightness.

In and around that rubble, a small group of filmmakers who had been active before the war created brave new works that explored the human struggles of the moment—actually got right down into them and painted them with vigorous respect for realism, with honesty and empathy. Their movies put a new face on a bruised nation and, almost incidentally, launched a new type of cinema that would become common the world over.

There were bona fide bohemians, freed of the overbearing yoke of fascism, creating demimondes in bars, cafés, and studios tucked into the center of the city: painters and sculptors and poets and novelists and musicians who had kept the flames of art kindled through the war, however dimly, and were ready to stoke them into a fire of making and sharing and being seen and heard and read.

There were other creators, of elegant and stylish things to wear—because it was Rome and Italy and how one looked mattered, as it always had since togas were the fashion. You could always, but *always*, count on a Roman at least to try to present a *bella figura*, a beautiful form, even when everything else in his or her life was a wreck.

There were renegade lifestylists, people who were intent on bringing to Rome some of the vitality that had invigorated Paris and Berlin and New York in previous decades but who had been stifled by moralists and Blackshirts and the Catholic church, aristocrats and rebels and avant-gardists, often from other countries, other worlds, with a shared passion to avoid the usual thing and to embrace the sensual, the iconoclastic, the daring.

And there was a small clutch of young men with cameras and flash bulbs, freelance photographers whose depictions of the city and its people and its extravaganzas and its crimes and its sensations and, most of all, its celebrated visitors were greedily gobbled up by a media culture that, too, was operating with new vigor now that the pall cast by Benito Mussolini and his Fascist censors no longer loomed.

In the first years of Rome's recovery from the war, these claques of innovators and strivers and revolutionaries worked on parallel, independent tracks; even those with an eye focused on more than one of them couldn't see that they would soon converge. From that vantage, it wasn't readily evident that there was a crescence, that something new was being created in more than one nook of the city or the culture, that there would soon come a blending, a catalysis, an explosive knocking-together of people and projects and incidents from all of these areas of activity into a single cultural moment—a boom. But it would happen, and all within a few square miles of the city, in its watering holes, studios, hotels, cafés, courthouses, darkrooms, and, famously, on one tree-lined boulevard mostly noted theretofore for being a place where very little worth noting ever happened. The things that would be done and made and, especially, photographed in Rome in those years would transform the city, at least in reputation, from the symbol of a vanquished empire into a font of new and enviable energies, artworks, ways of living.

It was a relatively sweet and naïve time when it was something of a novelty to peek into the actual private lives of celebrities (as opposed to the public relations versions of their lives); when widely imitated ideas and tastes in everyday fashion came from the workshops of clothing designers; when the shooting of a movie could be an event in and of itself; when travel to a world capital was a once-in-a-lifetime dream; and when the idea that packs of photographers would roam a city at night attempting to capture images of famous faces in flagrante delicto was almost too unimaginable to be taken for real.

In later days, everything a bold-faced name said or did would be potential fodder for revelation, scuttlebutt, shaming; the dominant fashion influences emerged from the streets; the entertainment industry ballyhooed itself numbingly, endlessly; and the media, as pervasive as bacteria, pried into every niche and navel, feeding itself gluttonously and discarding the icons it created with all the ceremony and deference one might accord a used tissue.

But in the fifteen or twenty years after World War II, when filmmakers and movie stars and fashion designers and street photographers and hedonists were colliding in the cafés, nightclubs, salons, ateliers, back lots, and cobblestoned streets of Rome, the combination of those strains of culture—high and low, official and illicit, elegant and crass—was a unique and in many ways unprecedented blend. For a few years, Rome was, once again, the capital of the world—a new world, built of stardust and chic clothes and the titillation of scandal and the buzz of motor scooter engines and the flash of camera bulbs. Bits of it had existed elsewhere previously, even in Rome, but never before had it all come together in the particular form which it took in that place and time, a form that would still dominate popular culture more than a half century later.

This is the story of how that came to be, how an unlikely but inevitable collection of people, businesses, incidents, and artworks combined into something that would be easily recognized later but had no precedence, no form, no name previously.

It's a story that begins with a destitute man and his son looking for a bicycle, follows with a newspaperman on a Vespa scooting an errant princess through picturesque ruins, and ends with another newspaperman, among a throng of hungover aristocrats, staring at the bloated corpse of a sea monster on a wind-swept beach.

It's a story of how a nation and its capital emerged from a decade of war—both global and civil—and, amid the loss and ruin and pain, gave rise to the contemporary mélange of glitter, scandal, commerce, style, and sensation that we recognize as "popular culture," of how the city of the caesars and the popes and the Blackshirts managed, for a decade or so, to galvanize the world's attention as a showcase of elegance, modernity, sophistication, license, and style.

It's a story of film stars and race-car drivers; of fashion plates and paparazzi and slumming nobles; of murder and movies and celebrity and shadows; of rebirth and glory and decay; of Fiat convertibles and sharp lapels and plunging necklines and big sunglasses and endless cigarettes; of jazz and stripteases and parties until dawn; of a Rome as decadent, as world-wise, as sensual as that of Nero: the Eternal City, yes, of course, but very, very *now*.

It spans an era that ranged, on screen and in life, from *The Bicycle Thief* to *Roman Holiday* to *La Dolce Vita*; from the new looks in ski and beach clothes designed by Emilio Pucci to the classically luxurious couture gowns of Valentino; from the emergence of curvy Italian actresses typified by Gina Lollobrigida to the triumph of the Neapolitan ugly duckling Sophia Loren; from the laughable Latin lover Rossano Brazzi to the most reluctant and charming of leading men, Marcello Mastroianni; from the neorealism of Vittorio De Sica, Roberto Rossellini, and Luchino Visconti to the rococo dreamscapes of Federico Fellini and the austere nightmares of Michelangelo Antonioni; from a few photographers taking pictures of a wedding and a murder trial to an omnipresent cadre of ravenous cameramen who'd stop at nothing to get a compromising photo; from a simple movie about the Resistance shot on stolen film stock to a gargantuan epic that would bankrupt a Hollywood studio; from an Italy that was staggered, bloodied, and decimated by war to an Italy that was swank enough and savvy enough to host the most modern Olympic games ever seen.

Throughout these years, as Rome's position at the acme of modern style and high living and filmcraft grew increasingly evident, certain threads resonated like motifs in a symphony: the Roman love of personal beauty and self-presentation, of the *bella figura* and *bellezza*; the intricate back-and-forth symbiosis of Italy and America, in fashion, in cinema, in shared heritage; the inscrutability and immutability of Rome in and of itself, eternal not only because of its age but because some fundamental aspects of it would simply never change, no matter the vagaries of surface activity; and the birth of a new type of modern popular culture, where innovations in fashion and social manners, in the liveliest of twentieth-century arts, and in insatiable forms of news media all came together in a single petri dish, as it were, for the first time.

Si fueris Romae, Romano vivito more, said St. Ambrose centuries ago: "When in Rome, do as the Romans do."

And as easy as it might be to dismiss the sentiment as a cliché, it has, like so many clichés, a germ of truth. Romans, before St. Ambrose and often since, have had a knack for making people everywhere, whether they've ever been to Rome or not, want to live *alla Romana*. And in the years after World War II, between the bomb and the Beatles, they did it afresh in a way that still resonates today.

Dolce Vita
Confidential

Buzzing Through Ruins

In many ways, Rome would always be defined by ruin, by what has been left behind, by the layers of the past on top of which subsequent incarnations of the city have been built, often with bits and pieces cannibalized from the debris of prior civilizations and regimes. Etruscan Rome gave way to Imperial Rome and then, in turn, proto-Christian Rome and Papal Rome and Baroque Rome and Risorgimento Rome and Fascist Rome. Each epoch produced new strata of urbanization and architecture and culture and habit that became part of the Romes that followed, and those later Romes availed themselves freely, in the manner of heirs everywhere, to the heritage and patrimony that lay literally at their feet. Ruins, to Romans, were a basic condition of life, neither wonders to be admired nor obstacles to be overcome: a given, an inheritance, a resource to feed upon in the creation of yet another new Rome.

In 1945, just as after invasions by Visigoths and Ostrogoths and Vandals and Huns, Rome was a fresh landscape of destruction, a war zone that had endured occupation by Nazis, incursion by the Allies, and, most grievously, a civil war between cadres of the Fascist Blackshirts and the Partisan Resistance. Like cities all across Europe, it had been pummeled from the air, as well as by artillery attacks, by small-scale street fighting, by vendettas and looting. It was a city depleted of resources: food, medicine, fuel, and building materials were all in short supply if not nonexistent; scores of thousands of the displaced from throughout Italy were living in shacks, cellars, vacant schools, barracks, even caves on the city's outskirts; black marketeers of the most predatory sorts thrived (even salt was a precious commodity). Other sites on the Italian peninsula had, arguably, suffered more: the port city of Naples, the industrial center of Milan, and the medieval monastery town of Monte Cassino, virtually obliterated by Allied bombing. But Rome, as the capital city, was the most visible and palpable symbol of a nation brought to its knees in utter defeat.

It didn't matter, on the level of simple humanity, that Italy had been one of the bad guys, a black-shirted antagonist on the world stage even before officially joining Germany in the Axis pact of 1939. Rendered in numbers, the war's toll on the country was grave. A nation of 44.4 million, Italy lost 291,000 servicemen and 153,000 civilians as a direct result of the war. The survivors faced huge challenges in carrying forward. In cities with more than 50,000 residents, a total of 1.2 million homes had been destroyed; in Milan alone, nearly 70 percent of all housing was damaged or obliterated; nationwide, nearly half the surviving domiciles had no functioning kitchens, and three-quarters had no indoor bathrooms (by one accounting, fewer than 7 percent of Italians lived in homes with the trifecta of electricity, running water, and flush toilets). Up and down the peninsula, 40 percent of bridges and railway lines were incapacitated or in ruins. A full third of Italy's national wealth had been wiped off the books in less than a half dozen years, and the cost of living had increased more than twentyfold. When peacetime routines resumed, 20 percent of the workforce had no jobs to report to, and those who were lucky enough to find positions or return to their previous employment were working for wages roughly half those of prewar levels. Almost 95 percent of the ordinary family's income went to pay for food, and even that was subsistence level: the average caloric intake of an Italian adult in the immediate aftermath of the war was three-quarters of what it had been twenty years earlier, with almost no meat or sugar included in the typical family's regular diet.

The situation was as dire as the global depression of the 1930s had been, and it fomented political uncertainty. With Mussolini's Fascist regime crushed, Italians had to choose among several paths in reconstituting their government: monarchy, democratic republic, and communism all seemed viable. The latter was, of course, anathema to the war's Allied victors, who sought through various means to sway Italy and other recovering nations to the Western side of the incipient Cold War. The Americans, in particular, were keen to keep Italy in the democratic fold, and they were especially well suited to the job. Not only had the United States emerged from the war victorious, wealthy, and alliance minded, but it had strong ties to Italy thanks to the immigration surge of the late nineteenth and early twentieth centuries, when more than four million Italians arrived in American harbors—the largest influx from any European country, some four times the number of Irish immigrants who came to the United States in the wake of the potato famine. Throwing in the historical curiosity that the Americas were discovered (so to speak) by one Italian (the Genoese Christopher Columbus) and named for another (the Florentine Amerigo Vespucci), adding the coincidence that among America's cultural heroes were a singer (Frank Sinatra), a baseball player (Joe DiMaggio), and an elected official (Fiorello La Guardia) of Italian descent, and considering the American political and humanitarian will to help a hobbled nation back onto its feet, it was no surprise that Italy should be wooed into the Western fold with the twin lures of cultural kinship and raw economic incentive.

From the very end of the war, the United States supported Italy with food and medical aid, military assistance, management and manpower for reconstruction, and imports of raw materials, all of which helped the defeated nation's hobbled economy back onto steady footing. When the European Recovery Program, better known as the Marshall Plan, began in earnest in early 1948, Italy was the third-highest recipient of U.S. funds (after Great Britain and France, both wartime allies). In its first four years, the Marshall Plan delivered upward of $1.2 billion in aid to Italy,[1] helping the nation recover materially and, not coincidentally, helping to steer the Western-leaning Christian Democratic party into political power.[2] Every boatload of grain and cotton and manufactured goods was a big occasion, and the U. S. ambassador to Italy, James Clement Dunn, celebrated the arrival of each hundredth ship with a ceremony and a speech. For more than a half century, Italians

---

1 Equivalent to $11.9 billion in 2016; by 1962, the combination of Marshall funds, military support, and other contributions totaled some $5.5 billion, or $43.5 billion in 2016 dollars.

2 The Christian Democrats would lead or play a key role in every government formed in Italy into the twenty-first century.

had nurtured the myth of the immigrant going off to the States and returning home wealthy; now, in a sense, all of Italy was in the shoes of that fortunate pilgrim, enjoying American largesse without having to undertake the arduous journey to Ellis Island and back.

If it was easy to credit Italy's American cousins with the nation's turnaround toward recovery, it would also not be entirely true. Some forms of Marshall Plan aid were sparks for Italian industries that had managed to survive the war in something like viable form. For one, the textile industry, long a source of Italy's economic strength and cultural influence, was ready to ramp up into productive gear soon after the fighting ended, and would become part of a lucrative symbiosis. American raw materials such as cotton and wool, shipped to Italy, would be transformed into fabrics and, later, styled into garments that became popular in, among many places around the world, America—a true win-win that spiraled upward for decades.

And there were other native industries that not only resulted in industrial growth but in improved quality of life for Italians—as well as in a new sort of cultural cachet for the nation that, somehow, would be almost entirely forgiven for its role in World War II not long after the last shots were fired. Among the most visible, in Italy and beyond, was the manufacture of motor vehicles, especially automobiles. Italian luxury and performance cars from such manufacturers as Alfa Romeo, Maserati, Lancia, and Isotta Fraschini were highly esteemed before the war and presently recovered much of their prestige. More impressive, the big daddy of Italian carmakers, Fiat,[3] had been and would soon be again one of the largest producers of automobiles in the world, and Enzo Fer-

3 The name is an acronym for Fabbrica Italiana Automobili Torino—roughly, the Italian Automobile Works of Turin.

rari was about to launch his world-conquering marque in the tiny town of Maranello, a few miles east of Bologna.

But those were small steps compared to an Italian innovation that combined practicality, affordability, style, and flair and achieved international renown. In 1946, the Piaggio company, which had produced locomotive and aviation equipment near Genoa since 1884, introduced a new product that turned personal transportation into something specifically and emphatically Italian. After a few designs were rejected, an aeronautical engineer named Corradino d'Ascanio crafted what patent papers referred to as a "motorcycle of a rational complexity of organs and elements combined with a frame with mudguards and a casing covering the whole mechanical part." It was a motor scooter, built on an engine that had been conceived (but never used) as a starter for airplanes, and it was known commercially, when it hit the marketplace, as the Vespa (or "wasp") for the buzzing sound of its motor.

With its sleek styling and low cost, the Vespa 98 (so named for the displacement of its engine) became a massive best seller throughout Italy and, soon, everywhere else. Its distinctive look—with a thin front shield connected by a flat floorboard to a rounded rear unit, where the saddle sat above an enclosed engine—was widely imitated and recognized as a symbol of Italian style, ingenuity, and vitality. The modern appearance of this new-generation motor scooter, like a comma on its back, was also practical. Because the rider didn't straddle the engine like a horse but rather sat atop it somewhat daintily, and because its front shield offered some protection from the elements, the Vespa could be used by men in suits or women in skirts—by working grown-ups, in short. It was inexpensive (Piaggio was a pioneer among Italian companies in offering installment plans), and it was relatively easy to maintain or repair. Its characteristic playful appearance and rattling buzz soon became familiar throughout Italy and Europe and beyond—one of the first true heralds of a youthful, fashionable new world.

Only a few thousand Vespas were sold in 1947, but that number rose every year. In 1956, not a decade after the first model was released, Piaggio marked the sale of its one millionth scooter, a figure boosted, no doubt, by the spectacle of the Hollywood stars Gregory Peck and Audrey Hepburn getting around town by scooter in *Roman Holiday* (1953). The second million took less than four years to sell. Other brands followed: Lambretta, founded in 1947, which produced a similarly popular line of motor scooters, and, three years later, Ducati, which began business by mounting small engines on bicycle frames before switching after several years to motorcycles. The other brands had their ardent adherents: there were Lambretta owners who wouldn't be caught dead on a Piaggio scooter, and owners of all brands formed groups with identifying badges and codes of conduct vis-à-vis those who favored rival models. But the Vespa was the archetype and the eponym. And it was an epitome of Italian design and resourcefulness combining to turn what might have been liabilities (a rainy day scooter ride was no one's idea of fun, and two was a crowd on the tiny seat) into an emblem of élan.

2 "An Old River Among the Great Hotels"

The Rome of 1948 was hardly a likely site from which a new blend of modern popular culture might start to emerge. Four years after the city was liberated by the Allies, three years after the execution of Benito Mussolini, two years after the abolition of the monarchy, and the year after the enactment of a new constitution, Italy was remaking itself from scratch, and Rome was the place where many of the energies of reconstruction, especially the cultural energies, were born.

Birth—or, more properly, rebirth—was a fitting place to start. Some aspects of the economy and infrastructure had been so decimated by the war that, to the casual eye, recovery seemed impossible. The government hadn't been truly representative in a quarter century. The people had been sapped in spirit by decades of fascism and worn, maimed, and beaten down by warfare and occupation and resistance. And yet, in a sense, there was liberation in it: Italy would be permitted to govern, reconstruct, and redefine itself, on its own terms, in its own image, if it could.

It was hardly an overnight thing, but in 1948 enough of it had begun to gel that the outline of a future state, a future culture, could be seen. In April, the Marshall Plan, named after its chief architect and advocate, Secretary of State George Marshall, had been signed into law by President Harry Truman. That same month, the first properly democratic election held in Italy in more than twenty years led to the installation of the conservative Christian Democratic party, which netted a 48 percent plurality. In November, Vittorio De Sica's masterly poignant *Ladri di Biciclette* (*The Bicycle Thief*), was released on Italian screens, forming with Roberto Rossellini's *Germany Year Zero* and Luchino Visconti's *La Terra Trema* a powerhouse trinity of movies revealing to the whole world the vitality of Italian cinema. The year saw the birth of the Centro Italiano della Moda, the Italian Fashion Institute, which aimed to unite the production of textiles with the creation of high fashion. It also saw the first racing victory of a car built by Enzo Ferrari in his quest to create the world's finest Grand Prix vehicles. It saw Gino Bartali, the most beloved athlete in the beloved sport of cycling, win the Tour de France, an international triumph in which the entire Italian population could bask.

And on Via dei Condotti, in the shadow of Trinità dei Monti, in the Antico Caffè Greco, where Goethe and Keats and Liszt and Byron and Ibsen and Wagner and generations of Italian intellectuals and musicians and writers and painters had taken their coffee and wine and leisure, an insurrection was underfoot. The Greco was like a museum, dating back to 1760 and hushed and reverent in a way that was at once charming and obsolete. "Everything is chaste and refined and measured," the novelist Ugo Moretti recalled of the café. "It's the atmosphere created by the old plush, or by the portraits of romantic souls hanging from the moldings or stuck in the frames of the mirrors, or by the sneezes of English poets that condition the air." Like many things in Rome, the Greco was as it had always been, which was part of its allure. But things outside the café weren't standing still, and Moretti and his art-mad friends, who had survived the war and had begun to revive themselves as a community, could no longer feel at ease in a place that seemed so intent on eschewing the pulse of modernization.

So, on an unrecorded date in 1948, they revolted. En masse, they decided that the time of the Greco was over, and they decamped around the corner to Via del Babuino, the half-mile-long avenue that connected Piazza di Spagna to Piazza del Popolo. The place they chose to gather in, mere paces from the Spanish Steps, was a spot called Il Baretto, and the scruffy band of writers and painters associated with the neighborhood began to haunt it almost nonstop. Il Baretto became famous and even notorious in the coming years as the center of the first underground culture to blossom in Rome after the war—arguably its first of the twentieth century. Fascism had cost Rome the bohemian heyday that other European capitals—Paris, London, Berlin—had enjoyed in the 1920s and '30s. Now, however, the city would have something to compete with decadent demimondes elsewhere, right in the bit of Rome that had, for centuries, been a hub of tourism, painting, fashion—an injection of iconoclasm, sensationalism, vice. By leaving a fusty old coffeehouse and making a new home in a dive bar, the *gente al Babuino*, as Moretti called them—the "people of the Babuino"—were helping push their town and their nation into a new era.

The Baretto was extremely well situated to become the home of a new flavor of Roman culture. It was located[1] in the midst of the Campo Marzio *rione* (or district) of the city, the traditional "foreigners' quarter," which was enlivened by a continual infusion of outsiders, with their imported ideas, clothes, and habits. It sat amid the fashion houses of the Piazza di Spagna and, more crucially, almost directly across the road from the southern end of Via Margutta, Rome's equivalent of Paris's Montmartre, London's Chelsea, or New York's Greenwich Village.

Via Margutta looked just the way an enclave of artists ought to. It was short—just a few hundred yards—and narrow and cobblestoned and lined with shade trees. The buildings were painted ocher and mustard and tomato and burnt orange and covered with ivy. They lined the Pincio hill side of the street without cross traffic, allowing pedestrians to walk the middle of the road freely and painters to set up easels outside without being interrupted too often by the flow of autos. It was almost too picturesque—one of those locations that would've been favored by artists as a subject even if they hadn't lived there—and surprisingly hushed in comparison with Via del Babuino, where cars and trucks and taxis careered just a short block away. Via Margutta was home to low-priced cafés and framing shops and an artists' club—the Associazione Artistica Internazionale (also known as the Circolo Artistico), which the young artists said they hated but secretly wished to belong to so that they could sit by its fireplaces in comfy chairs during the worst of the winter.

For several centuries, because it was built along a fetid stream

---

1 And, as of 2016, still was.

that ran down from the Pincio hill, Via Margutta had an unfashionable air, the site of stables for the palazzos of Via del Babuino and, later, the shops and living quarters of stonemasons, woodcarvers, and metalsmiths. Drawn by the tradition of artisans in the street and the very low rents, painters and sculptors—Italian and foreign—had begun to gravitate into Via Margutta as early as the eighteenth century, forming a thriving community and, over time, encouraging the establishment of art galleries and art supply shops and of bars, restaurants, and clubs catering to the creative class.

By 1948, Via Margutta and the surrounding area were uncontested as the mecca for artists aspiring to careers in Rome, and when Moretti and his chums decided that they would shun the Antico Caffè Greco, the street and the nearby Baretto became the focal point of the scene around them: a decadent, sensual, hardscrabble, melodramatic world infused with sex, booze, drugs, criminal undertones, the high and low comedy of people with great ambition and little money, and the youthful sense, so common after the war, of having the wind at one's back and a dazzling, modern future ahead.

The Baretto wasn't much to look at: ten or twelve tables, a mirror over the bar, a cross-eyed waiter; maybe forty customers could be accommodated comfortably. But in its heyday it felt there were as many as two hundred people in the place, according to Moretti, "as if its walls were elastic." And the crowd consisted, almost entirely, of painters, writers, models, dilettantes, posturing existentialists, slumming aristocrats, bohemian foreigners, and local underworld types: drug dealers, prostitutes, pimps, thieves. For a few years, when Rome still seemed sleepy, destitute, mired in its past, the Baretto was undeniably up-to-date, a hot spot to rival anything New York or Paris could offer at the time.

The art crowd gravitated toward other spots: La Tazza d'Oro, another bar off Via dei Condotti, which also drew customers who had declared the Greco dead to them; Gelobar, not far from the Greco, a small tavern that would eventually be home to Rome's first jukebox; Rosati and Canova, both in the Piazza del Popolo, long favored by a tonier crowd as well as by writers (per Moretti, Canova was "frequented by high-class intellectuals and hence by third-rate poets with the proofs of their new books in their pockets"); the restaurants Peppino's, aka Filthy Peppino's, where it was rumored that the dishes were cleaned by hungry cats, Taverna Margutta, which offered credit to artists, and Menghi's, which also let artists run up tabs but was far more persistent in collecting payment; and Piccolo Slam and Siviglia, a pair of nightclubs in which the law was broken so frequently and openly that police raids were common and, in both cases, terminal.

But Baretto was the centerpiece of the scene, and it developed an international reputation. "The Baretto was so famous," Moretti recalled, "that even foreign artists, especially those from Paris and New York, got off at the Stazione Termini, took a taxi, and said 'Au Baretto' or 'To the Baretto' to the driver, and there wasn't a driver who didn't know where to take them." Even *The New York Times* took note of it, citing it, somewhat disingenuously, in a 1950 article on cheap dining options in Rome as "one of the little coffee shops which in Italy replace the corner drugstore (or at least the soda fountain)." Milk shakes were one of the few addictions in which the patrons of Baretto *didn't* indulge, but the point was made: every bohemian in Rome, from all of the city's blossoming creative fields, was, if only occasionally, on hand.

For those who found Baretto too louche, or the cafés on Piazza del Popolo too filled with third-raters, there was another redoubt in which to idle and kibbitz and pass away the hours of a slightly more genteel bohemian life, a street not far from Piazza di Spagna but at a sufficient distance that there might as well have been a moat separating them.

Via Vittorio Veneto was a sinuous boulevard that began at the Piazza Barberini and rose toward the Porta Pinciana, the ancient city wall at the foot of Pincio hill. In ancient times, the area was part of an imperial park where, it was said, Messalina, the wife of the Emperor Claudius, held orgies. In the seventeenth century, the land was enclosed within the Villa Ludovisi, an immense private estate and garden built by a cardinal and frequented by nobility, clergymen, and wealthy foreigners. The commanding height, looking out over the city toward St. Peter's and the setting sun, was an attraction—and it ensured that the villa was free, relatively, of the disease-carrying mosquitoes that plagued the low areas of the city around the Tiber. In 1873, no less a visitor than Henry James declared the Villa Ludovisi "the most delightful [place] in the world."[2]

But a little more than a decade later, during a real estate boom that followed the unification of Italy into a single nation, developers carved the Villa Ludovisi into parcels and built a new neighborhood, the Ludovisi district, with streets named for the regions of the new country: Campania, Sardegna, Sicilia, Liguria, Friuli, Lazio, Toscana. The main drag, which ran north/south with a pair of doglegs—one right, one left—along its course, was named for the Veneto region, and its upper reaches, nearest the Aurelian wall of the old city, were lined with horse chestnut trees and large apartment blocks for working-class families, with shops and cafés on

2 And he was quite aware of those mosquitoes, which carried what was known as "Roman Fever," the condition that killed the heroine of his novella *Daisy Miller*, who contracted it while dallying in the Colosseum by moonlight.

the street level. (The "Vittorio," or "victory," of the street's official name was added after World War I, in commemoration of an Italian military triumph at a town called, aptly enough, Vittorio Veneto, but nobody ever used the street's whole name when talking or writing about or visiting it.)

By the end of the nineteenth century, the upper end of the street, which had been designed for low-cost housing, became, contrary to the intentions of city planners, home to a more monied set. In the apartment blocks, small flats were combined into larger apartments or, in several cases, refitted as hotel rooms, and the restaurants and places of business on the street became more elegant and expensive. Among the debuts of the era was the Hotel Excelsior, at the northeast corner of Via Veneto and Via Boncompagni, with a signature cupola on its rooftop and five-star accommodations within. And several other deluxe hostelries sprang up: the Hotel Ambasciatori, the Grand Hotel Flora, the Regina, the Savoia.

If the upper end of Via Veneto took on a bourgeois and cosmopolitan hue that reminded visitors of Paris, the lower end, with the older buildings, remained distinctly Roman. Almost at the very bottom, just off the Piazza Barberini, stood Santa Maria della Concezione dei Cappuccini, a church that dated back to the seventeenth century and was home to a famous cemetery where the bones of thousands of monks had been used to form sculptures, architectural features, and dioramas illustrating moral lessons (which, of course, few of the habitués of the boulevard ever heeded). Just up the street was the Ministry of Industry, filled with politicians, bureaucrats, and lobbyists, and farther uphill still, at the northernmost bend in the road, was the Palazzo Margherita, built after the breakup of the Villa Ludovisi and purchased in 1931 by the United States for use as its embassy, a function it would serve into the twenty-first century.

During World War II, Via Veneto and its hotels changed hands along with the rest of Italy. The Nazis took over the Grand Hotel Flora and the Hotel Excelsior while they occupied Rome, looting the hotels of paintings and silverware and hosting all-night parties that were occasionally punctuated by furniture flying out of windows into the street. When the Allies arrived in 1944, the Germans retreated to the Villa Borghese and were permitted to leave without a shot, in accordance with a twenty-four-hour cease-fire requested by the pope. For a time after that, the Allied troops commandeered the big hotels as headquarters, behaving similarly riotously but spending money and, if only by contrast with the Nazis, earning the affections of the locals.

With the end of the war, Via Veneto came slowly back to life as a posh street. Near the hotels there was a celebrated barbershop, which one famous patron thought of as "a comforting, nineteenth-century place," so quiet that it resembled "a Swiss clinic for nervous disorders . . . an island in the pointless uproar of our lives."[3] But the street began, as well, to evince a small blush of bohemia. At the very top (and, technically, around the corner on Via di Porta Pinciana) was Mario's Bar, one of the first spots in Rome to offer jazz regularly. Down the hill there was Zeppa's, once a creamery but, by the late 1940s, the cheapest restaurant on the street, favored by students and by artists who, wandering over from the Campo Marzio, would often trade their work, to then be hung on the walls, for food and drink. A similarly long-haired atmosphere could be found at Rossetti's bookshop, for a time the most celebrated spot on Via Veneto, which sat between the tony cafés and shops around it like a crusty old uncle at a noisy family gathering. Rossetti's was

3 Another customer, Tennessee Williams, would immortalize the shop in *The Roman Spring of Mrs. Stone.*

the daily haunt of a large number of the city's best-known poets, novelists, and journalists, who took Via Veneto as their own and visited the cafés and bars along the street for meals or a drink or a coffee and then wandered back into the bookstore to gossip about the excesses and inanities they'd witnessed.

A staggering array of literary talent wandered up and down Via Veneto and spent hours sipping coffee and parsing one another's arguments around tables at those cafés: Alberto Moravia, Carlo Levi, Giuseppe Ungaretti, Salvatore Quasimodo, Cesare Zavattini, Cesare Pavese, Mario Soldati, Natalia Ginzburg. Combined they would sell millions of books, start hundreds of critical debates, and win every single writing prize that Italy (and in the case of the Nobel laureate Quasimodo, the world) had to offer.

An early eyewitness to this Parnassus was the struggling journalist and cartoonist Federico Fellini, who arrived in Rome as this activity was reaching a boil. But he never felt entitled, with his paltry credentials and white canvas shoes, to eavesdrop on, much less add a word to, such rarefied conversations. For him, Via Veneto, with the arches of the Porta Pinciana at its top and its hushed cafés and grand hotels, was like a forbidden paradise. "To my scared provincial eyes," he recalled, "it wasn't even Rome—it was some fairy-tale vision, Monte Carlo or Baghdad." He dared, he said, "put my nose into a café near Porta Pinciana only once," and, immediately feeling himself regarded by the waiters as if he were Charlie Chaplin's Little Tramp, he spun on his feet and left: too rich for his blood.

Among the most celebrated participants in the scene, and its greatest chronicler, was Ennio Flaiano, the gimlet-eyed journalist, novelist, playwright, screenwriter, essayist, and diarist who was born in 1910 in Pescara on the Adriatic coast of Abruzzi. Flaiano was one of those provincials who was destined to come to the big city, which he did in 1922 as a student. After high school, he briefly studied architecture but quit, finding enough work as a journalist to make a living. He did military service in the African campaigns of the mid- to late 1930s and, after being demobilized, returned to Rome to marry, start a family, and resume his writing career.

Flaiano was the sort of cynic who perceived deeply and immediately the pretenses, follies, and failings of his fellow humans and yet nevertheless was almost compulsively drawn to be among them. He fashioned himself a twentieth-century Martial or Juvenal and, in their vein, composed pointed, acid, unforgettable adages about the foibles of modernity, humanity, and, especially, his countrymen and fellow Romans: "In Italy, the shortest line between two points is an arabesque"; "One trait of the Italians is to hasten to the conqueror's aid"; "The Roman doesn't need to feel that he is different from what he is to exalt himself; he admires himself enough already"; "Never was there a period so favorable to narcissists and exhibitionists. Where are the saints? We will have to content ourselves with dying in the odor of publicity"; "The hairs in the soup are always there even if they are invisible to the naked eye."

When not pondering the dubious qualities of his fellow man or banging the typewriter or hustling for assignments, Flaiano passed days schmoozing with Levi, Soldati, and, especially, the poet Vincenzo Cardarelli along Via Veneto. He was paying bills with work as a freelance film critic, and, like many others, eventually found himself drawn into writing movies instead of writing about them. By the time the war shut down film production, he was making a name as a screenwriter, and when the Italian cinema revived, he was busily back at work.

But he always had eyes on a more indelible sort of fame. "'To do cinema,' for many, or for everybody, is a subsidiary and secondary activity," he wrote, and he spoke of his envy of Mario Soldati, who had two desks, one for screenwriting, one for writing fiction. Flaiano, too, had two desks, if only in his head, and on the more literary of them he wrote a novel, *Tempo di Uccidere* (literally *Killing Time* but translated into English as *The Short Cut*). On its publication in 1947, Flaiano received the very first Strega Prize, now considered the most prestigious award in Italian letters but at the time a matter of uncertain distinction, granted by a jury who were friendly with all the nominated writers and named for a liquor company whose owner happened to be a chum of the chief juror.

Flaiano never published another novel, perhaps because he was too busy writing movies. He was credited on a film per year from the war's end until 1950, when he was among the screenwriters on *Luci del Varietà*, a whimsical story about a theatrical troupe that was codirected by Alberto Lattuada and, in his debut, Federico Fellini. It marked the first of ten films that Flaiano and Fellini would write together over a span of fifteen years—during which time Flaiano received a whopping *fifty* screen credits in total.

But at the dawn of that extraordinary period of creativity, Flaiano was just another of the literary boulevardiers who gravitated among the central meeting places of his clan: the Greco on Via dei Condotti (the more domesticated writers never quit it), Rosati and Canova on Piazza del Popolo, and the string of cafés along Via Veneto. There, Flaiano reveled in his regular encounters with Cardarelli, by then an aged figure always decked out in a fur-lined coat, scarf, and hat, no matter the weather or time of day.

Cardarelli had come to Rome as a young journalist at the dawn of the twentieth century and then, after decades, remade himself as a poet, and a prize-winning one: A book of his verse took the second Strega Prize, in 1948. He was living out his final years in a small flat off Via Veneto, and he passed his days shifting between two spots: the one comfy chair in Rossetti's bookshop and the table nearest the door of the Caffè Strega, where he took all his meals and was doted upon by the ownership, who charged him the old prices even when the street became famous and the customers the sort of folks who didn't give a thought to money and might even have sniffed at bargains. Cardarelli had ceased writing, but he was a revered figure and an absolute staple of the scene. He could be caustic, belittling the purchases made by customers of Rossetti's or engaging in banter with his chum the painter and cartoonist Amerigo Bartoli. Bartoli was a short man, and one day, asked by a mutual acquaintance how the painter was getting on, Cardarelli replied, "He's not growing, he's not growing! At night he's nervous, he can't sleep, so he paces back and forth underneath his bed!" Bartoli got his revenge with an even more famous jibe, introducing Cardarelli, three years his elder, as Italy's "greatest dying poet."

This was the sort of back-and-forth that Flaiano relished, and during the years of his ascent as a screenwriter, there was no better place for it than Via Veneto. By day and early evening, he would visit Rossetti's; later he would wander up the hill to the string of cafes which had begun to dominate the strip: Caffè Rosati, Caffè Strega, Caffè Doney, and the Golden Gate. Like many such spots around the city, these offered outdoor seating at small tables that were protected from the sun by large umbrellas, adding a carnivalesque touch to the tree-lined boulevard and giving it an appearance that was even more deluxe and, in ways, for an ordinary Roman, unapproachable.

And there was another attraction on Via Veneto that no other street in Rome could offer: movie stars. Because there were modern luxury hotels at the top end of the street, because there was a Cook's Travel store and offices of various airlines and cruise companies near the bottom, because the American embassy was right there, because they had heard its praises sung by returning GIs, and because there were *two* dining spots nearby that replicated American menus and *two* nightclubs along the strip in a city in which such were scarce, wealthy foreigners, including Hollywood celebrities, would often encamp on Via Veneto, and the street became known as a place where Americans—and, especially, American movie stars—would stay and play.

Among the very first recorded recognitions that there was a bona fide international scene blossoming on Via Veneto appeared in the pages of *The New York Times Magazine* in August 1950, under the byline of Tennessee Williams, who wrote about his belief that Rome was the new Paris in an article entitled "A Writer's Quest for Parnassus":

> In Rome there is only one street where people make a social practice of sitting on the sidewalk. That is Via Veneto. It seems, at times, to be given over almost entirely to Americans, streetwalkers, and boys picking up discarded cigarette butts. But it's a beautiful street. It winds like an old river among the great hotels and the American Embassy and the fashionable places for Americans to sit in the sun.[4]

To some degree, this renown preceded the war: the posh hotels and cafés were so genteel and so distinct from much of Rome that Italian movie people had made the top end of the street into something of a clubhouse, much as the writers had colonized the lower half. In the Fascist era, gigolos and lounge lizards were known to

---

4 The democratic Williams also wrote fondly of a late-night joint called Caffè Notturno, not far from Via Veneto on the Piazzale Porta Pia, where he liked to sit and watch prostitutes, pimps, and thieves passing away the small hours.

prowl Via Veneto looking for foreign women to prey upon, and the various cafés around the hotels became favored by movie producers as a hunting ground where they could meet investors, directors, and, especially, pretty girls who worked in nearby fashion houses or had come to the city to make a go at acting careers. After the war, this activity revived; Via Veneto was posh, if low-key, and those impressive hotels had their bars and restaurants and cafés attached to them, and the street still held a gilded luster even as Italian filmmaking focused on heart-wrenching portraits of people who couldn't afford so much as a coffee on such a high-toned street.

With the end of the 1940s, a few American film productions were based in Rome—costumers, as they were called in the trade, like *Prince of Foxes*, about intrigue among the Borgias—and the reputation of Via Veneto as a center of the international movie business, or at least the Roman corner of it, was established. The street began to be dotted with movie stars sipping espressos or browsing at the twenty-four-hour newsstand or simply strolling in the mild Roman air: Orson Welles, Tyrone Power, Eduardo Ciannelli. Wander up the street, especially at night, and you might bump into someone you'd only ever seen on a movie screen.

As the presence of Hollywood stars portended, Italy had begun to reclaim its long-standing status as a destination for travelers from abroad. That stature was boosted, if only inadvertently, when Pope Pius XII declared that the one-year period starting at Christmas 1949 would be a Holy Year, or Jubilee, calling Catholics to come to Rome for a variety of spiritual aims. Those who made the pilgrimage and who visited the city's four basilicas would receive a special Jubilee indulgence. There would be scores of commemorative masses and celebratory events. And the call went out around the world for the faithful to make the journey.

By November 1, 1950, some four million pilgrims had visited the city, including more than 100,000 Americans, many availing themselves of special tour packages offered by Catholic travel agencies. Those trips, in the days before jet travel, could take as long as two months, with side journeys throughout Italy, France, and other destinations tacked on. American magazines and newspapers ran travel guides to Rome, extolling the city's beauty, history, holiness, and customs—and assuring readers that the natives were quite friendly despite the recent hostilities.

Among the spectacular sites that the pilgrims saw on their epochal trip—one that would become an icon of Rome and its postwar renaissance—was a new iteration of Roma Termini, the central train station that connected the city to the wider world. Located on the Esquiline hill, Termini got its name not from its status as a terminus (which, being in the middle of the country, it both was and was not), but because it sat across a piazza from the ruins of the Terme di Diocleziano, the Baths of Diocletian, the largest public bathhouse in ancient Rome. The station had operated in some form since the 1860s and had been updated several times, most recently in the midthirties during one of Mussolini's building sprees. After the war, Termini, which had suffered bomb damage, required both repair and enlargement. An architectural competition was held, resulting in the selection of a hybrid design incorporating elements suggested by as many as seven designers. The result was a massive, low-slung, streamlined building composed of strong, flowing lines leading to a portico that opened onto the city and suggested the wing of a massive bird. It was dedicated on December 20, 1950, and would prove to be a launching point or fated destination for millions of vacationers, migrants, pilgrims, politicians, clergymen, and dreamers; eventually it became the second busiest railway station in all of Europe, behind only the Gare du Nord in Paris.

Roma Termini was built, like so much of the city, on top of something old; the architectural brief called for preservation of Etruscan-period walls on the site. But it was unmistakably new and forward-looking. Step into or out of the station at any time, in any weather, coming or going, whatever your disposition, and you couldn't deny the obvious declaration embodied in it: Rome was, once again, a center point.

The question remained, though: Of what?

3 Made in Italy

There would come a day when it would be impossible to think of fashion and not think of Italy: the catwalks of Milan; the acres of real estate in Manhattan and Tokyo dedicated to Italian clothing brands; the names of Armani and Versace and Prada and Dolce & Gabbana.

But there was a name that preceded them all and, in fact, made all those names possible: Giovanni Battista Giorgini, known to his friends as Bista.

He was born in 1898 to a family that owned marble quarries and sold stonecutting equipment in the Tuscan seaside town of Forte dei Marmi, about seventy-five miles from Florence. His family line was venerable, and he looked the part of the Florentine gentleman he was. "[His] profile is reminiscent of certain knights that can be found in the paintings of the old Tuscan masters, with a falcon on the shoulder," wrote a friend. He was courtly, well dressed, educated, worldly, and charming, but, in the eyes of another observer, "behind his gentle appearance there is a grip of steel."

He left school to volunteer in the Great War and returned home to find that rather than be allowed to attend university he would have to enter the family business. That spelled doom to Giorgini. He wanted to travel the globe, to serve in the diplomatic corps. But that would require additional schooling, which his family could no longer afford. He persevered unhappily with his duties.

And then a lifeline: a cousin in Florence opened a ceramic export firm and offered him a job. He would still, in a way, be a diplomat. He would see the world, or parts of it, as a traveling salesman of fine Italian crafts. Within two years, he reckoned he knew the business well enough to set up shop on his own, selling a wide range of Italian-made products abroad: glassware, embroidery, leather, linens, ceramics. Starting in 1923, he regularly visited America, building a clientele of department stores and specialty shops and beginning to understand the American market, so alien in so many ways to Italy and yet, in its embrace of simplicity, ease, and value, not entirely dissimilar. He developed a real feel for what Americans liked. At the same time, traveling his own country to seek products to sell, he grew in his conviction that the quality and creativity of Italy's craft work was unsurpassed; he wondered what sorts of Italian goods could be sold abroad, and he saw no ceiling.

The stock market crash of 1929 tempered his ambitions, but only in one direction; seeing that Americans could no longer splurge on Italian-made luxuries, he simply reversed his business model, importing American-made goods into Italy and selling them in a shop in Florence. The business was eventually scuttled by another world war, and despite his age and the fact that he was now a father of three, Giorgini served again. When the Allies drove the Nazis out of Florence, he emerged on his feet once more, making his home, just outside of the city center, available as a headquarters for the victorious Americans. In turn, they licensed him to open a kind of minimall in the heart of Florence called the Allied Forces Gift Shop, a large space where Italian craft makers produced and sold their work to stupid-rich (by local standards) American and British soldiers. That enterprise was so popular that Allied command asked him to open similar enterprises in Milan and Trieste.

Once again, Giorgini had understood which products of Italian creativity and artisanship would find favor with American buyers. And when it was possible again to travel overseas, he put his combination of skills and connections to a more rigorous test. In his long drives around Italy seeking new products for his shops, he conceived a vision of Italian craft and inspiration that went beyond pottery and knickknacks and decor. He had an idea that there was a potential market in the United States for Italian clothing—and not just knitwear or accessories or cheap goods, either, but real haute couture.

But there was a problem: nobody, not even in Italy, had ever heard of Italian haute couture.

There was historical precedent to build on. As far back as the togas of the caesars, Italian clothing had influenced European dress in at least two important ways: the style and look of garments, which is to say, *fashion*; and the manufacture of textiles and the actual construction of clothing, which is to say, *craft*. In the Renaissance, production of and trade in textiles helped Florence and Venice rise as European centers of power. Nobles, courtiers, and pretenders to their ranks all over the Continent imitated some aspect or other of Italian fashion, following the clothes worn by such tastemakers as Catherine de Médici and visible in the works of influential painters such as Botticelli and Raphael. Connoisseurs distinguished with prejudice between clothing made in the Italian style and clothing actually made in Italy, the latter being especially noted for the fineness of fabrics and other materials and the patent skill of the production. Not only was Italian clothing favored for its dash, flair, and beauty, but it was noted for its quality. On through the eighteenth century, Italy was a prolific source of fashion inspiration and direction for both women and men—witness that famed peacock of song, Yankee Doodle, who referred to the affectation of a feather stuck in his hat as "macaroni," a slang term then denoting sartorial splendor *alla italiana*.

But fashion means change, and among the changes in the favored dress of Europeans after, roughly, the dawn of the Enlightenment was a shift from Italian to Parisian style, particularly in women's apparel (men's clothing, less obviously subject to whims and trends, retreated to relatively somber London). This was partly a question of the pursuit of novelty, partly a question of a collapse of Italian influence in political and cultural matters, partly, even, a question of concerted effort by French interests to pry away for themselves provenance over the world of haute couture (it's no coincidence that the language of high fashion would be almost entirely French). Italy never lost its reputation for the quality of its materials, for its textiles, its leatherwork, its production of subsets of fashion such as shoes and hats and handbags. The phrase "Made in Italy" wasn't only a badge of honor but the actual slogan of a concerted campaign of the Fascist government to promote the export of Italian crafts and goods. But save for those connoisseurs who recognized the quality of Salvatore Ferragamo's shoes or Guccio Gucci's purses (to name two fashion concerns that thrived between the world wars), nobody with an interest in fashion as an art or a form of expression or a status symbol or a luxury business gave much thought to Italy as a place from which new looks and talents emerged. The one great Italian couturier of the 1920s and '30s, for example, the Roman Elsa Schiaparelli, worked exclusively in Paris, never in her homeland. Fashion was a French thing; Italians, in contrast were mere *makers*.

*B*efore he could remind the world that Italy was one of history's great founts of fashion, Giorgini would have to remind Italians themselves. And as for haute couture, well, almost nobody in the country had the money for evening gowns or cocktail dresses, let alone anyplace to wear them. (A small handful of fashion shows held in Venice and Rome as early as 1947 were more akin to charity galas for the ultrawealthy than proper exhibitions of new creations intended to generate headlines and business beyond word of mouth.)

In his travels, though, Giorgini had seen a number of things that gave his inspiration life and nourishment. He knew that Italian textiles were among the finest in the world, certainly in Europe, and that the country's textile factories had largely been spared destruction during the war, surviving more than 90 percent intact. He knew that there already were some Italian couturiers—often of noble origins with little inherited money—and that there was a larger group of fashion designers at work in virtually every sartorial métier, from swimwear to shoes to men's suits to millinery to formal dresses. He knew that there was a real correlation between the clothing that Italian designers made for domestic clients and the taste and lifestyles of ordinary Americans.

At the same time, he knew, too, that the very idea of fashion was almost exclusively connected to Paris in the minds of buyers, retailers, and the press in both Italy and America. Most Italian designers—dressmakers, really—simply and slavishly reproduced the works of the great Parisian ateliers, albeit with very high standards of material and tailoring; they would physically trek to Paris to see the new collections, purchase (at dear prices) detailed instructions on how to reproduce them, and then return home to make them, without variation, for customers. There was no thought among either Italy's clothiers or their clients that it was possible to achieve truly fine and truly fashionable results without passing through Paris. If Giorgini was going to share with the world the quality and style being offered by Italian clothiers, he would have a particularly daunting French dragon to slay.

Ironically, some of the groundwork on which he could build had been laid by, of all people, Benito Mussolini. Il Duce hated conceding precedence in *any* field, however frivolous, to outsiders.[1] Among his government's efforts to fortify Italian cultural identity were the establishment of a national fashion office (the Ente Nazionale della Moda Italiana); the imposition of strict quotas limiting reproduction of foreign designs; centralized control of textile and clothing manufacture; and even the publication of a government-sponsored fashion magazine, *Bellezza*. There was precedence, in short, for Giorgini's vision of Italian fashion presenting itself to

---

1 For example, Italians called soccer *"calcio,"* partly because Mussolini's government insisted that the sport derived from an ancient Florentine game of that name and not from the English sport known virtually everywhere else—except in the United States—as football. To bolster this theory, which was hogwash, they revived the old game, which is more or less a brutish melee of two teams of twenty or so kitted out in fancy dress. It would still be played, in historical costume, mainly for tourists, as *calcio storico*, in the twenty-first century.

the world with a single identity, and, as in other areas in which Italy was attempting to rebuild itself after the war, the foundation laid by fascism could be turned to serve a new kind of cultural and economic project.

In 1947, still peddling his grab bag of Italian goods, Giorgini made an unlikely inroad into the world of American museums with an exhibition of furniture, glassware, ceramics, and leather goods; entitled "Made in Italy," the show toured the United States for several years. He reckoned he could likewise bring a group of Italian designers and their work to America for a similar showcase, and in 1950, he approached one of his best clients, the B. Altman department store in New York, asking if they would sponsor it. They declined.

So Giorgini devised a second plan, arguably more ambitious and far-fetched. He would round up a number of Italian designers and present their work in Italy—at his villa in Florence—in early 1951. And he would bring American eyes to the clothes by piggybacking on the annual February fashion shows in Paris, offering travel, lodging, and hospitality to buyers from the most prominent American department stores, who would be just seven hundred miles away and maybe charmed by the chance of visiting Florence. He *knew* that there was a real harmony between the clothing that was being designed and made in Italy and the taste of the American public, not only in the airy stratum of haute couture but in the more ordinary (and more price-friendly) realms of daily clothing and sportswear; a few Italian designers were even starting slowly to make small names for themselves abroad. Now he was going to extend himself, his reputation, even his home in an effort to get the rest of the world to see it as well.

All he needed were designers with work to show and customers to show it to. And he had just a few months to whip it all up.

* * *

*G*iorgini began a letter-writing campaign directed at American department store buyers and Italian designers. In writing to both groups, he bent the truth a bit, telling them, not entirely accurately, that their competitors and colleagues were already engaged to exhibit work or to attend as buyers.

To the Americans he sounded the notes that might be expected of a salesman who didn't quite have a product on hand to sell, stressing his long association with their stores, his understanding of the buying habits of Americans, the high quality of Italian goods, and the chance he was offering them to be the first retailers in their markets with something truly new and exciting for customers—without ever detailing exactly what would be on display or which designers would be participating. The letters brimmed with confidence and the promise of marvels; the responses were polite, interested, even enthusiastic, but, to a one, noncommittal. Never discouraged, Giorgini kept the lines of communication open, even as the show was but a few weeks away.

To the Italians, he adopted a tenor more like that of a general rallying troops for a challenging campaign:

> *Since the United States is now quite well disposed toward Italy, it seems to me that the time has come to attempt to establish Italian fashion in that market. . . . We must organize a presentation of our own collections. . . . It all depends, therefore, on our determination to show that Italy, which has demonstrated her mastery in the field of fashion over the centuries, has preserved her genius and can still create style with a wholly genuine spirit.*

Giorgini often delivered this pitch in person, appealing to a shared sense of national pride and insisting that the designers participate using wholly original work—no imitations of the French. He presented the opportunity as if he were a cousin trying to make the case that it would benefit the whole family. And, like many momentous family decisions, it incited much internecine struggle.

Among those he beseeched to join his crusade were the members of an actual family who were already, by some ways of reckoning, Italy's best-known couturiers—all on the strength of a single dress worn one single time.

"The Three-Sided Mirror"

For a romantic setting, it was hard to beat.

In the middle of the Roman Forum, in the shadow of the Colosseum, just beside the Temple of Venus, stood a tiny church named for a fifteenth-century saint, Francesca of Rome. It had a dainty look, with a baroque wedding-cake portico, a Romanesque campanile, and a commanding view of the rubble of antiquity. Despite its location in the midst of an archaeological site, it was a functioning church, with priests and monks of the Olivetan order holding regular masses and seeing to the upkeep of the premises—

more a monastery than a parish, but neither a ruin nor a tourist monument.

Still, it was a puzzlement to the white-robed monk who answered a knock at the door one afternoon in January 1949 when a handsome foreign couple wondered if it was possible for them to marry there. "No one has ever been married here," he told them, adding, "Well, not in my memory." They wondered whether they could ask his superiors for permission, and they did, and within a few days it was granted.

It was conceived of as a small wedding—the couple didn't have family or very many friends in Rome; they were in town because the groom had business there. But it wasn't going to be chintzy, and it was even creating a bit of buzz. Among those expected to attend were such fashionable nobles as Count Rodolfo Crespi and Prince Dado Ruspoli; the wedding mass would be celebrated by Monsignor William Hemmick, the famed "patriot priest," an American serving as canon of St. Peter's; the reception, to be hosted by Ambassador James Dunn, would be held at the U.S. embassy on Via Veneto.

The groom, as it happened, was royalty of a kind: Hollywood leading man Tyrone Power, who was working in Rome and Tuscany on the adventure film *Prince of Foxes*. And his bride-to-be was also a performer, Linda Christian, the twenty-five-year-old star of the previous year's *Tarzan and the Mermaids*, nicknamed by movieland wags, for obvious reasons, the Anatomic Bomb, and reckoned to be one of the most beautiful girls in the world.

So there was more attention focused on this particular ceremony than a typical wedding might draw. On the morning they were to exchange vows, the couple had to fight their way into the church. An estimated eight thousand people, straining for a glimpse of the glamorous pair, had turned up outside, with a small but vigorous clutch of photographers and newsreel camera-men staking out positions close in. Traffic crawled; the ceremony was delayed for more than an hour.

Once the couple had been declared husband and wife, they exited the church, en route to a wedding breakfast and then, despite the groom's recent divorce, a private audience with Pope Pius XII. On the church steps, they were engulfed by a clamor of applause and cheers and by camera snaps that would, in the coming days, enable the whole world to peek in. It was later recalled as the first news-reel wedding of the postwar years. And in the center of it all was a wedding dress—50 yards of satin, 70 yards of lace, more than 1000 pearls, a 15-foot train—conceived and created by the Sorelle Fontana, the Fontana Sisters, a trio of designers who had opened their own atelier just a few years earlier and who had the audacity to think that Italians could produce custom, haute couture as good as anything that came out of Paris.

It was fitting that the Fontanas should become known to the world in a setting so like a scene from a storybook, as the tale of their lives and work could itself be mistaken for romantic fiction.

The sisters—Zoe, Micol, and Giovanna, in birth order—hailed from Traversetolo, a small town about fifteen miles south of Parma. Their father, Giovanni, had a construction business that had built the house where he and his wife, Amabile, raised their family. Amabile had been born into a line of women who worked outside the home in one of the very few arenas in which they were then permitted to: dressmaking. She passed down the trade, teaching her daughters needlework, cutting, and design from a very early age, and the girls were put to work in the family shop whenever they weren't in school ("The dressmaker's was run with military, even Prussian precision by my mother," Micol later recalled). It wasn't ordinary sewing and mending they were learning, either: the exact techniques of beading, embroidery, and other specialty skills that Amabile drilled into her daughters had been passed down for generations; the girls would come to master ways of making that, in some cases, hadn't changed significantly in hundreds of years.

The elder girls had a real aptitude for the precision tasks they were assigned, and when Zoe was wed at age twenty-three, in 1934, she and her new husband reckoned that her abilities would guarantee their household an income—but not in Traversetolo, where one dressmaker was plenty to meet demand; it would have to be Rome or Milan. The decision of where to set up their home was the stuff of fate, as Micol often told it: "[Zoe] left Traversetolo, went to Parma station, and asked what was the first train passing through. The ticket clerk replied that it was headed south to Rome. 'Very well, two tickets for Rome it is.'" Zoe promised that she would send word to her sisters so they could join her once she had settled, and one month later Micol and Giovanna were boarding a southbound train themselves, headed toward a future they couldn't even imagine. "How do you think everything will turn out?" Micol asked her baby sister. "Fine," Giovanna answered. "How else should it turn out?"

At first, each worked on her own: Zoe for the famed dressmaker Zecca; Micol for a rival, Battilocchi; Giovanna at home. By 1943, they had saved enough money and met enough potential customers to take the risk of opening their own shop on Via Liguria, a quiet, neat street just off Via Veneto, convenient to many prospective clients. It was still wartime, Micol remembered, and the action was still hot: "We could hear the distant booming of guns while we worked." But they were able to attract trade with the quality of their handiwork and their ability to whip up smart imitations of Parisian fashions with the limited resources available to them, going so far, at times, as to exchange food for fabric so as to meet orders.

Their combination of technique, taste, and resourcefulness was, said the fashion writer Elisa Massai, essential to their success. "They had the knowledge and skill of true craftsmen and the intuition of those who have risen through the ranks," she wrote. "Not everything came completely from their own ideas, but they were among the first to create an embryonic type of Italian fashion." The Fontanas made no secret of the fact that many of their creations were reproductions of French models, which was what the smart Italian women of the day wanted. But they were also able to interest their clientele in creations of their own that, not straying too dramatically from the dominant French styles, exhibited an individualism which appealed to more than one wealthy Roman eye. Very quickly, the sisters learned to rely on a business model based partly on reproductions and partly on originals; Zoe and Micol designed the clothes and oversaw production, quite often with their own hands, and Giovanna handled the mechanics of the business, including, crucially, publicity.

Of course, in postwar Rome, the only real publicity available was word of mouth. By this means they came to the attention of Gioia Marconi (daughter of Guglielmo, the father of wireless radio), a style icon who had an entire wardrobe designed by the Fontanas and bragged all over town about the quality, speed, and reasonable cost of their work. By *that* means they came to know a genuine Russian princess, Irene Galitzine, who started modeling for them and discreetly promoting their designs among her set as soon as the atelier on Via Liguria opened and who would, in the course of her work as envoy, learn enough from the sisters to open her own house of fashion some fifteen years later. And through Galitzine they came to the attention of Linda Christian and, through the word of mouth, as it were, of the international celebrity press, of the rest of the world.

With Linda Christian's wedding dress seen and admired everywhere, the Fontanas were suddenly renowned, celebrated, and in demand. They were known as "the three fountains of Rome" (*fontana* being the Italian word for "fountain") and "the three-sided mirror," reflecting the close collaboration of the sisters. Along with the growing throng of society women, there now came a slow but steady stream of actresses—not only Italian but American ones. Myrna Loy requested Fontana dresses for her wardrobe in the 1949 film *That Dangerous Age* (aka *If This Be Sin*), which was shot partly in Capri and Naples. When *Quo Vadis* was being shot in Rome the next year, star Robert Taylor was visited by his wife, Barbara Stanwyck, who ordered a wardrobe of dresses from the Fontanas. Irene Dunne, touring Italy that same year, stopped by Via Liguria and selected a variety of outfits. A joke circulated around Hollywood: To see Rome properly, you needed a day for the Forum, a day for St. Peter's, and a day for the Fontanas.

From movieland royalty, the sisters moved on to dressing *real* royalty. In 1951, Princess Nariman of Egypt, on the eve of marrying King Farouk, ordered a trousseau of *seventy* formal evening dresses from the Fontanas.

Little wonder that the first fellow to dream up an all-Italian fashion show came calling at Via Liguria when it was time to find designers willing to exhibit at his event. When Giorgini approached them with his proposal, the Fontana sisters weren't immediately convinced. "We were hesitant," recalled Micol. "The French were an institution, and we were just some Italian dressmakers with an idea." They understood that if they threw in their lot with a wholly Italian production, they would run the risk of alienating the French, denying themselves the ability to re-create the Parisian collections that their clients expected of them. At the same time, Micol said, "We were already creating a bit of Italian fashion. . . . And yet it was not an easy decision. Turning our backs on Paris meant giving up a mechanism that we knew worked."

The Fontanas wrestled with Giorgini's invitation for weeks, calling on the counsel of their kin to help them make a decision. "We had long family discussions," Micol recalled. Giovanna was particularly reluctant to take a risk: "I would always say, 'How can we do this? It's too difficult to compete with the French,'" she remembered. But Zoe and Micol were ready to take the leap. "In life, you cannot stay in one place," Micol declared. "You have to move forward." Giovanna remembered her sisters telling her flat out: "'Your opinion doesn't count. You're the minority and we're going ahead with this.' What could I do but follow?" The Fontana sisters were in.

*N*ot very far from the Fontana atelier, on the Via Gregoriana near the Piazza di Spagna, Giorgini courted another designer of haute couture whose work and personal appearance were becoming known throughout Rome and beyond. By American standards, she was a fantastical creature, a bona fide noblewoman who looked like a movie star and created art out of fabric. But to the newly emerging Italy, she was more like an emblem of the nation's finest qualities rolled into one elegant ball.

The postwar constitution adapted in 1947 had declared Italy to be "*una Repubblica democratica, fondata sul lavoro*" ("a democratic Republic founded on labor"), and both nouns in that phrase would have been seen as something of a threat by the country's large cohort of titled nobles, be they descended from Black (monarchical) lines or White (papal) ones. Titles had long been reckoned a precious commodity in Italy, and under fascism they could be a sinecure; even if an aristocratic family had no wealth to go along with its name, that name in and of itself entitled its owner to a standard of living that, if not exactly regal, was often far more comfortable than warranted by the actual work or merit of those who bore it. In the new Italy, though, the balance between comfort and effort that some aristocratic families had long enjoyed (i.e., much of the former and little of the latter) became, at least in theory, untenable. The building of the new republic would entail genuine labor, and regardless of who your grandparents were, you were expected at least to make a show of chipping in.

For some people born to high names, however, work wasn't a duty but a calling—indeed, a mission. One such was the Duchess Simonetta Colonna di Cesaró, born in 1922 from a line of Sicilian nobles and raised in the heart of Rome in a family that was openly anti-Fascist. During the war, Simonetta and her parents and siblings were imprisoned by Mussolini's police in a village in Abruzzi, where the teenager kept her mind and hands occupied by acquiring skills in what might, in another aristocratic family, be termed demeaning chores: cooking and, especially, sewing and dressmaking. Simonetta had always been interested in clothes, and she discovered that she genuinely enjoyed designing and making them. When the war ended and the family returned to its home on Via Gregoriana, she decided she would do something unique with her newfound abilities: she would practice them professionally.

In 1944, she married—a nobleman, naturally: Count Galaezzo Visconti di Modrone. But that didn't deter her from going ahead with her plans to design and create a line of clothes. With quality textiles impossible to come by, she scrounged materials from around her home: dishcloths, aprons, towels, drapes, and the uniforms of maids, butlers, and gardeners, adding bits of lace and ribbon that she was able to find in street markets. In all, she produced fourteen items, mostly daywear and sportswear, and she dared to show them to women of her social circles, using the name Simonetta as a trademark. On the strength of the original-ity, vitality, and fine tailoring displayed in her work, she took some orders and was commissioned to do some one-off pieces. A career, if a small one, began.

There was no doubt as to Simonetta's talent, but she might have remained a secret—a noblewoman with a taste for making clothes for her friends—if it weren't for the fact that she was also a great beauty. In 1947, the American edition of *Vogue* planned a photo shoot on the most attractive women in Rome, and Simonetta came to the editors' attention. Not only were they struck by her dark eyes, aquiline profile, and elegant bearing, but they noticed her clothes and were amazed to learn that she herself had not only designed but actually made them. Her outfits were as fashionable as any-thing coming out of Paris, but they had their own style: the cut, the draping, the layering, the sleeves, waists, and details. These clothes were fresh, feminine, modern, original, and, somehow, truly Italian—Roman—and they were gorgeous. *Vogue* published images of Simonetta modeling her own pieces over two pages of their story, and suddenly she was being talked about in New York as a hot young Italian designer. Even those Roman aristocrats with the most refined senses of snobbery were impressed, and Simonetta's business grew, requiring her to convert the bottom floors of the building in which she was raised into a workroom and showroom.

Approached by Giorgini about his grand scheme, Simonetta roused with characteristic mettle. As she later recalled, Giorgini "outlined his plan to me, a plan that was ambitious, difficult, and in some ways revolutionary. . . . The plan that Giorgini had in mind broke with tradition. It was potentially a boomerang." But she proceeded without fear:

> I accepted without thinking twice. . . . I was already designing original fashion, and I did not copy the French. . . . For me, Giorgini's project was not a risk. It was a lifesaver. It was even more than that. It was a rocket ship.

With Simonetta and the Fontanas aboard, three other Roman designers joined in: the flamboyant and already semifamous Emilio Schuberth, a Neapolitan whose personal presentation—pouffy hairdo, shirts open to the waist, jewels on his fingers, wrists, and neck—was as spectacular as his work, which had been catching the eyes of connoisseurs for a decade-plus; Carosa, a label created by Princess Giovanna Caracciolo Ginetti; and Alberto Fabiani, who had studied in Paris and whose atelier, on Via dei Condotti, was noted for the exquisite quality of its handwork ("a classic coat and suit man," said an admirer in the American press). Particularly reliant on French inspiration, Fabiani was at first uncertain about Giorgini's plan, but Simonetta persuaded him. "I almost forced him," she recalled. "Thanks to French fashions, he had acquired a rich and numerous clientele. It was understandable that he was doubtful, but my prodding made his fortune."

From Milan, Giorgini landed another four designers of notable talent and pedigree: Germana Marucelli, Vita Noberasco, Vanna (the trade name used by the dressmakers Anna Carmeli and Manette Valente), and Jole Veneziani. And he fleshed out the show with a real thunderbolt of inspiration. Well aware that Italy was ahead of Paris in such daily clothing categories as knitwear, sportswear, and the lower-cost designer lines that would soon become known as ready-to-wear, Giorgini secured the presence in his show of four creators of those styles, which he lumped together under the rubric *boutique fashion*: from Milan, Giorgio Avolio, Franco Bertoli, and Baroness Clarette Gallotti (who worked under the label Tessitrice dell'Isola, the "Weaver of Isola"); and, as the sole representative of Florence, a designer who was becoming well-known and who was so chary of Giorgini's enterprise that he determined to invite the visiting North Americans to his *own* nearby palazzo for a private showing after the main event, a Florentine marquis named Emilio Pucci.

5 "Paris Didn't Move Us Like This"

Two questions Emilio Pucci was repeatedly asked throughout his career of nearly five decades: "What is fashion?" and "How did you come to be involved in it?"

To the first he gave a number of answers, often philosophically nuanced and filled with historical and cultural citations, as might be expected of a man with several postgraduate degrees. "Fashion is the essence of modern life," went a typical one. "It is movement. We must capture it but give it freedom. It is the vision of tomorrow realized today."

To the second, there was only ever one response, proferred again and again, always with a smile, and consisting, pretty much, of the truth: "How did I get to my work? Well, I'd have to admit to one great weakness: pretty girls."

Emilio Paolo Pucci dei Marchese di Barsento was born in Naples in 1914 and was reared in Florence, where his family had long counted among the highest nobles in a city particularly top-heavy with such. The Pucci line ran back more than a millennium; they owned estates and a grand palazzo, they were patrons of Botticelli, and, it was said, they were the first great family to use forks at the dining table, creating a fashion that never went away.

Pucci's father, Orazio, was the 11th Marchese di Barsento, and his mother, born Augusta Pavoncelli, was a Neapolitan princess. The Puccis lived off the profits of their extensive landholdings, the men hunting and riding and perfecting their sporting skills (Pucci's older brother, Puccio—yes, *Puccio Pucci*; it was an old family name—was an Olympic sprinter), the women running the household, shopping, planning and attending fetes and luncheons, and so forth. Pucci liked to joke that he was the first member of his family to work in a thousand years, and it was one of those jokes that was, in truth, more serious than not.

From his teens, Pucci was notably active in both body and mind. He played tennis and swam and fenced and raced cars and skied, the latter so well that he competed on the Italian Olympic team in Lake Placid in 1932. But he was equally devoted to academics, pursuing finance, politics, industrial science, art, literature, and languages: a true Renaissance man and one of the very few who it could be said was literally born so. He attended university in Milan with an emphasis in business. But he transferred in 1935 to the University of Georgia to study methods of cotton production. There, he honed his English by joining the debate team and kept up his skiing, representing the school in national collegiate competitions.

The following year, Benito Mussolini, claiming colonial provenance over east Africa, ordered an invasion of Ethiopia, occasioning sanctions against Italy by virtually all Western democracies. As a result, Italian nationals living abroad found themselves cut off financially from home and, if they were of military age, unable to return without risking conscription. Pucci wanted to continue studying in the United States, and he was able to turn his passion for sport and his willingness to work hard into a means of doing so. On a ski trip to Oregon's Mount Hood, he happened to meet the president of Reed College, in nearby Portland, and the two struck a deal: in exchange for tuition, room, and board, Pucci would serve as coach of the college's ski team.

At Reed, Pucci earned a master's degree in political science with a thesis about his country's political ideology. "Fascism: An Explanation and Justification" was a passionate defense of the ideal of centralized government, which he would come to reject once he returned to Italy and lived under a particularly brutal and corrupt one. He was remembered by his classmates for his social zeal ("Some women were just delighted to see him again and others wouldn't come within ten feet of him," recalled a classmate), for his diligent hard work (he took jobs as a waiter and dishwasher to augment his modest stipend), and, most of all, for his stylistic flair. The chief instance of this would be his design for the uniforms of the Reed ski team. Rather than the bulky winter clothes that most skiers wore, he had personally favored stretch fabrics and form-fitting cuts, which provided warmth and flexibility; to keep the pants' cuffs from riding up the wearer's legs, he sewed elastic stirrups to the cuffs. Working with the Portland outdoor clothiers White Stag, he produced a design of lasting influence—the first recognizable modern skiwear.[1]

When he graduated from Reed and returned to Florence (where he would eventually earn a doctorate in political science and law), Pucci was, as he expected, drafted into the Italian military. He served as a fighter pilot throughout the last days of the Ethiopian campaign and the first years of the ensuing world war. In 1943, recovering from a tropical disease in Capri, he became involved in a plot to smuggle Mussolini's daughter Edda Ciano out of the country after her husband, Foreign Minister Galeazzo Ciano, turned on Il Duce and found himself facing execution on a charge of treason. It was an episode of great drama, involving secret diaries, terrifying Gestapo agents, nighttime escapes by boat, even a hidden pouch that Pucci hand-sewed into Edda's coat, which she smuggled safely across Lake Lugano into Switzerland.[2] Having turned on the regime himself, Pucci, too, waited out the end of the war in Switzerland—where he socialized and, naturally, skied.

After the liberation of Italy, Pucci returned home and he continued to tinker with sportswear. In 1947, he was in Zermatt when he ran into a friend—female, *bien sur*—whose ski apparel he simply couldn't abide. He dressed her in one of his form-fitting outfits, and she was noticed by the photographer Toni Frissell, who snapped a shot that wound up in *Harper's Bazaar*. The following year, the magazine's editor, Diana Vreeland, ran pictures of several models and Pucci himself in his ski clothes, creating a small sensation. The New York department store Lord & Taylor wanted to buy the exclusive right to sell the designs, and several American

1 In time, the operators of Reed's home circuit, Mount Hood, would memorialize his innovations by naming a chair lift and a ski trail, the Pucci Glade, in his honor.

2 Her husband wasn't so lucky, meeting his death at the hands of a firing squad in January 1944.

companies offered themselves as manufacturers. In the end, Pucci chose to produce the clothes himself, contracting with his old friends at White Stag and completely reinventing the way people dressed for winter sports.

And then he did the same for the summer. Another holiday, this time on Capri, and another girl; for her he designed shorts and tops and swimwear in playful cuts and bright colors. These sorts of things, more commonly worn than ski clothes, were even more successful; soon there were knockoff imitations on the market all over Italy and in the United States, where a vogue blossomed for what were known as "Capri shorts." But those who sought to copy Pucci's inspirations were readily found out: it turned out that his genius for cuts and lines was augmented—and maybe outdone—by his genius for color and patterns, which no one could imitate readily. Fleurs-de-lis and harlequin diamonds and the scrolls from Doric columns rendered in turquoise and peach and topaz and magenta and puce, all in one flowing or angular design: a Pucci looked like no other piece of clothing, more like a Picasso or a Kandinsky than a Dior or a Chanel.

He began to design scarves—bright panels with as many as sixteen hues in a single piece, inspired by the light and tints of the Tyrrhenian Sea and by the ancient architecture and frescoes that had been before his eyes since he was a baby. A friend, the department store magnate Stanley Marcus, encouraged Pucci to adapt these designs into blouses and dresses, and he took a few gingerly steps in that direction. Working out of a tiny atelier in a disused chapel in his family palazzo, he produced playful and dazzling pieces of the finest silk, cotton, and, for the ski slopes, synthetic materials. He opened up a boutique in Capri's famed Piccola Marina, where he sold his creations under the label Emilio of Capri, which was the name he gave the shop. They were beautiful, they were fun, they were exclusive, and they were a sensation in both Europe and the United States. The marquis with the eye for women's sportswear was becoming, of all things, a fashion world star. And he was happy to throw in with Giorgini's proposed show, aware that he didn't necessarily need for it to succeed.

As 1951 dawned and the date of his daring gamble neared, Giovanni Battista Giorgini still lacked the one key element to his scheme to launch Italian fashion as a worldwide phenomenon: foreign buyers. A few of his American contacts had expressed noncommittal interest in attending the show being planned for Florence, but none would say for certain that they'd be there. Giorgini cut them deals: Parisian shows required a deposit, applicable against purchases, as an entry fee, but admittance to Giorgini's show would be free. He worked the telephone lines furiously, using all the wiles he could summon. Sometimes he joked: "Be my doctor. Come to take my temperature," he told people who thought he'd gone mad with his campaign. To others, he flat out lied: "I convinced them to participate fraudulently," he admitted years later. "I assured each one that their direct rival would be present."[3]

In early February, he was at last able to confirm the participation of buyers from four major North American stores: B. Altman and Bergdorf Goodman from New York, I. Magnin from San Francisco, and Henry Morgan from Montreal.[4] That was it: no foreign press, no Italian buyers, no clutches of photographers or celebri-

3 Pointedly, Giorgini did *not* invite the American press, chary of having any possible failure aired abroad. The five journalists he invited were Italians, handpicked and friendly, although one, Elisa Massai, served as the Italian correspondent for *Women's Wear Daily*.

4 Two other Americans, manufacturers of ready-to-wear clothing, happened to be in Florence that week and, literally bumping into their colleagues in the street, were invited along.

ties or jet-setting clotheshorses. The first international show of Italian fashion would be more like a private party at someone's home (which, technically, it was) than like a media event.

When the buyers arrived from Paris, Giorgini remembered, they ribbed him for being lucky that they'd made the trip at all, "practically making fun of me and emphasizing how much of a favor they had done by coming." He met them with spectacular hospitality, providing cars and drivers and plush hotel suites, dotting their visit with grand dinners and cultural tours. "He was a gentleman and knew how to treat people incredibly well," recalled an Italian journalist, "especially the Americans, who were so very important then. He treated them like foreign princes."

The first showing was on February 12. In the salon of his home, Villa Torrigiani, in a room with no elevated catwalk, Giorgini presented, to the accompaniment of a piano, what had been termed the "boutique" collections: morning dresses, knits, and sport-, beach- and leisure-wear, some of it produced by the designers who would also be showing couture work, but most by those, like Pucci, who created *only* less-than-formal clothing. This was another of Giorgini's brilliant stratagems: not only were Italians well ahead of Parisian designers in the materials, craft, and styling of such attire, but nobody in Paris even showed such stuff to the American buyers. The Yanks would be seeing wholly new looks in wholly new categories of clothes.

The decision paid off. The buyers found the change of genre palate-cleansing, and they were genuinely impressed with what they saw: the colors, the youthfulness, the vitality, the wearability, and, in particular, the prices—bargain-basement by Parisian standards—were all new and inviting. They understood, too, that a lot of what they were looking at was at once very Italian—bright, lively, stylish, elegant, relaxed, and well made—and very American, for many of the same reasons. French clothes could often feel stuffy and highfalutin to ordinary Americans, but the things Giorgini had assembled for the buyers on this day seemed homey and familiar and, everyone noted, salable. Most important of all was the fact that there *were* no Parisian standards for what they were seeing: as Gianni Ghini, Giorgini's longtime assistant, remembered, "The boutique was innovative because the French did not have it." And as Elisa Massai reflected, Giorgini knew that this stuff was "in line with the taste and costume and lifestyle of Americans." The buyers agreed: they bought heaps of what they saw, and their appetites were whet for the more traditional couture designs.

After a day off for sightseeing and relaxation, the second part of the exhibition was held, a formal cocktail party and dinner with the crowd at Villa Torrigiani swelled with invitees from outside the world of fashion, including a cohort of Florentine nobles, a perfect teaser for Americans who could still be dazzled by a title, even if it had neither power nor wealth behind it.[5] After drinks and small talk, everyone took seats for the formal showing of the couture lines.

Giorgini's library had been turned into a combination dressing room and workshop, and the entire tiny world of Italian high fashion was on hand, focused on presenting their designs in the best possible light to an audience who barely knew their names: Fabiani, the Fontanas, Schuberth, Simonetta, Veneziani, and the rest. In normal times they might consider themselves rivals, however friendly. But Giorgini's appeal to their sense of national pride, his argument that recognition of Italian fashion in and of itself would boost them all, encouraged them to leave their competitive instincts at home. Now they worked alongside one another

5 Ever on guard against the hegemony of Paris, Giorgini had sent invitations to his high-titled Florentine guests with the proviso "Ladies are kindly requested to wear dresses of purely Italian inspiration."

as a casually united federation. And they sent their models out, one by one, to face judgment.

At first, there was silence: "unreal," as Micol Fontana recalled. Then, after the final model returned to the workroom, there was applause. But Giorgini had worked himself into such a state that he couldn't tell if it was sincere or polite. He summoned the courage to ask the Americans outright, "Does it work?" And the representative of I. Magnin replied for them all: "Paris didn't move us like this."

By every measure, Giorgini had crafted a huge success. The boutique lines had already sold well, and now several of the couture designers did substantial business: Simonetta placed her entire collection with Bergdorf Goodman, and Fabiani, the Fontanas, and several others struck similarly significant deals with specific retailers. Again, the color, the cut, the needlework, and the creativity of the designs met with universal approval—and the prices made it all irresistible. Almost every clothier who displayed in the show came away with some sort of deal, if only for the rights to have their designs replicated in the United States. And because it was a group event and not a showcase for a single designer, the impression it created was that Italy itself was a fount of fashion creativity—a legitimate alternative to the collection of sometimes feuding couturiers know collectively as "Paris." The effect, ultimately, would be to lift a whole industry, not just an individual star or two.

With the show a bona fide hit, Elisa Massai felt able to report favorably on it to her American editors at *Women's Wear Daily*, who ran a front-page article entitled "Italian Styles Gain Approval of U.S. Buyers" just days later. And after the celebratory backslaps and cordialities subsided, Giorgini went right back to work. He had originally envisioned an Italian fashion show to piggyback on *each* Parisian season, meaning that he'd have to organize it all over again for the coming summer.

That show, however, couldn't be held at his home, as more than 150 American retailers and journalists had reached out to him to express interest in attending. (Bettina Ballard, the fashion editor of American *Vogue*, wrote to Giorgini, "I had very good reports of your show. Everyone seems interested in Italy.") The summer event, held in Florence's Grand Hotel, and, crucially, *before* the Paris shows, was another success, featuring upward of six hundred dresses and outfits and attended by buyers from stores in Chicago, Dallas, New Orleans, Philadelphia, Montreal, Zurich, and Johannesburg, as well as a much larger press contingent. *The New York Times* declared, "Italian Fashions Command Praise," and *Life* magazine reported to its readers, in a lavishly illustrated feature, "Italy Gets Dressed Up: A Big, Hectic Fashion Show Attracts U.S. Style Leaders, Poses a Challenge to Paris." That last bit was debatable, but one influential buyer assured Giorgini that the competition with France was real: "Had we known what the Paris collections were going to show and what the Paris prices were going to be, we would have bought a lot more in Florence."

There was another winter show in early 1952, also at the Grand Hotel, and it was the biggest success yet: in sales (every one of 150 department stores attending made purchases); in critical response ("Italian fabrics are superlative, the Italians' sense of color is marvelous, and their clothes are fresh and beautiful," said Carmel Snow, the famed editor of *Harper's Bazaar*); and as an event reported on in newspapers and magazines throughout Italy, the rest of Europe, and the United States.

Then came Giorgini's final masterstroke: for the July 1952 show, he secured use of the glittering Sala Bianca of Florence's Pitti Palace, a ballroom in one of the most romantic settings in a city filled with them. Amid several days of shows of the latest works of sixteen designers, a formal ball was held in the Boboli Gardens adjoining the palace, with nearly 300 American journalists and buyers intoxicated by the aperitifs and mild air and lofty views of the Arno River, the red-roofed city, and the surrounding hills.

It was otherworldly: a fifteenth-century palace filled with Raphaels and del Sartos and Titians and miracles of silversmithing and tapestry weaving and furniture making, perched on the south side of the river alongside the vast, terraced gardens, with their ornamental statues, all amid one of the most beautiful cities on earth. Merely arriving on the grounds of the Pitti Palace put American buyers into something of a swoon.

The Sala Bianca itself resembled the ballroom from an animated movie about a princess and her love. (Giorgini, so familiar with American culture, might well have been inspired by Walt Disney.) As its name indicated, it was white, its walls laced with ornate stucco moldings and lined with large mirrors highlighted in gold; below, a shining parquet floor; above, a high arched ceiling from which hung an array of Bohemian crystal chandeliers. Lit up, the room sparkled like a skyscape on a moonless winter night. With the visiting buyers, manufacturers, and reporters pampered and wined and dined and entertained, with the exhibitions broken up by formal balls and receptions held in classical gardens or palaces, with Florence itself a more romantic backdrop for work and socializing than even Paris, Giorgini could have had the models wear potato sacks on the catwalk and they may well have found approval.

But what he showed was some of the most exciting new fashion of its time, and not just high-toned stuff but also the sorts of things that people everywhere could wear or emulate: appealing, original, affordable, chic. From the moment of that first Sala Bianca show, the Italian fashion and clothing industries ranked among the most important in the world, representing, in a country still wobbly from the war and its aftershocks, a vital new stream of style and creativity and, yes, profit. Years later, Italy's economic rise would come to be known as *Il Boom*; those fashion shows mounted by Giorgini had, in retrospect, lit the fuse.

And yet it transcended commerce. The chief impression that the out-of-town buyers and writers took away, that kept bringing the stylish women of means to gaze and shop, that gave the whole enterprise an air of possibility, energy, sparkle, and delight, was the sense that, somehow, in the wake of the calamities and privation of fascism and war and reconstruction, Italy had retained the *bella figura* and the *bellissima*, that the people who had so often ruled the world with their style as much as with their might had once again tapped into the mood of a moment and found a way to make everyone take notice and say, We'd like some of that. The Italy that would be so influential in the latter half of the twentieth century was born.

6 "Motion Pictures Are the Most Powerful Weapon"

Like so many other Italian cities, it had been occupied and bombed and burned and looted during the war, and it stood in a state of semiruin, populated with the homeless and the destitute—a shell of its bustling glory of just a few years prior. But even though its fallen state was familiar, its squalid condition brought a pang to people who had never been anywhere near it. It had been a city of dreams, miracles, and fantasies, a wonderland where the impossible was realized every day, where past, present, and future were simultaneous, the real and the imaginary inseparable. And now it was a skeleton of itself.

Technically, it wasn't a city, even though its name, Cinecittà, meant "Movie City." A compound of seventy-three buildings sitting on 145 walled acres on the southeastern outskirts of Rome, Cinecittà had been the uncontested hub of Italian cinema before the war. By 1945, however, it was no longer a movie studio but a refugee camp. It would have been hard at that time to walk through the famed gates on Via Tuscolana and imagine anyone making a movie there. It was no wonder that Italian filmmakers were choosing to work in the streets rather than try to shoot inside of what was left of what was once Europe's biggest movie studio and the home of what was, after the government and the church, Rome's largest and most visible business.

At the end of the war, Cinecittà wasn't even ten years old. Its dedicatory ribbon-cutting had been held on April 28, 1937, a mere 475 days after the cornerstone for the project had been laid— impressive efficiency even for a Fascist-run project. The opening ceremony was a spectacle, with soldiers in full pomp and hordes of laborers and masses of bureaucrats and officials and bunting and flags and a band and newsreel cameras. In the center of it all, chin and chest forward, engaged with what he saw and clearly proud of having made it all come to be, was Benito Mussolini, who declared himself the father of many aspects of Italian life but had real claims to paternity when it came to the cinema and, specifically, to Cinecittà.

Mussolini *loved* the movies. He liked Laurel and Hardy films; *Ecstasy*, in which Hedy Lamarr appeared in the nude; anything featuring Hollywood silent star Anita Page, to whom he wrote long fan letters and once proposed marriage; epics about ancient Rome, such as the Italian silent blockbusters *Cabiria, Gli Ultimi Giorni di Pompei (The Last Days of Pompeii)*, and *Quo Vadis?*; and cowboy pictures from America. Still greater than his fandom, though, was

his understanding of the power of the moving image as entertainment, as catharsis, as an occasion for community, as a vehicle
for political messages, as a means of fostering a cult of personality. He often, it was said, passed nights studying newsreel footage
of himself and refining his posture, his gestures, his delivery of
speeches in a mirror.

Inevitably, as in so many things, he sought to claim preemi-
nence in the movies for Italy, to remind the world of the undeniably great Italian films of the silent era, to foster an Italian cinema
that could create celluloid monuments to the civilization that he
was constructing on top of the ruins of ancient glory. A student of
both Lenin and Goebbels in matters of propaganda, he wanted, in
short, for Italy to rule the world, if in no other way, through film.
"Motion pictures," declared one of his grandiloquent mottos, "are
the most powerful weapon"; another encouraged greatness in
cinema "so that Fascist Italy can spread the light of Roman civilization more rapidly through the world."

But as everyone knew, the global cinema was effectively owned
by Hollywood, and Italy's great foundation of silent cinema—both
the epic and the experimental once thrived there—meant nothing compared with the onslaught of iconic American stars and
the popular musicals, westerns, crime stories, and comedies in
which they appeared. Italy was but a tiny producer of films, and
they were often of a nondescript sort, pale imitations of American
inspirations, with performers who carried no cachet outside Italy's
borders. As far as the rest of the world was concerned, the Italian
cinema had died when the talkies were born.

Mussolini worked to change that. Encouraged by his son Vittorio, who had an active interest in making films and sought to
produce and direct before being pulled into service in his father's
military, Il Duce spent a good deal of the 1920s and '30s organizing

the Italian film industry into the sorts of guilds and associations that he used to centralize and control so many other aspects of business, culture, and daily life. There were censors, predictably, and state-made movies and newsreels, and ministries to oversee financing, production, and distribution, but there were also film festivals and a film school and a film archive and even a state film magazine—all very forward-thinking for their day. Still, the scale of actual filmmaking in Italy faced the hard limit of finite production facilities, and those that existed were privately owned, which wasn't the way a Fascist government liked to run such things.

At the time, the biggest and busiest movie studio in Italy was Studi Cines on Via Veio, just south of the center of Rome. But in September 1935, that facility was almost completely lost in a fire, the origin of which was never entirely explained. At the time, Mussolini's government was busy building La Terza Roma ("the third Rome," after those of the caesars and the popes), tearing up neighborhoods, laying down new boulevards, building train stations and ministries and even a model city, later known as EUR (for Esposizione Universale di Roma), to show the world how modern the new Fascist Italy was. So they added a movie studio to the to-do list, and planned to make it the biggest outside of Southern California in the bargain.[1]

In January 1936, Mussolini went out to lay the cornerstone of the new studio on Via Tuscolana, southeast of the city center, where the necessary land had been acquired for nearly 3 million lire (in a deal as shadowy as the Studi Cines fire). He declared that the facility would compete with the great film studios of Hollywood, London, Paris, and Berlin, that it would be a place particularly

---

1 Vittorio Mussolini went to Hollywood to learn the components of a major movie studio.

suited to enormously scaled stories of Rome's imperial history, and that its productions would reveal to the world the excellence of life under fascism. Barely fifteen months later, he was back to cut the ribbon, to speak to the amassed crowds, to watch his son Vittorio direct scenes for one film and oversee production meetings for another, to witness the postproduction work on the epic *Scipione l'Africano* (*Scipio Africanus*), which was shot, in part, on the site of the new studio even as it was being built.

From the start, Cinecittà was one of the busiest workplaces in all of Rome, hosting dozens of productions a year until it was shut down by the war: 279 films in all, about half of which were style known as *"telefoni bianchi"* ("white telephones")—romantic comedies about wealthy folks in Art Deco homes played in the vein of (but well short of the heights of) films made by Ernst Lubitsch or starring Fred Astaire.

It was a boom time in Italian cinema. The country had never produced more than 36 films in any year before Cinecittà was built. But by 1938, that number had climbed to 59, and it would rise steadily, even in wartime, to 120 in 1942. In part, this was thanks to the consolidation of the industry under the various Fascist guilds and initiatives; as Hollywood's moguls could have attested, centralized control of moviemaking really did result in efficiencies and profits. In part, it was due to the possibilities afforded producers at Cinecittà and a handful of independent studios that sprang up to catch the spillover of the activity on Via Tuscolana. And in part, too, it resulted from a series of edicts that organized the import of foreign films into Italy under the hand of the government, all but daring Hollywood's studios to pull out of the country, which they eventually did, thus ensuring space on Italy's screens for native films and guaranteeing respectable box office for even middling local productions.

In this atmosphere, some talents worthy of notice by the rest of the world started to emerge: the directors Alessandro Blasetti, Alberto Lattuada, and Mario Soldati; the fist-faced, roly-poly actor Aldo Fabrizi; and a fiery Roman actress with unconventional looks but undeniable charisma and astonishing talent named Anna Magnani. Through their work, and that of a few others, Cinecittà became a symbol of modernity, glamour, and riches. It drew aspirants, connivers, and dreamers from all over Italy, enticed by the chance to see a movie star, to earn a pay envelope without doing backbreaking work, or, if they were lucky, to rise above the mob and become, whether in front of the camera or behind it, stars in their own right.

One of these was a skinny, goggle-eyed journalist and cartoonist from Rimini, on the Adriatic coast, who arrived in Rome in 1939 with hopes of making the things he saw in his dreams come alive on the page or—dare he imagine?—on the screen. His name was Federico Fellini, and he would someday become synonymous with the fabled movie studio. But on that first day he entered its gates, he was just another unknown, hopeful rider on the rickety blue tram that ran from central Rome to the semipastoral area where Cinecittà sat.[2]

Fellini was nothing more than a kid reporter, there to interview actor Osvaldo Valenti, then making a costume epic under the imperious command of the famed Blasetti,[3] who'd been in

2 At the time, few Italians owned cars and few actors made truly large salaries, so this famous tram often carried the top screen performers of the day along with all the anonymous aspirants.

3 From Fellini's half-recollected description, he likely was on the set of *La Corona di Ferro* (*The Iron Crown*; 1941), a biblical story with lots of action that would become a footnote to history upon its debut screening at the Venice Film Festival when Joseph Goebbels, on hand to scout talent for propaganda films, dismissed it as "not even worth commenting on."

movies since the silent era. From the very first, Fellini felt a rush of sensations—wonder, amazement, déjà vu, nostalgia, yearning, ambition, inspiration—that would perennially be part of his experience of Cinecittà, even as he became a fixture of the grounds in the decades to come. At the moment he arrived, he recalled, "I had exactly the same strange sensation that I remembered having as a little boy when I was taken for the first time to see the circus." He was overwhelmed by the sheer numbers of people working on the set, by the chaotic energy, by the blend of modern technology and costumes and props from ages past, by a massive crane jib rising and rising in the middle of the melee, and by a godly voice which, like that at a train station, bellowed out instructions to the cast and crew from who-knew-where.

"All of a sudden, everything went quiet," he remembered. "Somebody lent me a telescope, and through it I saw a man thousands of feet up in the air, on a chair firmly bolted to the platform of the crane, and wearing shiny leather breeches, a helmet on his head, and an Indian silk scarf, with three megaphones, four microphones and about twenty whistles round his neck. It was him. Blasetti. The director."

Fellini would soon return, talking his way past Pappalardo, the hulking, terrifying, infamous guardian of the front gate, hoping to catch a glimpse of Vittorio De Sica, who was acting on the lot that day. And then he would become a regular visitor, working as an idea man for comic screenplays, revising scenes that were being shot right then, in real time, camping with his portable typewriter inside the crowded and noisy bar where actors came to dine and schmooze, often still in costume: "cardinals, revolutionaries, SS men, troglodytes, green lizards more than six feet long, and concubines." There was nowhere else he would rather have been.

But in 1943, war put an end to production at Cinecittà, twelve hundred people were dismissed without severance pay, and the three films that were in front of the cameras were simply shut down. That summer, Allied bombing destroyed three of the studio's sixteen soundstages. Soon after, Mussolini's dream factory was occupied by the Nazis, who used it for a logistical headquarters, a storage facility, and, when they were forced to flee, a rummage sale at which everything was free. The Germans stuffed a freight train with the studio's heavy equipment and sent it home, but it was, fatefully, waylaid, and almost all the cargo was returned. That much couldn't be said for the tons of furnishings, fixtures, and materials that the Nazis left behind and which were subsequently looted by the locals, who didn't, it was said, leave a single bathroom faucet in its place.

No wonder, then, that Cinecittà served in a new capacity at the end of the war and the start of the slow recovery: as a camp for refugees displaced by the bombing and fighting that had rendered their homes, and even whole towns, unlivable. Hundreds of families were still living on the grounds of the studios when film production resumed. As work ramped up, Cinecittà reclaimed its place as one of the largest employers in Rome, an enormous factory in a town dominated by the government and the church and at the heart of a region that was more agrarian than industrial.

The Italian cinema would have to be rebuilt from scratch, and it wasn't at all evident that it could do so on its own—particularly as Hollywood movies came pouring back onto the country's screens and started, as before, to soak up all the limelight and money available. Imported films were still held to quotas, but even with that handicap, Hollywood made more money in Italy than any local film entity could ever dream of. The native film industry felt itself under siege: among its responses was a massive rally in the Piazza del Popolo at which various filmmakers and actors spoke, including Anna Magnani, who famously shouted to anyone in the government who was listening, *"Aiutateci!"*—"Help us!" In response, within two years of the end of the war, a new means of protecting the fledgling Italian film industry would emerge, a program that would have important ramifications in Rome and in Hollywood. Per an edict championed by Giulio Andreotti, an undersecretary in the Department of Entertainment and Tourism (and later prime minister), and with the assent of the administrators of the Marshall Plan, the profits that Hollywood studios made in Italy were frozen there and could be spent, by law, only in projects aimed at reviving the Italian film industry. In practical terms, this meant that American movie studios, once again permitted to show their films in Italy, had to leave their profits in Italian banks, to invest in the works of their Italian counterparts (something none of them had ever done or wished to do) or to make their own movies in Italy, another apparent nonstarter.

While the matter of these "locked funds," as they came to be called in Hollywood, was being pondered, though, an avenue opened up for Italian filmmakers that had nothing to do with movie studios—neither those in Hollywood nor Cinecittà. In mid-1944, a director who had made a few nonfictional films on Fascist themes under the supervision of Vittorio Mussolini had begun work on a project that would depict life under the Nazis, when the secretive machinations of Fascist collaborators and the Resistance turned the lives of ordinary Romans into a deadly game of cat and mouse. Roberto Rossellini had no secure financial backing for the film, no completed script, no sets or props, and no reliable source of film stock—just a determination to show life as it was being lived in Rome in the last months of the war and a few true stories of heroic self-sacrifice—one involving a priest (played by Aldo Fabrizi), one a housewife (Anna Magnani)—upon which to hang his narrative.

Rossellini was born in 1906 into the upper-middle class, growing up comfortably in the Ludovisi district. His father, a construction executive, built what might have been the first cinema in Rome, and young Roberto was given a pass to see all the movies he wanted to, which was quite a few. He received an unusual education through hired tutors—he never attended secondary school or university—and extensive travel.

By his twenties, Rossellini was working in movies; really, he never thought of any other career for himself. He started as a gofer, then moved on to the sound and editing departments, and he wrote about film for a number of publications. His work caught the attention of Vittorio Mussolini, and soon Rossellini was getting credits on films intended to promote the Fascist political agenda, including support for its war in Africa. He made a couple of stabs at independent productions—one, his first directorial credit, *Prélude à l'Après-midi d'un Faun*, suggested by the music of Claude Debussy, was banned by censors for erotic content. But by the time the war was starting, Rossellini was a full-fledged director of propaganda films being made on substantial budgets at Cinecittà and even on location in war zones.

He lived well: large homes, fast cars, a pair of marriages (the first, to a Russian-born actress, was annulled; the second, to the costume designer Marcella De Marchis, produced two children). But despite his bourgeois lifestyle and his work for the Mussolinis, he was a conscientious leftist. And once he no longer had to curtsey to Fascists for patronage, he turned himself fully toward his humanist impulses as subject matter for his work.

The limitations he faced in his new project, which might have stopped him before the war, when he relied on the largesse of

Cinecittà to provide what he needed, proved to be assets. Rossellini's film, his first feature, went before the cameras in January 1945, with around $20,000 as a budget.[4] He shot it in the actual streets and buildings where some of the events took place, during stolen snatches of time when the crew and cast could assemble, on leftover bits of unexposed film stock, and with electricity mooched off of American military facilities. Entitled *Roma: Città Aperta* (*Rome: Open City*), it took its name from the status that the Nazis had disingenuously bestowed upon Rome during their occupation of the capital—a designation of demilitarized control that was meant to assuage global fears of Hitler running the Vatican or looting the Colosseum but which was a complete misnomer, as Rome was ruled by the Germans with the same iron fist they wielded anywhere they planted their flag.

The film opened in Italy in September 1945 to a mixed critical response and indifference at the box office. Overseas, though, it proved a sensation. In the United States, where it premiered the following February, it took in an estimated $2 million in ticket sales (one New York theater showed it nonstop for twenty months) and won prizes as Best Foreign Film from the New York Film Critics Circle and Best Actress, for Magnani, from the National Board of Review; it would eventually be nominated for an Oscar for Best Screenplay as well. Rossellini himself was awarded a prize at the Cannes Film Festival that spring.[5] *Città Aperta* garnered the most enthusiastic reception by far that any Italian film had enjoyed since the silent era, and it was hailed almost immediately and unanimously as a breakthrough in the language of cinema: naturalistic, human, raw, daring. It would cement a global idea of Italy and

4 Approximately $263,000 in 2016.

5 As if in response to its international successes, Italian critics reversed their initial stance and named it best film in their annual awards for 1946.

its movies for years to come, changing the generally held impression of the Italians and their wartime experience and turning the eyes of cineastes toward a country whose films hadn't really made a strong impression in decades. More deeply, it gave filmmakers around the world a new idea of what sorts of subjects cinema could depict and how such movies could be made.

Several qualities made *Città Aperta* unique: its blend of borrowed-from-the-headlines stories and fiction; the nonprofessional players mixed into the cast; the use of real locations and snatches of newsreellike footage of life in the streets during wartime (in an opening sequence, a platoon of actual Nazis marched right through the actual Piazza di Spagna); and a focus on human-scale struggle that made its characters and their stories readily understandable to audiences everywhere. The pregnant widow and the parish priest weren't heroes in the Hollywood vein but ordinary people living under unimaginable stresses and challenges and nevertheless finding the courage to stand up for the causes of liberty and dignity.

Rossellini followed up in 1946 with *Paisà* (*Paisan*), another war story, this one composed of six vignettes that followed chronologically, from Sicily north almost to Venice, the path of the Allied armies, telling a variety of stories of love, death, resistance, and revenge. Once again, Rossellini filmed in actual locations using many nonprofessional actors and telling stories that had circulated as fact or legend during the fighting; once again, his film won prizes and acclaim, at home and abroad. This time, the world was ready for what he had to offer, and a name was coined for it—*neorealism*—suggesting a form of art based in reality and in the new economic and social conditions of the postwar era. Rossellini always rejected the term, claiming that neither the "neo" nor the "realism" was entirely appropriate. But it would stick.

In 1948, Rossellini would release a third wartime drama: *Germania Anno Zero* (*Germany Year Zero*), centered on a young boy scratching out survival amid the rubble of Berlin. By then, his works numbered among a small throng of Italian films that circulated around the world under the *neorealism* rubric, most notably, *Sciuscià* (*Shoeshine*) and *Ladri di Biciclette* (*The Bicycle Thief*), both directed by Vittorio De Sica, who was principally known as an actor. These deeply humane films about the struggles of ordinary Romans to maintain a shred of hope or dignity in the face of brutal poverty and official indifference struck an even deeper chord with audiences than Rossellini's films had. Again, they were made not in film studios but in the streets and buildings of the city; again they starred nonprofessionals in virtually every key role; and, again, they were met with acclaim around the world, including, respectively, the first and third Academy Awards ever bestowed for Best Foreign Language Film.[6]

The depiction of poverty, desperation, and helplessness in De Sica's famous pair of neorealist films was unforgettable: families and orphaned children nearly starving; masses of unemployed men wearing rags and smoking cigarette butts found in the street; boiled cabbage dinners; pawnshops filled with ordinary household goods; predatory black marketeers; callous policemen; and a bombed-out cityscape of ruins. There were thick layers of pathos—cynics might have called it schmaltz—but the human reality of the situation was palpable. With his lead actors plucked from the streets (Lamberto Maggiorani and Enzo Staiola as the father and son in *Ladri*, Franco Interlenghi and Rinaldo

6 In those years, the Foreign Film Oscar was more like an honorary award for special merit than a competitive, elected prize. It wasn't until 1956 that the category would be opened to voting like those for the other Academy Awards—and an Italian film won that year, too.

Smordoni as the ill-fated bootblacks of *Sciuscià*), De Sica was using the raw material of suffering as the stuff of art, and the simple dreams of his protagonists—a job, a filling meal—as rays of hope. The films were beautifully made: atmospheric, handsome, tight. There were other (and earlier) fine works to emerge from the moment and the movement known as neorealism, but this pair of films caught the world's attention and imagination vividly and for very good reason; they would still feel fresh and vital decades on—as good a definition of a classic as could be.

In a remarkable cultural turnaround, a country that had allied with Hitler to wage the most destructive war the world had ever known was now celebrated as a source of sympathetic portraits of human resilience, love, aspiration, and, sometimes, redemption. The themes of poverty, endurance, and yearning ran through a string of acclaimed neorealist films that emerged from Italy in the coming years, including De Sica's *Umberto D*, Giuseppe De Santis's *Riso Amaro* (*Bitter Rice*), and Luchino Visconti's *La Terra Trema* and *Bellissima*. They created an image of a nation on its knees with which audiences everywhere could empathize. There was no braggadocio to them, no sense of excusing away Mussolini and his wars, no traces of nationalism or even, really, of any political agenda. They were simple stories of simple people facing titanic difficulties. And they were made in a way that seemed palpably more vital and true than the typical studio-based film from Hollywood or Rome. In the years after neorealist films from Italy first appeared on American screens, their influence could be seen in Hollywood productions ranging from prestige titles (*A Streetcar Named Desire, On the Waterfront, Call Northside 777, Marty*) to B-level film noir thrillers, with their real-life locations and frequent use of nonactors for atmosphere. Not since the silent era had U.S. filmmakers found inspiration in Italian movies.

And there were more and more new movies emerging from Rome once again after Cinecittà slowly ground back into action in 1948. The first megaproduction to be made there after the war was *Fabiola*, a costume drama about the conversion of Rome to Christianity directed by Alessandro Blasetti. It was exactly the sort of spectacle the studio had been built to create: massive sets, elaborate costumes, thousands of extras, the sort of thing that only Hollywood could do on a similar scale. When Hollywood executives saw the film, they took note of the high level of craft and industrial accomplishment it evinced. The Italians could make a certain type of movie well, they noted. . . .

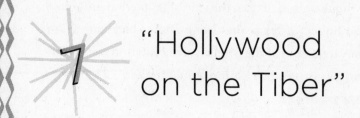

7 "Hollywood on the Tiber"

At the same time that their estimation of Italian cinema and, even more, the capabilities of Italian studios were on the rise, American moviemakers were puzzling out what to do about the monies they were making in Italy but couldn't, because of the laws concerning locked funds, bring back home. It was almost inevitable that they should take a flier and shoot a film in Italy, using the box office frozen there as the budget for a production that would employ the resources of Cinecittà for technical needs and the unmatched locations of Italy as a backdrop. In June 1948, 20th Century Fox sent director Henry King and a full crew of technicians and actors to Rome and Siena to make *Prince of Foxes*, an adventure film about honor and subterfuge under the rule of the Borgias. Tyrone Power, then at the height of his stardom, was cast in the lead as an assassin; Orson Welles, already profligate but still somehow bankable, received a reported $100,000 to play Cesare Borgia. When it opened, the film made a respectable $2-million-plus gross, and the production conditions were of sufficient quality that it managed Oscar nominations for its cinematography and costumes. Almost accidentally, an entirely new sort of production was born: a Hollywood movie—if not, ultimately, a particularly memorable one—shot entirely in Italy.

Encouraged by *Prince of Foxes*, Metro-Goldwyn-Mayer decided to bet a large sum of locked funds on an epic, sending an expedition, as it were, to Italy to film a full-fledged Hollywood production. Since Cinecittà was essentially up and running, MGM decided to make a satellite of it, renting out almost the whole studio for almost all of 1950 in order to remake the 1924 silent epic *Quo Vadis?*,[1] a story of early Roman Christendom, with Mervyn LeRoy set to direct and Elizabeth Taylor and Gregory Peck set to star, at least at first.

Those two would eventually be replaced by Deborah Kerr and Robert Taylor, but that didn't mean that MGM was stinting on the film. The production of *Quo Vadis* cost more than $7 million,[2] and it would, as they liked to say in the movie biz, all show up on the screen. More than 30,000 extras were used in the largest scenes, and LeRoy remembered them with both awe and fondness: "The crowds of job-hunting Romans were so vast and so vigorous that they once nearly overturned my car," he wrote in his autobiography. "The Italians, I found, were born actors. They loved being in

1 The 1924 title included a question mark, which the remake dropped.
2 The equivalent of $68.9 million in 2016.

front of the camera, even if they were with 59,999 others, and each one of them felt it was his picture."[3]

A total of 32,000 costumes were made to order, still a record for a film, as were ten hand-carved wooden chariots, which would be used in other productions for years to come. Cinecittà's electrical system couldn't handle the demands of the imported American lighting rigs, so generators were brought in from Great Britain and from decommissioned warships. And equipment wasn't all that MGM sent to Italy: Virtually every speaking performer and every department head in the crew was a non-Italian. Louis B. Mayer and company may have trusted the Roman weather and been desirous of such authentic backdrops as the Colosseum and the Via Appia Antica, but they weren't going to gamble on Italian technical skill, even if, at the level of seamstresses, carpenters, electricians, animal wranglers, and the like, all hands were local.

In effect, *Quo Vadis* was a Hollywood production parachuted into Cinecittà and availing itself of only those human skills so cheap as not to be worth the money to fly overseas. That made it unique. What made it revolutionary, though, was that it was a big hit, making more than $45 million at the global box office, generating eight Oscar nominations (including Best Picture), and proving to the moneymen of Hollywood that there was a demonstrable upside to using locked funds as the basis of a budget for big-scale moviemaking of the sort at which the Italians were particularly able. In the spring of 1950, writing about the production and the promise of overseas filmmaking it embodied,

3 Among the throngs, legend had it, were Elizabeth Taylor herself, visiting the set and dressing up, without credit, as a slave girl, and a pair of Neapolitans, also uncredited, who had recently arrived in Rome to have a go at the movies: Romilda Villani and her daughter, Sofia Scicolone, who would soon change her surname professionally to Lazzaro and, later, to Loren.

Time magazine coined a phrase, "Hollywood on the Tiber," that had an undeniable ring to it.

By then, a more sensational collaboration of Hollywood and Italian cinema was unfolding. In the wake of his first international successes, Roberto Rossellini received the most remarkable fan letter.

"Dear Mr. Rossellini," it began.

> *I saw your films* Open City *and* Paisan, *and enjoyed them very much. If you need a Swedish actress who speaks English very well, who has not forgotten her German, who is not very understandable in French, and who in Italian knows only "ti amo," I am ready to come and make a film with you.*
>
> *Ingrid Bergman*

And with that began a keystone episode of the modern age, a moment bringing together the intimate lives of two headstrong, talented people, the gigantic sensation-making machinery of the commercial cinema, and the acid splash of mass media.

Bergman, who had left her native Sweden to become an Oscar-winning Hollywood star, was married to her compatriot, Dr. Petter Lindström, with whom she had a daughter. Rossellini not only was married, with a son of his own, but was romantically involved with Anna Magnani, among others. They met in New York and agreed to make a film together, *Stromboli*, a story about a war refugee married to an Italian soldier and forced to live with him in his home village on a tiny volcanic island off of Sicily (Bergman took Magnani's role in it, which sat quite poorly with the Italian star, who presently went off and made her *own* volcano movie). Together on a nearly unpopulated island equipped with almost medieval accommodations, director and star became lovers. She got pregnant, and by the time their baby, Robertino, was born neither would yet be divorced; newspapers and magazines everywhere reported it, with pictures and blaring headlines. Right-wing movieland gossip queen Hedda Hopper launched a vendetta against them in her enormously popular column, and people who had never met them were excoriating them in private meetings in Hollywood and in public sessions of state in Washington and Rome. (Of course, this fueled ticket sales: by some estimates, *Stromboli* grossed nearly $1 million on its opening day in the United States.)

At the height of their artistic and commercial careers, with home lives that had been depicted in publicity as content and stable, two of the most prominent names in world cinema rushed headlong into a love affair that ended their marriages, yielded three children, produced five films, and was shared with the global public virtually in real time via a sort of media that had never been seen before: a nexus of newsreels, picture magazines, and tabloid newspapers that actively sought to ferret out and broadcast intimate details about the lives of celebrities, baring, in the most damning language and with lavish illustrations, private matters that had always been airbrushed out of public accounts of the lives of movie stars. In two countries, news outlets of various degrees of sobriety carried stories about the affair; in Hollywood, Bergman was more or less blackballed, unable to work for a major studio for years;[4] throughout the United States, civic and state authorities banned the showing of *Stromboli*; in Rome, Washington, and Stockholm, politicians denounced the couple as immoral (a Colorado senator called Bergman a "free-love cultist" and Rossellini a

---

4 She would eventually win a second and then a third Oscar, and she worked in movies almost up until her death in 1982, but she never made a film in California again.

"love pirate"); and there was condemnation from the Vatican. For the better part of a year, Ingrid Bergman and Roberto Rossellini were the most notorious couple in the world.

Some of the outrage could be put down to the mores of the times, when public behavior that suggested private sexuality was widely condemned in the United States. Some was surely due to the fact that Bergman, packaged by her American producers and publicists as a kind of pure, natural, ideal woman (she had most recently been nominated for an Oscar for her performance in *Joan of Arc*), had proved herself quite human. Some could be attributed to lingering feelings of ambivalence toward Italy in the wake of the war. But some, too, could be ascribed to differences between the news-gathering cultures of Hollywood, where virtually every media outlet cooperated with the studios, even choosing not to report on the potentially criminal activity of movie stars in exchange for exclusive interviews and privileged access, and Rome, where competition among journalists for scoops was becoming increasingly cutthroat as the economy showed signs of revival and more and more Italians splurged on gossipy publications.

It happened, in fact, that the very first inkling the world had of the Bergman-Rossellini affair came in the form of surreptitious photos of the couple published in Italian magazines. Being that most of *Stromboli* was shot on location off of Sicily, as Rossellini's neorealist aesthetic demanded, there were few opportunities for anyone to see, much less photograph, the couple at work or relaxing together. But late in 1949 they were back in Rome, dining at a restaurant near the Porta Pinciana, right at the summit of Via Veneto, and word of their presence made its way to a news agency. Straightaway, a pair of photographers, Ivo Meldolesi and Pierluigi Praturlon, were dispatched to get snapshots of the lovers. Unexpected, they found the pickings easy; Praturlon, who had made a name for himself two years earlier by spotting Greta Garbo walking anonymously at a Tuscan resort and getting a series of pictures of her, crept in close to Bergman and Rossellini and took several photos. Rossellini, catching sight of him, reacted with seriocomic violence, hurling a plate of spaghetti and taking off in an angry huff.

Praturlon, though, knew exactly where Rossellini would be going—his apartment in a large palazzo on Viale Bruno Buozzi in Pinciano, beyond the Villa Borghese—and he was piqued enough to do something about it. He took off on his motor scooter and was in place for an ambush when Rossellini and Bergman arrived home. When Praturlon popped out to get more shots, Rossellini, with advantageous knowledge of the terrain, lured him into the foyer and trapped him in a corner behind a door. The photographer, unable either to shoot pictures or to flee, shouted for help until another tenant of the building came downstairs to see what the ruckus was, forcing Rossellini to free his prisoner.

Despite the wild details, the incident wasn't much noted at the time, maybe because it looked like a personal matter between the photographer and the filmmaker, who had already been burned by bad publicity. But even a neutral observer would have had to wonder, What the hell kind of melee was that?

8 *Scattini* and *Fumetti*

Snaggletoothed, jug-eared, and thin as a blade, Pierluigi Praturlon wasn't by nature predatory, so it was deeply ironic that he first became widely known for invading the privacy of movie people.

Born in Rome in 1924, he barely escaped the war by virtue of being conscripted just days before the armistice, and in 1945 he began eking out a living taking pictures of tourists and selling photographic equipment out of a shop near Piazza Navona.

His specialty was street photography in the vein of the great French snappers Brassaï, Cartier-Bresson, and Doisneau—candid shots of ordinary people engaged in the quotidian or eye-teasing tricks of light, space, texture, shape. Before long, he was drawn toward shooting news events, and he began freelancing for various Italian newspapers and magazines.

But he was destined to touch stardust. In 1947, he was shooting a conclave of the Communist party and spotted Garbo. The episode led him into a subject matter: movie people. He was hired to shoot portraits of the comic actor Walter Chiari, among others, and he worked for the Venice Film Festival as a semiofficial photographer.

In 1949, the year in which he had his run-in with Roberto Rossellini, Praturlon, who was by then known professionally simply as Pierluigi, was hired by the Roman film company Lux to shoot official publicity photographs of its productions, launching a career as a designated set photographer that would last for decades.

But that was after he'd made his name and earned the trust of editors, movie studios, even celebrities. Before that, he was . . . well, there wasn't really a name for what he was. "Photographer" felt too formal, suggesting well-lit studios and official portraits; "photojournalist" seemed too serious, given the sorts of things he shot. And as for the phenomenon in which he sometimes participated— of multiple photographers stepping up to the line where celebrities' public and private lives met and then crossing it—that had no name, and almost no precedent. Wherever there were notables and celebrities and pretty girls, there were men with cameras, yes, and sometimes packs of them. But actively chasing down subjects in situations in which they might reasonably expect privacy, or deliberately inciting incidents with them that would make for more sensational images: What was that? And who were the guys, Praturlon chief among them, who were showing up like toadstools after a rain and doing it?

* * *

*W*hen they were young, in the hardscrabble years after the war, a fair number of these photographers worked as *scattini*—a word meaning "tics," "jerks," "things that pop up," or, in this case, "snappers," that is, of photos. In a day before people traveled with their own cameras, the *scattini* of Rome worked for—or, as often, *as*—professional photographers, scratching together a few lire a day by enticing tourists to have their pictures taken in front of the Colosseum or Spanish Steps or some other eternal Roman site. A *scattino* would charm and amuse and cajole tourists into posing; the snapshot would be taken; and the subjects would be given an address to which they could report the following day to purchase a print. The percentage of people who bothered to come around and buy pictures was pretty low, though, which meant that the *scattini* did a lot of shucking and jiving for not very much pay.

For the young men who did it, part of the compensation was learning something about photography, maybe falling heir to a camera, and, almost as if they had apprenticed themselves in the old-fashioned way to a master shoemaker or baker, acquiring a set of skills that would allow them to make a living. The composition and lighting of shots; the chemicals and techniques of the darkroom; the best times and places to solicit business; the tricks to jerry-rigging a bit of gear; the best way to handle the authorities; the honing of lines of palaver and hullabaloo to entice customers: it all got passed down in a legacy of collegiality and mentorship that a Renaissance painter would have recognized.

But by the time some of these *scattini* grew up, the world immediately around them had changed and the chance to practice the trade they'd studied was nearly lost, like that of a pony express rider. There were more tourists, yes, but increasingly they had their own cameras. A young man who wanted to be a photographer would have to find new moneymaking venues for his talents.

Fortunately, a few quirks of Italian culture and history had combined to make photograph snapping into something like a going concern for the *scattini* who stuck with it. Even though Italy still labored under one of the lowest literacy rates in Western Europe, the country's magazine publishing business experienced a boom in the wake of the war. In part this was because of the lifting of press restrictions that had smothered journalism during the years of fascism. In part it was because radio hadn't gotten quite the same foothold in Italian houses as it did in, say, the United States or the United Kingdom.[1]

After the war, dozens of new magazines appeared on newsstands throughout Italy, appealing to a variety of specific audiences: men, women, children, those with various political or religious orientations, special interest groups, and those with diverse levels of education. There were serious magazines and picture magazines; men's magazines, sometimes with slightly (and only slightly) risqué tones; and women's magazines, often characterized by a combination of fashion and home-decorating tips, sunny encouragement about the grind of daily life, and sentimental stories about the lives and loves of famous women.

In a sense, the ultimate expression of the latter were the magazines built around what were known as *fotoromanzi*: stories told in something like comic book style, but with actors in costumes on sets enacting the events of the narratives, which were invariably the sorts of tales that fueled soap operas on radio and, later, TV. A *fotoromanzo* could go on for many episodes, spanning many issues

[1] The regular broadcasting of television wouldn't begin until January 1954: a full half decade after the TV set started to become a staple of the modern household elsewhere.

of a magazine, with artfully posed actors acting out tales of lust, passion, and betrayal and speaking through dialogue balloons.[2] The genre was launched just after the war with the introduction of the magazine *Grand Hotel*, which was quickly joined on the news-stand by *Bolero Film* and *Sogno*.

But those magazines were staged and scripted and run almost like movie studios; there was no place in them for spontaneously captured images or even submissions from outside the production line. The magazine boom that would encourage the careers of *scat-tini* into street photographers was modeled more on the line of the American picture magazines *Life* and *Look* and became a competition in which editors and photographers scratched and clawed at one another and at the people whose images were in demand.

Several of these were legitimately news-oriented weeklies, with political slants toward the left, the right or the Catholic church, filled with serious writing, edited and contributed to by some of the greatest minds in Italy, and, to meet the rising tastes of the day, publishing bigger and bolder and *more* photographs than Italian magazines of the prewar era had ever used. In time, public taste pushed some of them toward celebrity news and other forms of gossip and sensation. But by and large they were founded with sober intentions and upheld something like traditional journalistic standards and practices. They included *L'Europeo* (founded in 1945), *Oggi* (1945), *Tempo* (1946), *La Settimana Incom* (1948), *Epoca* (1950), and *L'Espresso* (1955)—many of which would still be published into the twenty-first century. They fed on newsy images—

---

2 Superimposed onto photographs in a way that made them seem to be emerging from the actors' mouths, these balloons so resembled cigarette smoke (*fumo*) that the magazines were also referred to as *fumetti*, which itself became a familiar term for all comic strips and graphic novels.

dozens of them a week—and they relied on freelance street photographers to provide them.

$\mathscr{A}$mong the throng of *scattini* turned pro photographers, nobody would have taken note of slight, meek-looking Tazio Secchiaroli, who bore himself like a civil servant or the keeper of a small shop. Like so many others in the pack, Secchiaroli was born during fascism and came of age in wartime. Before his birth in November 1925, his father, Pietro, a bricklayer, built a home for himself and his wife, Rosa, in Centocelle, later a suburb not even six miles from the Trevi Fountain but then a semipastoral town where sheep still flocked in unfenced meadows. Tazio and his two sisters were born and raised in that house, learning skills expected of them: housekeeping and cooking for the girls, carpentry and building for Tazio. Tazio liked to read, and always would: poetry, history, philosophy. But school came second: the Secchiarolis worked.

In 1941, Pietro died suddenly, and Tazio left school for good, finding a job first as a coal stoker on railroad trains, then as an errand boy at Cinecittà, which sat about two miles from where he lived. That brush with movie life was his first glimpse of cameramen at work, and he decided to try his hand at the game. He borrowed a camera from a friend and spent a sunny afternoon shooting pictures of a soccer match on a nearby field; one shot, an image of a ball flying right at the lens, a young man on a bicycle following behind it, and the field and players in the background, all in focus, revealed a real gift for composition, composure and, crucially, capturing action clearly and crisply in the heat of the moment.

That serendipity—freezing a specific instant into an object of fascination and even beauty—took hold of Tazio's imagination. He found himself drawn into the life of the *scattini*, making his way into Rome to join the squirrelish packs of entrepreneurs who shot photos of soldiers and tourists in front of famous landmarks and learning the various tricks and skills by which professional photographers made a living. The hours were long, the pay inconsistent and meager, and, within a few years, the job itself was dying off: The soldiers were gone, replaced by those tourists and those cameras of theirs.

But there were other avenues of opportunity for a young man with ants in his pants and a fascination with photography. In 1951, Tazio became acquainted with the photojournalist Luciano Mellace, then employed by the International News Service, for which he shot images, especially of papal events, that appeared in American newsweeklies. Through Mellace's endorsement, Tazio, too, started working for the photo agency, once again doing odd jobs and running errands, and it was in that role that he first made his mark.

In June 1952, left-wing protesters massing against U.S. domination of NATO clashed with police at the Piazza Colonna—a hot news story and a great occasion for photos. Tazio gave Mellace a ride to the scene on his Lambretta motor scooter, and they had an inspiration: they rode directly into, through, and around the skirmish, Mellace taking pictures, Secchiaroli scurrying them away, avoiding both police and demonstrators. The protest and Mellace's photos of it lasted in the collective memory for maybe a day, but a far deeper impression was made by a pair of images taken by another photographer, Franco Pinna, who captured, inadvertently, a couple of shots of Tazio driving Mellace around while the latter snapped away. The two were dressed in suits and good shoes; Tazio, driving with both hands, had a cigarette between his lips and his eyes sharply focused on potential trouble; Mellace was almost smiling as his flashbulb exploded and he captured a shot of a protester trying to escape the grasp of a policeman; the news event was, for a split second, less interesting than the behavior of the people trying to record it. Protests, even modestly raucous ones such as this, were common enough in postwar Italy. But the spectacle of a photojournalist careering into a news event on a scooter like a centurion aboard a chariot was a novelty—if you knew enough about the business to recognize it.

Among those who would have appreciated the inventiveness and cheek of what Tazio and Mellace had done was Adolfo Porry-Pastorel, widely considered a forerunner of the modern photojournalist, still working in his early sixties, with his own agency, Vedo (the Italian word for "I see," but technically an acronym for Visioni Editoriali Diffusi Ovunque, or "Editorial Visions Distributed Everywhere"). Porry-Pastorel, a Barnumesque self-promoter, was famed for his speed as a shooter and, especially, a developer of news photos—he could get from shot to print, even in inhospitable locations, in as little as fifteen minutes. He was known, too, for acts of sabotage against rival photographers: he was caught sticking postage stamps on their camera lenses, and he once used carrier pigeons to transmit pictures of Adolf Hitler's visit to the Italian fleet in the Bay of Naples ashore so rapidly that newspapers featuring his photos were being sold on the streets before he, Hitler, and the rest of the photojournalist corps arrived back in port.

Porry-Pastorel surely recognized in Secchiaroli a kindred spirit of competitiveness and resourcefulness, along with a nose for news, a sharp eye, and a steady hand. He hired the younger man as a staff photographer, giving him entrée into a world where he could learn tricks, meet editors, and be invited to events worth shooting rather than having to figure out how to crash them. Secchiaroli was always keen, responsible, diligent, and productive. Under the guidance of a maestro, he would have the opportunity to blossom into a model professional—*if* the right opportunities fell his way.

9 A Girl on a Beach

She lay so still in the rising sunlight that the first person who saw her took her to be asleep.

She was facedown on a stretch of beach outside the village of Tor Vaianica, about twenty kilometers south of Ostia—Rome's ancient seaport and modern beachfront playground. She wore a coat and blouse and underwear, but she had no skirt, no garters, no stockings or shoes or handbag, and she offered no clue whatever as to who she was. Even closely examined, she could still be mistaken for a sleeper—she wasn't bloody or bruised or wounded in any visible way. She had apparently drowned and done so almost peacefully. It was eerie.

After forensic examination of the scene, the body was moved to Rome, where it was positively identified a few days later as that of a girl who'd gone missing approximately thirty-six hours before being discovered on the beach—and whose parents, thunderstruck and grieving, had no idea what she might have been doing so far from home or what could have happened to her.

She was Wilma Montesi—a girl whose name meant nothing in life but would become recognizable in police stations, forensics labs, courtrooms, and, especially, tabloid newspapers throughout Italy and elsewhere for almost a decade to come.

On the morning she was discovered—April 9, 1953—Wilma was a twenty-one-year-old of no special status. She wasn't born to a prominent family, didn't aspire to be an actress or fashion model, had no creative or entrepreneurial ambitions to mark her as a modern Italian girl. Shortish, dark-featured, round-faced, she was an ordinary young woman who lived with her parents and did chores and shopped in the neighborhood and had a fiancé, a rookie policeman whom she'd met only a handful of times and who lived some two hundred miles away. Her father, Rodolfo, was a carpenter; her mother, Maria, a housekeeper. They lived, along with Wilma's sister, brother, and grandparents in a proper and nondescript working-class home in the Trieste district of Rome, a little way northeast of the tourist center.

Her semidisrobed state on the beach puzzled the police, but it didn't compel them to a deep inquiry. Responding to a traumatized family and an inquisitive press, the coroner deemed Wilma's death accidental. The body evinced signs of neither sexual assault nor fatal trauma, and—perhaps to placate her parents, who insisted that their daughter was a paragon of virtue—authorities theorized that Wilma had gone to Ostia to soak her feet in salt water because her new shoes had given her blisters, that she'd waded into the waves, succumbed to exhaustion, passed out, and drowned. That she hadn't mentioned trouble with her feet to anyone at home, much less the idea of taking a trip to the ocean to treat them, and that her body had come to rest miles away from Ostia—*and against the predominant flow of the tide*—mattered not in this judgment. Officially, the case was sad, unfortunate, of no more than passing interest, and closed.

But in the coming weeks and months, in the zabaglione of rumor and gossip that enlivened conversation in cafés and bars in Via del Babuino and Via Veneto, other accounts of Wilma's demise started to emerge—if only in the form of innuendo and hearsay. She had been present at a drug-and-sex orgy involving gangsters, prostitutes, noblemen, and politicians, and either (1) she overdosed and her rich and powerful playmates had her body dumped by the shore, or (2) she did too much, saw too much, and knew too much, and she had been killed in order to be silenced. Nobody in the chic cafés knew her, but she was assumed to be nothing more than the most unfortunate of a growing population of decent girls lured into and then ruined by a depraved upper-class demimonde whose inhabitants would become more sinister and brazen than ever now that they had apparently, with the collusion of policemen and medical examiners, gotten away with murder.

The hum of talk grew louder and more frequent in the weeks after Wilma's death. An obscure drowning would simply not rest in peace. None of the gossip could be proven, not in conversation, much less in court. And even in the scandalmongering tabloid newspapers and magazines of the day—of which Romans were greedily fond—none of it could be published for fear of ruinous libel action by parties whom the gossips suggested were behind the girl's death. But the chatter persisted and grew in detail and soon took on a hue that made it irresistible to certain editors and publishers: One of the bold-faced names being whispered about in connection to Wilma's death belonged to the son of a prominent politician. The story was evolving into something beyond mere titillation; it was, at least potentially, a white-hot scandal.

The rumors first came to public light about a month after Wilma's death and in the most arcane way imaginable: a cartoon published in a satiric magazine showed a flock of pigeons arriving at a police station, one carrying a garter belt in its mouth. The ordinary reader would need a degree in symbology to recognize what was intended: an allusion to Wilma's missing undergarments, and, less directly, to Attilio Piccioni, foreign minister and deputy prime minister in the right-wing Christian Democrat government. Piccioni's surname meant "pigeons" and his son, jazz pianist and bandleader Giampiero Piccioni (aka Piero Piccioni, aka Piero Morgan), was rumored in louder and louder tones to be involved somehow in what was becoming known as *il caso Montesi*—the Montesi case.

Perhaps a few score of Romans would have looked at that cartoon and understood right away the connections it implied between Wilma and a politician's son. But in the tiny, overheated society in which gossip and scandal thrived like mold in a damp cellar, the small circle of people joking about the alleged truth behind the girl's death expanded steadily, furtively, until knowing whispers metamorphosed into bold averrals of fact. In October 1953, the left-wing magazine *Attualità* published specific claims and questions about the case, pointing out, among other things, that the strand upon which Wilma's body was found was a notorious smuggling site and sat a mere kilometer away from Capocotta, a private wooded estate used by noblemen and their guests (and, occasionally, paying customers) for hunting and, the article claimed, parties involving drugs, girls, gambling, and, in at least one instance, it was insinuated, an inconvenient death. It was implied that Wilma died as the result of nefarious doings at Capocotta, where her fellow revelers—in effect, her murderers—included the young Piccioni and a shadowy and altogether dubious Sicilian nobleman named Ugo Montagna, by title the Marchese di San Bartolomeo and by lease the operator of the Capocotta estate.

These were sensational charges and they quickly launched the magazine's publisher, Silvano Muto, a stolid and reserved young lawyer with a fascination for bohemian life, into the public light. Piero Piccioni was a fairly well-known name, even without the benefit of his father's position. He led a New Orleans–style band in regular gigs around Rome and abroad, worked occasionally as a film composer, sat in on jam sessions with the likes of Louis Armstrong, and enjoyed, despite an appearance that suggested a haggard bureaucrat, a reputation as a ladies' man, squiring, among others, the actress Alida Valli. Montagna's name, by contrast, was a new one to most of Muto's readers. Despite his grand title and the trappings of wealth amid which he lived, Montagna was chiefly a *rimediatoro*, a fixer or middleman who made his money through connections to those who held real power, amassing his own clout through theatrical acts of generosity toward his acquaintances; he introduced people to one another, coordinated business deals, helped steer the careers of the sons of rich families, and so forth. He was tall and trim and silver-haired, with impeccable manners and clothes. He seduced powerful men—and their daughters and wives—with confidence and ease. He drove sports cars and traveled widely and had a dog named Marijuana. His connections included politicians, businessmen, and Vatican insiders; his conquests included actresses, heiresses, fashion models, and the sorts of pretty girls who came to Rome from throughout Italy and beyond in search of glory and riches.

Among the women who passed through Montagna's hands were two girls of disparate backgrounds but with similar stories— Adriana Bisaccia and Anna Maria Moneta Caglio. Bisaccia was a provincial southerner whose sojourn to Rome was a dispiriting tale of powerful men, casting couches, broken promises, and vanished opportunities that had ended with her working as a typist and artists' model on the fringes of the Via Margutta bohemia. Caglio, on the other hand, came from a respectable Milanese family with estates and titles and centuries of history including a great-grandfather, Ernesto Teodoro Moneta, who won the Nobel Peace Prize in 1907. An unhappy adolescence had led her into a series of dramas and misadventures, even suicide attempts, and she had come to Rome to find her a career as a model or an actress, neither of which had blossomed.

Both of these women spent time drinking and smoking and gossiping in the bars and cafés around the Piazza di Spagna that were frequented by artists, existentialists, small-time criminals, and tabloid journalists—the Baretto crowd and its hangers-on and sniffers-about. In the months following Wilma's death, in various haunts of the demimonde, Bisaccia hinted broadly and often, with the frank air of someone who wants to be recognized as worldly, that she knew the "real" story of what had happened to the girl found on the beach, asserting that the goings-on at Capocotta were at the heart of the mysterious death and even claiming to have seen Wilma at parties/orgies involving the Capocotta set. Muto met Bisaccia during one of these confessional jags, and her claims prodded him to investigate the case. Soon after he first published his charges in *Attualità*, the publisher met Caglio and from her learned even more about the shadowy world of Capocotta, which she had come to know when she'd been romantically connected to Montagna. She was, in short, an eyewitness to the depravity and criminality of the *marchese's* world. And Muto would need friends like her, because not long after he printed his sensational story, he found himself on trial for libel.

Even in the wildcatting world of partisan tabloid journalism, accusing a pair of prominent or even semiprominent men with complicity in a death that had been ruled an accident was an eye-raising gambit. At first, presented with a demand to recant his articles by authorities working under the command of Attilio Piccioni, who'd leapt immediately to his son's defense (not to mention that of his own good name), Muto agreed to withdraw his claims. But by March 1954, he had chosen to retract his retraction, face his accusers, and reveal what he took to be the facts about Wilma's death in open court. As one of his team of attorneys he chose Giuseppe Sotgiu, a Communist politician with a reputation for florid and dramatic speechifying. Sotgiu, recognizing the opportunity to put the systems of wealth and power represented by the Capocotta set on trial while nominally defending his client, planned to make a great theatrical event of the proceedings, to call both Bisaccia and Caglio as witnesses, to assert that there were corrupt and evil forces at work behind Wilma's death, and to claim that the authorities, cowering to power, had killed the girl a second time by failing to mount a proper investigation of her fate. She hadn't drowned, Sotgiu argued; she had been murdered—he produced forensic experts who agreed with that assertion—and the police and medical examiners had covered it up because her killers were men of influence.

At first, the death of Wilma Montesi had been one sort of news story—a teary tale of an unfortunate girl's strange, unfortunate demise. These new charges, though, coming not in the pages of some scandal sheet but in open court, and bolstered by the testimony of attractive young women telling lurid tales of sex, drugs, power, and corruption—well, *that* was the stuff that sold newspapers. The discovery of Wilma's body and identity had passed through the media briefly and routinely in the spring of 1953. In the early months of 1954, as Sotgiu thundered and schemed in Muto's defense, the Montesi case morphed from sad human-interest story to outright potboiler. Editors, writers, and, especially, photographers responded to the demand for news about it with unprecedented zeal and vigor. The press had one of those periodic "trials of the century" on their hands, and they were determined that the sensation would be as loud and intense and long-lived as they could make it.

Enter the *scattini*.

In the days after Wilma's death, identification, and funeral, photographers had, as expected, hovered discreetly on the periphery to capture images of the death scene, the bereaved family, the mourners, and the police. But the Muto trial engendered a slightly greater frenzy, with pretty girls on the witness stand and potentially explosive political implications. And that meant more lenses, more bodies, more competition. The small pack of photographers who had showed up at the wedding of Linda Christian and Tyrone Power multiplied in sheer numbers and intensified into a fraught and pushy little mob. They were emboldened in their tactics—confronting or sneaking up on lawyers, witnesses, even the Montesi family, whether outside the Palazzo di Giustizia, where the trial was taking place, or at their homes or offices or at any public place they visited to dine or shop or relax. The public devoured images and stories related to the case; coverage spread from the tabloids to the respectable daily and weekly news organs; crowds at the Palazzaccio (or the "Ugly Palace," as the courthouse was commonly known) grew in number and passion with each day. Sotgiu, knowing that anything at all might pop out of the shadows if he kept the spotlight sufficiently bright, encouraged the media attention, and his courtroom performance was designed to intensify it.

And then: a bombshell. Sotgiu had chosen to defend Muto, in large part, by attacking the received theory of the case: that Wilma had gone to Ostia to wash her feet in the sea, fainted, drowned, and floated to Tor Vaianica. He turned an accusatory lens on Montagna, Piccioni, and Saverio Polito, the Roman police commissioner, who, he insinuated, was in the pocket of powerful interests and had covered up the true facts of the girl's death. And his parade of witnesses (several more had emerged in the wake of the publicity surrounding the case, swearing to sinister goings-on involving Wilma and/or the Capocotta crowd) was designed to draw the attention of the three judges away from the question of Muto's alleged libels and toward the chance there really was a fire of illegal behavior beneath the smoke that his client's newspaper had spewed.

But all he needed was Anna Maria Moneta Caglio, whose comely face and flair for drama would, more than any of Sotgiu's stratagems, turn the trial into a circus. Of all the personalities involved in the trial, she was the photographers'—and newspaper readers'—favorite subject. Nicknamed the Black Swan, she was the subject of speculation, rumor, and joking among the crowds outside the Palazzaccio, in the usual haunts of gossip, and in the press. And she lived up to the renown surrounding her: being led from the courthouse to a waiting car one day by a police escort, she nearly fainted, overwhelmed, apparently, by the trauma of her testimony and the crush of photographers and gawkers trying to get a glimpse of her. Tazio Secchiaroli was in that crowd of snappers, working for the Vedo agency, and he got a remarkable shot of Caglio overcome by the moment: eyes squinched mostly shut, mouth slightly open, head atilt, upper arms gripped by a man standing behind her, overcoat crumpled open to reveal a sober suit of clothes beneath, she had a look that could be agonized or sexual or otherworldly, not unlike that of Bernini's famed sculpture *Ecstasy of St. Teresa*. The picture went everywhere.[1]

And her behavior *inside* the courtroom was equally sensational. She spoke of the dark activities at Capocotta; the brutish and predatory words and deeds of Montagna; the drugs; the not-always-willing women; the creepy men of power and station like Piccioni. It all climaxed in the introduction as evidence of a letter Caglio had left with her landlady the previous fall with instructions only to open it on the occasion of her death or disappearance. Read aloud in court, it said, in part,

> *Do not believe any other letter I may have written, only this one. All the others have been extorted from me. My Christian principles are too strong for suicide, but because I know the character of Ugo Montagna and Piero Piccioni, the son of the Minister, I am afraid of disappearing and leaving no trace behind. Alas, I know that the head of the gang of drug traffickers is Ugo Montagna. He is responsible for the disappearance of many women. He is the brain of the gang while Piero Piccioni is the murderer. . . .*

The prosecutor, astonished and flustered, called straightaway for a postponement of the proceedings, which the judges granted, and those present spilled into the street to spread word of this

---

1 Including the offices of film producers: Caglio would appear, in 1955, in *La Ragazza di Via Veneto*, a forgotten melodrama that would be her only film appearance.

shocking new turn. The whispers that had begun in bars and cafés and which had been gathered by Muto in the pages of his magazine were now being blasted throughout the media and the land as fact. A new investigation into Wilma's death was begun; Montagna, Piccioni, and their friends in the police and political circles began desperately to mount defenses; and the media, baying and panting and blaring out each new revelation, innuendo, and hypothesis, gobbled it up and spat it out with unprecedented vigor and glee.

The peaceful body on the beach was now the center of a full-blown media storm.

10 A Nose for *the* Shot

You can't be a photojournalist unless you're enterprising, and you can't be a great photojournalist unless you're also something that Napoleon liked his generals to be: lucky. As he proved as soon as he was hired on at Vedo, Tazio Secchiaroli was both. At first he was only sent out to shoot soccer matches: foolproof, low-risk assignments. But before long he showed the value of his instincts, his initiative, and his photographic skill. That shot of Anna Maria Moneta Caglio outside the Palazzaccio, for instance, was a delicious bit of serendipity: a moment, a posture, a lashing of drama, a sly allusion to fine art, a pretty girl, all wrapped up in a blazing scandal, with the alluring but evanescent smoke and flash of a firework display. It was, in a sense, *perfect* photojournalism.

But it was nothing compared with what Secchiaroli pulled off next. With the Montesi case and its myriad spinoffs, he was, like scores of Rome's photographers and journalists, following a hot story almost around the clock. On a Sunday in the fall of 1954, he went from shooting the news to making it.

Vedo had a contract with a tabloid paper, *Momento Sera*, requiring that a photographer be present in the newsroom at all hours; often there would be two or three on hand. The job involved a lot of sitting around and a lot of routine assignments. But one day Secchiaroli noticed several editors engaged in hush-hush little meetings and his instincts started to tingle. A request was made for a photographer to head out on an assignment, and Secchiaroli stepped forward ahead of his peers to volunteer.

He was driven out to an apartment block on a quiet street in the Prati district, north of the Vatican, where a waiting reporter told him what was going on: there was a brothel on the premises and a famous person—he didn't say who—would be arriving soon; Secchiaroli was to get a picture of him going inside.

Secchiaroli picked out a spot and waited . . . until he got a shot of Giuseppe Sotgiu—Silvano Muto's grandiloquent lawyer, president of the Rome provincial council *and* of the Automobile Club, a leader of the Communist party, the man who had operatically decried the immoral upper class that had killed Wilma Montesi—strolling into the building with an air of familiarity. Secchiaroli snapped him from his hiding place, unseen.

Ordered to stay until he got pictures of Sotgiu leaving, the photographer waited four hours for another shot. By then it was dark, and he needed a flash. Sotgiu exited the building nonchalantly, and Secchiaroli caught a shot of him by surprise. The attorney asked what was happening and Secchiaroli, thinking on his feet, explained that he had recognized a newsworthy face and thought he should take some up-to-date pictures for the files; Sotgiu, thus stroked, posed.

When he returned to the newsroom with his shots, Secchiaroli learned what was going on. Rumors had been circulating that Sotgiu and his wife, the painter Liliana Grimaldi, were using the brothel as a love nest where Liliana and her lover, a young accountant, could make love while Sotgiu watched. The couple had been engaged in this behavior for some time, using the names Signor Mario and Signora Pia, with Liliana enjoying the favors of various men and women. And Secchiaroli's shots would be a key in revealing the politician's secret life to the world.

Based in part on the photographs, police raided the brothel a few weeks later when Sotgiu and Grimaldi were inside. Along with Liliana's lover and several partymates of the moment, the couple were taken into custody for questioning. Sensational headlines resulted, accompanied by Secchiaroli's images: a landslide of ruinous attention. It didn't matter that not a single law had been broken or that nobody claimed any torts or damages. The Communist moralizer had been revealed as a pervert and a hypocrite. Sotgiu was dismissed from the party and removed from his various positions of prominence, and Grimaldi, who had never shared her husband's love of the limelight to begin with, quietly excluded herself from the social whirl around Via Margutta and Via del Babuino that had been a significant part of her life.

The spectacle of Sotgiu's fall diverted the public for a little while, and then attention returned to the Montesi case, which had been reopened as a homicide investigation. In the mind of the larger public, the combined events proved the depravity and shamelessness of the rich and the powerful of Rome. But what wasn't fully appreciated yet was the way in which the impact of both stories had been magnified and protracted by the photographs that accompanied the screaming headlines. There was a paying audience for accounts of any manner of scandal or outrage—so long as they were accompanied by images of the transgressors. An enterprising young man with a camera and his own transportation could put together a nice living simply by feeding off the more outré goings-on around town.

*N*ot long after he photographed Sotgiu, Secchiaroli made legitimate news headlines once again with a scandalous and potentially dangerous set of images. A judicial inquiry had been completed, and a trial was scheduled, with Ugo Montagna and Piero Piccioni having to defend themselves against charges of actions leading to the death of Wilma Montesi and (along with Police Commissioner Saverio Polito) of conspiring to cover up their deeds. Montagna and Piccioni were said, by their attorneys, friends, and partisans in the press, to be strangers to each other, but most people in Rome suspected strongly that that was hogwash.

Another afternoon, another tip phoned into a newsroom: Montagna and Piccioni would be meeting at Piccioni's home, and a photographer named Velio Cioni was sent to stake out the spot. After some time, he watched Montagna's car drive up, Piccioni emerge from his home, and the two men get into Piccioni's vehicle and speed away. On his motor scooter, Cioni pursued them to a street near the Stadio dei Marmi, the Fascist-era athletic facility north of the Vatican. He phoned Secchiaroli, who raced over to the site in his Fiat.

"The city streets were empty in those days," Secchiaroli later said,

and you go could from one place to another in just a few minutes. . . . They had driven into a dead-end street and would
have to come back the same way. I parked my car so as to block
half the street. When they were done talking and doubled
back, I blocked the rest of the street with my body. They realized right away that I was a photographer and that to avoid
having their picture taken they would have to run me down.
And in fact they came right at me, as if they were trying to do
just that. But I didn't move.

He came away with a half dozen shots in which the defendants in
the upcoming trial were clearly identifiable and clearly going out
of their way to have some sort of secretive talk—a huge headline-
maker in a case that was still selling papers and magazines up and
down the Italian peninsula.

In the end, Secchiaroli's scoop didn't affect the trial: the prosecution's case was built on insinuations, suppositions, the testimony of a variety of unreliable witnesses, and even the insights
of psychics. All three defendants were eventually acquitted. Ultimately, the majority of jail time spent and monetary penalties paid
after the death of Wilma Montesi would fall to the *witnesses* for acts
of perjury and other convolutions of the course of justice. But if the
prosecution and the Montesi family had lost, Secchiaroli had, in a
sense, won: his daring, his speed, his nose for news, and his ability to take sharp, telling photographs under pressure were, once
again, peerless.

11 The Curvy Girls

Hollywood on the Tiber wasn't built in a day.

After the production of *Quo Vadis*, American movie studios took a gingerly approach to using Cinecittà and other Italian studios as regular settings for their work. In 1951, a small caper comedy, *The Light Touch*, written and directed for MGM by Richard Brooks and starring Stewart Granger, George Sanders, and the Roman starlet Anna Maria Pierangeli, who used the stage name Pier Angeli, was shot partly at Cinecittà, but it was a relatively small production that hardly fulfilled the promise of employment and largesse signaled by *Quo Vadis*.

However, more than ten Italian films were made at the studio in that same year, and that number doubled in 1952. In a nation still recovering from the war, in a city that had never fully industrialized, not only did the movies provide a fantasy of escape, but they were a vital and viable business employing thousands. In Rome, moviemaking was one of the most labor-intensive enterprises, and Cinecittà was one of the largest employers that wasn't an arm of the government or the church. Thus began a heroic era filled with legendary stories: families living inside the walls of the studio in makeshift homes that security guards never discovered (or didn't care to report); packs of semiferal dogs roaming the back lots and fighting one another for territory; extras appearing in three or four costumes in a single day so as to claim multiple dining chits or pay envelopes; stage mothers clustered on Via Tuscolana thrusting their children at cars entering the famous gates in hopes that a producer or director inside would see a face he could use. On a given day, productions at the studio might call for upward of one thousand bodies, either to dress in costume or to do manual labor, and the whole of Rome, it appeared, had at one time or another queued up to get a chance at the golden ticket to fill those slots.

In 1951, director Luchino Visconti, one of those potential starmakers in the big cars, made *Bellissima*, a film about a Roman housewife (Anna Magnani) so desperate to get her daughter a part in a movie that she spends the money that she and her husband had saved to move out of their tenement flat on acting lessons and audition clothes and the like. It was a film about filmmaking, but not so much a backstage story as one about trying to knock down the doors to *get* backstage. With its urchins and its bare-bones apartments and its fear of destitution and its grimy locations and nonprofessional actors, it felt like a neorealist film. On the other hand, it was slick and polished work (always named with Rossellini and De Sica in the pantheon of neorealism, the aristocratic Visconti generally produced work of high formal refinement, even when his subjects were in no way genteel). The family at the center of the story wasn't as badly off as the one in *The Bicycle Thief*, with their bed linens in hock; they had food in the pantry and savings to call upon and tickets to soccer matches and, especially, the promise of the movies to inspire them.

By 1952, in fact, the movies had spawned a gold-rush mentality among Romans, and Cinecittà had become a kind of Klondike calling out to an impoverished populace still healing from the wounds of the war but filled with hopeful stars (or carpenters or electricians or seamstresses). Another film, Dino Risi's 1953 melodrama *Il Viale della Speranza* (*The Boulevard of Hope*), told the stories of hopefuls lured down Via Tuscolana with dreams of making successes of themselves. And there were plenty of real-life stories of nobodies who became big somebodies to buoy their aspirations.

*O*ne of the most inspiring of such stories was that of Magnani herself, an ordinary Roman who was anything but ordinary. Magnani was a volcano, a tempest, a devastating performer who seemed to live and breathe her art and whose best performances would rank among the most vivid and immediate and emotion-rich ever filmed. She was born in Rome in 1908 (and would die there in 1973), and she was a living symbol of the city: its she-wolf, its spirit goddess, the voice of its streets, the face and body of its native population.

Her parents were never wed—she would never know for sure who her father was—and her mother left her to be raised by aunts and uncles and a grandmother in a series of flats in the Roman slums. She had a spotty education, including musical training, and she was encouraged to pursue a career in theater. She enrolled in the Regia Scuola di Recitazione "Eleanora Duse," the nearest thing Italy had to a national dramatic academy, named for the great star who was considered one of the first practitioners of what would be recognized as a modern acting style. But she didn't last very long and didn't apparently glean much from the experience. Forced to work, she supported herself by singing in nightclubs and then with acting jobs in stock theater. By the mid-1930s, she was appearing regularly in films.

The piazzas of Rome may have been filled with women like Magnani, but on screen, particularly among leading ladies, there was nobody to compare. She would never be mistaken for a beauty pageant contestant or some producer's girl on the side: she was full-bodied, shaggy-maned, often slightly disheveled, with a long nose and a tendency to sport bags beneath her eyes. She projected no vanity and few pretenses. But she had a raw, titanic talent, especially for screen acting, where the camera could get close in on her and reveal her wondrous ability to channel the disparate emotions of a moment.

When she was in the throes of a scene, whether romance or comedy or drama or even a meaningless bit of busywork like setting a table or selling fruit from a stall, she was absolutely magnetic. Fears and lusts and furies and griefs cascaded organically across her face, through her eyes and voice, in her very posture and gait. She was protean, mercurial, profound, and deeply original. At the time she was starting to create a career, avant-gardists in Moscow and New York were developing what would become known as the Stanislavskian system of acting, more commonly known as the Method, designed with an aim toward teaching actors how to express, naturalistically, the emotions of their characters. Magnani, her own best teacher, was living and breathing and, most obviously, *feeling* that way of performing before it ever had a name.

Eventually she would work with a pantheon of great directors: Rossellini, Visconti, Jean Renoir, George Cukor, and Sidney Lumet among them. And she would win an Oscar for acting, in English, in *The Rose Tattoo*, which was written for her by her chum Tennessee Williams. But for all that, she would never be considered a break-out star or a hot girl or an emblem of the modernization of Rome. She was a glorious anomaly—and the world, it seemed, preferred something more predictable from the women it turned into icons.

There was another emerging star, who, in a sense, didn't really want to be an actress at all. She wanted to be an artist, and, in time, she would become just that. But first she would have to become other things—a sex symbol, a screen icon, an international celebrity, a wife and mother, a photojournalist, a living vessel for a variety of ideas about Italy, female beauty, and the Mediterranean temperament, and even one of the first widely noted specimens a new species of girl: the *maggiorata*, or "curvy girl,"[1] a physical embodiment of everything that other Europeans and, especially, Americans thought of when they thought of an Italian woman. She even had a perfect name for the job: Gina (shortened from Luigina) Lollobrigida—or, more sensationally, La Lollo, as the Italian press, quickly followed by the French and English and American, would think of her.

She was born in 1927 in Subiaco, Lazio—a mere fifty miles from the heart of Rome and the birthplace, as it happened, of Lucrezia Borgia. Her father was a furniture maker and moved the family to Rome in search of work when the war was coming to an end. Young

1 The term was derived from the phrase *maggiorata fisicha*, which became popular after appearing in the 1952 anthology film *Altri Tempi*, one episode of which involved an accused murderess whose lawyer argued that convicting such a statuesque woman as his client would mark the jurors as prudish and cruel.

Gina first hoped to pursue art, maybe studying painting or sculpture. But she was fated by her beauty and her physique to be the model, not the maker. She drifted into drama classes and had her first stage role in 1945. Soon after, she was being urged to enter beauty pageants, an institution that had died away during the war but which had been revived spectacularly in 1946, when the shapely Silvana Pampanini, who would go on to fame as a pinup girl and actress, came very close to being named Miss Italia (the English word was, in fact, used). The following year, Gina participated, and she finished in third place in a competition that included several soon-to-be celebrities, including the winner, a Milanese bakery assistant named Lucia Bosé.

Many beauty pageant contestants were offered contracts to model clothes, to make movies, to be on magazine covers and in advertisements. Bosé herself would go to on a notable career in films: she would become romantically involved with a young writer-director named Michelangelo Antonioni, who cast her as the lead of his first feature, *Cronaca di un Amore* (*Story of a Love Affair*) in 1950, and she starred in a bona fide smash hit, *Le Ragazze di Piazza di Spagna* (literally, *The Girls of the Piazza di Spagna*, but known in English as *Three Girls from Rome*) in 1952.

But Gina became the bigger star. When she appeared on the Miss Italia stage, she had already been in about a half dozen films, none of which had much impact, artistically or commercially. By 1950, though, she had the lead in several movies, most notably *Miss Italia*, a quasi-autobiographical story ginned up with some melodrama. The films still weren't particularly memorable, but Gina had become famous, and her natural beauty, her rags-to-riches story, and her aura of sexuality paired with moral decency all combined to make her an ideal of young Italian girls, who all wanted to follow in her footsteps.

She was also, of course, pursued by men. And in 1949, one of them captured her, a Slovenian physician named Milko Skofic, who, somewhat presumptuously, took over her career as her agent and manager. It was in that capacity that Skofic agreed, amazingly, to send his wife by herself on a flight to the United States, where a Hollywood producer who had seen pictures of her thought he could make her into a real star.

His name? Howard Hughes.

Even in the annals of the many women wooed, pursued, won, and dumped by the talented and fickle Mr. Hughes, Gina Lollobrigida is a noteworthy entry. She was ensconced by the not-quite-yet reclusive Hughes in a Beverly Hills hotel suite, where she was attended by a full-time staff, including maid, chauffeur, acting coach, and English tutor. She was assigned a scene to learn—in which, incredibly, a wife asked her husband for a divorce—and underwent repeated screen tests in different wardrobes, hairstyles, and settings. She was miserable, she didn't like Hughes much (she called him "interesting" but was unhappy with the slovenly appearance he cultivated and the low-market places he preferred to dine and dance), she missed her husband (to whom she would swear she was faithful the whole while), and she simply didn't fit in: she wanted to go home. Hughes let her, in exchange for her signature on a contract forbidding her to work with any other Hollywood producer.

Initially, that concession didn't seem to matter. Not only was Gina in demand at home, but she was being sought by producers from elsewhere in Europe. Her first truly important international film was a 1952 costume action romp, *Fanfan la Tulipe*, a Franco-Italian coproduction set in prerevolutionary France. But as her stock rose in Italian films, particularly with the smashing success of the romantic comedy *Pane, Amore e Fantasia* (*Bread, Love and Dreams*; 1953) and its sequel, *Pane, Amore e Gelosia* (literally, *Bread, Love and Jealousy*, but known in the United States as *Frisky*), her arrangement with Hughes was thwarting her ambitions. Other Italian actresses were free to break into the American cinema, but Lollobrigida wasn't. She did appear in one semi-Hollywood film, John Huston's half-baked 1953 farce *Beat the Devil* (in which she could appear because it was independently financed outside the United States and thus fell outside the bounds of her agreement with Hughes). But that wasn't the big Hollywood career that had once beckoned her.

And by then, frankly, she had stiff competition for the title of the most sought-after *maggiorata* in the movies, even at home. In fact, she would be trumped as Rome's most famous actress by a girl who was as far from a *maggiorata* as could be imagined.

12 "She Will Be a Sensation"

Despite the best efforts of Gina Lollobrigida, her manager-husband, and, for the brief time that he cared, Howard Hughes, the actress remained a star only in Italy. She could therefore be forgiven if she got a little miffed when a twenty-three-year-old with one notable credit to her name was cast in a big-budget Hollywood on the Tiber film, which would turn her into a huge international star and Oscar winner.

Audrey Hepburn was born in Belgium and raised in Holland and England. She had trained as a dancer and, after flopping out, segued into acting. She appeared, nearly invisibly, in a few Dutch and English films and on the London stage, and then she won the title role in a Broadway adaptation of Colette's novel *Gigi*, a light (non-musical) comedy that ran for more than 200 performances and brought her to the attention of Hollywood.

At the time, director William Wyler was in preproduction for Paramount on *Roman Holiday*, a bubbly little sort-of romance about a princess on a world tour who escapes her handlers and spends a couple of days gallivanting around Rome in the company of an American journalist. Gregory Peck was cast as the reporter and Eddie Albert as his photographer chum, but for the leading lady Wyler wanted an actress who was, in his view, an anti-Italian, physically unlike the curvy *maggiorate* who had become synonymous with Italian films—and the world's perception of Italian women—in recent years. He was aware that he needed to draw audiences, though, so at first he let his producers try to persuade him to hire Elizabeth Taylor. When she proved unavailable for the shoot, which was set for the summer and early fall of 1952, he tested Hepburn. She was perfect: as he told some Roman acquaintances, his new star had "no arse, no tits, no tight-fitting clothes, no high heels. In short, a Martian. She will be a sensation."

With a budget of approximately $1.5 million, the film was another windfall for Cinecittà, although, once again, the Hollywood studio sent along a huge crew (including, at the birth of Italian high fashion, Edith Head, who would win one of her eight Oscars for the wardrobe she designed for Hepburn). It was another parachute project, dropped in on top of whatever the Italians were doing at the time, availing itself of Rome's picturesque locations but not necessarily its salaried workers and performers, and then flying back out. But there could be little resentment about the production or the resultant goodwill and largesse it brought to the

Roman studio or, for that matter, to Rome itself: *Roman Holiday*, set in the here and now and headlined by an insanely charming pair of stars, would prove a far bigger boon to the capital than *Quo Vadis*. It painted a portrait of a city steeped in novelty, romance, gaiety, and vitality, with the emblematic motor scooters zipping through scenic streets and piazzas, and colorful colonies of bohemians, journalists, nobles, and ordinary folk mixing together in a chummy minestrone of merrymaking. It featured gelato and wine and an open-air market and streets crowded with picturesque faces and the most glorious Vespa ride through and around it all, still an iconic image of freewheeling liberty and swank style decades later. From the Colosseum to the Trevi Fountain to the Spanish Steps to the *Bocca della Verità*, the array of the city's tourist spots was on display, and there were glimpses of a more modern Rome: the American journalist lived at 51 Via Margutta, which marked him as arty, and he took the princess dancing on a barge in the Tiber where a jazz band played Dixieland in the shadow of the Castel Sant'Angelo.

Roman Holiday grossed $12 million worldwide in 1953 and was nominated for ten Academy Awards, including Best Picture, taking home the prizes for Best Actress and Best Motion Picture Story in addition to Edith Head's prize.[1] It made Rome look like the very best place on earth to cut loose for a few days, just a few years after all the world took pity on the Romans with their stolen bicycles and handmade shoeshine boxes and pawnshops filled with bed linen and socks. And it made Hepburn a superstar, an icon of cinema and fashion and of Rome itself: she would go on to make several films there, become associated with a number of Roman fashion

---

1 That screenwriting Oscar went to Ian McLellan Hunter who had, in fact, signed his name to the script in a secret agreement with the real author, the blacklisted Dalton Trumbo, who was finally awarded the prize in his own name some forty years later.

designers, and, eventually, live and raise children in the city. It didn't seem to matter to international audiences—or to Romans— that her tiny frame and elfin features bore almost nothing of the earthy sensuality that made Anna Magnani and Gina Lollobrigida so magnetic. Hepburn was the ideal girl of a moment, and that moment would be at one with the Rome which she made her fictional playground and chose as one of her real-life homes.

$\mathcal{B}$ut the 1950s were allowing for a brassier and more overtly sexual image of feminine allure to emerge on movie screens than previously, and Hollywood would send a specimen of that sort to Rome in November 1953: Ava Gardner flew in after divorcing Frank Sinatra, to blow off a little steam at the nightclubs that were starting to pop up around town, to acquire a hand-fit wardrobe of couture dresses, and, almost incidentally, to play the title role in Joseph L. Mankiewicz's *The Barefoot Contessa*, a story of a poor girl turned man-eating diva that was, apparently, personally tailored to Gardner as a bespoke gown. The film was shot at Cinecittà and a variety of locations around Rome and a few nearby cities, but, uniquely for an American film, it used Italy to stand in for a number of other locales,[2] indicating a level of trust on the part of an American production company (in this case, a one-off collaboration between Mankiewicz and a collection of investors, including the Italian publishing mogul Angelo Rizzoli) in the technical expertise of an Italian crew. For this reason, *Contessa* had a slightly larger contingent of locals on board.

Or maybe it was just getting too expensive to send technicians from Hollywood to Italy, especially as the trip was becoming more

2 The only scene in the film that would be set in Rome was an interior of a screening room—which could have been shot at any movie studio on earth.

and more frequent. While Gardner was getting acquainted with Rome, Paramount was wrapping up the filming of *Ulysses*, a costume epic by veteran director Mario Camerini, working with a largely Italian cast and crew but with Kirk Douglas and Anthony Quinn as his stars—an interesting model for making movies abroad while retaining creative control and ensuring something like reliable box-office returns.[3] At the same time, on the same Cinecittà lot, 20th Century Fox was in production on *Three Coins in the Fountain*, a frappe of wan melodrama and flat comedy directed by Jean Negulesco and featuring among its star-crossed lovers Dorothy McGuire, Jean Peters, Louis Jourdan, Clifton Webb, and an Italian actor whom Hollywood executives had been touting for stardom for a couple of years without luck, a big-jawed, big-haired, square-shouldered sportsman, lawyer, director, Freemason, accused (and acquitted) arms dealer, and (he claimed) clairvoyant named Rossano Brazzi.

Born in 1916 to a shoemaking family in Bologna, Brazzi was raised in Florence by a doting mother (two previous children had died) and participated seriously enough in sports to achieve semipro status as a soccer goalkeeper and to be ranked as an amateur boxer. He studied law at San Marco University in Florence, where he dabbled in school theatricals. As an apprentice attorney in Rome (his first big case was the defense of a woman accused of stealing a chicken), he continued to pursue acting, appearing in stage melodramas and in small roles in films. Very quickly, his manly chest (accentuated by use of a girdle), strong jaw, corona of hair, aquiline profile, and haughty bearing made him a popular screen presence ("Sometimes my face is more beautiful than the leading lady's," he

3 There were other benefits: if a film was deemed to be of a certain percentage of local origin—whether that consisted of funding, casting, or crew—the Italian government provided its makers with tax breaks and other subsidies and considerations.

gallantly boasted to a fan magazine). Soon enough, he was starring in, among other films, *Noi Vivi* (1942), a two-part adaptation of Ayn Rand's *We the Living* and, more promisingly, *Aquila Nera* (*Return of the Black Eagle*), a 1946 remake of the 1925 American film *The Eagle*, which had starred the cinema's first great Latin lover, Rudolph Valentino.

In that latter role, Brazzi was "discovered" by David O. Selznick, who thought he'd found a second Valentino. Selznick brought Brazzi to Hollywood, despite his thick accent and his lack of renown outside his own country.[4] It was a disaster. Despite launching a robust publicity campaign about the hot new leading man he'd imported, Selznick, stymied by the actor's dodgy English, wound up selecting for Brazzi's American debut the role of Professor Bhaer in the 1949 production of *Little Women*, an older man falling in love with June Allyson's Jo while wearing a powdered wig and (oh, the indignity!) a pillow stuffed under his costume to simulate middle-age spread. Humbled, Brazzi asked to be released from his contract, which favor was granted him, and he went home. This smackdown was greeted with no little relish in Roman film circles. "He was full of himself when he set off for Hollywood," recalled the veteran American agents Hank Kaufman and Gene Lerner, who had offices in Rome, "and came back with his tail between his legs. Italians are very unforgiving toward the 'prodigal son' who doesn't make it abroad and doesn't return loaded with money." Brazzi's first film back home didn't exactly rekindle his career: he was cast opposite Anna Magnani in *Volcano*, the awful, hurried-up film that

4 And despite the fact that Brazzi had a wife, a Florentine baroness named Lidia Bertolini, whom he'd met at university and married in 1940 and who was so short, plump, and plain-looking that she was often taken to be his mother. Their marriage, childless, lasted until her death in 1981.

had been built around her after Roberto Rossellini replaced her in *Stromboli* with Ingrid Bergman.

But Brazzi, possessed of an athlete's confidence, persevered. He returned to a place of prominence in Italian films and then, with *Three Coins in the Fountain*, to American movies—or, more specifically, American movies set in Italy, where he could play something like his established screen image and his thick accent wouldn't be a hindrance. His nearly cartoonish embodiment of the manly Latin lover (a role that, he insisted, had nothing to do with his life) might have proved a barrier to his progress in Hollywood; the figure held an attraction/repulsion for American audiences who were fascinated by what they saw as Continental charm and sexual libertinism but preferred to think of it, apparently, at a remove of a few thousand miles rather than on the streets they walked. Brazzi couldn't convince as a hero or a wolf: he was too stiff and formal and looked uncomfortable except when photographed in profile with an actress in his arms. As an icon of his nation and his people, he was like Maurice Chevalier: a gentle caricature of stereotypical traits. But he could fill the role of Mediterranean Romeo adequately for the purposes of melodrama.

He followed *Three Coins*[5] with a role in *The Barefoot Contessa* as an impotent Italian prince (who has lost his virility in a wartime episode in Benghazi) and then, with his surest footing yet in a Hollywood production, as a Venetian antique dealer wooing

---

5 Which, in one of those inexplicable turns, was nominated for an Oscar as Best Picture, alongside *The Caine Mutiny*, *The Country Girl*, *Seven Brides for Seven Brothers*, and the eventual winner, *On the Waterfront*—and ahead of such non-nominees as *Rear Window*, *Sabrina*, and *A Star Is Born*. *Three Coins in the Fountain* won in the only other categories in which it was nominated: Best Song (sung, uncredited, by Frank Sinatra) and Best Color Cinematography (which, showing Rome in Cinemascope, was genuinely lovely).

Katharine Hepburn's American spinster in David Lean's Venice-set 1955 melodrama *Summertime*. From there, he was cast as Emile De Becque in the 1958 screen adaptation of *South Pacific* (he didn't actually sing "Some Enchanted Evening"—Giorgio Tozzi did), and he became a genuine star outside of Italy, if never exactly an icon and not for long.

The decade-long struggle to make Brazzi a star in American films ought to have been a cautionary tale for Hollywood producers scouring Italy for the *next* next Valentino, but they kept trying. In 1953, it was the turn of Vittorio Gassman, a serious stage actor with a hawkish profile and a jittery energy who had remarkable vocal and physical range and had been in the movies since the end of the war. Though he was known among his countrymen as the Laurence Olivier of Italy (both were, it happened, directors of note), he never quite made a similar impression in Hollywood, where he appeared, sometimes in the lead, in a series of forgettable B movies, a sojourn that found him returning home and resuming his career with one particularly notable American credit to boast: he had married and fathered a child with the American actress Shelley Winters. He would keep running at international stardom like a man trying to build up enough speed to leap over a gap, but he never quite made it.

Great things were imagined, too, for Walter Chiari, a rugged-looking specimen who was rubber-faced and adept at comedy and who never did find his way to Hollywood even though he spoke English well and appeared in several American films shot in Rome. Ditto Alberto Sordi, a stout, big-eyed comedian who held such a prominent role in the hearts of his fellow Romans that they would eventually name a shopping gallery in the heart of the city for him; he appeared in small roles in a few English-language films and starred in one of the most popular Italian comedies of the fifties, *Un Americano a Roma* (*An American in Rome*), which he cowrote, playing Nando, a typical Roman of his time who strove to emulate the Yanks infesting his hometown by speaking American slang, walking like John Wayne, eating cornflakes with ketchup, even threatening to kill himself if he couldn't get a visa to travel to the United States.[6] He had a bit of Jackie Gleason in him, and a bit of Robert Mitchum, but he had nothing that Hollywood needed, and they let him thrive in his homeland unbidden.

It wasn't just Italian leading men whom American producers couldn't quite slot into their world-conquering schemes. Despite a long train of beautiful and often talented actresses coming up within the Italian system, there was still not a bona fide film icon to have come out of Italy. Along with the efforts to turn both Anna Magnani and Gina Lollobrigida into Hollywood (and, therefore, international) stars, there was David Selznick's "discovery," Alida Valli, a sharp-featured beauty who appeared in Alfred Hitchcock's *The Paradine Case* and Carol Reed's *The Third Man* before returning to more familiar habits of living and working back home; there was Silvana Mangano, whose role as a tempestuous field worker (also named Silvana) in Giuseppe De Santis's 1949 *Bitter Rice* caused an international sensation but who chose to stay in Italy and work alongside her husband, producer Dino De Laurentiis.[7] And there were Elsa Martinelli and Lucia Bosé, who transitioned from early appearances in beauty pageants and work as fashion models to

6 In the wake of the film's extraordinary success, the Neapolitan bandleader Renato Carosone had a blockbuster hit with a song "Tu Vuo' Fa' l'Americano" ("You Want to Act American") about the pathetic life of just such a fellow; it would appear on screen in 1960's *It Started in Naples*, with Sophia Loren singing, and then again in 1999 in a memorable scene in Anthony Minghella's *The Talented Mr. Ripley.*

7 Among their grandchildren would be the food TV star and cookbook author Giada De Laurentiis.

modestly successful careers on screen, with some interruptions, as was almost required of Italian actresses, to raise families.[8]

*I*t was almost as if Italian screen talents—and there were plenty of them—had some intangible weakness that mitigated against success abroad, or, at least, in Hollywood, where the studio system had decades of experience in molding the raw material of aspiring actors into larger-than-life successes. And it wasn't any better for the filmmakers. In 1953, David Selznick tried to make a movie with one of the moment's most celebrated directors, Vittorio De Sica, and the result was a catastrophe of clashing egos, intentions, visions, and methods. *Stazione Termini*, conceived by the great novelist and screenwriter Cesare Zavattini, was set during a ninety-minute wait between trains at Rome's sleek central railway station, still the most visible architectural sign of recovery from the war and the symbol of arrival in Rome not only for foreigners but internal migrants. In this case, it would be a point of departure: a Philadelphia housewife, visiting her sister in Rome, fell into an affair with a half-American/half-Italian schoolteacher and was leaving town so as not to endanger her marriage any further; the film would depict their tortured adieu.

Selznick was famed as Hollywood's most insufferable meddler, notorious for sending novella-length memos explaining the gap between his objectives and the work in progress to directors and screenwriters. As this film was to star his wife, Jennifer Jones (opposite that exemplary Italian, Montgomery Clift), he was more attentive than usual, dispatching epic missives regularly from Hollywood to Rome—where De Sica, who couldn't read a lick

8 Bosé left films in 1956 to marry the celebrated *torero* Luis Miguel Dominguín, not long after his split with Ava Gardner. Their three children included the future Spanish pop idol and actor Miguel Bosé.

of English, ignored them. In one of the great case studies of conflict between a director with a strong voice and a producer with the
purse strings, the result was two distinct films. De Sica's movie,
Stazione Termini, which showed in Europe, was approximately
ninety minutes long and filled the space around the melodrama
with dozens of amusing and acute observations of the behavior of
the mass of humanity that passed through the train station; Selznick cut almost a third of it, mostly the fascinating portraits of
daily life whirling around the parting couple, and, at barely an
hour in length, released it in the United States under the title *Indis-
cretion of an American Wife*. With its earnest ardor and actors who
are at once deeply committed and deeply miscast, De Sica's film
was a bit liberal in laying on the melodrama, but it was a satisfy-
ing experiment in real-time storytelling and a lovely time capsule
of actors, characters, and human moments of a certain place and
time. Selznick's film was more like a sketch, lacking any feel for a
world around its characters, a lengthy anecdote that made viewers
wish for a breath of air and another face or two to look at. The picture performed poorly with critics and audiences, and in its wake
no other Hollywood producer would seriously consider working
with an Italian director—particularly a celebrated one—for years.

"She's Impossible to Photograph"

Finally, someone arrived on the scene who could break through, an Italian who would be recognized internationally, almost on first sight, as being not just a foreign curiosity but one of those superhuman creatures known as movie stars.

By the time she was twenty-nine years old, the child born Sofia Scicolone to an unwed mother from Naples had: changed her name twice; married and had her marriage annulled; miscarried a child; moved from Pozzuoli near Naples to Rome to Beverly Hills to Paris to Switzerland and then back to Rome; won prizes in beauty pageants; become a star of *fotoromanzi*; appeared top-less in two movies; and accrued more than forty mainstream film credits, alongside such costars as Clark Gable, John Wayne, Cary Grant (twice), Frank Sinatra, Alec Guinness, Peter Sellers, Alan Ladd, William Holden, Charlton Heston, Anthony Quinn (three times), Vittorio De Sica, Alberto Sordi, and Totò, and under the guidance of such directors as George Cukor, Carol Reed, Sidney Lumet, Martin Ritt, Anthony Mann, Michael Curtiz, Stanley Kramer, Anthony Asquith, Alessandro Blasetti, Mario Soldati, Dino Risi, and, once again, De Sica.

She had won an Oscar while speaking a language other than English (a first); she had received a $1 million payday to appear in a movie (a first for an Italian, male or female); she was held up as a living embodiment of Italian mores and style and, especially, movie art (even while she was unable to live in her own homeland); and she had become an international symbol of sex, glamour, and, in some eyes, shamelessness and vice.

She wasn't known as Sofia Scicolone by then, or Sofia Stuz-zicadente ("toothpick"), as childhood classmates had dubbed her for her gangly, stick-figure body, or Sofia Lazzaro, as she was known professionally for a few years (after Lazarus, who, it was suggested, would have risen from the dead anew in the presence of her beauty). She was known as Sophia Loren, a hybrid mon-icker inspired by a Swedish actress's surname and the English spelling of her Christian name.

That she should go through all those transformations to hit on just the right pair of words to be known by would reveal something of her desire to achieve worldly success. But at the same time, it was laughable, because, really, all Sophia Loren ever had to do to be a star was show up.

* * *

S he first showed up on September 20, 1934, at a clinic for unwed mothers in Rome. Her mother, Romilda Villani, whom everybody in Pozzuoli thought looked like Greta Garbo, had come to the big city to break into movies, only to meet one Ricardo Scicolone, a clerk for the state-run railroad and an inveterate rake. Their romance had resulted in a pregnancy but no promise of marriage, and Romilda reckoned that naming the baby Sofia after Ricardo's mother might sway grandma to the child's side and force a wedding. But all she got was Ricardo's signature on a document acknowledging paternity of the baby, thus passing along his name. Romilda was forced to return home and move in with her family, who barely eked by on the salaries that her father and brother earned working at a nearby munitions factory.

Even in that meager household, little Sofia was a bit of a desperate case: dark-complected and skinny, with features that seemed not to fit her face. The first worry was feeding her, a responsibility borne by the whole family, when they traded away the little portion of meat they could afford to a local wet nurse in exchange for nourishment for the baby. By the time she was a toddler, the child was well enough that Romilda returned to Rome, ostensibly to renew her pursuit of a career but, in truth, to find Scicolone. She caught him long enough to get pregnant once again. ("She was at the height of her physical splendor," he later said. "It was inevitable that there should be new outbursts of passion between us.") In May 1938, another daughter, Maria, was born, but Scicolone refused to acknowledge her, and thus she would be known as Villani—and, having been born out of wedlock, be ineligible to attend Catholic schools.

By then, the international sanctions imposed in reaction to

Mussolini's African invasions had begun to make themselves felt even on top of the privation that was typical in Pozzuoli. "Hunger," Sophia later recalled, "was the major theme of my childhood." And it only got worse when World War II broke out, with German occupiers and Allied bombardments (that munitions factory was, naturally, a target) and then, like a bad joke, a volcanic eruption that destroyed many of the bits of Pozzuoli that the bombing hadn't. With only the clothes on their backs, the Villanis evacuated to the home of relatives in Naples, where regular air raids forced them to spend nights in dark tunnels teeming with rats, lice, and scabies.[1]

The arrival of Allied troops meant a return to what was left of the family home, where Romilda, ever hearing the siren call of show biz, set up a little cabaret in the living room and entertained GIs, mom playing piano, the little girls singing and dancing, grandma selling homemade wine and simple meals. It was a modestly popular spot,[2] and Romilda was a sufficiently appealing hostess to attract repeat customers, some of whom brought gifts of food, cigarettes, toys for the kids, and nylon stockings for the ladies—and some who bore marriage proposals (none of which, apparently, included a place for her daughters, so she declined them all). This small success once again made Romilda hungry to pursue a life on the stage or the screen, and she was off to Rome again, with fourteen-year-old Sofia, who was taken out of school never to return. The big attraction was news that an enormous Hollywood production of *Quo Vadis* was being made at Cinecittà and they were hiring hundreds—*thousands*—of extras with the possibility of even bigger and better.

---

1 These episodes so traumatized the girl that she would sleep with a light on every night for the rest of her life.

2 Years later, a British acquaintance of Sophia would recall stopping in while a young soldier—fellow by the name of Alec Guinness.

Lodging once again with relatives, Romilda and Sofia reported to the famous gates on Via Tuscolana and succeeded in getting through the preliminary rounds of culling from among the many thousands of aspirants. Sofia, in particular, was noticed, and she was selected to be interviewed by the film's director, Mervyn LeRoy. Romilda had picked up a little English during her brief career as a home entertainer, but Sofia had none, and so her mother told the child simply to answer yes to whatever she was asked. That strategy worked well enough when the question was "Do you speak English?" but not so much when it was "How old are you?" Mother and daughter got jobs, but only as extras, and though the pay was meager it was encouraging enough to keep them (and, presently, kid sister Maria) in Rome as part of the throng of movie business hopefuls.

There was always some small bit of work—Sofia may have appeared in as many as twenty films without billing[3]—and there were other avenues available to a pretty girl. Because a pretty girl is what Sofia had become: the skinny ugly duckling with the mismatched features had grown, by age fifteen, into a tall, voluptuously proportioned knockout. True, she had a big nose and a gap between her front teeth and unusual planes and angles to her face. And yet those discordant details somehow harmonized, and anyone with a discerning eye could see that she was a rare beauty—raw, yes, and without any immediately obvious talents as an entertainer, but eager, fearless, and determined—and with an even more eager, fearless, and determined mother propelling her.

In addition to film work, Sofia found jobs as a photographer's model, which led her to the world of the *fotoromanzi*—the graphic

3 Including 1950's *Luci di Varietà* (*Variety Lights*), the first film on which Federico Fellini would receive (technically, share) credit as a director—and the only film of his in which she would ever appear.

novels that told soap operatic stories of intrigue and amour using photographs of real actors rather than drawings. Back in Pozzuoli, Sophia had studied a kind of pantomime acting, learning how to express a variety of emotions using just her face and simple hand gestures, making her a natural for this kind of work. Taking the stage name Sofia Lazzaro, she became a sensation, appearing as a vamp and femme fatale in popular narrative series in *Bolero Film* and *Sogno*. Although later on she would dismiss it as "the most stupid job imaginable," it was a path that Gina Lollobrigida, among others, had taken to fame. And it gave her experience in taking direction, playing to a camera, and filling a role.

There was yet another avenue of activity open to a girl of her age, experience (or, rather, inexperience), and allure: beauty pageants. In a beauty pageant, after all, particularly one with a swim-suit competition, Sofia had advantages that few of her competitors could marshal. There was no career attached to these contests, and the prizes could often be something as minor as supplies of food or household goods. But they were frequent, they were easy to enter, and they were, for her, knock-overs. Romilda dragged Sofia up and down Italy to enter these contests, and while she didn't win them all, she made an impact each of the many times she entered one. At the 1950 Miss Italia pageant, barely sixteen, she was crowned Miss Elegance, a title invented on the spot by the judges so as to give her *something* for her evident merits.

She was often asked to take part in beauty contests even when she wasn't intending to, such as one evening in 1950 when she was dining with friends on a restaurant terrace near the Colosseum and there happened to be some sort of pageant in progress in the adjoining gardens. Sofia paid no mind, but soon a waiter came by with a note from one of the judges inviting her to join the competi-tion. Her friends urged her on, suggesting that a lot of movie people frequented the restaurant, but she was uninterested. And then a second note came, signed with a name that meant nothing to her. This time, though, she had a sense that she should consent, and so she left her group and joined the throng of aspiring beauties.

She came in second. But when it was over, the fellow who'd invited her to join the contest introduced himself. He was short, bald, roly-poly, and a good twenty years older than her if he was a day. He said that he was greatly taken with her beauty and that he was a movie producer responsible for the careers of Gina Lollobrigida and Lucia Bosé. He asked her to join him on a walk through the garden, and when she agreed, and much to her surprise, he behaved like a perfect gentleman the whole time they were alone. When they parted, he gave her his business address and told her to come see him the next day to talk about her plans and to make a screen test. He had high hopes for her, he said. His name was Carlo Ponti. She'd never heard of him.

Carlo Ponti came to be a movie producer for the usual reasons: he liked money, and he liked girls.

He'd been born in 1912 in Magenta, not far from Milan, where his father ran a print shop that specialized in sheet music. Carlo had his eyes on bigger things, imagining a career as an architect, but he found the course work difficult and switched to law, in part, he confessed, because it offered a quicker path to riches. In 1939, he was a full-fledged attorney in Milan, with a specialty in contracts, when a family friend recommended him for a position in a newly formed film company.

Two years later, the first movie bearing his imprimatur (if not his name) as producer appeared: *Piccolo Mondo Antico* (*Old-Fashioned World*), directed by Mario Soldati and starring Baroness Alida Maria Laura Altenburger von Marckenstein-Frauenberg, better known by her stage name, Alida Valli. The film drew praise from the press but was mainly forgotten, though Valli launched her brief international career on the strength of it, a success for which Ponti readily took credit.

When the war put film production in Italy on pause, Ponti was engaged in another project, Alberto Lattuada's *La Freccia nel Fianco* (*The Arrow*), which was completed (with its director and even leading man replaced) after the war and became one of the first Italian films to reach the screen in peacetime.

Soon after, Ponti was hired by Lux Film of Rome, Italy's most prestigious and prolific production company, and he worked exclusively in movies from then on. He liked to brag that he discovered and/or launched and/or created every notable Italian actress of the time, and while each of those claims could be disputed, it was incontestably true that he had a hand in the early careers of Gina Lollobrigida, Lucia Bosé, and Silvana Mangano—all of whom were, like Valli, known throughout Italy and making names for themselves abroad by 1950.

Ponti had taken a bride by then—his college sweetheart Giuliana Fiastri, who preferred to stay at home while her husband saw to business, whether that was on film sets during the day or in cafés and clubs at night. They had a daughter and would soon have a son, but there was no illusion that their marriage was sacrosanct. Ponti had a reputation as a wolf, and, like many married Italian men, he took few pains to hide it.

In that sense, he was like his business partner, Dino De Laurentiis, a fellow producer at Lux Film with whom Ponti formed an independent company, Ponti–De Laurentiis, in 1950. De Laurentiis was the younger man by seven years, but he had been in the movies almost as long as his partner and he had built an equally impressive résumé.

He was the son of a pasta manufacturer from Torre Annunziata, near Naples, and he had been working as a salesman for his father's business in 1935, a mere sixteen years old, when, on a whim, he enrolled in classes at the Centro Sperimentale di Cinematografia, the Italian national film school. There he discovered his taste for producing, and by 1941 he was working on his first credited film, *L'Amore Canta* (*Love Song*). After the war, he, too, was hired at Lux Film, and he and Ponti combined as a team, driven by ambition, tireless in their work habits, and partial to the ladies.

Despite his relative youth, De Laurentiis had also married, a union that he managed to have annulled in 1949 when he "discovered" a girl who had been working in films without credit or notice since the end of the war. Curvy, dark, with a palpable sexual charge, she was cast by De Laurentiis, Ponti, and director Giuseppe De Santis in the lead role of *Bitter Rice*, a melodrama set in the rice fields of the Po Valley. The story combined a neorealist tale of poverty and labor with a potboiler about untamable passion and opportunistic crime. The girl, Silvana Mangano, became an overnight star on the basis of the film, in which she appeared in skimpy outfits suited both to rice gathering and to showing off her body. And, presently, she became Mrs. De Laurentiis, forsaking a major movie career to raise a brood of four children.

Ponti had a front row seat to his partner's private life, and he apparently couldn't help but imagine a similar situation for himself. And maybe he saw it on that fated night in the summer of 1950, walking through a garden with a gorgeous girl who appeared capable of standing alongside—if not above—Mangano, Lollobrigida, and the rest. What matter that she was twenty-two years younger, and a full head taller, than him? It was Italy and he was a man, married or no, and he had all the cards. Why not toss a few on the table and see what happened?

* * *

Sophia had been filmed before, but always as a background player, and when she showed up to Ponti's office for her test, the cameraman warned the producer to expect the worst: "She's impossible to photograph. Her face is too short, her mouth is too big, and her nose is too long." Ponti looked at the footage and agreed: without the proper hair, makeup, and wardrobe, she was simply too unshaped and unusual for the screen. When she returned to hear his verdict, he suggested, delicately, that she have a nose job, and she resolutely balked. They reached a polite impasse, and he bade her adieu.

Then, unable to forget her, he called her back for another test under better conditions. This time she passed muster, and they reached an accord. Sophia agreed to let Ponti guide her career—which meant guiding her life. She would receive a stipend, a clothing allowance, diction lessons (her Neapolitan accent, which would have limited her to regional roles, had to go), acting lessons, and more. The exact nature of their relationship would be somewhat mysterious: the rakish Ponti, married with two children, was already romantically involved with another of his protégées, the Swedish actress Maibritt Wilkens.[4] Sophia, still living with her mother and sister, wasn't really the get-about sort. Long after they let the whole world know that they were a couple, Sophia would insist that Ponti served her strictly as mentor and father figure in this first phase of their relationship. "He gave me a rootedness and stability that kept me grounded," she said, "while the world around me seemed to swirl dizzyingly, excitingly."

4 Who, as May Britt, would go on to work in Hollywood, where she would meet, marry and have two children with Sammy Davis Jr.

And swirl it did. Under the guidance of Ponti (and not, pointedly under contract to Ponti–De Laurentiis), Sophia started appearing in higher-profile roles in higher-budgeted films. By 1952, she was acting not as a background player but as a credited actress—and using the name by which the world would ever more know her. She made two other films that year, and then, with Ponti doing exactly what he said he would, no fewer than ten in 1953, including the three that would make her into an actress recognized by audiences and sought after by filmmakers: *Aïda* (the Verdi opera, in which she played the title role, lip-synching for the voice of Renata Tebaldi), *Due Notti con Cleopatra* (*Two Nights with Cleopatra*, in which she played both the title character *and* her slave girl look-alike), and *Attila* (an epic about the barbarian general, who was played by Anthony Quinn).

These films all performed modestly well in Italy, and they would all eventually be released around the world, some after a few years as Sophia's fame created audiences for them. But they weren't particularly notable as movies, and she was still quite unpolished in them. Granted, she was still only twenty years old and had almost no formal training. But she was getting by on sheer beauty, brass, and charm—and she and Ponti knew it. They encouraged the hullabaloo surrounding her now famous physique—Roman police had to be called to clear a crowd away from a lingerie boutique when it was announced that she would be shopping there. And while she wasn't ashamed of such publicity, she and Ponti determined that she was running a risk of overexposure—in every sense. They tapered off on the amount of work she did and tried to be more selective about the material and, especially, about her directors and fellow cast members. So, in 1954, she made only four films, and with them she forged a screen image of herself and found a teacher and collaborator who would come to mean almost as much to her life and career as Ponti—namely, Vittorio De Sica.

Cunningly, Ponti realized that De Sica, who was also a larger-than-life character from Naples, could teach Loren how to channel her natural charm into genuine performances, and, conveniently, he was about to direct an anthology of six short films based on the stories of the Neapolitan author Giuseppe Marotta—*L'Oro di Napoli* (*The Gold of Naples*). Sophia would star in the second of them, *Pizze a Credito* (*Pizza on Credit*), in which she played the promiscuous wife of a *pizzaiolo* who leaves her wedding ring at her lover's house during a tryst and, once her husband notes that is is missing, pretends to have lost it in the pizza dough. Sashaying around rainy Naples in a clingy dress that emphasized the character's bold-cheeked sensuality, she was sensational—and she was, by her own confession, merely imitating her director, who demonstrated how he wanted her to move and emote and speak before each take and then encouraged her during the actual shooting, acting along with her from his director's chair. (He didn't have to work too hard, he later said: "Neapolitans, like children, always look good on camera.")

She was a smash, stealing every second granted her in what turned out to be a hit film, and Ponti readily saw that his instinct about De Sica and Sophia was right. Of her next six films, De Sica would costar with her in four, two of which, though directed by Dino Risi, could also be thought of as De Sica's, according to contracts which specifically stated that Loren's work would be done under De Sica's hand: "The supervisor of direction will be Vittorio De Sica who, it is agreed, will be present, as in all the preceding films, at all times when you [i. e., Sophia] are required to be on camera." Accordingly, Risi's *Il Segno di Venere* (*The Sign of Venus*) and *Pane, Amore e . . .* (*Bread, Love and . . .*) were, in reality, codirected by De Sica. He would have no impact on her work in *La Donna del Fiume* (*Woman of the River*) by the formidable Mario Soldati, a revenge drama. But he would, once again, offer a guiding hand as costar and coconspirator in *Peccato Che Sia una Canaglia* (*Too Bad She's Bad*), directed by the venerable Alessandro Blasetti, in which the final important male figure in Sophia's career would turn up, playing opposite her for the first of what would turn out to be eleven films spanning forty years of work: Marcello Mastroianni.

Fairy tale wedding: Linda Christian in a Fontana Sisters gown at her 1949 marriage to Tyrone Power.

Living dream: the Sala Bianca in 1952.

The Fontanas size up Lucia Bosé in *Le Ragazze di Piazza di Spagna* (*Three Girls in Rome*, 1952).

Micol Fontana, aka The American Sister, off to conquer the world again.

Renaissance man: Emilio Pucci.

Jet-setters: Simonetta, with her husband Fabiani.

"Enter in silence and in orderly form. Read carefully the instructions in the leaflet that you've been given": Extras queue at Cinecittà for work in *Quo Vadis* (1951).

Anna Magnani as the mother of a Cinecittà hopeful in *Bellissima* (1951).

Ingrid Bergman and Roberto Rossellini, first targets of the paparazzi.

Street of dreams: Via Veneto, looking north from the intersection with Via Ludovisi.

Anita Ekberg
(center) and Pier-
luigi Praturlon on
the Spanish Steps.

Tazio Secchiaroli, the Fox of the
Via Veneto, in his element.

Boulevardier:
Ennio Flaiano.

Kid journalist
Federico Fellini.

Gina Lollobrigida, first of the *maggiorate*, as curvy Italian starlets of the postwar era came to be known.

Sophia Loren, age 16 and billed as Sofia Lazzaro, in *Era Lui, Sì, Sì . . .* (*It Was Him, Yes, Yes . . .*, 1951).

14 "I'm a Peasant"

They come for you in the morning in a limousine; they take you to the studio; they stick a pretty girl in your arms; sometimes they earn something off you and give you some of the profits. They call that a profession: Come on!

 *Two things distinguished the young Marcello* Mastroianni, according to those who knew him best and longest, and they remained essential truths about him, in important ways, throughout his varied and extraordinary life and career.

One, in the words of his mother, was "He never

really knew how to lie. . . . I'd tell him not to bother to go on. He had such a simple face, like an open book."

The other he himself declared in interviews for decades: "I am," he would say, explaining some decision he'd made (or, more often, *hadn't* made), "lazy."

Both traits—an inability to dissemble and an inveterate indolence—were, it happened, perfect tools for the profession in which Mastroianni would become famous. On the one hand, he was at his absolute best as an actor when cast as someone whom he understood instinctively, someone whose experiences and attitudes were so natural to him that they might as well have been his own. On the other, his aversion to preparation, to study, even to learning scripts, lent his work an air of spontaneity, discovery, and immediacy that might have been lacking if he had put in more effort.

As he would accrue more than 140 screen credits over not quite fifty years, plus a considerable stage résumé, "lazy" doesn't feel like the right word. But he used it to describe himself again and again. His workaholism, he explained, was a stay against his indolence: "I have an absolute need to be occupied. If I stop, I fall victim to my own laziness and to daydreaming." His need to keep busy manifested itself in more than a busy schedule. He was an inveterate fidgeter, worrying his hair, his socks, his eyeglasses, his shirt cuffs, his coffee cup, the crumbs on a tablecloth, and the ever present cigarette ("Probably a million of them," he reckoned when asked late in life about his tobacco intake, "enough to obscure the sky of Rome.")

He had been born Marcello Vincenzo Domenico Mastrojanni (the spelling was altered later by a press agent) in the hamlet of Fontana Liri in the Ciociara, a rural region straddling the Roman state of Lazio and Neapolitan Campania. The area had been annexed or conquered repeatedly over the centuries, and its inhabitants were as noted for their native cynicism as for their shoemaking, which they practiced more as a folk craft than a business and never on an industrial scale. At the time Mastroianni was born, the locals, the *Ciociari*, were very much as they had been since the birth of the great Roman orator Cicero in the neighboring village of Arpino, two millennia prior. "We are an indolent, lethargic bunch of people, filled with an ancient 'why-try-and-change-things' attitude," Mastroianni once told a reporter. As for himself, he would frequently say, he was just like the others in his homeland: "I'm a peasant."

The Mastroiannis were a vaguely artistic clan, including a few sculptors and a painter. But Ottorino, Marcello's father, was a carpenter and cabinetmaker. He and his wife, Ida, lived very modestly, chasing opportunity after the birth of their first child, Marcello, in 1924, to Turin, where a second son, Ruggiero, was born five years later. Four years after that, the family moved to the outskirts of Rome, to the Tuscolano neighborhood—not far, almost inevitably, from the spot where Cinecittà would soon be built.

Ottorino worked doggedly, but his family was always needy. Marcello made his own toys and wore hand-me-down clothes from an uncle and stood by restaurant windows salivating at the fare on offer, and when his shoes wore out his father repaired them with strips of aluminum, so that the boy's footsteps rang like a horse's when he walked down cobblestoned streets. "Until I was twenty-five," he later said, "I accepted poverty as a natural condition. I was taught as a child to accept everything as a fatality." He had only one image of wealth and ease in his mind, and it was as modest as could be: "I always thought a gentleman was a person who had a radio and a maid."

He had an aptitude for numbers, though, and he loved the smell of sawdust in his father's workroom and clothes (even though he saw how devastating a life of hard labor was on Ottorino, who barely lived past his elder son's twenty-fifth birthday). He harbored hopes of becoming a technical engineer—honest work—but he was out to earn a little bit of money from the time he was a kid. When he was eleven or so, that meant showing up at the gates of Cinecittà to work as an extra—as, in the case of his first film, a peasant boy stomping grapes in a musical starring the singer Beniamino Gigli (the grapes the extras stomped happened to be real and so, naturally, skinny Marcello ate so many that he made himself sick). He was an attentive student, but he always made time to get over to the studio and get paid, appearing uncredited in about twenty films over the years.[1]

He followed grade school with a technical education that could have led him to a number of respectable professions: engineer, accountant, graphic designer. But he remained enamored of acting, and when it came time to get a college degree, he made sure to choose a school that offered both an accounting program *and* a theater program, and he kept pursuing the stage even as he made progress toward a more traditional degree. Lazy or not, he had an itch for acting, returning to Cinecittà regularly and making himself known to people who could forward his career: when his mother took work in a bank and learned that her new colleague was the sister of Vittorio De Sica, Mastroianni importuned her for a letter of introduction to the great director, who granted him an audience, dismissed him with "Keep studying," and, if only to shut him up, gave him a role as an extra in his *I Bambini Ci Guardano* (*The Children Are Watching*; 1942).

By that time, Mastroianni was of age to serve his country, and

1   Including Alessandro Blasetti's *La Corona di Ferro*, during a crowd scene of which the young journalist Federico Fellini visited Cinecittà to interview the director. The future collaborators might have stood eye-to-eye and not known it.

he was put to work as an army cartographer, drawing maps for Italian troops retreating from the Allies' northward march. When Italy surrendered, he and his fellow mapmakers were rounded up by the Nazis and sent to the Alps to dig trenches. Word came that they would be transferred yet again, possibly to Germany, and Mastroianni forged papers for himself and a friend and fled, carrying a mattress on his back so that he looked like anything *but* an AWOL soldier and he always had a ready place to sleep. Eventually the pair arrived in Venice, where they scratched out a living selling sketches of Venetian sites to the handful of tourists then about. Learning that Rome had been liberated, they headed south on a train ride that Mastroianni would remember for the rest of his life. He tried his best to look nondescript and innocent in the overstuffed rail car, and he was shocked when, upon the train's entering a pitch-dark tunnel, a woman kissed him passionately and scurried off before he could see who she was. ("How many years have passed," he asked, remembering the incident a half century later. "And yet that moment, even now, is one of the most vivid of my life. Memory is bizarre, yeah?")

Back in Rome, he continued to haunt the movie studios and various theater troupes, looking for roles, while taking steady work in the accounting department at Eagle-Lion Films, the local offices of England's J. Arthur Rank film organization. "I hated my job," he remembered, but he found a way to make the most of it, rehearsing potential acting parts for his colleagues: "I was one man with five women in one room. One day I read some poetry for them, and they liked it. I said, 'I'll read for you and you do my work, okay?' For two years they counted and checked off, and I read for them. Then the boss discovered that I wasn't good at accounting, only at poetry for girls, and he kicked me out." Cute, but not entirely accurate. He *had* been getting somewhere in his efforts toward building an acting career: he had his first speaking part on-screen in 1947 in an adaptation of *Les Miserables*, and the following year he appeared as the male lead in a production by the University of Rome's theatrical troupe, opposite a young actress named Giulietta Masina. She brought him to the attention of Luchino Visconti, the great stage director who had begun making films just before the war but was still presiding over the most artistically prestigious theater in Rome.

Visconti sent his assistant, Franco Zeffirelli, to ask Mastroianni to come around for an interview, which was a nervous-making event for the young actor. "I was told you are talented," the maestro said at their meeting. "Very well. If this is true, you will be Mitch in *A Streetcar Named Desire*. If not, you will be an extra." The audition was good enough that Visconti offered him a place in his troupe. Initially, Mastroianni balked: "I have a job," he said, "I can't just walk out of it without being sure of walking into something else." Told he would be receiving a salary that was more than triple what he earned at Eagle-Lion, he signed on. But he dared not tell his parents that he was risking his future on so uncertain a career as acting. Indeed, until he invited them to his first opening night (a modern-dress adaptation of *As You Like It*), he led them to believe he was still working as an accountant, parceling out his pay as they would have expected and leaving the house hours before he'd ever be due at the theater.

His workmanlike diligence didn't impress Visconti, an actual aristocrat and a fastidious aesthete who ran his theater under strict control, dictating to his performers exactly how he wished them to perform every scene, line, gesture. Mastroianni, gamely essaying Shakespeare, was far from his director's ideal, and he withered as Visconti ridiculed him for sounding like a tram conductor or Johnny Weissmuller. But years later Visconti admitted that he saw something ineffable in the young actor that application and training could, perhaps, elicit: "I saw Marcello being born as an actor. He brought forth a deep and natural sensibility that I developed in him through work. But if he hadn't had the sensibility, then nothing would have come out."

Visconti's theater was Mastroianni's graduate school. Alongside the cream of Rome's stage actors—Vittorio Gassman, Rina Morelli, Paolo Stoppa—he appeared in the Italian debuts of *A Streetcar Named Desire* (playing, as promised, Mitch to Gassman's Stanley and Morelli's Blanche) and *Death of a Salesman* (he was Joey, the friend of the Loman boys). He appeared in Chekhov's *Uncle Vanya* and *The Three Sisters* and a variety of contemporary Italian plays. He was blessed by Gassman with private lessons in reciting verse dialogue (giving the lie, incidentally, to gossip-page suggestions that the two were professional rivals; Gassman admittedly envied Mastroianni's gifts in admiring and collegial tones: "He had the great gift of being lovable. . . . I had to make thirty ugly films before becoming comfortable in front of a camera. For him it was simply natural."). He met Flora Carabella, an actress and daughter of the composer Ezio Carabella, and started a romance that led to marriage in August 1950, and a child, Barbara, born in December 1951. He stayed with the company for almost eight years, improving his craft, graduating to better roles (he would eventually play Stanley and Biff, respectively, in revivals of *Streetcar* and *Salesman*) and, inevitably, taking mornings and days off to haunt Cinecittà and Rome's various film offices looking for work.

And he got it. Three or four times a year, he appeared on-screen in virtually the same role: an ordinary young man, often a returned soldier or prisoner of war, working at some menial profession and in love with a girl who seemed not to notice him. The epitome of these was his role in Luciano Emmer's *Le Ragazze di*

Piazza di Spagna, in which he played a big-hearted cabbie pursuing a girl who already had a fellow, only to win her when her boyfriend was revealed as a cad and she tried to kill herself. It was a largish part and a popular film—and it doomed him to play taxi drivers for the next several years.

As luck would have it, he was playing a taxi driver just two years later when he achieved sufficient stature in the movies to leave the stage, this time in Alessandro Blasetti's *Peccato Che Sia una Canaglia* (*Too Bad She's Bad*), alongside Vittorio De Sica and Sophia Loren.

Loren and Mastroianni were, in many ways, a perfect match: the voluptuous Neapolitan minx and temptress and the weary, earthy Roman who, it appeared, would rather work and sleep and eat than dally, even with a goddess. In *Too Bad*, they meet when Sophia's character, in cahoots with thieves who had their eyes on Marcello's taxi, shamelessly schemes and lies and then wriggles her way out of each scheme and lie when it fails. She sings in the cabbie's ear, invites him to skinny-dip, and exposes him to a perilous meeting with her father and grandmother and kid brother—also con artists and pickpockets and thieves. Only in the last act does the cabbie start truly to fall for her wiles, and by then the affection is mutual. The film was pure marzipan—light comedy, light romance, swift and spry as a Hollywood picture but shot in picturesque Rome. It was a hit at home and abroad, including in the United States.

Mastroianni won a Golden Goblet prize from Italian film critics for his work in this film and the more dramatic *Giorni d'Amore* (*Days of Love*) and, given the vagaries of movie financing at the time, had to pawn the trophy when his salary for the films was too slow in materializing. That particular honor, though, served as proof that his stock as a player and a name was rising. He was considered a capable hand in both comedy and drama, and if his naturalness could sometimes be mistaken for a lack of effort, he was nonetheless a plausible presence in a variety of roles.

Too Bad was a big enough hit that a sequel to it, more or less, was made the following year: Blasetti's *La Fortuna di Essere Donna* (literally, *Lucky to Be a Woman*, but released in the United States as *What a Woman!*). This time, Mastroianni is the one on the make—a photographer for tabloid newspapers and magazines who catches a candid shot of a girl (Loren) fixing her stocking and places it on the cover of a glossy magazine, causing scandal but sparking in the girl the desire to be a movie star. As the two hide their attraction for each other behind screens of worldliness, cynicism, and white lies, a third figure emerges, a count who spends his days grooming young ladies for stardom. (The role was played not by De Sica, who would've shone, but rather Charles Boyer, a charming fellow, yes, but with no real sense for the florid or the playful.)[2] Once again, the romance is delayed for farce and screwball situations and sillinesses of plot (Blasetti had a light touch but no filter for inferior material), and once again the inevitable is put off until the last possible moment—a happy ending that any fool could see coming from the very first frames.

The two Blasetti pictures found their way to the United States, where they—or, more specifically, Loren—were greeted rapturously: "Forget the story, forget the subtitles, just watch the dame," drooled Bosley Crowther in *The New York Times*.

The world would soon do just that.

---

2 The original trio all acted together in one other film at this time, *La Bella Mugnaia* (*The Miller's Beautiful Wife*), a sex farce set in the seventeenth century that received little love from critics or audiences.

15 Signor Sigarone

By the time Three Coins in the Fountain proved a hit, however undeservedly, Hollywood productions were shooting in Rome almost without pause. *The Barefoot Contessa* was followed almost immediately by *Helen of Troy*, which, with scale and ambitions more modest than those of *Quo Vadis*, set a standard for many productions to follow. Director Robert Wise and a core crew of thirty-five department heads and technicians flew into Rome to direct a cast of, mainly, Brits, with the little-remembered Italian actress Rossana Podestà in the title role.

Those films were followed by yet another Paramount

epic, King Vidor's adaptation of *War and Peace*, a $6 million production starring Audrey Hepburn, Henry Fonda, Mel Ferrer, Herbert Lom, and Vittorio Gassman, and featuring the Swedish starlets May Britt and Anita Ekberg. Dino De Laurentiis and Carlo Ponti received producing credits on the film, which was, technically, an international coproduction. Yet despite the size of the budget and the big Hollywood names in the cast, the crew, with the exception of cinematographer Jack Cardiff, featured Italians at the head of virtually every technical department: art, sound, electrical, costumes, and music. Following the pattern it started with *Ulysses*, Paramount had found a way to make movies in Italy and achieve reliable standards of work without the expense of sending over large crews.

Once it became clear that there was a legitimate method for making successful productions in Rome without deploying American technicians, Hollywood on the Tiber went from being a clever catchphrase to a legitimate financial, social, and cultural phenomenon. In 1956 and 1957, Hollywood studios and producers made more than a dozen films in Cinecittà and at other Roman and Italian locations, including *The Little Hut* (directed by Marc Robson, with Ava Gardner and her flame-of-the-month Walter Chiari), *Ten Thousand Bedrooms* (Richard Thorpe, with Dean Martin in his first—disastrous—film without Jerry Lewis), *The Seven Hills of Rome* (Mario Lanza as an expat Italian-American singer), *A Farewell to Arms* (Charles Vidor, with Rock Hudson, Jennifer Jones, and her former director Vittorio De Sica, this time as an actor), *Legend of the Lost* (Henry Hathaway, with John Wayne seeking a fortune in ... Timbuktu), and *The Quiet American* (Joseph Mankiewicz, with Audie Murphy and Michael Redgrave, and Cinecittà providing interiors for a film set in Vietnam).

Those stars and many others—Orson Welles, Lauren Bacall,

Marlon Brando, Elizabeth Taylor, Cary Grant, Marlene Dietrich, James Stewart, Grace Kelly, Gary Cooper, William Holden most brightly among them—thronged through Rome's Ciampino Airport, conveniently located southeast of the city center on the route that took them right past Cinecittà. They filled the hotels, restaurants, cafés, and nightspots around Via Veneto, with excitable clutches of photographers snapping away at them whenever they were visible in public, from the moment they stepped off the plane. Some were there to work, some to vacation, some passing through to other destinations. But the word about the scene in Rome had become a huge draw for American film people—far more than, say, Paris or London. Rome was a combination of a getaway and a work opportunity, with a favorable exchange rate, a mild climate, and great food and shopping and sightseeing.

In time an expatriate community of Hollywood not-quite icons, aspirants, and has-beens sprang up: the actor Mickey Knox, who fled the Hollywood blacklist and counted Norman Mailer and James Jones among his friends and who styled himself the American mayor of Rome; Robert Alda,[1] the vaudeville, Broadway (he created the role of Sky Masterson in *Guys and Dolls*), and film star born in New York as Alphonso Giuseppe Giovanni Roberto D'Abruzzo; Mario Lanza, another Italian-American who came to Rome to try to reignite his movie career only to douse it, as he had in Hollywood, with his stubbornness and truculence and overindulgence in food and drink (he would die in Rome, perhaps of a heart attack, perhaps of the effects of diet pills, perhaps of a busted gut—for real—in 1959); and a pair of British starlets, Dawn Addams and Belinda Lee, whose performances in undistinguished Italian films seemed secondary to their private lives, which were far

---

1 Father of actor Alan Alda.

richer in real drama. There were dozens like them, and they made Rome appear to be as exciting a moviemaking climate as any place in the world.

In Hollywood, this phenomenon looked dangerous: "runaway production," they called it, and there was talk of how many jobs it was costing and dollars it was siphoning away. But at the same time, the cost of Italian labor was low, the quality of the work was good, the spectacle of foreign locations made a nice inducement for Americans to leave their TV sets and see a movie, and there were those locked funds that weren't going to spend themselves. Just as many American films were being shot in England, but no particular social or cultural scene of note grew up around London-based film productions, and London itself wouldn't fully emerge as a cultural hot spot for a few more years. In Rome, however, the presence of Hollywood stars and moguls and hangers-on, coinciding with the resurrection of Italy's economy, the high quality of its native movie culture, and the revival (if not invention) of other modern media and art forms made for a unique phenomenon.

This was the heyday when one could suspect that every movie star and celebrity on earth made the haj to Via Veneto and Cinecittà, where stories abounded of the clash of filmmaking styles and human temperaments. American producers were known, generically, as *Signor Sigarone* (Mr. Big Cigar), and served as the sort of comic embodiment of parsimony, naïveté, greed, temper, appetite, and incomprehension that Romans had been lampooning—and circumventing—since the age of the caesars, a foreign pretender to power who only *thought* he was in charge of things. There were stories of insurance scams arising from little staged accidents (favorite ploys including cutting oneself with a sterilized shard of Coca-Cola bottle glass or faking a lump on the head by careful use of a sand-filled nylon pouch); of extras gorging on multiple sack lunches and then becoming seasick during naval scenes shot in one of Cinecittà's massive water tanks; of crew members volunteering themselves for stunt work without any previous experience or safety-enhancing knowledge; of fistfights between the locals and the Hollywood imports who were asked to work side by side at identical tasks but who received massively disparate paychecks.

It was a boom time, with more work for more people on Via Tuscolana than even Mussolini could have envisioned. Per a contemporary *Time* magazine account, "movie producers . . . were just as common as cats in the Forum, and just about as noisy. . . . As many as three pictures were being shot at once with the same cast. . . . Drinking orgies, studio spies and gorgeous villas with swimming pools were the rule of the day. The purple sports shirt had replaced the purple toga." It would have been easy to conceive that the Hollywood behemoth was liable to suck all the available nourishment and talent from the scene. But Italian filmmaking still had something of a wildcatting aspect to it—an inversion of the Hollywood model, with independent producers invested with more prestige than studios and the best work being done by individuals with strong voices rather than by a system designed along industrial lines. At times, Italian filmmaking was a communal venture, a loose confederation of creatives (writers and directors, especially) who often worked together, as evidenced by the appearance of one another's names in the writing credits of so many films or by the popularity of anthology films to which four, five, or even six directors and sometimes twice as many writers contributed short movies.

Rather than blot out local production, the unignorable presence of Hollywood fed it. There was more money in the Italian filmmaking economy; there were more Italians gaining real-world work experience on movie sets; there were expatriates from the

United States and various European countries showing up with projects and, sometimes, funding; and there were more locals aspiring to get into the business—writers, producers, agents, directors, actors—than at any time anywhere since the rise of Hollywood itself.

In this climate, the Italian directors who had already established important careers thrived. Vittorio De Sica rebounded from the difficulties of *Stazione Termini* (which wasn't a flop in Italy) with *The Gold of Naples*, a tremendous hit, and *Il Tetto* (*The Roof*), another neorealist portrait of life in the lower rungs of the Roman economy. He also acted in as many as ten films a year and was successful in almost everything he touched ("A fantastic man," remembered Marcello Mastroianni. "Beautiful, beautiful! He was like a pope!"). Roberto Rossellini made four more films with Ingrid Bergman, including *Europe '51* and *Viaggio in Italia* (*Voyage in Italy*), which, with *Stromboli*, constituted what became known as his "solitude trilogy." Luchino Visconti, always slightly apart from the throng in his nobility and disdain for fashion, made films at a more deliberate pace, taking time off to work in the theater but continuing to produce exceptional movies such as the tragic love stories *Senso* and *Le Notti Bianche*. In the wake of *Stazione Termini* there might not have been opportunities for Italian directors to work in or for Hollywood, but they had the attention of anyone in Italy—or France or Germany or England, for that matter—who could help them finance a new project.

Among those who particularly benefited in this environment were the members of a younger generation of filmmakers who were rising to the levels of the widely recognized postwar masters. They had worked underneath and alongside the prior generation— with very few exceptions, Italian auteurs were particularly generous and collegial with one another and always would be—but they were less likely to tackle themes of grand social import or to devote themselves monkishly to what might be thought of as the tenets of neorealism.

Michelangelo Antonioni was a writer and director from Ferrara who had been making small and often grim tales of passion, violence, and ennui since just after the war, sometimes writing for and with others but most often generating his own ideas for such melodramas as *Story of a Love Affair*, *I Vinti* (*The Vanquished*), and *Le Amiche* (*The Girl Friends*). Dino Risi, from Milan, had toiled at short films and documentaries and then transitioned into romantic comedies, such as the smash hits *Poveri ma Belli* (*Poor but Handsome*), a story of penniless Roman boys on the make, and its follow-ups, *Belle ma Povere* (*Beautiful but Poor*), about girls in similar circumstances, and *Poveri Millonari* (*Poor Millionaires*), in which all of the above get lucky in love and business. Pietro Germi, from Genoa, had been writing films since before the war but didn't start directing until after, when he made crime dramas with more than a hint of film noir about them such as *In Nome della Legge* (literally, *In the Name of the Law* but released in the United States as *Mafia*), *La Città se Difende* (*Four Ways Out*), and *Gelosia* (*Jealousy*). All of them would have been notable directors in any country, particularly Antonioni, who was developing a style and point of view that seemed his and his alone.

But none of them stood out as much as the cartoonist, journalist, gag writer, script doctor, and shambling man-about-town from Rimini named Federico Fellini.

16 "Sit Down, If You Dare"

In retrospect, it might be likelier that he came from Mars or Parnassus or Cockaigne or (and this would have been perfect) from one of his own fantastical movies.

Intimates knew him as FeFe, a nickname that was at once boyish and cuddly and clever, being comprised of the first two letters of both his Christian and family names.

But he preferred an even more elaborate puzzle: *Io, FF, il Re Del Cine*—"I, FF, the King of Film"—in the Italian, an anagram of "Federico Fellini."

Fellini came into the world—a "born liar," by his own

admission—on January 20, 1920, in Rimini, a small city some 220 miles north of Rome on the Adriatic coast of Emilia-Romagna that bubbled to life each summer with an influx of tourism. At the time, his father, Urbano, who had been born in the nearby village of Gambettola, was starting up a wholesale cheese and coffee business in Rimini, where his wife, Ida, née Barbiani, had roots on her father's side. But Ida's mother was Roman, and Ida was herself born in the capital, which was where she was living when she met her future husband soon after the Great War.

It was a love match, disapproved of by Ida's parents, and in August 1918, the young couple eloped to Gambettola. A few months after Federico was born, Urbano and Ida tried to make a go of living in Rome, but her family refused to give them any help and his business ventures never quite succeeded. Back to Rimini they went, where they would make their home permanently, filling it with two more children, a boy and a girl, in the following decade.

Young Federico wasn't much of a student. He liked to draw, and he was particularly fond of comic strips, but those weren't passions encouraged by his teachers. He was thin and dark-complected (classmates called him Gandhi), and he avoided sports. He was, in a very real sense, addicted to his own dreams, both the nocturnal and daytime varieties; decades later, he would take up a habit of sleeping with a sketch pad and colored pencils by his bedside so that he could record his fantastical night visions immediately upon waking. He was fond of the movies, and the Fulgor cinema in Rimini would forever hold a special place in his heart. There he first beheld so many of his cinematic heroes, love objects, and inspirations. But despite the fame he would achieve in film, the boy Fellini wasn't as keen on movies as he was on the circus: he even briefly—for a couple of hours, that is—ran away from home to become a clown.

That impulse to get out of Rimini and see the world was strong in him, and it drew him especially to Rome, the city of wonders for which his mother continually pined. The family visited the capital twice during Federico's early teens, which only served to intensify his desire to live there full-time. After graduating high school, he arrived in Rome to stay in the spring of 1939, ostensibly to study law but really to pursue a career as a journalist or a cartoonist or a storyteller of some sort—to do something, in short, that might feed his lifelong desire to create, to entertain, to provoke, to arouse.

There were limits to his Roman spree. For the first two years in the city, his mother and sister lived with him. He focused on work, contributing regularly to newspapers within weeks of showing up in town; soon he was writing gags and, later, whole scripts for radio, then punching up comedy scripts for the movies. Within a few years, he was winning awards for journalism and radio plays. He collaborated with some of the Italian cinema's best-regarded writers, directors, and actors. And he accrued a valuable reputation within the small but buzzy movie business as a useful fellow around a production office and a film set—able to employ his brains, his hands, and his guile to deal effectively with problems.

In 1942, he met and wooed a girl, a small, spry, gifted actress named Giulietta Masina. She was then twenty-one, just a year his junior, and she was building a notable acting résumé on stage, first in student productions and then in small but well-regarded troupes. She interpreted an impressive variety of roles, including, no doubt due to her tiny stature, a fair number of young boys. She, too, came from Emilia-Romagna but was schooled in Rome, where she lived with her aunt and uncle in a solid and monied household filled with music, literature, and art. When she met Fellini, she was still learning her craft but was already being celebrated by theater people as a rising talent.

They first met in the offices of a radio show for which Fellini was a regular writer, and he asked her to lunch, ostensibly to speak about a film he was helping to cast. Almost from the start they were an item, and they married in October 1943, under the shadows of the Nazi occupation of Rome and Allied advancement up the Italian peninsula. The wedding was held at the home of Giulietta's aunt and uncle, and Fellini designed the invitations himself, little cartoon booklets that celebrated the couple's coming together and anticipated their future as parents. (That future, cruelly, would never come: a few months after their marriage, a pregnant Giulietta took a fall and suffered a miscarriage; one year later, she bore a son, Pierfederico, who would live not quite two weeks, dying of encephalitis; the couple remained childless thereafter.)

Fellini managed to dodge the draft, partly by avoiding official registration as a citizen of Rome—a tactic that meant, on the one hand, the authorities had no means to track him down or even know of his existence, but, on the other, he was a non-person, ineligible to receive books of ration cards. He had a couple of near scrapes: for instance, one day in the Piazza di Spagna he was rounded up in a Nazi sweep and placed in a truck headed who-knew-where; he improvised an escape, leaping from the truck to accost a passing German officer as if he was an old friend, "Fritz! Fritz!" By the time he finished making apologies to the startled Nazi—who didn't know him from Adam—the truck had driven off.

Eventually, conditions in Rome made impossible most of the avenues of work on which he had come to depend, and so Fellini returned to the sketch pads and pencils that had fueled his creative urges as a young man. Together with some of his fellow newspaper illustrators, he opened up a business on Via Nazionale: the Funny-Face Shop, selling drawn-on-the-spot caricatures to Allied soldiers. Banners advertising the store promised a ten-minute turnaround on the work and enticed customers thus: "Watch out! The most ferocious and amusing caricaturists are eyeing you! Sit down, if you dare, and tremble!"[1]

In the summer of 1944, a man of substantial bearing—a Roman native, well dressed, with an air of being accustomed to having things his way—turned up at the shop, not to have his portrait drawn but to make a proposition to the proprietor. During his time rewriting the work of others for the radio and the movies, Fellini had made a name for himself, so it was no surprise that a stranger would wonder whether he might be interested in rewriting a new script. But then the fellow revealed the *real* reason that he sought Fellini as a collaborator: Fellini was known to be friendly with the comic actor Aldo Fabrizi. Did Fellini, the visitor wondered, think Fabrizi would agree to appear in the film?

Had it been somebody else asking, Fellini might have taken the fellow's tactics as clumsy, naïve, desperate, underhanded. But he knew who his visitor was even before he introduced himself. He was Roberto Rossellini, known in the small Roman movie world as a rising figure of import. His new project was a story about Roman civilians struggling under—and, in truth, *against*—Nazi occupation. As a work in progress it was known as *Storie di Ieri* (*Stories of Yesterday*), but it was released, famously, the following year as *Rome: Open City*. By accepting Rossellini's offer, which was based on the sheer happenstance of his knowing Fabrizi, Fellini would gain entrée to the ground floor of postwar Italian cinema.

---

1 The standard price for a caricature was a few thousand lire, which was almost nothing to the American soldiers, who were beloved by Fellini and his colleagues for leaving generous tips, including such luxury items as cans of food and packs of cigarettes. The latter especially impressed him: "If we'd smoked those American cigarettes, in those wonderful packages, before the war, everyone would have known that no one could defeat America," Fellini recalled.

* * *

*F*ellini helped write the script of *Open City* (along with Rossellini and Sergio Amidei, all of whom would share in the film's Oscar nomination for screenwriting), as well as that of Rossellini's follow-up, *Paisan*, and he worked on a handful of the director's other films, sometimes serving as assistant director in addition to his writing chores, and once, in the short film *Il Miracolo* (*The Miracle*), even acting—opposite none other than Anna Magnani. During the same period, he worked several times with two other notable directors, Pietro Germi and Alberto Lattuada. In 1950, he and Lattuada would coauthor and codirect *Luci di Varietà* (*Variety Lights*), a slight, charming tale of a traveling troupe of vaudevillians faced with the inevitable obsolesence of their medium and a dramatic and costly episode of backstage romance. The film, which Fellini and Lattuada funded themselves with loans, was a box-office flop despite some nice reviews.[2] It served, however, to ignite a thirst in Fellini to take control of the camera rather than just write for the screen or assist someone else. He realized that he had a personal vision—had had one since he first started drawing cartoons as a boy—and that he could realize it in the cinema, but only if he was able to direct films on his own.

Two years after the commercial disappointment of *Variety Lights*, he took the director's chair by himself on a lightly satiric romantic comedy about love and pop culture and the bedazzlement of Rome called *Lo Sceicco Bianco* (*The White Sheik*). As in so many cases in the Italian cinema, the script was a collaboration among a handful of writer-directors who wouldn't actually have produced pages

2 Giulietta Masina was singled out for accolades in only her second speaking role in a film.

together but who were often willing to help one another. The original story was by Michelangelo Antonioni, with the assistance of Fellini and the playwright and screenwriter Tullio Pinelli, who'd had a hand in *Variety Lights*. For the screenplay, Fellini and Pinelli were joined by the screenwriter and boulevardier Ennio Flaiano, forming a troika that would remain together for more than a decade of stupendous scripts.

The White Sheik was a fabulously entertaining film about provincial newlyweds visiting the big city on their honeymoon only to be separated by the bride's infatuation with an actor (Alberto Sordi) who portrayed a lusty Arabian prince in her favorite graphic novel series; while she runs off to meet her beau ideal, the groom is forced to deflect the attentions of his Roman relatives who want, naturally, to meet their new niece and have made arrangements for the couple to be blessed at an audience with the pope. It was thoroughly winning,[3] but, like *Variety Lights*, it disappointed commercially, perhaps because the public found Fellini's comedy too fantastical and broad (his mature style could be seen bubbling up in the film), perhaps because Sordi, appropriately unctuous and hammy, had not yet become beloved by audiences. Critics, too, were largely dismissive. But Fellini had acquired a taste for directing, he persisted in writing ideas for new movies he wanted to make, and, in the boom times that Italian cinema was enjoying, he found new backers to help him realize a new project.

This time, Fellini would tell the sort of story that, for a lot of novelists and filmmakers, would usually be a first work: a portrait of a group of young men idling away their lives on petty schemes and paltry romances in a provincial seaside town not unlike the

---

3 And influential: an episode of Woody Allen's 2012 anthology film *To Rome with Love* borrowed heavily from its plot.

Rimini of his youth. Having left the city of his birth for good at the age of nineteen, Fellini would have been too young to be one of the gang of fashionable layabouts who were known in the local dialect as *vidlòni* or, less idiomatically, *vitelloni* ("calves"). But he had observed them with admiration and jealousy. They were the cool older brothers he never had: well dressed, romantically savvy, game for new adventures and sensations, a proto–Rat Pack embodying, with an Italian savor, a brand of midcentury male privilege and self-indulgence that looked glamorous from afar but up close revealed itself to be shallow and a little sad.

The film, entitled *I Vitteloni,* was shot mostly in Viterbo and Rome, with Ostia standing in for coastal Rimini and a few indoor sequences shot in various locations where one of the stars, Alberto Sordi, was performing during a national variety tour. Sordi appeared as one of the ensemble alongside fellow *vitelloni* Leopoldo Trieste (the hapless groom from *The White Sheik*), Franco Fabrizi, Riccardo Fellini (the director's brother and remarkable look-alike), and Franco Interlenghi. No longer the teenage waif of *Shoe-shine*, Interlenghi played Moraldo, the sensitive youngest member of the crew and, it would appear, a stand-in for Fellini himself, a dreamer with artistic yearnings and an ambition to move to Rome.

Each of the *vitelloni* had a bit of Fellini in him: ham, poet, womanizer, romantic, scene-stirrer, and wallflower. The story was episodic, with the tale of Fabrizi's shotgun wedding, abortive affairs, and home life forming a spine, but with each character being afforded a moment in the spotlight and each of the lead actors given a showcase to play. If *The White Sheik* felt like a sketch of a future Fellini film, *I Vitelloni* felt like the full thing, teeming with wild revelries, late-night encounters, backstage show biz shenanigans, brief amours, grotesque cameos, carnival music, and recurring reminders of the gaps between the real world, the longed-for world, and the world of unbridled imagination. It was the first Fellini-Fellini, and it was thoroughly entertaining, resonant, and fresh.[4]

Finally, Fellini had a hit. At the Venice Film Festival of 1953, the film was awarded a Silver Lion (technically the second-place prize, for which it tied with five other films, including Kenji Mizoguchi's *Ugetsu* and John Huston's *Moulin Rouge*; oddly, no film was awarded the top prize). Reviews outside of the festival were strong, and the box office was good. In time *I Vitteloni* would receive wide international distribution and acclaim (when it reached the United States in 1957, under the awful title *The Young and the Passionate*, Fellini, Flaiano, and Pinelli would be nominated for a screenwriting Oscar). The film would influence a number of younger filmmakers, including Martin Scorsese, who would always acknowledge the debt his 1973 breakthrough, *Mean Streets*, owed to Fellini's work, and Barry Levinson, whose 1982 *Diner* was another film about a group of dreaming young men who never get far from home.

Almost inevitably, Fellini was asked to follow up his hit film with similar material—*Le Vittelone*, say, about a pack of restless young women, suggested one producer. Instead, he, Flaiano, and Pinelli started to work on a story about Moraldo's arrival in Rome, his efforts to make a career as a journalist, his encounters with women and the bohemian life, his spiritual crises, his search for meaning. *Moraldo in Città* they called it—*Moraldo in the City*. But they didn't quite get around to making it, not exactly, anyhow, and not just yet.

4 The finale afforded substantial evidence that the quiet Moraldo, of all of the film's many characters, was a stand-in for the director, even if it would only have been evident to those who knew the real Fellini and who paid very careful attention to the sound track: as the train left town carrying Moraldo to a future of who-knew-what who-knew-where, the director very briefly dubbed his own voice in the midst of Interlenghi's farewells, as if bidding adieu to his own provincial past.

17 "Florence Is a Lost Cause"

In the aftermath of the triumphant debut of Italian haute couture at the Sala Bianca, Emilio Pucci found he had a problem on his hands. His boutique clothing lines, which included sportswear, blouses, and day dresses made with his characteristic vibrancy and color, were still being produced in a centuries-old artisanal method: He sketched out designs and then oversaw their execution in his palazzo workshop, where his preferred seamstress, Signora Ida, and her crew of a dozen or so labored under his careful attention. Fittings were done directly onto models' bodies, à la haute couture, and sizes weren't standardized. Pucci was making sportswear, but he might as well have been designing ball gowns, so particular were his products and deliberate his methods.

Frankly overwhelmed by the response at that first show, Pucci accepted far more orders than he could honestly fill and turned the private showing he had planned to host at his home into a party for the out-of-towners who had already seen—and fallen for—his work. His potential customers wined and dined, he broke the news that he couldn't meet their demand, promising that he'd be ready for them when Bista Giorgini's next exhibition was mounted. And he made good on his word: he set up a more modern system, with regular sizing and greater-scale production. With a small corps of Florentine home seamstresses contracted to assemble garments according to carefully prepared patterns, he was able to meet a larger number of orders and still turn out high-quality items. After a few more years had passed, Pucci engaged a local factory to mass-produce ready-to-wear shirts and blouses, garments of simple enough design to be made reliably using industrial methods.

By then he had replicated his tiny Emilio of Capri boutique in other spots where he could count on socialites and wealthy travelers to wander into them: Rome, the Tuscan spa town of Montecatini, the resort island of Elba. None of these mattered more to his growing business, though, than the market available to him in America. His ski clothes and beachwear had percolated down from an elite clientele to a wider public, and his brilliantly colored dresses, separates, and scarves sold well and were widely imitated. Ever the gallant, he claimed that the American market was not only his most lucrative sales ground but one of his great inspirations. American women, he said, had the perfect figures to show his sportswear to its most flattering effect.

And the American energy for business and hullabaloo was, he explained, at the core of his enterprise: "After the war there was a great hunger for color, novelty and newness," he told *The New York Times*. "We Italians have been very much shaped by America. It was you who gave us the push to create without forcing what we created. I never knew what a press show meant, and, of course, Italians are very poor at being efficient. But because Americans have a need for excitement and novelty in their clothes, it was like a seed planted in our minds."

That seed was nourished by a seemingly bottomless well of innovation, taste, and flair. Pucci used all the colors in the crayon box, working in geometric shapes or floral bursts or motifs of classical architecture or stylized visions of nature. He combined hues that few others who worked with such rich materials dared—plum and orange and turquoise and gold and cardinal in a single silk top, say. And the lively palette he often favored suggested the realms of psychedelia and Day-Glo before those styles ever came to market. He was a genuine fount of new ideas and looks and vibes—and the things he was doing in the 1950s would be imitated in fashion all around the world as the '60s and '70s unrolled. Often he changed the future by absorbing something of the past: a Sicilian collection, a collection inspired by the Palio festival of Siena, a Botticelli collection. Pucci could make a garment, and the person who wore it, feel classical and modern at the same time. The very look of his work—the color and tenor and spirit of it—changed the idea of fashion going forward. Other clothiers may have had more impact with specific items of clothing. But Pucci's most sensational innovations came in what were, arguably, the first thing that most people noticed: color and pattern. Had he merely helped to invent modern skiwear and beachwear he'd be a memorable figure in the history of fashion. But his aesthetic would have an enormous impact on the appearance of the westernized, industrialized world for more than a half century.

$\mathcal{A}$nother breakout star from that first Sala Bianca show was Simonetta. After Bergdorf Goodman bought everything she showed, the department store invited her to the United States to present a complete collection, an event that was covered thoroughly by the fashion press. "Countess Visconti," as *The New York Times* called her, "handles fashion with a light hand. Her clothes are created with an eye to wearability, but they also are chic." Just as the boutique show had been such a hit in Florence, so, too, did Simonetta's noncouture pieces strike a chord in Manhattan. "The Visconti play clothes are a delight," the *Times* continued. "Here color sense and fun mingle."

"I make my fashions to suit myself," she said of her work. "They are things I like to wear." Happily for her, "I find they are the type of things American women like to wear." In the coming decade and beyond, Simonetta would repeatedly visit the United States, which provided a fertile market for both her couture and her boutique lines. Back home in Rome, business proved substantial enough to require that two floors of her Via Gregoriana residence be devoted to it: a retail shop on the street level and, just above it, a salon for couture.

And there were changes, as well, farther upstairs, in the private residence: By the time she became a regular visitor to New York, Simonetta was no longer a Visconti, having divorced her husband, by whom she had a son. In 1952, she married once again, this time to someone who, not born an aristocrat, understood her taste for work: Alberto Fabiani, the same designer whom she had persuaded to show in Florence just the year before.

Fabiani was born in 1910 to a pair of tailors in Tivoli, just east of

Rome, and was, according to family legend, destined to follow in their steps after an accident in their shop at age six: a long needle punctured his chest, nearly piercing his heart. He apprenticed in Paris and returned to Rome in 1931, taking over his parents' business five years later. He moved the business twice, first from Tivoli to Rome's Via Frattina, just off the Piazza di Spagna, then to the more upscale Via Condotti. His work, which was widely recognized for the quality of the cut and the elegance of the line, earned him the nickname the Surgeon of Suits and Coats, particularly as he shook the shadow of Paris and devised what would eventually come to be seen as a more Italian style. He had a reputation as an innovator: more than once some new look he created was rejected by buyers and press alike, and then, a few seasons later, would be imitated by another designer and met with acclaim and sales, accounting, in part, for Fabiani's widely noted air of ironic melancholy.

The marriage of two up-and-coming stars of the fashion world proved irresistible to the press. In the span of just a few years, *The New York Times* would run articles on the couple with the headlines "Happily Wed Pair Compete for Rome's Fashion Trade" and "Happily Married Couple Success in Fashion, Too." Much was made of their status as competitors—though Fabiani's designs appealed to a slightly more conservative clientele than that which went for the sparkling femininity and youthful pizzazz of Simonetta's work. He was also less frequently photographed and celebrated than his wife: "It's not important that people know me," he said. "To know the coat is more important."

They lived together on Via Gregoriana with what would eventually be a household of three children: a child from each of their previous marriages and one they had together. Simonetta worked downstairs in her boutique and studio while he kept his atelier on Via dei Condotti, a brief walk away. Their attitudes toward each other's work were much commented on. As they explained often to the press, they talked about details of business and of craft all the time, they sketched on scratch pads and scraps of paper in each other's company, but they kept their actual designs secret from one another until the last possible moment, revealing them at dress rehearsals within a week, or even days, of the runway premieres of their collections. "By this time," Simonetta explained, "both of us are sick of our clothes. We need a fresh eye. We criticize. We often make changes on the other's say-so. We are jealous, too." Despite the fact that their designs were often of completely distinct genres and styles, there was a bit of a rivalry in the air, she admitted. "Our workroom employees hate each other. If I've finished my collection first and want to help my husband, my girls won't let me. They'd rather die than let anybody in from the house of Fabiani."

Fabiani, possessed of a far more low-key personality than his wife, would laugh off the suggestion that they could possibly collaborate. "Of course we discuss design ideas and criticize each other's clothes," he said. "I don't know why, though. We never pay any attention to what the other says."

Each was at once a business executive *and* a creative designer, and they each cut a figure, Fabiani with an understated formality that was so thoroughgoing that he would work in a tie even on the stuffiest of Roman afternoons (he did, a reporter observed, open the cuffs of his shirt), Simonetta with her legendary beauty and energy and zest for life (she was an avid skier, on both snow and water). Fabiani liked to tease his wife about the time she spent two days and a night preparing for a costume ball in Paris—designing a gown, sewing it herself, having her hair and makeup done to match it, and eschewing meals so that it would fit her better—only to faint dead away from exhaustion and lack of nourishment soon after her spectacular arrival. "Fabiani was depressed," a reporter wrote, "because he had missed the fun of the party. Not his wife. She had enjoyed her grand entrance, so to her the evening was a roaring success."

The Fontana sisters had already made a name for their work before Giorgini persuaded them to join his shows, and their success afterward was proportionally phenomenal. They already had a select clientele of Hollywood actresses, and through the publicity and excitement over Italian clothes and the connections they so carefully cultivated, they were able to gain a foothold in the United States. Soon after the first Florence show, Micol Fontana traveled to Los Angeles as a guest of Linda Christian and Tyrone Power, who threw a party at their home in her honor (Cary Grant took the bedazzled designer for a moonlight ride in his convertible at the evening's end), and helped her organize a fashion show at a Beverly Hills hotel. "They wanted the movie stars to see Fontana clothes," Micol recalled, and the show was such a hit that attendees "jumped on the runway afterward, because it was new and different."

Very quickly, the Fontanas' work became famous for a combination of qualities: the designs were fresh without being trendy; they were very like Parisian fashions but were far more affordable; and they exhibited the mastery of craft—beading, stitching, embroidery—and a fineness of material for which Italian products were perennially noted. A large cadre of celebrities became customers: Grace Kelly, Elizabeth Taylor, Merle Oberon, Joan Fontaine, Rita Hayworth, to name a few. In 1952, the sisters designed a wedding dress for Audrey Hepburn, who was then engaged to James Hanson, an English Tory who would later gain fame as a corporate raider; when Hepburn called it off, the dress was given to one of the Fontana employees for *her* wedding. Alongside these high-wattage names, Linda Christian was something of a second-stringer, but the loyal Fontanas always developed genuine bonds with clients. During Micol's debut visit to Hollywood, for instance, Christian gave birth to the first of the two daughters she had with Power, and Micol brought the clothes to the maternity clinic for a private showing. When Christian bore her second daughter, she asked Micol to serve as godmother.

Micol took a lot of·orders at that Beverly Hills show, but those who missed it didn't have to travel all the way to Via Liguria to buy a Fontana dress: In the coming years, Micol became a regular visitor to the United States, opening a workshop and salon in Manhattan, tirelessly promoting not only the Fontana brand but the very idea of Italian fashion and placing clothes in top-flight department stores all over the country—New York, Philadelphia, Miami, Chicago, Dallas, Los Angeles, San Francisco. She learned English, made friends everywhere, and played the publicity game like a pro: when she was to attend an opening night at the Metropolitan Opera in New York, her press agent suggested that she dye her hair green and wear a white and red outfit—the colors of the Italian flag—to make a splash; she loved the idea and did it and, as predicted, was noted throughout the media for her playfulness. The Fontanas were once again in American headlines in 1956, when they were commissioned to design a wedding dress for Margaret Truman, the former president's daughter.[1] Soon after, Micol was a guest at the Eisenhower and, later still, the Kennedy White House. She became so well-known and well liked that she would eventually make an estimated ninety-five trips to the United States, earning

1 In 1955, the Fontanas had designed the wedding gown for the Italian crown princess Maria Pia di Savoia, in her exile in Portugal, and a massive haul of more than one hundred dresses for Angelita Trujillo, the daughter of the Dominican dictator Rafael, for her ceremonial coronation as "Ideal Queen of Peace, Progress and Culture," whatever that was.

her the nickname the American sister and even, in time, receiving an honorary degree from the State University of New York for her contributions to *American* fashion.

Back in Rome, the Fontanas' successes were just as substantial. The 1952 release of Luciano Emmer's *Le Ragazze di Piazza di Spagna*, whose lead characters worked in the Fontanas' Via Liguria atelier, occasioned an international publicity tour for Micol, who crisscrossed America when the film opened there, showing a new collection that was heralded by three models wearing identical dresses in white, red, and green.[2]

But it was a Hollywood production and a Hollywood star that gave the Fontana sisters their greatest boost of all. When Ava Gardner arrived in Rome in late 1953 to play the title role in *The Barefoot Contessa*, the Fontanas made thirty custom pieces for her wardrobe—as many as they might create for an entire season's collection. The Fontanas' work delighted Gardner, suiting her larger-than-life personality as well as her screen role. In the coming years, she would have clothes made for her regularly by the Fontanas: they created pieces for her wardrobes in *The Sun Also Rises* and *On the Beach*, and two dresses that they made for her to wear to the wedding of Grace Kelly and Prince Rainier of Monaco were particularly celebrated in the fashion press. Over time, Gardner and Micol would visit each other's homes and become genuinely close, which, Micol explained, was an inevitable outcome of the way she and her sisters worked: "When you dress people you become their friends, because you have to understand them inside."

Gardner even helped the Fontanas drum up publicity with some particularly splashy fashion moments. In 1954, she indulged a fan-

---

2 Antonioni's *Le Amiche*, adapted from a novel by Cesare Pavese, was set in a dressmaker's shop in Turin and featured Fontana clothes in the fashion scenes.

tasy of walking the runway as a model, appearing unannounced at the end of their winter show and drawing some mixed responses. One Roman newspaper claimed that Gardner "cavorted hoydenishly before and after the show," which would have surprised no one, but may not have been exactly true. As another observer, the prolific Italian fashion writer Irene Brin, described the scene in the monthly *Bellezza*:

> The artfully wicked Fontana sisters have the knack of always keeping a trump card up their sleeve. . . . Surrounded by rough wooden tables, buckets of French champagne on ice, cans of hairspray, and slices of lemon, Ava Gardner, dressed in green satin, was waiting for her cue to appear on stage. . . . She paced up and down in her small cage, she wrung her hands, she cleared her throat, she adjusted the bodice, she sighed, she allowed Zoe Fontana to hold her face in both hands and plant an encouraging kiss on her forehead . . . and when her cue came, she made the sign of the cross. Then, like someone going to the guillotine, she went to face the applause.

The Fontanas and Gardner pulled off an even greater bit of ballyhoo in late 1955, when the star appeared in photos wearing a form-fitting black sheath dress with a high collar, a broad-brimmed round black hat, and a large cross hanging around her neck on what looked like a set of rosary beads. The dress, called the *pretino*, or "novice priest," was clearly designed after a clerical cassock and was part of a collection the Fontanas called *la linea cardinale*, "the cardinal line," which drew sufficiently shocked reaction from some quarters that it was withdrawn from circulation—not, however, before several of the designs had been sold and had made a lasting impression on a number of sharp-eyed observers. Federico Fellini, for one, was so tickled by the image of a woman dressed nearly like a priest that he kept it in mind for use in a movie just a few years later.

The miniscandal of the *pretino* line didn't stop the Fontanas from being called to the Vatican in July 1957, when Pope Pius XII recognized the fifty years that matriarch Amabile Fontana and her daughters had put into what had grown into a significant Italian business by holding a special audience for them and their employees. The pontiff had learned that the Fontanas did a nice business in austere black dresses that visitors wore for private meetings with him: "We are glad that we, too, bring you some work," he joked. Along with Amabile and her daughters, a dozen models, sporting those black dresses, and eighty or so members of the Fontana staff, their traditional white aprons worn with matching veils, received blessings. There were, predictably, admonitions; the pope urged the Fontanas to keep designing "modest" and "healthy" clothes. And there was at least one classic banality: "Where do you take inspiration for your ever-changing styles?" he asked the sisters, who compared their creative process with that of painters and musicians. It was, according to a papal spokesman, "the first time in Roman Catholic Church history a Pontiff officially took note of women's fashions without condemning them."

By then, the Florentine fashion shows had simply come to be known as the Sala Bianca, a phrase denoting not only a specific place but all the activity surrounding a certain field of business, like Wall Street or Hollywood. The shows of 1955 drew in the neighborhood of five hundred buyers and two hundred members of the press, and as many as thirteen hundred new pieces were displayed: couture, boutique, ready-to-wear, jewelry, shoes, accessories, and textiles. The emergence of Italy as a major producer of contemporary fashion was complete. And if there was nothing like the surprises of 1951 and 1952, there were new talents, new products, and new ideas emerging virtually every year. Florence had a legitimate claim to being the chief rival of Paris.

That was a remarkable achievement. But there was another rival for Florence (and for Giovanni Battista Giorgini, for that matter) to contend with: Rome. As soon as the international scale of the Florentine triumph became evident, a group of Roman politicians and businessmen, sensing a combination of opportunity and threat, created the Sindacato Italiano Alta Moda, the SIAM, or, as it was known in the American press, the Roman Center of High Fashion. In part the body was meant to promote *all* Italian fashion and textile manufacture, but, more specifically, it was designed as a way to keep Roman designers, their work, and the foreign money and attention they garnered, in the capital—and out of Florence.

Nominally a trade lobbying group that worked to improve conditions in the fashion and textile businesses, SIAM was founded under the aegis of the Christian Democratic government (the ranks of which supplied the union's officials) in the immediate aftermath of the first Sala Bianca show, and it held its initial exhibitions in Rome in the early months of 1953. There was unquestionably a lot of Roman talent to draw upon—not only the quintet of Carosa, Fabiani, Fontana, Schuberth, and Simonetta, whom Giorgini nabbed for his first show, but newer names such as Brioni, Capucci, Gattinoni, and Giovanelli. SIAM said that it wanted to showcase the special skills of Roman couturiers; to spare its members the expense of traveling to Florence to show their work; to allow designers greater freedom to exhibit than Giorgini allowed in his carefully curated shows; and to eliminate interference from the textile manufacturers of the North who helped subsidize Giorgini's exhibitions and who, the Romans whispered, ensured that designs showcasing their product lines were featured. It also, inevitably, marked a modern episode in the long-running struggle between two Italian cities that had vied for centuries for supremacy over the peninsula, an internecine war which the American buyers and press were largely ignorant of and indifferent to.

And war it was. SIAM's constitution explicitly forbade its members from showing in Florence, and it deliberately scheduled its exhibitions in the days right before Giorgini's, in part to cherry-pick from his foreign guest list, in part to muffle some of his thunder. The strategy had a real impact. In the first few years of SIAM shows, held in ballrooms of the hotels along Via Veneto, a good number of Roman designers stayed away from the Sala Bianca, leaving Giorgini's shows mainly to the Milanese and Florentines. Although the Roman cohort had participated avidly in the initial shows in Giorgini's home and at the Grand Hotel, by the time of the first Sala Bianca exhibition, they were almost entirely absent: no Fabiani, no Simonetta, no Fontana sisters, no Schuberth. If Rome was trying to send a message, it was surely heard.

At first, it wasn't clear who was on which side: Simonetta and Fabiani showed with Giorgini for his first seasons, then switched allegiances; siding with SIAM was a choice, Simonetta explained, born of civic pride. "One day, we told ourselves that Rome was just as good as Florence and that every place had the right to its own exclusive revolution. Individualism is a typically Italian weakness." In practice, though, she and Fabiani and others wavered several times in their commitment to one or the other city's exhibitions, one season showing in Rome, the next in Florence, and such was the chaos of the moment that neither the Roman nor Florentine authorities sanctioned them for disloyalty.

After a while, the idea of a feud between the two cities became a regular topic in fashion circles—a little bit of juicy drama amid the glitter. If it seemed to some that the airing of bad blood could threaten the viability of the blossoming business, repelling outsiders, say, who feared choosing sides, others saw the family squabble as a sign of health. Simonetta, speaking at a time when she was once again showing in Florence, said, "People love to grumble and whisper about feuds in the fashion world. The Americans are feted in Rome, and then Florence tries to make them happier. We Italians are not famous for our organization anyway. . . . Besides, what does it matter where a new designer presents his clothes? If they are good, people will know it, even if he shows them in a cornfield or little village."

The idea of factions at war proved irresistible to the American press. In the decade after the founding of SIAM, almost every year brought a headline about the feud in *The New York Times*: "Two Cities Bury the Hatchet," "Roman Couture Is Still Divided as Shows Open," "Fashion Shows Set in Florence Despite Revolt," and the like. Years on, the battle between the Florentine faction and their Roman cousins had lost none of its fire. The Romans, Pucci said, "are trying to kill the Florence festival. It is not going to be killed." "Dirty lies!" responded Count Rodolfo Crespi, the publicist and editor who ran the Roman fashion group, adding, "Florence is a lost cause." Despite the harsh language, very little in the way of dire consequences fell to the designers who went back and forth between the two cities. And the rumbles of war really did create a sense of excitement, with each city's fashion elite trying to outdo the other both on the catwalk and in the hospitality suite. The American buyers and journalists enjoyed the squabble as much as they did the clothes, and both the reputation and the balance sheets of the Italian fashion world benefited from the attention.

In particular, one collaborative pair of Roman designers prospered happily during the celebrated feud. In the January

1952 show at the Grand Hotel in Florence, several of the models wearing Simonetta, Fontana, and Fabiani dresses walked the runway accompanied by a dapper, handsome man, a model named Angelo Vitucci. He wore strikingly cut and fitted formal suits created by the team of Nazareno Fonticoli and Gaetano Savini, who had met almost twenty years prior as a young tailor and marketing manager, respectively, at a Roman men's shop called Satos. Almost immediately after the war, they decided to go into business on their own, making bespoke menswear of the most exacting specifications—forty-five to fifty hours of fitting, cutting, sewing, pressing, and detail work for a single suit. They named their enterprise for an island off the Dalmatian coast of Croatia that was enjoying a vogue as a getaway for the wealthy: Brioni.

Italian men's suits had always been noted for their fine fabrics and for the exemplary handiwork that went into them. Tailors in Rome and Naples were regarded as among the best anywhere. But the undisputed capital of men's high quality suitings was Savile Row in London, where the style was always precise and understated. In the British view, dominant throughout the Western world before 1950, a man's clothing was meant to complement that of the woman he accompanied—*never* to draw attention to itself. Men were, by and large, straitjacketed into boxy, almost military suits of stiff lines and a finite palate of materials, colors, and details—just as London ordained.

At Brioni, a different idea took hold. Just as women's couture emphasized a stylized silhouette, so did Fonticoli and Savini put forward a style of more form-fitting suits for men. The shoulders were pitched naturally rather than straight across; the waist of the jacket was tapered to meet the trousers, which fit the hips precisely; the drapery of both pieces of the suit was natural and fluid, rather than solid and resilient; there were elements of shantung silk, of velvet, even of bright color. The finished product was elegant, impeccably made, and undeniably formal. But it was relaxed and natural and unpretentious as well. The vibrant and playful air that characterized the clothing that Italians were designing for women felt like a refreshing breeze; this breakdown of the Savile Row men's suit into a more form-fitting look was more like a tornado. And its force was felt nowhere more powerfully or more immediately than in the United States, where the formality of British tailoring for men felt as artificial and Old World as Parisian couture could for women; the American mentality of men of even lofty position called out for something natural, dynamic, and flowing, and Italian suits turned out to be just that thing.

The sight of Vitucci accompanying the models in Florence was tremendously exciting to the American buyers. No one had ever put a man on a fashion runway like this before, and nobody from the United States had ever seen clothes like those Vitucci was wearing: tuxedos made of silk, shantung smoking jackets, sleek and modern lines, and attractive materials. Almost overnight a new phenomenon was born—the so-called Continental look, a hip redoubt to the formalism of Savile Row. The New York department store B. Altman put a display of Brioni suits and jackets in its Fifth Avenue windows and created a sensation.

The following summer, when the first show was held at the Sala Bianca, Brioni was given an entire showcase of its own—another first—and enjoyed another tremendous breakthrough. Vitucci, gaining renown as the world's *only* male runway model, wore a dozen suits and ensembles, and he worked the catwalk like a huckster, chatting with the ringside crowd, allowing them to handle the fabrics he was wearing, smiling, kissing hands.[3] The American fashion press went all in on the new look, calling it "a second

3 By day he worked in marketing at Brioni; he would leave the house in 1963 and open his own fashionable atelier, Angelo Roma, eventually earning that most desirable of jobs for a men's clothier: designing a suit for James Bond.

Italian renaissance" (the *Boston Herald*) and hailing Brioni as "the Dior of men's clothing" (*Life*). Word quickly spread among the Hollywood crowd that was filing through Rome, and star after star stopped by Brioni's Via Barberini atelier—just down the hill from Via Veneto—to have a custom suit made: Henry Fonda, Clark Gable, John Wayne, and Victor Mature among them.

The Brioni style was quickly taken up and imitated in Rome, in Paris, and, most surprisingly and influentially, in London, where it was embraced not by the venerable tailors of Savile Row but by a new set of designers who were creating inexpensive but fashion-conscious clothing for young men who wanted to look smart but also up-to-date. Calling themselves "mods" after the modern jazz music they preferred to traditional jazz, or "trad," these young hepcats rode Italian motor scooters, abandoned the British cuppa tea for espresso, the newly imported Italian beverage that was becoming the preferred elixir of London's bohemia,[4] and ignored the fusty dictates of Savile Row in favor of a sleek Italian look. None of these style rebels could afford a Brioni suit, but a whole culture of snappy fashion based on the new Italian looks rose up around a nondescript thoroughfare of London's downmarket clothing district, a few blocks of dusty retail spaces known as Carnaby Street—the first place where Italian men's style met the widespread demand of with-it young men on the make.

But it wasn't only on Carnaby Street, and it wasn't only in menswear. In the first five years of the Florence shows, exports of Italian clothing to the United States rose by a factor of five. By 1960, *Women's Wear Daily* was reporting a continuing rise in imports of Italian clothing and declared, "More Americans are visiting the

---

4 The first Gaggia espresso machine in England showed up on Frith Street in Soho in 1953.

Italian market than ever before, they are coming earlier, and they are buying in greater depth." Almost regularly, new records were being set in American imports of Italian sportswear and knitwear. In 1950, approximately $600,000 worth of sewn goods from Italy came into American markets; by 1961, that figure had risen to $83 *million*. Even though that $83 million represented only 2 percent of what Americans spent on clothing that year, it meant a massive inflow of cash to Italian coffers and an enormous boon to the Italian economy. It meant, too, that Italian taste—and, as well, a taste *for* Italy and things Italian—was spreading rapidly in the biggest market in the world. From Columbus and Vespucci through Sinatra and DiMaggio, America had always had a strain of Italian DNA in its cultural bloodstream. Now it was wrapped in it, from head to toe.

18 "A Fine Race Horse and a Goat"

In the mid-1950s, the Italian cinema was arguably at its historical healthiest. The great directors from the immediate postwar years—De Sica, Visconti, Rossellini— had been joined and sometimes even surpassed in the ranks of international auteurs by the next generation. Fellini and Antonioni, as well as Pietro Germi, Mario Monicelli, Dino Risi, and Francesco Rosi, were all making films that featured international stars and that were exported to commercial and critical success in Europe and the United States. At the same time, a healthy genre industry was bubbling up in the places where the sunlight of international acclaim and awards may not have shone but audiences and profits were to be found.

In the years after *Quo Vadis*, American producers had come to trust not only the infrastructure of Cinecittà but the workforce. There were scores of technicians and craftspeople and specialists. And there were all the things they made, enough props and sets and costumes to fuel what would become a whole industry of *sandaloni*—low-budget, Italian-made, sword-and-sandal movies, bowdlerized rehashings of tales from Greek, Roman, and Judeo-Christian history and mythology about Hercules, Samson, Ulysses, and other classical heroes.[1] Those *sandaloni* movies, though critically derided, sold tickets and provided training for a number of filmmakers who would take the lessons they learned working on ritzy Hollywood productions and cheap Italian knockoffs and create their own films—and sometimes their own genres—in the years to come.

But even the most action-packed sword-and-sandal film was tame compared to a particular struggle that was taking place elsewhere in the film world. To speak of it as bad blood, or as a vendetta, as a feud would be, in a certain light, ludicrous. But through the mid-1950s, egged on by the tabloid press, by publicists, and by movie producers, the various *maggiorate* were pitted against one another in the forum of public opinion for the title of prettiest, curviest, most popular, most famous. And after a little while it became clear that it was a two-woman contest: Gina Lollobrigida vs. Sophia Loren.

Various magazines ran charts comparing the details of the actresses' ages, heights, weights, and vital statistics (and those of such eventual also-rans as Silvana Mangano, Silvana Pampanini, Rossana Podestà, and, occasionally, a foreign interloper like Anita Ekberg,

[1] These films were also known as *peplums*, for an outer robe commonly worn in ancient Greece and Rome.

Brigitte Bardot, or even Marilyn Monroe). Careful attention was paid to who was seen in whose company, who was cast in which role, who got a bigger reception at a film premiere or on a radio or television broadcast. The brouhaha was sufficient that it made headlines overseas; in Cartagena, Colombia, of all places, several stories about the Lollo-Loren "feud" appeared under the byline of a young journalist named Gabriel García Márquez (who was a partisan of Gina, aesthetically, but cunningly saw that Loren would be the bigger star).

Some of this was strictly movie biz hoopla, designed to sell tickets and to keep people talking about new films. And some of it reflected the moral climate of the day. Lollobrigida, the more mature (by seven years) with her happy family life and characteristic "good girl" roles, was held by many, especially those aligned with the Catholic church or the Christian Democratic party, to be a paragon of Italian virtues; Loren, the southern girl born out of wedlock, with a history of appearing in vampish roles (sometimes unclothed) and a (semi-) public relationship with a married man, was castigated by the right but embraced by other factions as an embodiment of a more modern sort of Italian woman.[2]

---

2 This back-and-forth between cultural factions using public figures as their totems almost exactly mirrored the feud between Gino Bartali and Fausto Coppi, the greatest Italian bicyclists of the decades before and after World War II. Bartali, nicknamed Gino the Pious, was the older and, like Lollobrigida, apparently happily married and devoted to religion (he helped Jews escape detainment and persecution during the war and actively abetted the Italian Resistance); he became a national hero by winning the Tour de France in 1938 and 1948, in addition to the Giro d'Italia in 1936, 1937, and 1946. Coppi, an avowed atheist and leftist, openly escorted beautiful women around Paris and Rome even though he was married; an innovator in training techniques (including diet), he won the Tour de France in 1949 and 1952 and triumphed in the Giro in 1940, 1947, 1949, 1952, and 1953. The two were teammates briefly, then avowed and bitter rivals; Bartali spied on Coppi regularly, certain he was guilty of doping himself with performance-enhancing drugs, a charge that Coppi didn't exactly deny. The feud, which had the millions of Italians who avidly followed cycling taking sides, ended only in 1960 when Coppi, aged forty, died from complications of malaria.

But some of it, particularly on Lollobrigida's end, was real. "We are as different as a fine race horse and a goat," she once groused, tired of answering questions about Loren. When they met for the first time, at the Berlin Film Festival of 1954, Lollobrigida initially refused to pose for a joint photograph, agreeing only when American actress Yvonne De Carlo joined in to make it a threesome and stood between the two Italians. Later that year, Lollobrigida and Loren were part of a cohort of movie people visiting London to promote Italian cinema, and Lollo left a cocktail party at the Savoy Hotel in a huff rather than endure, as the event's promoters asked her to, a chest-measuring contest alongside Loren. (Loren, still only twenty, wondered aloud to the press disingenuously, "Why is Gina mad at me? I want to be friendly with her, why not? It's true that my measurements excel [sic] hers, but is that a reason to be furious with me?")

Soon enough, though, the challenger rose to become champion. Loren replaced Lollobrigida as the leading lady in the third and final *Pane, Amore . . .* film, and, by virtue of her tireless work ethic (including her devotion to English lessons) and the support of Carlo Ponti as her agent and manager and Vittorio De Sica as her frequent costar and personal director, she was able to build a Hollywood career while Lollobrigida was still forbidden to work in the United States by her contract with Howard Hughes. Worse yet for Lollo, she had acquired an unenviable reputation as a difficult customer to deal with. She was whispered about as "Lollofrigida" and, according to *Time*, which put her on its cover in 1954, "She has been involved in as many as ten lawsuits at once. Her most famous day in court came when she asked damages from an Italian movie critic who wrote a derogatory review about her 'udder.' He and his editor were fined $176 and costs." (Not long after, she moved for a brief period to Canada in part to escape Italian taxes.)

Other new faces would soon emerge: Claudia Cardinale, a gorgeous, doll-faced beauty pageant winner from Tunisia already working with some of the Italian cinema's greatest stars and directors by the time she was twenty, and Monica Vitti, Italy's answer to Jeanne Moreau and muse, as the world would soon discover, to Michelangelo Antonioni. But none would ever quite ascend to the aerie where Lollo and Loren battled (or were imagined to be battling) for supremacy.

There was a similar—if less sensational—competition among Italy's directors. The great neorealists were still active: Roberto Rossellini had gone off to India, where he'd soon be making films; Luchino Visconti still wavered between the theater and the cinema; and Vittorio De Sica kept so busy as an actor and a director that he seemed more like a movie studio than a man. And two of the next generation were emerging as equally important voices: Federico Fellini was starting to be recognized outside of Italy, and Michelangelo Antonioni was gaining a significant constituency of his own.

Antonioni was, in many ways, the anti-Fellini, cool and austere where Fellini was gregarious and cluttered, taciturn and intellectual where Fellini was garrulous and fantastical. The two respected each other and got along well professionally, but they were destined to run on parallel tracks, never intersecting and, at least in the eyes of the world, always competing with one another: an auteurist incarnation of the civil wars between Vespa and Lambretta, Coppi and Bartali, Loren and Lollobrigida.

Antonioni was the older, born in 1912, eight years before Fellini. And he grew up in Ferrara, in Emilia-Romagna, not far from Fellini's Rimini but more industrialized, wealthy, northern, and, in a sense, courtly: people didn't go there to blow off steam but to live and work. Antonioni's father was a self-made man who managed to acquire income-producing lands around the region, and Michelangelo, raised in a solidly middle-class household, was expected to attend university and acquire a profession. He went to school in Bologna and studied economics, during which time he came to embrace Marxism, which would provide him with a lifelong set of convictions and ideas (committed atheism would provide another stream of his thinking). While still in school, he published some writing infused with the spirit of his studies, and he stayed in Bologna for several years, engaged in intellectual pursuits.

At the same time, though, even since boyhood, his imagination had been captivated by the idea of making things, particularly buildings and cities; as a youngster, he was fond of creating miniature towns filled with tiny figurines that he would manipulate in stories of his own devising, creations he once called "*happenings . . . little films.*" While at school in Bologna he painted as a pastime and attended movies avidly, eventually publishing some film criticism.

In 1940, he went to Rome, in part because he had the opportunity to work at the film magazine *Cinema*, which was unabashedly Fascist and edited by Vittorio Mussolini. The job lasted only a few months, but Antonioni made the acquaintance of several of the creators of the neorealist aesthetic. He followed his short-lived magazine stint by enrolling as a student at the Centro Sperimentale di Cinematografia, the state-sponsored film school, another awkward fit that lasted only a handful of months.

He barely survived the war, siding with the Resistance but being drafted by the Fascists, who deemed him treasonous and might well have executed him if they'd maintained power longer. Spared, he worked with Rossellini on his short documentaries about the war and apprenticed with Marcel Carné in France. In 1943, he directed his first short film, a documentary about the daily lives of impoverished fishermen in the Po Valley of Northern Italy.

In the next half decade, he kept working at short documentaries while dreaming up story ideas, some of which became feature films. (One of these was the basis of *The White Sheik*, Fellini's 1952 solo directorial debut, which the younger man made with the older's blessing.) He'd made his fictional feature debut in 1950 with *Story of a Love Affair*, starring Lucia Bosé, with whom he had a romantic connection. It was a thoroughly credible melodrama: grown-up, erotic, tense, with some relation to the potboiling novel *The Postman Always Rings Twice* (which Visconti had loosely adapted as *Ossessione* in 1943); you could sense the artist's mature work in the textures, if not the plot, and the acting, photography, and editing were top-notch. The film was received warmly by critics—Antonioni was awarded a special Nastro d'Argento (the Silver Ribbon, the Italian film critics' top prize) for "the human and stylistic values" it embraced—and from that point he was able to continue working as a writer-director for another half century.

In the coming years, Antonioni continued to make short films. His next credit, *I Vinti*, was composed of three discrete tales of imperiled modern youth in England, France, and Italy; his contribution to the anthology film *L'Amore in Città* (*Love in the City*) stood out for the stark fashion in which it depicted its subject matter, *Tentato Suicido* (*Suicide Attempt*).[3] Compared with his peers, Antonioni focused on establishing a mood with the camera, creating a spare and static aesthetic that made his characters appear a little like experimental subjects in a laboratory, a strong contrast to the

---

3 The other directors included Fellini, Alberto Lattuada, Dino Risi, and the screenwriter and novelist Cesare Zavattini, whose inspiration the project was. Just as they were willing to share story ideas and write scripts in big teams, Italian directors of the 1940s, '50s, and '60s often contributed short films to such group projects, sometimes with a common theme, almost as if they were engaged in a workshop exercise.

emotional, sympathy-wringing figures, often drawn from real life, who populated neorealist films.

He made a second feature, *La Signora senza Camelie* (*The Lady Without Camelias*), also with Bosé, in 1953. And then two years later, he crafted his real breakthrough: *Le Amiche*, an adaptation of a Cesare Pavese novel about a group of women in Turin including a dress-shop manager, a model, a sculptor, a tomcatty gal who lives on the largesse of her absent husband, and a depressive who has survived a suicide attempt. It was a traditional melodrama with a lot of chatter, but it was fully steeped in what would soon be recognizable as Antonioni's idiosyncratic style: long takes; deep, flat focus; sharp, often terrifically handsome frames; idle bourgeois characters concerned with their emotional lives rather than the daily needs that tormented the people in neorealist cinema; and a strong sense that economic success can't cure loneliness, heartsickness, or despair. The film won the Silver Lion at the Venice Film Festival, and it took three Nastro d'Argento prizes from the Italian film press: Best Cinematography, Best Supporting Actress (Valentina Cortese), and Best Director.

After another two years came *Il Grido* (released in the United States under its Italian title): the first truly Antonioni-ish Antonioni, a story of wandering, alienation, and despair, with a loosely built narrative, an overwhelmingly stark visual aesthetic, and a sense of modern ennui as viewed through the cool detached eye of what James Joyce called the "God of the creation . . . invisible, refined out of existence, indifferent, paring his fingernails." It was an episodic narrative about a man wandering the countryside with his young daughter after being abandoned by his wife. It relied less on plot than on emotional nuance; waiting for something to happen, audiences could grow restless. But if they sat with it, steeped themselves in it, absorbed it, gave into it, it could fill them with a strange blend of melancholy, wonder, pain, and even a little hope. In its vagueness, its slow pace, its artful compositions, and its satisfaction with an enigmatic ending, it felt like art-art. And it was a tantalizing taste of where its director would soon go.

*F*ederico Fellini was quicker to discover his native idiom and his audiences—both at home and abroad. He had made his mark with *I Vitelloni*, which launched one of the most extraordinary careers in twentieth-century art.

After contributing a charming episode about a matrimonial agency to the anthology film *L'Amore in Città*, Fellini produced a milestone of world cinema. In *La Strada*, his humor, his pathos, his native humanism, his fantastical imagination, his love of the circus, his ability to orchestrate all aspects of film craft, his gifts as a commercial artist, and even his wife were all deployed to powerful effect. It was a success for everyone who was involved with it, but principally for Fellini, whose vision and execution were universally recognized as singular. His name would be listed ever after alongside those of the great directors who rebuilt Italian film after the war—Rossellini, Visconti, De Sica—but also among those of the rising generation of global directors who were changing the face of cinema everywhere: Ingmar Bergman, Akira Kurosawa, Satyajit Ray, and the little mob of French New Wave directors who would appear in a few years' time.

The story of strife between three itinerant circus performers— a brutish strongman, a whimsical acrobat, and a simple, good-hearted girl who finds herself caught between them—*La Strada* was written by Fellini and Tullio Pinelli (with a rewrite from Ennio Flaiano) over a span of two years and shot around Rome and Abruzzi beginning in October 1953. In her most visible role yet, Giulietta Masina played Gelsomina, a waifish young woman sold by her mother into the service of the strongman, who, in a coup for the production, was portrayed by the Hollywood star Anthony Quinn, newly minted as an Oscar winner for his work in *Viva Zapata!* The key third member of the cast was also American: Richard Basehart, a B-movie star who worked occasionally in Rome in part because he was married to Valentina Cortese, the Milanese star who had joined the chain of Italian girls who made their way to Hollywood.

La Strada is a curious hybrid of neorealism and fantasy, set, barely, in the here and now. The temper-prone, boozy, womanizing Zampano is unable to see that Gelsomina considers herself his; he uses her simply as a prop in his act, as a maid, and as a bed warmer (if not, explicitly, sex partner). When she runs from him and encounters the clownish tightrope walker known as Il Matto (The Fool), she seems to find a lifeline. But Zampano returns, engages in an ugly rivalry with Il Matto, and leads the trio into an awful and, ultimately, poignant fate.

The film debuted at the Venice Film Festival in September 1954, where it was recognized with the second-place Silver Lion,[4] on an awards night that broke out into actual fistfights in the audience when it became clear that Luchino Visconti's *Senso* would be shut out entirely. In the polemical atmosphere that surrounded Italian cinema of the day, murmurs circulated that a Fellini camp had mounted a boycott of the Visconti film, leading to a cold war between the two filmmakers, who refused to speak for nearly a decade. In this context, it was no surprise that *La Strada* was greeted by Italian critics and audiences with a partisan mix of reverence and hostility.

---

4 This time, Fellini's film was tied with three other masterpieces: Elia Kazan's *On the Waterfront*, Akira Kurosawa's *Seven Samurai*, and Kenji Mizoguchi's *Sansho the Bailiff*.

Abroad, however, it was almost universally hailed as a major work of art. There was a dreamlike, fairy tale quality to the film despite the earthy textures (you could almost smell Zampano's dirty clothes and wine-soaked breath); it perfectly balanced a simple tale, complex art, and powerful craft. And the performances of Masina, evoking Chaplin and even Shirley Temple, and Quinn, crude and animalistic, with a human core occasionally asserting itself, were stupendous. The box office was massive in Europe and Asia; there were prizes and official accolades from critics and filmmakers everywhere; and when it appeared in the United States in 1956 it was greeted with almost unanimous praise. Not only would it win the first competitive Oscar for Best Foreign Language Film (previously the prize was awarded without a vote as a special honor), but Fellini and Pinelli would be nominated for their screenwriting. Offers came for Fellini to work in America and for Masina to star in a sequel about the adventures of Gelsomina—also, if he wished, to be made in Hollywood.

But Fellini had fallen under the spell of a new project of his own devising, a story about con men posing as priests that would eventually be released as *Il Bidone* (*The Swindle*). Once again he wrote it with Flaiano and Pinelli. Once again he had an American leading man—this time the genial but alcoholic and unreliable Broderick Crawford. And once again Basehart and Masina costarred, he as Crawford's accomplice, she as Basehart's wife. There were hints of Fellini's signature themes and techniques (as well as a scene of upper-class debauchery that would prefigure his later work). But it was a far more realistic and worldly movie than *La Strada*, it was rather grim and a bit drab, and it was greeted with little enthusiasm at home upon its debut at yet another Venice Film Festival and with similar ambivalence abroad.[5]

5 It wouldn't debut in American movie houses until 1964.

While *Il Bidone* was something of a setback for Fellini, he was almost immediately at work on a new project with an enthusiasm that drowned out any disappointment. During the making of *Il Bidone*, Fellini became fascinated by the criminal and bohemian underworld on the fringes of Rome and the prostitutes, thieves, and drug users who inhabited it. In pursuit of a new story idea, he would spend nights visiting the haunts of these shady characters, conversing with them over drinks and meals, picking their brains, divining their hearts. Predictably, his film world colleagues included more than a few men who were acquainted with this milieu, and he availed himself of their services as guides, among them a young novelist and screenwriter named Pier Paolo Pasolini who was apparently intimate with every stripe of vice available to sample or observe in and around Rome.

*P*asolini had been born in 1922 in Bologna, where his father, a military officer, helped discover a plot to assassinate Mussolini but squandered much of the glory that resulted by being arrested for gambling debts. Pier Paolo was schooled all over the North of Italy, as his father's service demanded, and several of those years were spent in Friuli, a province north of Venice where his mother's family was based. Eventually, the boy attended high school and university in Bologna, where he played soccer and wrote poetry, both lifelong passions. He published two books of poetry in Friulian, specifically in the dialect of Casarsa, which he preferred to the dialect of Udine: of such split hairs could he kindle raging fires in himself. He was drafted into the war almost at its end and never actually served, escaping his barracks and hiding in the countryside, where, when peace prevailed, he and his mother worked as schoolteachers. He engaged in politics, writing about the cultural advantages of communism, but when his homosexuality was revealed in an incident involving a student, he lost his teaching job and was expelled from the Communist party, forcing him into exile from the region with which he would identify deeply all his life.

In Rome, he continued to write essays and poetry, adding the local Romanesco dialect to his repertoire of voices. He got a job as a gofer at Cinecittà, sold books from a street stall, began to frequent the circles of Roman intellectuals, and landed a teaching position in a nearby *borgata*, one of the new proletariat neighborhoods on the outskirts of the city where the poverty and desperation contrasted stunningly with the high life being lived by foreigners, tourists, and swells just a few miles away. He was drawn, as he would be his whole life, to the underworld. So at the same time that he was becoming acquainted with such luminaries as Alberto Moravia and Ennio Flaiano at the intellectual oases of the Piazza del Popolo and Via Veneto, he was also getting to know the pimps, drug dealers, and prostitutes, male and female, in the area referred to as the Passeggiate Archeologica, a picturesque stretch of ruins south of the Circus Maximus that hosted tourism in the daylight and illicit activities at night.

In 1955, he published a novel, *Ragazzi di Vita* (literally, *Boys of the Life*, but often translated as *The Ragazzi*), which became a succès de scandale, drawing positive reviews, heated sales, hostile editorials, and even legal action for obscenity. It was unflinching and scandalous and written in the Romanesco of the streets, and it drew the attention of Fellini, Flaiano, and Pinelli when it became clear to them that they didn't know the world of Roman prostitutes well enough to write convincingly about it. Fellini contacted Pasolini, enlisting him to help render the life of the Roman underworld—and, even more specifically, its language—in a new film project.

Pasolini may have been noted for his familiarity with a dark world, but he looked the part of an intellectual: square-jawed, stony-visaged, and always dressed impeccably in suit and tie, his large eyeglasses adding to the overall impression of angularity, austerity, sobriety, even nerdiness. The tap on the shoulder from Fellini was just the thing he needed to evolve into a movie world figure. Once he'd gotten a credit alongside a major director, Pasolini was increasingly in demand as screenwriter.

Fellini's nocturnal excursions with Pasolini resulted in a script entitled *Le Notti di Cabiria* (*Nights of Cabiria*), about a prostitute who, despite the horrible conditions of her life and work, believed in the redemptive power of love, ultimately to her downfall. Masina was the only actress considered for the lead, this time without the support of an American star to bolster her at the box office. The film was shot throughout Rome—using locations Fellini had visited during his tours of the underworld—in the second half of 1956. Upon its debut at the Cannes Film Festival the following year, Masina was awarded the prize as best actress and Fellini was cited for special recognition by the jury.

Even more than *La Strada, Notti di Cabiria* was a showcase for the remarkable Masina, who danced, argued, flirted, dreamt, swooned, lost her heart, and sought solace and courage with a vivid fluidity. She was a singular presence in Italian cinema, not overwhelmingly sexual, one of those *maggiorate*, but impossible not to watch and admire and love and empathize with. And the film probed even further into the shadows of modern Rome than *Il Bidone*, including sequences near the Terme di Caracalla, the famed thermal baths, where the city's prostitutes sought clients, and along Via Veneto, where Cabiria flaunted herself in front of high-end call girls and caught the eye of a drunken movie star (played by Amadeo Nazzari, the Italian Errol Flynn) who took her nightclubbing and then to his home.

Partly encouraged by its triumph at Cannes, Italian audiences and critics responded rapturously to the film, even though it depicted Roman life so disreputably. Export to the United States resulted in commercial and critical success, culminating on the night of March 26, 1958, when Masina walked up the aisle of the Pantages Theatre in Hollywood to accept the Academy Award for Best Foreign Language Film—Fellini's second in two years. (He himself stayed behind in Rome, despite also being nominated that evening for the screenplay of *I Vitteloni*.) Giulietta returned home with the statuette and placed it, along with all the other trophies and certificates that her husband's films had won, in a room he called "the sanctuary of Divine Love" and refused to enter.

Fellini, meanwhile, had resumed his nightly explorations of the dark sides of Rome, fascinated simultaneously by the decadent modernity that had sprung up in certain parts of the city and by the idea, abandoned just a few years earlier, of revisiting Moraldo, the young dreamer who escaped the provinces at the end of *I Vitelloni*, and imagining how he was faring in the capital. He was contemplating a complete rewrite of the material then known as *Moraldo in Città*. But he required a spark of inspiration that he hadn't yet encountered—until, that is, he started to hear stories of packs of photographers chasing after celebrities around Via Veneto.

19 "A Charnel House Under a Green Marquee"

There was no single precipitating event—no battle or assassination or decree, no *Jazz Singer* or *Sacre du Printemps* or *Sun Also Rises*, no invention or extinction or paradigm-shifting moment of any sort. It evolved slowly, its essential strands and energies meeting gradually, at a pace you'd need time-lapse photography to chart, like vines twining together into a mesh on a trellis. If you were watching you could see it approaching, though nobody had ever seen anything exactly like it, nor could anyone have predicted how it would turn out.

Journalists from Italy and even the United States had been writing about the curious scene on Via Veneto for several years. In 1953, the magazine *Epoca* carried an article by the expatriate American writer George Nelson Page entitled *"Passa per Via Veneto la Gioventù Dorata"* ("The Golden Youth Pass Along Via Veneto"), describing the life of chatter and schmoozing up and down the street and illustrated with pictures of the aged poet Vincenzo Cardarelli and café terraces and intellectuals chatting over books in Rossetti's shop and drinks at Caffè Rosati. That same year, *The New York Times* published a similar story, "Grandstand for Rome's Passing Show," written by Melton B. Davis and touting various spots on Via Veneto, complete with prices of select menu items, descriptions of the crowd each café drew ("[to Zeppa's] come most of the artists who wander over from Via Margutta. . . . Doney's . . . is the favorite meeting place for Americans"), and recommendations about nightlife, lodging, and transportation.

Epoca returned the following year, this time with the young journalist Oriana Fallaci doing the reporting. The article, *"Via Veneto, Décolleté di Roma"* (roughly, "Via Veneto, Where Rome Bares Itself"), once again featured Cardarelli, seated in hat and overcoat at the Strega and complaining about the crowds, among whom were cited a few princes and movie stars and other *snobs* (the English word had been adopted by Italians). A tone of knowing cynicism and weariness crept into the text, which was focused mainly on the cohort of writers and journalists who made their home at Rossetti's, but it was more properly a sketch of life as it was then lived, a feature story rather than an exposé or an indictment. Like the previous articles about the phenomenon of Via Veneto, it bore a tenor mostly of curiosity: "There's a street in Rome where bohemians, intellectuals, movie people, and well-off foreigners rub against each other: Who'd've thunk?"[1]

In the handful of years since those articles, something had occurred that would create a rising pressure, in effect, underneath Via Veneto, and the street was on the verge of an explosive crescence, a volcano ready to blow smoke and sparks that would be visible everywhere within the popular media.

 $\mathcal{T}$ he energy that would ignite Via Veneto was known, in Italy, as *Il Boom*—a breakneck economic and cultural revival and expansion of the nation. Since the early 1950s, the Italian economy had mushroomed, transforming the lives of ordinary citizens up and down the peninsula, remaking the major cities, and recasting Italy

---

1 It wasn't all cheery news and delightful novelties. On a morning in November 1954, a man's nude body lay on the sidewalk outside the Hotel Eden on Via Ludovisi, just off Via Veneto. The dead man, who witnesses said seemed to be smiling, was Raimondo Lanza Branciforte, Prince of Trabia, thirty-nine years old, heir to one of the oldest titles of Sicily and a well-known sportsman, scenester, and skirt chaser in the swell spots of Europe. He had a title and money, and he lived like a nobleman of a bygone era: He was educated in England, spent some time serving as a diplomat in Paris, and he even wrote a memoir/treatise (never published) about his life and ideas entitled *Mi Toccherà Ballare* (*I Shall Have to Dance*). He included among his amours Rita Hayworth and Carroll Baker and among his friends Luchino Visconti, Aristotle Onassis, and Gianni Agnelli. He was known to spend freely, to live hard, to use cocaine, to drink and dance and dally until dawn rose. His apparent suicide confounded those close to him. He had just come to Rome from Sicily after a party in his ancestral castle in honor of Onassis, and on the morning of his death he had been to see a doctor, who noted nothing amiss. He may have been manic-depressive—he exhibited several classic emotional symptoms of the condition. But his death was a mystery—and not only the why, but the how: the accounts of the hotel manager, the police, and Lanza di Trabia's brother all disagreed as to which floor of the hotel he had leapt (or, as it was inevitably suggested in the newspapers, been pushed) from. The following year, the mystery inspired a song by Domenico Modugno, "Vecchia Frak" ("Old Tuxedo"), an evocative and melancholy ballad about an elegant man, wearily wandering the city in the wee hours and deciding, almost on a whim, to leap into the river and bid the world adieu.

from the buffoonish ally of Nazi Germany into a hive of style, culture, fine craft, genteel living, and even heavy industry. Through the rest of the decade, Italy's industrial production index grew at an astonishing 120 percent, the net production of its industry grew 103 percent, and its gross national income grew 78 percent. Even Americans, riding historically high, took notice.[2]

Ordinary Italians had done without many things when the war had ended, but gradually the country's industrial concerns managed to offer an economically hobbled population a selection of consumer goods that it could, albeit with effort, afford. Those Vespa and Lambretta scooters, for instance, were firmly established as a cheap mode of personal transportation. By the mid-1950s, however, with the industrial engine of the country starting to reach full operation, a substantial number of Italians were able to afford not only two wheels but four—and a chassis and seats to go with them.

In 1955, Fiat released its 600 model, designed by Dante Giacosa as Italy's answer to the Volkswagen, a small, reasonably affordable car not much bigger or more powerful than a motor scooter but a bona fide sign of its owner's having emerged from dark times into relative prosperity. More than a million of the little things rolled off the production line in the first five years during which it was available—an average of 1000 finished vehicles a day. (Another model, the smaller, more economical 500 Nuovo, also created by Giacosa, was introduced in 1957, and nearly 200,000 of them were sold in the first three years of production.) In the span of fifteen years, from 1950 to 1964, the number of privately owned cars in Italy rose from 342,000 to 4.67 million, and similar increases

2 They also took payment: by 1962, Italy would pay back all of its billions of dollars in Marshall Plan loans.

were seen in the construction of new homes and the ownership of televisions, refrigerators, and motorcycles.

With such popular products to manufacture, it wasn't surprising that the first and greatest flushes of Italy's postwar prosperity should be felt in the North, the traditional industrial center of the country. From that region emerged automobiles (Fiat, but also the luxury makes Lamborghini, Ferrari, Maserati, Lancia, and Alfa Romeo), motorcycles and scooters (Vespa, Lambretta, Ducati), tires (Pirelli), home appliances (Italian washing machines manufactured by Candy and Zanussi became the largest-selling in Europe, and their refrigerators weren't far behind), business equipment (Olivetti typewriters), furniture, molded plastics for household use, and textiles that were recognized—and purchased—the world over. (Industrial products such as petrochemicals, liquid fuels, and steel also saw huge upswings.) Italian goods were favored for their style, their quality, and, because the nation's labor was still relatively cheap, their low prices.

That labor came, mainly, from central and Southern Italy, especially the rural areas. The 1950s found many millions of Italians moving in search of work: as much as 30 percent of the entire population of the country migrated internally—some 200,000 per year, almost all from the agrarian South to the industrial North—during what became known as the "era of the cardboard suitcases" (so named for the stereotypical travel gear of the rural classes arriving in big cities). They arrived on the famed *treno del sole*, the train of the sun, which ran the length of the country, and they were such staple figures of modern Italy that a film, *La Ragazza con Valigia* (*The Girl with the Suitcase*), would eventually be built around an archetypal hopeful migrant. In Rome, Milan, and Turin, these influxes required the construction of huge new housing complexes on the peripheries, the famed *borgate* that ringed the cities and which resembled, for good and bad, public housing projects in the United States, Britain, and France.

The challenges presented by the shift of populations to urban areas were stark and real, and in Rome they were particularly acute; the city didn't have sufficient industrial capacity to put all of its new citizens to work. Even though these migrants found themselves struggling for decent living and working conditions in close proximity to the seats of government, church, and the country's largest media enterprises, they found that these powers often did little more than cursorily witness, dutifully chronicle, and, then, usually, forget the problems that were mushrooming just beyond the walls that marked the historic borders of the city.

What was happening *inside* those walls—more precisely, inside the couple of square miles defined by Via Veneto, the Piazza di Spagna, Via Margutta, and the Piazza del Popolo—couldn't have provided a starker contrast. There, in the traditional artistic and touristic hubs of Rome, *Il Boom* was less an economic event than a sociocultural one. It didn't matter that just a few miles away there was real struggle and suffering associated with the upward spiral that pulled so much of the country into the modern age with mixed results. There were bread and circuses and novelty and amazement on, it seemed, every corner of Via Veneto and its environs, and the distractions that ensued would captivate the world.

*E*ven just a few years prior, Via Veneto had been a quiet street, with its intellectuals engaged in friendly rivalry at the bottom and cafés discreetly humming with film producers and aspiring cinematic folk at the top. *Time* wrote about the street's "swarms of gnats . . . the hundreds of little middlemen, promoters, rumor touts and inside-kiters who do the dizzy business of making Italian movies." But by 1957, when the English travel writer H. V. Morton visited it, the street had undergone a transformation:

At the top of the Via Vittorio Veneto a great number of red and blue sun umbrellas dot the wide pavements each side of the street. This is American Rome, just as the Piazza di Spagna was English Rome a hundred years ago. Everything here is a little richer and more expensive than elsewhere; we are in the dollar area. Here you see the "milords" of the new age, the film stars and the celluloid caesars, and those executives whose names occupy such a tedious crescendo of type before a film begins. ... [The area] has a strong character which overflows into the side streets, where you find quick-lunch bars and American restaurants which specialize in club sandwiches, Chicken Maryland, apple pie, canned peaches, hamburgers, and American coffee. These haters of colonialism have indeed created a barefaced colony where they feel safe and at home, and into which they can return, as into a fortress, after raids into foreign territory! There is something quite fascinating about the Americanism of this part of Rome. It is, in its way, imperial.

Morton's tone was more wry and humored than that adopted the following year by, again, Melton Davis, who anatomized Via Veneto in a book about the death of Wilma Montesi: "Only in modern Italy could a single half-mile-long street contain so much grace and vulgarity, power and decadence, charm and arrogance as did this gilded alley. It was made to order for the fixers, for the dope-addled princes and dream-haunted paupers, for the whole fantastic parade that gathered there."

And Davis was positively rhapsodic in comparison to the tenor taken by some of those whose memories of Via Veneto were personal and even halcyon. Ennio Flaiano, who truly loved his time among the gossipy literati at the bottom of the street and even among the haughty film people at the top, looked upon the changes on Via

Veneto with an eye that was less bemused than horrified. Writing in his diary in 1958, he saw, first, the rise of a new social class:

> [T]his "café society" that frolics between eroticism, alienation, boredom, and sudden affluence ... flourishes a bit everywhere. But here in Rome, through a mixing together of the sacred and the profane, of the old and the new, through the en masse arrival of foreigners, through the cinema, it presents more aggressive, subtropical qualities. . . . Rome has expanded, become disproportioned, got rich. Scandals explode with all the violence of summer storms.

He saw, too, to his palpable despair, the conquest of his beloved Via Veneto by this sensation-seeking, superficial mob: "This is no longer a street, but a beach. The cafés, which overflow onto the sidewalks—how many are there? six? seven?—have, each one of them, a different type of umbrella for their tables. . . . Even the conversations are seaside resort: baroque and jocular; and they are concerned with an exclusively gastro-sexual reality. All that's missing is splashing water."

And his was a playful view compared with that of Sandro de Feo, a screenwriter and author whose novel *Gli Inganni* (*The Cheaters*) contained this damning passage:

> So tonight it's Via Veneto. The spectacle of a slaughterhouse under a green canopy is what it is, but undoubtedly my nerves have been flayed by the wind, making me exaggerate its obscenity and grotesquerie. If I had the strength to do anything, I would laugh, the way I do when I read the stories of the Marquis De Sade and reach the points where the author gets heavy-handed.

And to be fair, the once staid street had become crowded and garish, affording old-timers plenty to grouse about. On the eastern side—or Left Bank, as it were—where Rossetti's bookshop still anchored the bottom, stood a trio of hotels (the Ambasciatori, the Regina, and the Savoia); a skein of dining and drinking establishments, including the Golden Gate, Rosati's, and Harry's Bar (a sibling establishment to the famous watering holes in Paris and Venice); and two newsstands, both of which specialized in out-of-town publications and one of which had a policy of being open around the clock. On the Right Bank, where the Capuchin Catacombs and American embassy sat, were the Excelsior and Grand Flora hotels; the cafés Doney and Strega; the street's only two nightclubs, Bricktop's and the Jicky Club (which was little more than the converted back room of the Rupe Tarea restaurant); an all-night pharmacy; the American-style restaurant Jerry's Supper Club; and the offices of *Lo Specchio* and *Le Ore*, a pair of tabloid magazines that thrived on images of bold-faced names cavorting in the street outside their doors.

In the years since Via Veneto's stock began to rise, the establishments at the top of the street had become larger, as Flaiano suggested, taking over the sidewalks with concrete flower beds and scores of small tables, topped at first by umbrellas and then by massive awnings (a rare Roman snow in 1960 would cause some of these to collapse). And, as Morton suggested, the scene had spread into side streets. Within just a few paces of Via Veneto were other hotels, less deluxe, and such nightspots as Capriccio, Club 84 (formerly Victor Bar, a hugely popular jazz club that was forced to change ownership in part because police were continually frustrated by the drug trade on site), the Kit Kat (aka "the last beach," because it was invariably the last nightclub to close its doors, at around six a.m.), and Il Pipistrello. And there were at least three of what were considered "American" bars, because of the style of their layout and service and because of their menus: the Arizona, the California, and the Colony. This was a remarkable concentration of late-night destinations in a city that had at the time, by one count, only twenty-one nightclubs, a mere seven of which offered live entertainment. For all the noise and clamor that Rome could inflict on a visitor, it was still, at its heart, a somewhat sleepy town dominated by three businesses—the government (almost one-third of Roman employees were civil servants), the church, and the movies—that generally required employees to report to work early in the morning.

This societal boom drove the intellectual set from the bottom of Via Veneto to the cafés of the Piazza del Popolo, which, per Flaiano, was "topographically protected from the assaults of fashion by its ample spaces, by the absence of large hotels in the vicinity, by the few cafés." And that left the street to the new set of international scene makers—jet-setters, in the new term of the day—that included movie stars, movie hopefuls, and the rich and very rich who didn't need to be famous to earn a place at an exclusive boîte.

One of the earliest to take center stage in this scene was Egypt's King Farouk, deposed in 1952 and arriving not long after in Rome, where he found hotels, restaurants, and clubs to provide a pleasantly cushioned prison in which to bring himself slowly to the brink of dissipative death. Farouk gorged himself and whored and spent piles of money and was such a regular on the nightlife circuit that nobody bothered to note his presence anymore. He didn't drink—he was a Muslim—but he ate multiple meals per night, he kept himself surrounded at all times by an entourage, including bodyguards, and his companions always included a few women, dressed in couture and laden with jewels, often paid to keep company with him. (He was said to be generous with prostitutes and was known to drive them around on their calls, squeezing himself improbably behind the wheel of a Mercedes.) Obese, beady-eyed, goateed, with tiny round spectacles giving him an owlish aspect of inscrutability, he was a fixture on Via Veneto, showing up late and claiming premium tables and gazing out at the scene around him with a simmering air. He rarely looked like he was enjoying himself, and he rarely tolerated guests other than his girls (when he did, he made sure that they picked up the bill). It was a wonder that he bothered to come out at all. But he had settled in Rome, and the cafés and nightclubs at the top of the street were the local version of the high life, so he claimed himself a prize spot, and who was going to question the prerogatives of a king, even one without a throne?

As it happened, quite a number of nobles had begun to habituate Via Veneto: Italian princes, marquises, dukes, scions of families that in some cases dated back millennia and who had begun to visit the street in search of distraction, dissolution, romance, amusement, or simply to satisfy curiosity about what they'd heard had been happening there.

Two of the most notorious of these slumming aristocrats were members of what was known as the Black aristocracy—families with titles conferred by a pope and who were tied to the Vatican by specific privileges and obligations (the more traditional aristocracy, descended from landholders and army leaders of bygone eras, were known as the White aristocracy). The most colorful of these sensation-seeking Black noblemen was Alessandro Maria Galeazzo Ruspoli, ninth Prince of Cerveteri, ninth Marquis of Riano, and fourteenth Count of Vignanello—known to his friends as Dado. He was born in 1924 in the family palazzo, which sat where Via dei Condotti met Via del Corso, very near the heart of bohemian Rome. His father's family owned estates and a famed castle and gardens north of the city, and his mother, though born in Naples, was heiress to a large Brazilian industrial fortune. It had been centuries since any Ruspoli had felt the need to earn a living, but Dado's father, Francesco, would serve in both world wars and spend peacetime pursuing a career as a poet and sculptor, frequenting (and financing) various artistic endeavors—ballet companies, theater troupes, orchestras.

As a young man, Dado cut an eye-catching figure around Rome and Capri, walking barefoot in the summer (to show off his painted toenails), wearing loudly colored clothes (and, when weather made it necessary, matching shoes), and sometimes sporting a raven, which he had nursed back from injury, on his shoulder. He was, in the words of an acquaintance, "an effeminate, strange sort of chap with exhibitionist tendencies," but he was of a gentle and agreeable nature and possessed a curious and lively spirit. Like his father, Dado was passionate about culture. With his presence and his purse, he patronized several arts organizations and charities. He befriended the great artists and intellectuals whom he met as a young man, including Jean Cocteau, Salvador Dalí, and Orson Welles, who taught him magic tricks.

In 1947, he wed a fellow noble, Francesca dei Baroni Blanc, but it was a troubled marriage. A few years before, Dado had been introduced to opium, and though he set out more than once to give up drugs (Cocteau tried to help him kick his habit), he was caught in 1953 with approximately five pounds of opium in his car. It was, he eventually told a judge, a personal supply, and the court took pity on him, imposing a modest sentence for smuggling and then suspending it.[3] The incident did nothing to dim his luster in the

3 Even though Francesca also dabbled in drugs, the scandal and stress of Dado's arrest and trial (as well as his apparent addiction to women other than his wife) cost them their marriage, and she moved on, eventually to Milan, where she threw herself from a seventh-story window in 1962.

Roman demimonde; he was a regular at the artists' haunts around Via Margutta and the swell cafés atop Via Veneto, and no gathering of famous faces at a nightclub, a party, an opening, or a scandalous happening seemed complete without him.

Another member of the Black aristocracy who swelled the Via Veneto scene was Prince Filippo Napoleone Orsini, Duke of Gravina, Prince of Roccagorga, of Solofra, and of Vallera, Prince of the Holy Roman Empire, and Prince Assistant to the Pontifical Throne, the last title making him one of the highest lay dignitaries in the Vatican hierarchy, invested with the honor of accompanying and attending the pope at the most formal and solemn masses and ceremonies. Along with a reputable record in the war, Orsini was a flat-out playboy, a married man and father who unabashedly chased women throughout the finest resorts, hotels, and nightclubs of Europe. He had been wed in 1946, at age twenty-five, to the Marchesa di San Michele Arcangelo, Francesca Romana Bonacosi, who suffered his dalliances, in part, by pouring her energies into their two sons and running their palazzo on the Pincian hill. But a decade into their marriage, Filippo's skirt chasing yielded an international scandal: in 1957, he met the green-eyed twenty-one-year-old English actress Belinda Lee, who was herself married to a photographer fourteen years her senior, and they embarked on one of the most sensational affairs of the era.

Lee was a rising star: gorgeous, voluptuous, bold, and very modern. She had studied at the Royal Academy of Dramatic Art, been put under contract by the Rank Organisation, and been introduced to Queen Elizabeth at the Royal Command Film Performance in 1955, curtseying alongside Marilyn Monroe, Joan Crawford, Brigitte Bardot, and Anita Ekberg. She had come up playing schoolgirls, but she graduated to femme fatale and sexpot roles, and when she met Filippo Orsini, she had been voted one of

England's favorite actresses and was appearing as Aphrodite, lead character in the Italian production *La Venere di Cheronea* (*Goddess of Love*).

Sparks struck between the prince and the showgirl immediately, and they took few pains to hide their relationship, hitting such fashionable nightspots as Capriccio on Via Liguria (owned by another Orsini, Filippo's cousin Raimondo), traveling abroad together, walking openly in affectionate contact; Lee even rented a flat barely five minutes' drive from the palazzo where Orsini's wife and children lived. Before the end of the year, Lee announced that she would leave her husband, "a man I don't love," and that she would move to Italy to make films: "Rome has changed me. One day I was a quiet English girl. The next day I was a woman," she said. She continued working, but her habits became erratic. At Filippo's beckoning, she left a film set in South Africa and flew back to Rome to see him.

No doubt because of his high position at the Vatican, Filippo was spared having his affair dragged into the press. But it was an open secret and a shocking one, and he was privately called to account for himself by church officials. At the same time, his wife reached her limit, visiting Lee's home to demand that she stop seeing Orsini. That night, Lee took an overdose of sleeping pills; fortunately, she was discovered and brought to a hospital, where she was put in intensive care. Filippo raced over, but hospital officials wouldn't allow her a visitor other than her husband. Anxious about his lover's fate, he returned to his empty palazzo, and, two days later, took his own overdose of barbiturates and, for good measure, opened the veins on his wrists. He, too, was rescued, but the scandal of the following days and weeks might have made him wish he hadn't been.

The newspapers *finally* ran the story of the romance. Lee's husband flew to Rome to see her (and was forced to wait for hours while, still in hospital, she was questioned by police). When she was healthy enough to be released, Lee was expelled from Rome and flew back to London (city officials had the ability to order even Italian citizens to leave town). And Orsini felt the might of the Vatican fall upon him and his family in thunderous fashion. After his release from the hospital and a psychiatric ward, he was ordered by Pope Pius XII to spend time in a monastery and then had his papal title stripped not only from him but from his sons—from all Orsinis.[4] (His most serious sin, in the view of the church, wasn't the adultery but the suicide attempt.)

In the coming year, Lee and Orsini would reunite while fighting off divorce filings from both of their spouses. They attended the Cannes Film Festival, obviously a couple, besieged by photographers and reporters, set up house in Paris, and traveled throughout Europe: the Côte d'Azur, Munich, various resorts around Italy. They even made a film together: Lee was cast as the lead in *Messalina*, a melodrama about the debauched Roman empress, and Orsini had a small, nonspeaking role as a nobleman. (The ironies were astounding: the real Messalina disported herself on imperial hunting grounds that, in time, became the vineyards of Orsini's ancestors and then part of the Villa Ludovisi, which, fatefully, was converted into, among other places, Via Veneto, where Lee and Orsini first met.)

But the strain of all they'd been through weighed heavily; more than once they were reported to have split up and, inevitably, to have reunited. During this time, Filippo defended Lee's honor against a wisecracking fellow aristocrat who, in the ensuing fracas, smacked Orsini in the face with a riding crop, leaving a nasty cut

---

4. In time, Pope Paul VI would do away with the Black aristocracy and all of its titles.

under his eye. Lee began to make the scene around Rome with her latest costar, Walter Chiari, who almost always courted his leading ladies, and Filippo was seen chaperoning French actress Irene Tunc and, later, Hungarian actress Eva Bartok.

There was always talk of reconciliation between them, but it wasn't to be. In 1960, Lee met tabloid journalist Gualtiero Jacopetti, who had made lurid headlines of his own five years earlier when, as a prisoner in Rome's famed Coeli Regina prison, he was accused of having intimate relations with a thirteen-year-old gypsy girl and forced either to marry her or face criminal charges (he chose the former, then wriggled free). At the time of his meeting Lee, Jacopetti had begun making documentaries; together with his partners Paolo Cavara and Franco Prosperi, he was assembling a film of footage of extreme behavior by humans, animals, and even natural forces that would be released as *Mondo Cane*, which set international box-office records as the first "shockumentary." Lee and Jacopetti would become an item, traveling together while he and his team made a follow-up, *La Donna nel Mondo* (*Women of the World*), which they hired Rossano Brazzi to narrate.

In March 1961, after shooting in Las Vegas, they headed back to Los Angeles. Outside of Barstow, California, the driver of the car in which Lee and Jacopetti were riding lost control—he may have blown a tire—flipping the vehicle and ejecting Lee, who was in the front passenger seat. She landed in a terrible heap. A highway patrolman happened by the scene almost immediately and tried to rescue her, but there was nothing to be done. She died within minutes of the crash, age twenty-five.

The funeral in Los Angeles was sparsely attended. Filippo came from Rome, Brazzi and his wife were present, but most of the others in the documentary crew were still being treated for their own injuries, and Lee's parents were unable to travel from England.

After the cremation, Filippo tried to take her ashes back home with him, but the funeral directors wouldn't give him possession because he wasn't a relative. Before the end of the year, arrangements for the remains were made, however, and she was buried in the Cimitero Acattolico, Rome's Protestant Cemetery, not far from the graves of her countrymen John Keats and Percy Bysshe Shelley. And when Jacopetti recovered and finished *La Donna nel Mondo*, he dedicated it to her: the film's opening credits stopped, music and all, and a title card declared, "To Belinda Lee, who throughout this long journey accompanied and helped us with love."[5]

Romances between actresses and noblemen were a thing among the Via Veneto set: Dawn Addams married Don Vittorio Emanuele Massimo, Prince of Roccasecca; Elsa Martinelli married Count Franco Mancinelli di San Vito; Marisa Allasio married Pier Francesco Calvi, Count of Bergolo, the grandson of the Italian king Vittorio Emanuele III; Irma Capece Minutolo *claimed* to have married King Farouk; and, most famously, Grace Kelly and Prince Rainier III of Monaco thrilled the world with a royal wedding in 1956.[6]

Linda Christian, whose 1949 marriage to Tyrone Power only *seemed* like a royal wedding and was a harbinger of all the mad activity with which Rome was bubbling over, herself became involved with an aristocrat. Having been cruelly dumped by Power

5 In 1968, Muriel Spark published *The Public Image*, a novel about an English actress sucked up by the high life of Via Veneto and the Roman demimonde of infidelity, suicide, and wild parties. It was certainly inspired by Lee's story, and it was short-listed for the inaugural Booker Prize.

6 And there was a twist in the bunch: in 1957, Henry Fonda, then fifty-two years old, wed the Venetian baroness Afdera Franchetti, twenty-six years his junior (and only five years older than her husband's elder child, Jane). The marriage—his fourth; her second—lasted not quite four years.

in 1952 (while she was pregnant with their second child; their divorce came four years later), she resumed acting, chiefly in B movies, and had no shortage of suitors. One in particular caught her fancy, a gruff Spaniard who was more interested in cars and horses and bobsleds than women but who was brilliant and charming and cleaned up nicely and was, without a doubt, a catch—even though he was married, to *two* women, with both of whom he had produced children.

His given name was Alfonso Antonio Vicente Eduardo Angel Blas Francisco de Borja Cabeza de Vaca y Leighton, Grandee of Spain, Count of Mejorada, Count of Pernia, Marquis de Moratalla, Marquis de Portago and Duke of Alagon. But he was known as Fon de Portago.

*F*on de Portago was a character that a Hollywood screenwriter might have dreamt up—and had dismissed by his producers as being too unbelievable. Born in 1928 in London, he inherited most of his epic name—as well as the blood of conquistadors, explorers, and kings—from his father, Antonio, who had been a sportsman, adventurer, politician, and even spy in his time (he was imprisoned in France during the Spanish Civil War for trying to sneak a vial of deadly bacteria across the border in a plot to kill Loyalists). Antonio was a friend of Spain's King Alfonso XIII, godfather to little Fon, who was bounced on the royal knee as a baby. Portago's mother, Olga Beatrice Leighton, had been born in England to Irish working-class stock but had come into a fortune when her first husband, Frank Jay Mackey, committed suicide and left her his controlling interest in the Household Finance Corporation, which he'd founded.

Beginning life with the twin advantages of a title—*titles*—and a fortune, Portago had the makings of a true spoiled brat. He was schooled in France and the United States, but he never attained a diploma. And he was hell-bent, even as a teen, on flouting whatever conventions his breeding, station, and wealth might have set before him. He was loath to bathe, to shave, to wash or change his clothes, even to brush his teeth. He seemed to make a point of being rude in polite company. Once, at a Palm Beach society dinner, Portago was scarfing his food like a soldier. "Why can't you eat like a gentleman?" asked the woman beside him. "I don't have to eat like a gentleman, or drink like a gentleman, or dress like a gentleman, or do anything like a gentleman," he replied. "I was born a gentleman." She replied, calmly, "In America, we also like a gentleman to behave like a gentleman." His response was not noted.

And he was an absolute dog with women. At age twenty, he met a former fashion model, Carroll McDaniel, at the El Morocco nightclub in New York and proposed marriage to her within twenty-four hours of being introduced. She agreed, albeit after a year, and eventually bore him two children. But by the time the second was born, Portago had found another American model, the famed Revlon "Fire and Ice" Girl Dorian Leigh (older sister of the original supermodel, Suzy Parker), and had married *her*—without bothering to divorce McDaniel. He and Leigh had a son together, but before *that* child's first birthday, Portago had found a *third* beauty to court—none other than Linda Christian, who was still traveling the world in a spin after the collapse of her marriage to Tyrone Power.

Christian, who had been pursued by rich and famous men since her teens, wanted nothing to do with him at first, but he proved persistent once again ("Are you seriously turning down a Marquis of Spain who was held in the arms of a king," he asked her), and she let herself be wooed. He had "a shining quality," she recalled, and she succumbed to it. Throughout 1956, the two were seen together in Europe, the United States, and the Caribbean. "What had started out in fun and laughter," Christian said, "now seemed close to real affection."

In fact, for all that was outré about him, there was much in Fon de Portago worth falling for. Despite his uncouth habits and appalling rakishness, Portago was an impressively intelligent and even philosophical fellow, fluent in four languages and capable of writing, as he would in 1957, magazine articles in idiosyncratic but entirely colloquial English. He was dashingly handsome, with dark, curly hair and hazel eyes. And he was a ferociously competitive, fearless, and accomplished sportsman.

As a teenager, he played polo and jai alai and learned to pilot a plane (and, true to form, accepted and won a bet that he could fly safely beneath a twenty-foot-high bridge across a causeway in Florida). He had aspired to be a jockey, and he was good at it, twice being crowned champion amateur horseman in France. But he was prone to accidents—both times he competed in the famed Irish Grand National steeplechase, he was thrown from his horse. Eventually, he grew too tall (at six feet) and heavy (even at a lean 170 pounds) to remain competitive.

He gravitated to motor sports, encouraged by a friend, Edmund "Gunner" Nelson, a thrill-seeking World War II veteran who was working as an elevator operator at New York's Plaza Hotel when they met. Portago had always loved fast cars, even as a boy, and by 1953 he was racing, first in midget cars in France, next as a copilot in the multiday Carrera Panamerica road race in Mexico, and then driving cars of his own, which he bought (and, often, wrecked) as an independent racer.

As on horseback, Portago was *fast* as a driver, but again, as on horseback, he was accident-prone. "Every time he comes in from a race," Nelson told a reporter, "the front of his car is wrinkled where he has been nudging people out of his way at 130 miles an hour." Portago had a number of serious scrapes, and a couple of outright smashups, he regularly burned out engines and brakes, but he almost always walked away from these incidents unscathed.

He enjoyed similar luck in another sport he took up: bobsled racing. Nelson, who had become a constant companion, gave him his first taste, at the famed St. Moritz–Celerina track, one of the most challenging in the world. Having never been in a bobsled before, Portago insisted on tackling the course the very day he laid eyes on it and demanded, over Nelson's objections, that he himself navigate and that Nelson serve as brakeman. They hurtled wildly down the ice, and they set a blistering time. Encouraged, Portago bought the necessary gear, and formed a team, set on representing Spain in the 1956 Winter Olympics in Cortina d'Ampezzo in the Italian Alps. Portago had been at the sport for only a few months, but he wound up finishing fourth in the two-man competition.

Still, automobiles proved to be his true passion. He loved the masculine camaraderie in race pits, he loved the dirt and the noise, he loved the competition, and he loved the thrill of danger. "Racing is a vice," he wrote, in English, in *Sports Illustrated*, "and as such extremely hard to give up."

As he became a more accomplished driver, he sought to join a world-class racing team. Since there was no team with more romantic allure than Ferrari, he pursued a spot in its ranks just as he pursued beautiful women—and with a similar pattern. At first, Enzo Ferrari rejected Portago out of hand by sending him an envelope with two photos in it: snapshots of vehicles that Portago had wrecked the previous weekend. ("He's a dictator," Portago complained. "If he doesn't like you, he won't give you a car.") But before long things changed: Portago became more adept, for one thing, and Ferrari needed a replacement for an injured driver. Portago was given a Ferrari—the fourth-best of four—and joined the Formula One circuit in 1956. Sharing driving duties with Peter Collins, he took second at that year's British Grand Prix, and finished fifteenth in the overall competition despite racing only a half-season.

Even though it was a deadly pursuit, Portago spoke about auto racing with an almost chilling nonchalance. "I'm not interested in cars," he told a journalist. "To me they're a means of transportation or a machine for racing. When I have a racing car that I'm going to drive, I walk up to it, and I look at it, and I think, 'Now, is this son-of-a-bitch going to hold together for the next 500 kilometers?' That's the only interest I have in it. And as soon as the race is over, I couldn't care less what happens to it."

But that attitude, he explained, bled into all things in his life. "I want to live to be 105," he said, "and I mean to. . . . I'm *enchanted* with life. But no matter how long I live, I still won't have time for all the things I want to do, I won't hear all the music I want to hear, I won't be able to read all the books I want to read, I won't have all the women I want to have. I won't be able to do a twentieth of the things I want to do. And besides just the *doing*, I insist on getting something out of what I do. For example, I wouldn't race unless I was sure I could be champion of the world."

In order to do that, he would have to rise in Ferrari's stable of drivers, where he was usually reckoned no better than third or fourth best. And so he was subject to the bidding of the imperious Ferrari—which, in the spring of 1957, meant that he would have to race in the Mille Miglia, the famous (even notorious) race that covered 1000 kilometers of Italian roads, a harrowing test of cobblestoned pavements and sharp corners and sudden curves and rises and descents—the entire route lined with cheering spectators, often standing in the middle of the road to catch glimpses of their racing heroes.

It was an immensely difficult and dangerous race. In 1953, Roberto Rossellini, who fancied himself an amateur race driver as a side to his busy moviemaking routine, had decided to test his driving prowess in the Mille Miglia but quit when he got to the halfway point in Rome; Ingrid Bergman herself ran to his car and begged him not to continue. There were many similar stories of far more adept drivers choosing to skip and/or not finish the race.

Portago had no appetite for it: he cited the opinion of world champion Argentine driver Juan Miguel Fangio, "If you have a conscience you can't drive it really fast anyway. There are hundreds of corners in the Mille Miglia where one little slip by a driver could kill fifty people. You can't keep the spectators from crowding into the road—you couldn't do it with an army. It's a race I hope I never run in."

But his hopes and Ferrari's plans for him were at odds. Ferrari offered him a ride in the Mille Miglia of 1957: brand-new, with a 4.1 liter V-12 engine that would make it one of the most powerful vehicles in the field. Ambitious to prove himself to his patron, he accepted, despite his reservations. Not only would he be driving on a course he didn't know well and which he knew was pitted with danger, but he would be doing so with almost no preparation in an unfamiliar car with a capacity that might have been too strong for the course. About the only advantage that he would have would be the presence of Gunner Nelson in the copilot seat, but Nelson didn't know the route any better than Portago and couldn't control the car from where he sat. Portago was, in a very real sense, alone. He didn't like to talk about fear, but he wrote about his concerns in a note to Dorian Leigh, with whom he maintained romantic contact despite his other entanglements: "As you know, in the first place, I did not want to do the Mille Miglia. . . . My 'early death' may well come next Sunday."

The race was run on May 19, 1957, beginning, as was traditional, in the northern industrial city of Brescia, heading southeast along the Adriatic coast, then across to Rome and back up to Brescia via Tuscany and Emilia-Romagna. It was grueling, and Portago, as ever a touch on the reckless side, had a couple of near scrapes during the first several hundred kilometers. When he got to Rome, the halfway mark, he was near the lead but being challenged by not only his Ferrari teammates but drivers in considerably less powerful vehicles than his. He knew that he would have to call on the brute strength of the engine to push forward if he wanted to retain the esteem of Ferrari, let alone win outright.

In the pit stop in Rome, he and Nelson, exhausted by the effort of five hours behind them and the prospect of a similar amount of time remaining, found themselves suddenly burst upon: Linda Christian had been waiting in the unusually cool spring air, and she ran up to the car, dressed in polka dots and carrying a bouquet of roses, to wish her lover good luck. Portago, who knew a moment of glory when it was in front of him, craned his neck for a kiss. The photographers filling the pit area delightedly captured the moment, but for Christian there was little romance in it. "I had a strange sensation with that kiss," she remembered a few years later. "It was cold. And it caused me to look for the first time at Gunner Nelson seated beside him. He seemed to be like a mummy, gray, ashen, as if mesmerized. He had the eyes of someone who had suffered an enormous shock." There was no time for questions or explanations or even a second kiss. Portago got back to business and sped off.

There was rain and even snow in the remaining hours, and the pace was furious. When he got to Bologna, the final refueling point, Portago was running fourth, risking an out-of-the-money finish that would, he knew, discredit him as a champion racer in Ferrari's eyes. There was some concern about a tire on the driver's front side being rubbed by a control arm, and the pit crew wanted to address it, but Portago pulled away, intent on powering his way to a victory, or at least to a top-three finish. He was gaining when he approached Guidizzolo, a small town on the road between Mantua and Brescia, maybe forty kilometers from the finish line.

Something happened.

Spectators would later report that the car veered sharply left, and while they would agree that it had struck a road marker, they differed as to what happened first: Did the car blow a tire and lurch toward the shoulder, or did it wander too far out of the center of the road and *then* burst a tire against the stone marker?

It didn't matter. The speeding Ferrari ran off the road, plowed through a clutch of spectators, skidded into a ditch, and then, airborne, crossed the highway *again*, landing upside down in a drainage area on the *right* side of the road. Two bodies were ejected onto the pavement in the process, and one, Portago's, was cut almost in half. He had died instantly, as had Nelson, as had a dozen spectators, including two small children.[7] It was a horror show.

The consequences were felt immediately, deeply, widely. In the Italian parliament and press, there were significant calls to abolish road racing entirely; the Mille Miglia itself was shut down almost without protest; it would resume only decades later, and then as a gently-paced showcase for old-time race cars. In the United States, where Portago's article was in the issue of *Sports Illustrated* currently on the newsstands, a slew of stories about his amazing life

---

7 The exact death toll would never be settled; several of the most severely injured spectators would succumb over the subsequent months and even years.

and horrifying death appeared; *The New York Times* ran a page-one story about the crash, including an illustration of the course.

There was a brouhaha over the funeral: Carroll McDaniel was due the deference of the widow and mother of Portago's children, but Christian had been his companion for months, and the photos of the *baccia di morte*—the kiss of death in Rome—ran everywhere. She didn't claim precedence, but she made it known in the press that she expected a place. (Dorian Leigh avoided the madness altogether by traveling to St. Moritz to model fur coats.) In the end, Christian had to travel to the funeral in Madrid on her own, not with the body, as she had wished to (but not on her own dime; there was a wealthy friend who saw to her transport), and she attended the ceremony quietly, alone.

The deaths of Portago and Nelson and all those spectators marked an episode in what would eventually be the end of the era of the gentleman racer. For one thing, the sport was more dangerous than it had ever been—the cars were faster, the prizes greater, the calendar more choked with big races. The romantic idea of a dashing, handsome aristocrat who raced on his free weekends was increasingly incongruous in a sport filled with full-time professionals who took automobile racing as a life-and-death matter and faced one another down in sober, cold-eyed competition. The rich boys in their toys were simply outclassed.

And the reputation of the sport itself changed as the death total mounted. Only two months before the Mille Miglia, Ferrari team driver Eugenio Castellotti had died behind the wheel, exactly as his mentor Alberto Ascari, the greatest Italian racer of the postwar era, had done two years prior. In the two years following Portago's death, the Formula One standouts Luigi Musso, Peter Collins, Mike Hawthorn, and Wolfgang Von Trips (technically Count Wolfgang Alexander Albert Eduard Maximilian Reichsgraf Berghe von

Trips) would *all* also die driving Ferraris, causing the *L'Osservatore Romano*, the official newspaper of the Vatican, to denounce the automaker as "the modern Saturn, a captain of industry who continues to devour his children"—even those, sadly, who had bounced on the knees of kings.

$\mathcal{F}$on de Portago was but one of the more visible of a raft of international playboys who haunted the clubs of Via Veneto and environs whenever they were in Rome.

There was Don Jaime de Mora y Aragón, who looked like Salvador Dalí, with slicked back hair and a waxed mustache, and was the brother of Queen Fabiola of Belgium. He counted more than fifty kings in his bloodline, sang in nightclubs, acted in low-budget movies, and liked to be referred to as Jimmy.

There was Porfirio Rubirosa, whose career as diplomat, race-car driver, pilot, jewel thief, smuggler, bagman, polo champion, and husband to actresses (including the French star Danielle Darrieux) and heiresses (the Americans Doris Duke *and* Barbara Hutton), was all the more amazing because he had been born without money, without title, and, in of all places, the Dominican Republic.[8]

There were native Italian playboys like Carlo Acqaviva d'Aragona, Mario Bandini, Baby Borea, Gegé Della Noce, and Giorgio Sacconi, some with minor titles, all with money, a pack of hounds who, seemingly, sent flowers to every unattached actress working in Rome and escorted the ones who responded to their

8 Coincidentally, Rubirosa met Duke in Rome just after the war, where he was assigned to a diplomatic post and she was working as a correspondent for *Harper's Bazaar*. When, soon after, he left Darrieux, who had been billed, not without cause, as "the most beautiful woman in the world," the rumor was floated that Duke flat-out bought a new husband for herself from his former wife for a cool $1 million.

overtures to Via Veneto as showily as possible, as if to inflate the value of their stock.[9] There was even a name for this breed: *accompagnatore*—"escort," but also with the implication of Anglo-American society's "extra man"—a fellow known for being seen beside the famous women of his day. The most celebrated among them was Gianfranco Piacentini, a tall, lean, appealing young man who had spent time in Los Angeles (where he became friendly with Richard Avedon) and who was photographed up and down Via Veneto with, among others, Eva Bartok, Linda Christian, Anita Ekberg, Kim Novak, and, once, in a whiskey-fueled evening that ended up in the waters of one of the famed fountains of Piazza Navona, with the Swedish actress Astrid Johansson.

And there was Francisco Matarazzo Pignatari, known as Baby, the son of an Italian count and a Brazilian industrial heiress. A hard-nosed businessman (mining, metals, heavy industry) and inveterate Romeo, he had two ex-wives and a string of lovers—old, new, and prospective—whom he wooed with expensive gifts and regular phone calls from wherever he happened to be in the world. He was a big man—six foot three, with enormous hands ("I was often black-and-blue after dancing with him," said an acquaintance, presumably talking about actual dancing), and he drove large American cars around Rome.

In November 1957, he was out on Via Veneto celebrating his second divorce when he spotted Linda Christian, who had recovered from the shock of Fon de Portago's death and was back in the social whirl. Baby asked for a dance and then for a date. In the coming days and weeks they saw a lot of each other, and were so

9 Among this lot could be counted Maurizio Arena, who was born modestly in Rome and had an actual career as an actor and singer (and, later, before his untimely death, faith healer), which meant he had business reasons to be seen out and about with every starlet in town.

visibly together around town that Roman gossip columnists were predicting a wedding. But it was a volatile relationship. They had tiffs, after one of which he threw a party at a nightclub and invited every pretty girl in Rome, it appeared, *except* Christian, only to show up at her door at four a.m. in tears, begging forgiveness. They decided to take a trip around the world together: Germany, Greece, Cairo, Bangkok, Hong Kong, Tokyo, Honolulu, Hollywood, Mexico City, and, lastly, Rio de Janeiro, his hometown. Once again, there was strain: at a nightclub on the Copacabana, Baby somehow got it in his head that Linda was being stolen from him by Rock Hudson. She left, vowing not to see him anymore.

Which vow lasted about a fortnight. Christian went to Buenos Aires, then came back to Rio. Pignatari was out of town but quickly returned and requested to see her, asking her to meet him in the lobby of her hotel at a precise time. She ran late, and while she was getting dressed, she heard a commotion in the street below. Looking down from her room, she saw dozens of men, hired by Pignatari, picketing her hotel, chanting, banging drums, lighting firecrackers, and carrying signs that said "Linda Go Home!" She promptly did. Baby chased her to New York, where they arranged to sit together at the El Morocco nightclub as if on friendly terms and answer questions from the press about their "reconciliation" and "friendship."

It was the last time they saw each other. Christian went on to marry, again in Rome, the English actor Edmund Purdom. And Baby went on to another scandal, an affair with the heiress Ira von Fürstenberg, at the time married to the Spanish nobleman Prince Alfonso de Hohenlohe-Langenburg. This drama included a custody dispute over her children, an arrest in Mexico, and nude snapshots of the heiress; it climaxed with a wedding in 1961, even though Ira didn't have her *first* marriage annulled until 1969—five years after she and Baby (and could there be any wonder about how he got his nickname?) had already divorced.

$\mathcal{A}$mid all this overheated activity, there was something more like a fairy tale, if a tragic one: the story of a broken princess floating through the glitter and gaiety of the Via Veneto scene in a cloud of gloom.

Princess Soraya Esfandiary-Bakhtiari was, when she first came to Rome in the early 1950s, the wife of the shah of Iran, Mohammad Reza Pahlavi, who had previously been married to Princess Fawzia of Egypt, sister of King Farouk. As Fawzia had failed to produce a male heir to the Peacock Throne, the shah divorced her and then, seeking a new wife, was shown a photograph of Soraya, the daughter of the Iranian ambassador to West Germany. She was a great beauty, but she was only sixteen at the time and still in school in Switzerland. Still, he met her and chose her for his own, marking their engagement with a twenty-two-carat diamond ring. They wed in 1951 and looked very much in love when they traveled the world, Rome included, in a honeymoon that lasted almost two years. But their bliss faced an inconvenient obstacle: Soraya, too, was unable to provide an heir; she couldn't bear children at all, despite the ministrations of doctors throughout Europe and the United States. In 1958, reluctantly, the shah divorced her, too, although he provided her with sufficient income so that she could live the rest of her days in regal comfort; he was even said to pay intimate visits to her after marrying a third time (and successfully, at last, fathering sons).

Soraya wandered like a lost bird after her divorce: Paris, Greece, Capri, London, the Côte d'Azur, and, inevitably, Rome, where she stayed in opulent hotel suites and spent long hours chatting with Roman aristocrats and the occasional movie star at nightclubs and cafés along Via Veneto. She was lovely, still, and always beautifully dressed and self-possessed. But it was clear to everyone that she was in mourning for the life that had been stripped from her. Photographers hunted her down—they almost couldn't help themselves—and gossip magazines wrote elaborate (and often entirely fictitious) stories about the end of her storybook marriage.

But there was little glee in these efforts in comparison to, say, the willingness of the tabloids and their photographers to poke at King Farouk. Rather, Soraya became a symbol of lost love, a *memento amori*, as it were, brokenhearted and unapproachable and somehow purer than the earthy crowds of glitterati among whom she mingled. She was courted by some of the more notable bachelors among the Roman aristocracy, and she allowed herself to be flattered by the film producer Dino De Laurentiis into thinking she might have a movie career. But she merely dabbled, appearing in a minor role in a movie or two.[10] Soraya never remarried and died without heirs. Her most fitting legacy might well have been a modestly popular French song, inspired by her time amid the throng on Via Veneto, entitled *"Je Veux Pleurer Comme Soraya"*—"I Want to Cry Like Soraya."

The Via Veneto's most celebrated nightspot didn't even open its doors until 1958: the Café de Paris.

With the single "f" in its name distinguishing it as French (and, as with the prejudices of the fashion world, somehow more elegant than its counterparts, the Italian *caffès*), it sat high up on the eastern side of street, just beside one of the big newsstands and across from the Excelsior and its adjacent Caffè Doney. Because it stayed

10 She would play a character named Soraya in the 1965 version of *She* starring Ursula Andress.

open until dawn, featured an American-style bar and delicatessen, and was owned by Victor Tombolini, eponym of the original Victor Bar, the Café de Paris was destined to become the hippest spot on the strip, the default watering hole for visiting celebrities, ambitious moviemakers, slumming aristocrats, rubbernecking people-watchers, and the photographers who had become more numerous and more intrusive on Via Veneto as the street grew in reputation and in what was for them a precious resource: famous people with their guard down, sometimes behaving badly.

There was a crush to get into the place and a real hierarchy of status in the assigning of tables, inside and out. If any question hung over the place, it was to do with the timing of its opening. The Café de Paris debuted for business in early August, not long before the traditional emptying out of the city for the end-of-summer *Ferragosto* holiday. Who, it might have seemed fair to ask at the time, would be around to frequent such a swank joint in just a few weeks' time when Rome turned, if only for a fortnight, into a ghost town?

20 "Poor Starving Devils"

It was getting easier to make a dollar with a camera.

You could wander up Via Veneto and bump into a different international star almost every day.

Wandering celebrities weren't concentrated in New York in the same way, nobody walked around Hollywood, and neither London nor Paris nor any other city in the Western world had anything like the same amount of film work or allure for the glitterati. But Rome had all that in spades, and, as a result, a veritable *tavola caldo* of famous faces was served up, buffet-style, for the photographers who buzzed through that one small neighborhood to get pictures of them.

It was a litany of box-office names that, set in paving stones, would've provided Via Veneto with a Walk of Fame to rival the one on Hollywood Boulevard. In addition to the expected Italian stars and such foreign regulars as Ingrid Bergman, Linda Christian, Anita Ekberg, Ava Gardner, Audrey Hepburn, Princess Soraya, and King Farouk, Via Veneto photographers prowling the boulevard's clubs and cafés snapped candid pictures of Anouk Aimée, Ursula Andress, Paul Anka, Louis Armstrong, Charles Aznavour, Lauren Bacall, Chet Baker, Brigitte Bardot, Richard Basehart, Warren Beatty, Jean-Paul Belmondo, Claire Bloom, Humphrey Bogart, Ernest Borgnine, Charles Boyer, Marlon Brando, Jean-Claude Brialy, Yul Brynner, Richard Burton, Maria Callas, Coco Chanel, Charlie Chaplin, Cyd Charisse, Maurice Chevalier, Jean Cocteau, Joan Collins, Sean Connery, Gary Cooper, Xavier Cugat, Tony Curtis, Dan Dailey, Linda Darnell, Bette Davis, Sandra Dee, Alain Delon, Marlene Dietrich, Joe DiMaggio, Luis Miguel Domínguín, Kirk Douglas, Duke Ellington, Mel Ferrer, Eddie Fisher, Errol Flynn, Henry Fonda, Jane Fonda, Clark Gable, Zsa Zsa Gabor, Greta Garbo, Judy Garland, John Gavin, Ben Gazzara, Stewart Granger, Cary Grant, George Hamilton, Rex Harrison, Rita Hayworth, Van Heflin, Katharine Hepburn, Alfred Hitchcock, Rock Hudson, Jennifer Jones, Danny Kaye, Grace Kelly, Jacqueline Kennedy, the Aga Khan, Aly Khan, Fernando Lamas, Burt Lancaster, Abbe Lane, Mario Lanza, Laurel and Hardy, Vivien Leigh, Jack Lemmon, Liberace, Tina Louise, Clare Boothe Luce,[1] Shirley MacLaine, Jayne Mansfield, Dean Martin, Roddy McDowall, Arthur Miller, Robert Mitchum, Ricardo Montalban, Yves Montand, Roger Moore, David Niven, Richard Nixon, Kim Novak, Peter O'Toole, Jack Palance, Gregory Peck, Anthony Perkins, Walter Pidgeon, Ezra Pound, Anthony Quinn, Prince Rainier of Monaco, Johnnie Ray, Steve

1 To be fair, she was the U.S. ambassador to Italy and her office was in the embassy on Via Veneto.

Reeves, Edward G. Robinson, Jane Russell, Romy Schneider, Jean Seberg, Simone Signoret, Frank Sinatra, Barbara Stanwyck, Barbara Steele, Rod Steiger, James Stewart, Gloria Swanson, Elizabeth Taylor, Robert Taylor, Peter Ustinov, Roger Vadim, Robert Wagner, John Wayne, Orson Welles, Cornel Wilde, Esther Williams, Tennessee Williams, and Shelley Winters . . . all in a span of about six or eight years. The photographers would joke that it wasn't worth the effort to shoot a certain tier of star unless he or she did (or was provoked into doing) something outrageous. Amid such a cornucopia of celebrities, only the truly rare items could ever stand out.

To accommodate all the photographs that were coming in from the streets, Rome's newsstands were plump with publications that were trading in sensational images more frequently than ever. Some of these emerged from a category of magazine that was called *la cronaca rosa* (or "the pink press"), a blanket name for women's interest magazines that included *Settimo Giorno* and *Gente*. Others were labeled *cronaca nera* (or "black press"), a term that covered true-crime publications such as *Detective Crimen*. And there were other magazines that were designed outright to serve as conduits for the sensational new photography that was coming out of various corners of Rome (and, soon enough, the rest of Western Europe and the United States), chief among them *Le Ore* and *Lo Specchio*, the former of which had taken to running a weekly Via Veneto page.[2]

2 A similar phenomenon brewed in the United States, where Robert Harrison's *Confidential*, the most notorious of all of the "inside story" publications, debuted in 1952, followed by copycat titles such as *Exposed, Hush-Hush, Inside, On the Q. T.*, and *Uncensored*. Ironically, America's exposé-oriented magazines were constrained by a number of cultural factors: the strict monopoly on information about movie stars that was held by Hollywood studios; a gentleman's agreement between studios and journalists about publishing potentially harmful stories about stars; the tendency of law enforcement agencies to work more cooperatively with the studios than with the press in cases involving celebrities; and the fact that Hollywood had nothing to compare with the zealous photographers of Rome—and, really, no place did.

The most popular of these magazines sold upward of half a million copies a week, and that sort of success caused the phenomenon of street photographers to spread. Very few kept cameramen on staff, relying instead on freelancers who were becoming bolder in the effort to get exclusive shots of famous faces, preferably doing something memorable. In the early days of the magazine war, a photographer might find a good payday in a shot of Greta Garbo or Orson Welles simply showing up in Rome or elsewhere in Italy. But soon enough, there would be a market for more electric material, and in time, the promise of a big score—*un servizio*, as the photographers called it—could only be realized if there was something truly eye-popping in the image. The reality that a photo could in and of itself be news and could pay dozens of times more than a simply illustrative shot of a headline-maker would eventually lead Rome's loose legion of street photographers, the *scattini* of yore, to morph into a new species of photojournalist altogether.

*I*n tune with this new climate, the Via Veneto photographers had evolved into a sharp and hot and cool mob. Indeed, more than anyone else on the scene, they epitomized the moment. They were lean, they were hungry, they were cynical and cunning and alert, they had thick skin, and they didn't scare easily.

They dressed well or at the very least presentably—jackets, ties, clean shirts and shoes—so that they wouldn't look out of place shooting pictures in the Vatican or a courthouse or some other official building during the day and, more important, in case they found themselves in a position to sneak into a swank spot and grab some lucrative shots at night. They drove motor scooters at first, then graduated to small Fiats, and they were, like all young Italian men, deeply fond of their vehicles.

Likewise, their photographic equipment was up-to-date and chosen for the specific needs of their working conditions. Although they'd grown up assisting established photographers, some of whom still used the old-style tripod-and-hood plate cameras, they had fallen romantically under the spell of the famed Graphix Speed Graphic cameras used by tabloid photographers in the movies (and, in the real world, by their spiritual granddaddy, Arthur Fellig, aka Weegee, the most famous American street photojournalist of the time and a man whose love of sensation jibed with theirs). But they found that those weren't ideal for the sort of candid shots that became their staple food. For these, the 35mm Rolleiflex twin lens camera, made in Germany by Franke & Heidecke, allowed for quicker picture taking and even subterfuge. The camera could be held at, say, waist height, allowing the photographer to take a picture while pretending to look elsewhere or even while looking straight at the subject, feigning disinterest.

After a time, Leica single-lens-reflex, or SLR, cameras were preferred, for their even more compact bodies and their quicker mechanisms for focusing and for advancing the film. Photographers preferred electronic flash units, particularly those by Braun, which freed them from the need to carry around or change flashbulbs and which gave off a sharp, wide arc of light that largely eliminated shadows, giving their shots stark, flat textures that made whatever they captured look somehow like an illicit activity illuminated by a sudden bolt of lightning.

They used other cameras, too, mainly for subterfuge, hiding them in hollowed-out books, in briefcases, in suit jackets, and even, in the case of some particularly delicate jobs, in the beehive hairdos of female accomplices. Like many Italians, the Via Veneto photographers were mad for the new gadgets and devices that emerged throughout the 1950s, signaling the advent of a new age.[3]

And they were archetypical Roman *furbi*—practitioners of the ancient Italian art of getting ahead, even if only a half-step, even if at the expense of someone else. They bribed doormen and chambermaids and cabdrivers; they made pacts with some actors and scene makers who obliged them (and helped fill their own publicity scrapbooks) by telling them where to go for "exclusive" shots; they deflated the tires of celebrities' cars so as to get photos of them milling about waiting for a mechanic; there was nothing they wouldn't do to get what Tazio Secchiaroli termed a *flashiate*—a score, a scoop, an exclusive, a shot that could earn a photographer enough to buy a new car and make a name for him.

They had other lingo, too: *fare le vasche* ("make a sweep") meant to troll the upper reaches of Via Veneto looking for something to shoot; *trivellare* ("to drill") meant to get a shot of someone (as in "I drilled him"); and there were nicknames for certain celebrities and doormen and bodyguards and, especially, for one another. Secchiaroli was called, among other monikers, Il Mitragliatrice Umana ("The Human Machine Gun") for his speedy shooting and Il Bounty Killer for his ability to capture images of highly prized and elusive subjects; there was a fellow called Buster Keaton because he never smiled; another called Er Mondano ("The Worldly One") for his connections to high society; another known as Er Bugia ("The Liar") for his tall tales; a few bearing such names as Crazy Rocket and Speedy Gonzalez for their energy; and

3 One of the most fortuitous from the vantage of the photographers was the decision by the designers of the Fiat 500 to use what were called "suicide doors" for the driver and front-seat passenger. Hinged at the rear rather than in front, the doors opened toward the back, revealing the entire bodies of those inside the car and turning every curbside exit from a vehicle into an involuntary exposure to camera lenses and other forms of rubbernecking.

others called The Deaf One, The Hairy One, The Pastry Eater, The Snotty One, and The Needle, for various physical attributes and characteristic habits.

They were cultish and laddish, and they identified with one another with fierce loyalty. They were individual freelancers, almost all of them, but they were generally willing to work together as a team even if it meant that only one or two of them would get a well-paid shot. They leapt to one another's defense when a fracas broke out (unless, of course, they were the ones getting the photos of it). They took care of the people who helped them out with valuable information about the comings and goings of photo-worthy subjects. And they really did move like a multiheaded, multi-limbed pack of shouting and flashing and pleading and provoking, a beast of many backs impelled by the desire to track down, capture, and, in some cases, instigate rows with its prey.

In large part, they had such thick skin because they never forgot where they came from. After a night shooting celebrities, many of them would return home to cramped, ramshackle rooms in neighborhoods undiscovered by fashion or tourism—sometimes to the very places they had been raised and where their families, immediate and extended, still lived. They may have worked after dark photographing the bold-faced and the brazen in chic cafés and nightclubs, but often during the days they shot news stories and street scenes that kept them in immediate contact with a Rome (and with Romans) not being buoyed by the new sense of progress and opportunity. They didn't have to see neorealist films to understand the hunger, deprivation, anxiety, and struggle that infused the lives of ordinary Italians. They were, no matter where they were born, true Romans—that is to say, brash and clever and opportunistic, deeply suspicious of anyone who put on airs or flaunted high station or wealth, and delighted to cock a snook at big shots and, even better, turn a profit on it.

Secchiaroli was quite explicit about this aspect of his working mentality when he looked back on these years: "Of course there was some resentment on our part," he admitted. "We photographers were all poor starving devils, and they had it all—money, fame, posh hotels. The doormen and the porters in the grand hotels gave us information, tips—you could call it the fellowship of the proletariat." At other times he referred to himself and his cohorts as "paratroopers" and "a pack of Indians," and when you saw those wild action photos of their flare-ups with celebrities, it was hard to say that he was exaggerating.

There were, in the end, hundreds of photographers, particularly once they became a globally recognized phenomenon and young men of dubious (if any) photographic skill realized that walking around Via Veneto with a camera hanging from your neck made it easy to meet girls. But on a given night the 1950s, there were around two dozen or so who made up the mob, including Pierluigi Praturlon and Secchiaroli and, most reliably: Adriano Bartoloni, Giancarlo Bonora, Alessandro Canetrelli, Velio Cioni, Guglielmo Coluzzi, Licio D'Aloisio, Mario Fabbi, Quinto Felice, Marcello Geppetti, Umberto Guidotti, Ivan Kroscenko, Ivo Meldolesi, Luciano Mellace, Lino Nanni, Giuseppe Palmas, Paolo Pavia, Mario Pelosi, Gilberto Petrucci, Franco Pinna, Elio Sorci, Sergio Spinelli, Bruno Tartaglia, Sandro Vespasiani, and Ezio Vitale.

Those hardy souls accounted for virtually every famous photograph of a celebrity along Via Veneto taken during the era, whether it depicted the stars doing something ordinary like having a coffee or buying a newspaper, seeking attention by riding a horse or dancing on a table, or engaged in that most exciting (and, for the photographers, most profitable) of exercises: throwing themselves angrily at someone who provoked them with an ugly word, an unwelcome approach, or, especially, a blinding flash of light.

Because, more often than not, the Via Veneto photographers got exactly the shot they were looking for. Eventually, they became as much an inconvenient reality of Rome as walking up hills, fending off souvenir peddlers, finding bureaucratic offices closed in the afternoon, or getting stuck in traffic behind protest marches. In a sense, they had changed the little world in which they lived and worked, and that change would, in time, be echoed and enlarged all around the bigger world.

The first and most famous (or notorious) of them, Praturlon, was also the first, as it happened, to transcend the pack. Within four years of his wild run-in with Roberto Rossellini, Praturlon had established a full business—Pierluigi: Fotonotizie d'Attualitá per la Stampa (The Latest Photo-news for the Press)—with offices on Via Frattina, just off Piazza di Spagna. He had carte blanche to walk onto almost any film set in Rome and start shooting. He was particularly noted for his behind-the-scene shots. Prior to him, most on-set photography amounted to little more than posed images of a film's stars reenacting a scene; Pierluigi captured candid moments of movie stars being ordinary humans at work, or of directors and stars huddling, or of the action that went on just outside the view of the movie camera: fascinating, atmospheric stuff.

His work was valued not only by the film companies that hired him—Italian and American—but by individual stars. He shot on the sets of *War and Peace* and *A Farewell to Arms*, among many other Hollywood on the Tiber productions, and countless Italian films, including a few by his onetime nemesis, Rossellini. In the course of his professional life, he would develop authentic relationships with the likes of Sophia Loren, Audrey Hepburn, Kim Novak, Federico Fellini, and Frank Sinatra. He eventually ran a sizable staff in Rome and established satellite offices in London and Paris (he liked to hire Rolls-Royces to meet him at the airport when working out of town). He was known to his photographic colleagues as "Lux," his nickname taken from a soap that was advertised with the assurance that it, like he, was "the choice of nine stars out of ten." He was, in many ways, a star in his own right.

In 1958, he was out with one of his famous friends, the Swedish starlet Anita Ekberg, who had spent the night cutting rugs all around Rome, closing down the Rancho Grande nightclub in the wee hours. As Pierluigi drove her back to her hotel, she complained about sore feet. They happened just then to be passing the Trevi Fountain, normally surrounded by tourists tossing coins into the water so as to ensure, per the legend, that they would one day return to Rome, but deserted at that hour.

Anita asked him to stop so she could soak her aching arches.

"No, come on," he said. "You'll be home in five minutes."

But she insisted, and so he stopped, and she got out and hiked up her skirt and stepped into the water and then, her pain relieved, danced languidly in the dark.

"I got my camera and started shooting her," he said. "I remember two *carabinieri* standing on a corner who weren't more than twenty years old. They didn't say a word. They were completely entranced watching this beautiful woman in the fountain, with her long, lovely legs."

The shots were published in a magazine called *Tempo Illustrato*, and Pierluigi had, again, captured an image that would become famous. This time, though, the fame would come some time later, after that quiet, magical moment was transformed from reportage into poetry, through the imagination of Federico Fellini and his fellow screenwriters, who were working on a new film about the Roman high life, untitled at the time that Ekberg took her footbath but known, at least provisionally, as *Via Veneto*.

* * *

For Tazio Secchiaroli, the surfeit of activity in Rome—at Cinecittà, on Via Veneto, in the ateliers of fashion designers, or in the shadowy corners of the Montesi case—was like hot air pumped into a balloon lifting him higher and higher and giving him greater ability to see and master the scene around him. Although he was almost entirely unknown to the public, they knew his images, and their demand for more of the same created new opportunities for him and for the increasing number of fellows who did a similar kind of work.

In 1955, the year after he photographed Anna Maria Moneta Caglio swooning outside a courthouse and Giuseppe Sotgiu exiting a brothel and Ugo Montagna and Piero Piccioni meeting in secret, Secchiaroli was able to leave the Vedo agency and set up a business of his own, Roma Press Photo, with a partner, Sergio Spinelli, another Vedo photographer, who had particularly good connections with newspaper and magazine editors. Taking a couple of rooms on Via Nazionale for offices, they divided the workload predictably: Secchiaroli was the principal shooter and printer; Spinelli worked mainly as salesman and administrator. As their most profitable business was made in shots taken at night, the two partners saw each other only in passing: Secchiaroli would be out on the prowl until the early hours, then return to the offices to develop and print his work; Spinelli would come to work in the morning and hit the phones, peddling the images around town and beyond.

The pair did well for themselves, and within two years they moved to larger offices—on the Via Gregoriana; precisely between Via Veneto and the little bohemia of Via Margutta—and hired two more photographers. Secchiaroli was able to trade in his Lambretta scooter, the very one he had driven through the crowd of protesters in Piazza Colonna just a few years earlier, for a brand-new Fiat 600. He wore better clothes. He worked days a little more frequently. He even hit the town, after a fashion. He was photographed dancing with none other than Anna Maria Caglio one evening—though, to be fair, he had a camera bag hanging from his shoulder while he waltzed.

But he hadn't lost his appetite for the hunt, for the stakeout, for the thought that there was a big prize shot out there to be snapped. He would go where the work was, even if it meant being up all night or getting mud on his new shoes or suit. He may have been his own boss, but he was still one of the boys. And his work was still of a very high level of quality, invention, and, in the best sense of the word, opportunism.

A famous example: in June 1958, news accounts emerging from the Umbrian village of Maratta Alta said that the Virgin Mary had appeared in a tree at a dairy farm, presenting herself to a local brother and sister and turning the site into a mecca for pilgrims. Spinelli thought this would make a great subject for a photo spread, but Secchiaroli resisted. Just to get Spinelli off his back, he went off with Tarquinio Maiorino, a writer for *Settimo Giorno*, to see what was up.

A small army of rustics seeking blessings, intercessions, and cures from the Madonna had turned the open field near the farm into what looked like a refugee camp. The tree that drew their adoration was surrounded by flowers, photographs of the ailing and the recently dead, letters beseeching the Virgin for aid and succor. It was impressive, in its way, but in the light of day it was cluttered and sad and not at all photogenic.

Secchiaroli learned that the real action typically took place at night, when people who worked during the day arrived in front of the shrine hoping for another visitation, and that triggered his imagination. He found the children who had witnessed the miracle, and he convinced their parents to dress them in their best clothes. When night came, he positioned the children and their family kneeling in front of the tree, praying and pointing to where the vision had appeared. Around them, farmers and villagers—men, women, young, old—stared at the branches in a variety of expressions of expectation, hope, and yearning. At times the crowd roused, following every movement and gaze of the children, as if they might see the Virgin's divine energy surging through them. But as the Holy Mother failed to return, the gathering evaporated, anticlimactically, with a few pilgrims cutting branches from the tree to bring home, just in case, while others chose to stay and pray even more fervently to the partly denuded tree trunk.

Back in Rome, it was clear, once again, that the photographs were far more exciting than the banal facts. The images of religious fervor could have come from the Middle Ages, and they showed how little, in some senses, Italy had changed, despite the boom that was being felt in Via Veneto, a mere sixty miles away from that dairy farm. *Settimo Giorno* published an article, featuring the photos, in which church officials debunked the very idea that the Madonna had ever appeared to the children. It was a somewhat silly story, but once again, the eye and the entrepreneurial instinct of Secchiaroli found a way to make it powerful.

And then came the night that turned him from an underground success into something like a celebrity.

"We Take Their Pictures and They Beat Us Up"

It was August 14, a Thursday, the eve of Ferragosto, the late-summer holiday that had been marked as carnival period by Romans since about 18 BCE and into which the Catholic church had folded the celebration of the Feast of the Assumption—the bodily rise of the Virgin Mary to Heaven. For millennia, *Ferragosto* had been observed, often by law, as a time for businesses to close and workers to be allowed respite. Since the 1920s in particular, Romans had customarily left the city for the shore, the mountains, their hometowns. The city emptied, as if thousands of Assumptions had occurred all at once.

This particular *Ferragosto* had left the city so dead that even some of the Via Veneto photographers were out of town. The weather was torrid, oppressive, and there was almost nobody to shoot.

So it was a smaller than normal hunting party out for game that night. The majority of them spent their time loitering, gossiping with doormen, chatting up passing girls. After a few bootless hours, somebody suggested they go get dinner, and so four of them squeezed into Pierluigi Praturlon's Fiat and drove off to a nearby spot that catered not to tourists and celebrities but to real people. They ate, they drank, and, at around two a.m., sated, they decided to make one last pass of the strip to see if anything had sprung to life before they called it a night.

Praturlon slowed down as he cruised up the wide and mostly empty street. Then, at the corner of Via Ludovisi, he jammed on the brakes. "There's Farouk!" he blurted to his companions. "Let's get out!"

At that moment, six years into his life of exile in Italy, the former king of Egypt was hardly the stuff of headlines. He was known all around Rome to waiters, doormen, madames, and, yes, photographers. To find him sitting at a table at the Café de Paris, his back to a wall, a glass of mineral water in front of him, flanked by Albanian bodyguards, with a couple of garishly done-up young ladies at his table, was hardly newsworthy—not even worth the cost of a flashbulb. Over the years, Farouk had mellowed to the photographers, who had grown bored with him and left him in peace. But it was a dead night, and the photographers' spirits were high, so they bolted from Praturlon's car—left it idling right in the middle of the street—and sprung into action like a SWAT team, not needing to coordinate with one another, eyes (and lenses) squarely on the target.

Farouk sat on a terrace with his back to the wall of the café, flanked by his frequent companion, the aspiring opera singer Irma Capece Minutolo,[1] and her sister. ("The rumor had it that the two sisters didn't wear panties, and I wanted to find out whether this was true, to 'record' the evidence," Secchiaroli later explained, only partly in jest.)

Separating the tables from the sidewalk were several flower boxes. Praturlon strode briskly from his car to this border, shooting away; Umberto Guidotti did the same but from a different angle; and Secchiaroli, because it couldn't be a sensational incident without him, jumped over the barrier, scuttled between the empty tables, and took a close-up shot of the deposed king with a full flash.

The sudden commotion looked more threatening than a mere photo shoot. Secchiaroli turned heel, but Farouk's bodyguards caught him. As the photographer struggled to get free, Farouk, demonstrating remarkable agility for a 300-pound man, moved in, hoping to prise away the camera. "I felt myself being lifted up bodily by Farouk," Secchiaroli said. "I had been looking out for his bodyguards, but they were the ones saving me from the king's rage. Given the chance, he would have pulverized me."

At the approach of their boss, the bodyguards eased their grip on the photographer to allow Farouk at him, but that gave Secchiaroli the split second he needed to hightail it to safety. He hadn't caught Irma unclothed, but he'd gotten a fine, atmospheric shot of Farouk and his companions at table, Farouk staring straight into the lens, alerted to an oncoming threat. And Guidotti got something even

1 Her long affair with Farouk—whom she later claimed secretly married her before his death, in 1965—made a semipublic figure of Capece Mintulo, who claimed royal ancestry and had, in 1954, sued two journalists for telling the world that her parents were a Neapolitan taxi driver and housemaid. She was noted even in Rome for her thick, garish makeup and brassy fashions and was known to wags, in the flush of her fame, as "*Irma Capace de Totalo*"—"Irma Capable of Anything."

better: a shot of Farouk and one of his bodyguards grappling with Secchiaroli. It was fuzzy and dark, but when you put it side by side with Secchiaroli's shots, you could easily figure out who was who and what was happening: hot stuff.

The photographers scattered, laughing off the fright, feeling the adrenaline. But they didn't go very far and not for very long. They heard that one of their favorite nemeses, Ava Gardner, was on her way to Bricktop's, a nightclub just down the street owned by the famed singer and dancer Ada "Bricktop" Smith. Ava was in the company of Anthony Franciosa, who was starring with her in *The Naked Maja* (he played Goya, she the Duchess of Alba). Ava on the town with a new man wasn't exactly a headline, but as Franciosa was at the time married to Shelley Winters, there was the potential for a payday in shooting them.

Ava and the photographers had a long, tart history. She had reacted violently to her first encounters with the Via Veneto photographers a few years earlier, and she held grudges. One time she posed demurely for a shot and then kicked the photographer in the groin once he'd taken it. Another time she gave one of them a taste of his own medicine. She plucked Marcello Geppetti at random from among the pack of snappers and had him escort her around for an evening, going from club to club in a borrowed jacket, dancing with a movie goddess, and having drinks pushed upon him. The poor fellow spent the entire night in fear of setting off her temper and worrying about who would pick up the tab for their carousal. Worse, he couldn't shoot a single frame—nor, for that matter, could his colleagues, whom he kept at arm's length as he was led from club to club, inveigling them not to take his picture and thereby compromise his reputation for journalistic remove from his subject.

Secchiaroli, for one, never cared for Gardner. "Among the people we hunt, Ava Gardner is certainly the most hostile to photographers, the most peevish, the one who gets most annoyed," he said. "There's never been a truce between her and us, and every time we turn up to photograph her in an indiscreet moment, if we only just irritate her, we're satisfied with the deed. Because of her ceaseless rudeness to us, we'll do almost anything to photograph her against her will." In one of their first encounters, Gardner splashed a drink on Secchiaroli, and he revenged himself soon after, hiding inside a box in a corridor at Cinecittà and leaping out to snap several shots of her coming from a swimming pool, wrapped in a towel, her hair wet and stringy, some of the least glamorous images of her that would ever circulate—which they did, widely.

The thought of catching Gardner out clubbing with a married man was irresistible, and the four photographers were in front of Bricktop's straightaway. Secchiaroli once again took the point—not for nothing was he becoming known as the Fox of Via Veneto. As the movie stars approached the club, he got right into their faces and blinded them with a flash. Gardner swore and Franciosa grabbed the nearest cameraman, not Secchiaroli but Giancarlo Bonora. But he held on only for a moment before the photographer slipped loose and ran off with his scattering chums.

A night that had begun with no promise whatever had erupted into a memorable spree. The photographers regrouped outside Bricktop's to wait for the American stars to emerge, and Gardner kept them waiting for hours. At four-thirty, she walked out of the club on the arm of her publicist, David Hanna, and drove off. A little while later, Franciosa came out, smiling and waving at the cameramen, who got almost nothing useful out of the encounter.[2]

---

2 For his part, Franciosa would soon get a visit from Shelley Winters, who showed up in Rome as soon as she learned that her husband and Gardner had gotten chummy with each other. Franciosa was happy enough at that time to oblige the photographers by posing with his missus.

At this point in the night, Secchiaroli remembered, "Via Veneto was completely deserted. It practically looked like something out of De Chirico." But from out of the surreal emptiness there would emerge yet one more explosion.

The door to another hot spot, Vecchia Roma, opened, and out stepped Anita Ekberg and Anthony Steel, the latter looking, as so often, despite his rugged jaw and impeccable suit, a little worse for the evening's efforts. Their car had been brought around for them, and they were getting in with the help of their driver when Secchiaroli and company turned up.

The final act of the evening would be a comedy. Once again the tip of the spear, Secchiaroli got off a few quick shots of the couple, and his cohorts closed in as well. "Every time Steel sees a flash," Secchiaroli recalled, "he flies into a rage like a beast and throws himself at the nearest person." The actor turned to face his antagonists, his fists clenched, his gaze vague. Secchiaroli saw an opportunity: "I started shouting '*Borracho!*'[3] at him, because the term in English had slipped my mind. It hit home immediately, and Steel, who was roaring drunk, tried to jump on me." The actor started toward Secchiaroli but stumbled, as if he'd missed the final step of a staircase. There was a flash behind him, and he turned to see another photographer racing away. Steel took a step or two in that direction and then just gave up, too drunk to act on his anger. Anita sat in the car, maintaining a strain of dignity, quietly seething (her marriage to Steel would end within a year). Their driver stood motionless on the curb, staring into the distance as if to deny the reality of the incident while it was unfolding in front of him. Steel gathered himself and got into the car, which rolled off into the

3 Spanish for "drunkard."

approaching sunrise. The photographers, satisfied with a surprisingly lively evening's work, headed home.

When Secchiaroli got back to his darkroom and developed his film, he was looking at a jackpot: he had at least a half dozen vivid images of Steel's aborted rampage, with Ekberg alluringly sprinkled throughout, enough for an entire photo spread—very good money for what at first seemed destined to be a wasted shift of work.

But the profit on the night was to be far bigger than whatever money he made. In the coming days, several newspapers and magazines in Rome—and, following them, in Paris, London, and New York—reported on the wild goings-on with headlines like "In Via Veneto, a Photographer Is Assaulted by Farouk and Franciosa" (*Il Giornale*), "The Terrible Night on Via Veneto" (*L'Espresso*), and "Farouk of the Night" (*Paris Match*). A few weeks later, Secchiaroli wrote (or had ghostwritten for him) a story in *Settimo Giorno* entitled "We Take Their Pictures and They Beat Us Up"— giving the magazine another chance, as if it needed one, to run all those crazy shots.

*I*n the *Settimo Giorno* article, Secchiaroli presented himself and his colleagues as guerrillas engaged in combat: "Now, there's our target, our face," he explained, describing a typical night on the prowl.

> Who's going to let it get away? . . . On these occasions, nothing will stop us, even if it means overturning tables and waiters, or raising shrieks from an old lady who doesn't quite get what's happening. . . . Even if the police intervene or we chase the subject all night long, we won't let go, we'll fight with flashes, we'll help each other out. . . . Of course, we, too,

would like to stroll through an evening, have a cup of coffee in blissful peace, and see Via Veneto as a splendid international promenade, rather than one big workplace or even a theater of war.

The battle cries that wild August night had barely faded when Secchiaroli found himself in the midst of another memorable scene. It was almost fall—cool enough that he went to work with gloves on—and once again the evening's menu involved Ava Gardner. This time she was being escorted around the usual chain of nightclubs by Walter Chiari, the Italian leading man who had been connected in the gossip press with Lucia Bosé, Elsa Martinelli, and Anna Magnani. Surely she saw in Chiari's chiseled features a dark echo of Frank Sinatra. Chiari was no superstar, but he had charm and a light manner and was well liked around town, even by the photographers.

It was a dull night, with Secchiaroli and three other photographers following Chiari and Gardner from club to club, shooting the usual images of the stars walking from a car to a doorway and then, later, from a doorway back to a car. Tedium. The photographers worked dutifully but all they got, Secchiaroli recalled, were "worthless photographs, because there were so many just like them."

He got another burst of inspiration. While Chiari parked his car outside of Gardner's building near the Piazza di Spagna, Secchiaroli told his colleagues to get ready. "I went up very close to Gardner and set off a flash in her face; she screamed and Chiari immediately rushed me." Secchiaroli held his ground, eyes on the actor, both hands on his camera, intending to protect his gear and, if he could, to get off a few shots. Chiari, unlike Tony Franciosa and Anthony Steel, had his wits about him, more or less, and had, up to then, enjoyed agreeable relations with the Via Veneto photographers. He recognized Secchiaroli as he got closer to him and let go of his anger, satisfied that he'd made a vivid show of defending Gardner, with whom he promptly went inside.

Secchiaroli didn't manage to get any pictures of the tussle. But Elio Sorci did, and the images he captured were sensational, vivid depictions of the ongoing battle between the photographers and the stars they stalked. The prey, in this case, was turning tables on the hunter. In the most famous picture, Chiari, impeccably dressed and credibly athletic, runs from the camera toward Secchiaroli, a blur around his legs indicating his pace. Secchiaroli, dressed in sports coat, sweater, and tie, braces himself on the sidewalk in front of the security gate of a jewelry store. Ready to bolt, his mouth is slightly parted, his gaze firmly on Chiari, his gloved hands gripping his camera. It's an action image and a provocative glimpse of a mysterious story: Who was the angry man? What had the photographer seen or done? Would it end violently?

Sorci got a second memorable shot, moving forward to capture Chiari's face as he put the brakes on his attack and looked beyond Secchiaroli to see if there was anyone else he needed to fend off. In this image, Secchiaroli is stepping out of the actor's path and into the street, one arm up held up defensively, his body between Chiari and the camera. It's not quite as vivid as the first, but given the fact that everyone in Italy would recognize the actor's face, it was, in some ways, even hotter stuff.[4]

The pictures were published almost immediately in *Settimo*

---

[4] However meekly it ended, the incident in Piazza di Spagna marked a change in relations between Chiari and the photographers. The following spring, he was hounded all night while out with Anita Ekberg, finally getting his hands on someone's camera and busting it up. *Le Ore* ran a two-page spread of eight photos chronicling the evening under the headline "Operation 'Walter.'"

Giorno under the headline "Walter Chiari Has Lost His Patience," and that was undoubtedly true. But really, who could blame him? It was more than fourteen years since the Allies had liberated Rome, but in certain neighborhoods, at certain times of the day, it seemed as if there was an outright war being waged by packs of photographers against the famous personalities populating the city's nightlife. If it ended in bloodshed or worse, nobody would have been surprised. (As one member of Parliament said, it was fortunate for these photographers that they lived in "a peaceful country.")

For several years, the Italian and foreign press had been gobbling up the work of the Via Veneto photographers. Now the stories *behind* the photographs were making news. It was one thing to see the bacchanals of Rome up close; it was another to see how the chaos was made, to learn what it took to bring these lurid scenes to your breakfast table. The reporters were being reported on; the media was telling the story of *itself*. And the story was being shared around the world, in vivid black and white.

It was a powder keg.

And guess who was about to light the fuse.

22 "The Most Sinful, Transgressive Thing"

By all accounts, Anita Ekberg started it.

There was a band, there were drinks and laughs and revelers, and before anyone knew it, she was dancing barefoot on the stone floor ("The first sign of Anitona getting into orbit is when her shoes come off," said a witness, using the nickname the actress would soon be known by). She was improvising a mambo, twirling like a dream: an explosion of platinum hair; that broad, brilliant smile; a snug black velvet dress, spaghetti straps flouncing, cleavage teasing the neckline: gaiety, pleasure, and sex, vibrant and alive.

A German actor, elegantly dressed, built like a stiletto, ventured to join her, taking her hand with his fingertips, moving delicately as if trying not to scare off a wild animal he hoped to trap.[1]

The party had been something of a dud, despite the titillating mixture of movie people and art world people and young people from noble families, despite the lively music from the popular Roman New Orleans Jazz Band. Now, though, with a single visceral impulse, the Swedish dervish had kicked it into life.

Inevitably there was clapping in time to the music from the sidelines; inevitably a few more couples started to dance. And, just as inevitably, a number of men hovered on the perimeter, a cordon of leers, eyes locked on the erotic spectacle of the bosomy Nordic blonde.

Locked, that is, until something else drew their attention.

*L*ater on, no one would be entirely sure how she got there—who invited her, whom she was with, who, even, she was.

Later on, she would claim that she had been drugged by a suspect cigarette or had something slipped into her drink.

But first there would be a wild display that would make the earth shake throughout Rome and cause ripples all around the world.

Ekberg, feeling no pain, had tumbled during her improvised dance and decided to take a seat, tempering the atmosphere from boil to simmer. In the lull, a small, dark girl in a white dress approached the drummer and whispered to him. Signaling to his bandmates that he would play alone, he started tapping out a

---

1 His name was Gérard Haerter, and he had just completed acting in the low-budget potboiler *Caltiki: The Immortal Monster*, a feature directed by the uncredited horror master Mario Bava; Haerter went on to a decade-plus career of playing villains in war movies and westerns.

steady, pulsing, back-and-forth rhythm. The girl stepped to the front of the bandstand and began to dance.

The floor cleared around her, and the phalanx of leering men grew in number. Anita had danced to enjoy herself, on a spree, as a release. She was an eyeful, but she was also an icebreaker; people joined in with her. But this girl—whoever she was—was giving a performance, and an audience declared itself present and alert.

From her table, Ekberg asked if the girl, who looked Middle Eastern, was a belly dancer. Now the focus of all eyes, she replied yes, explaining that she couldn't belly dance just then because her dress was too restrictive. Anita shot back that if the girl would take her dress off, she would do the same—but only if the girl went first.

Now it was a party.

Flushed with the attention, the drumming, the buzz, the girl reached down to her shoes, giggling, rising to the challenge. She said she needed a rug to dance on, and tablecloths appeared on the floor before her. They weren't fine enough, she said, and she asked the men to lay down their jackets, which several did straightaway, forming a makeshift carpet of silk and wool.

Long, wavy hair shimmying, full lips in a dreamy smile, she reached for a zipper. Turning toward the band, always moving to the beat, she revealed her shoulders and then her nude back—she wore no bra—and let the dress fall altogether. This was no belly dance; this was a full-on striptease.

The girl turned and swayed and grinded and stretched. She removed her stockings one by one, flaunting them, tossing them to onlookers. Wearing only black panties, she lowered herself gradually to the floor, ending up on her back with her hands on her breasts, her legs folded beneath her, her knees spread, as if she was sliding under a limbo bar. By then, the drummer had moved himself to the floor as well, and his tom-tom now sat between her parted thighs.

Surrounding them, men in shirts and ties gaped, some literally with their mouths hanging open, too startled to look away or to attend to the cigarettes and drinks in their hands. Among them were sprinkled more than a few women, gazes more circumspect than ecstatic but no less riveted to the scene.

And at a remove of several meters, standing on a table so as to take in as much of it as he wished to, snapping shot after shot after shot of a moment that some people wouldn't want seen but many others would pay good money to look at, was Tazio Secchiaroli—Johnny-on-the-Spot yet again.

"What was happening before my very eyes was indescribable," Secchiaroli remembered, deeming it "the most sinful, transgressive thing that I had ever photographed."

Unlike the stripper, Secchiaroli had been invited to the party, along with four other photographers, by a press agent who had been hired to promote the event by its honoree. Her name was Olga di Robilant, and she had been born in Venice to a family of old-line monarchists who left Italy for Portugal along with King Umberto II after the Second World War. Her family had titles and lands but no money, and Olghina, as she was known, had come to Rome to make her way as an actress. She was tall and pretty with fair hair and bright blue eyes, and she had already worked on *The Nun's Story*, the Audrey Hepburn film that was shooting at Cinecittà but hadn't yet been released (and for which, ultimately, she wouldn't receive a screen credit). Seeking to make herself better known in the capital, she asked a chum, the American Peter Howard Vanderbilt, who had a name *and* money, to throw a party for her birthday, her twenty-fifth.[2]

2 Vanderbilt was the son of a woman who had married into the famous old family, and he was living in Europe under something of a cloud. He had been named as a participant in a homosexual love triangle by *Confidential* magazine two years prior and was trying to keep a low profile as he worked abroad as a portrait photographer.

They chose the night of Wednesday, November 5, 1958, and the restaurant Rugantino on a cobblestoned piazza in the Trastevere district. Di Robilant engaged the publicist Enrico Lucherini to help fill the room with top-shelf movie and art world types (she and Vanderbilt already knew the society mob) and to make sure that there were photographers on hand to record the event for magazines and newspapers. Along with the younger, hipper members of the Ruspoli, Borghese, and Pignatelli families whom di Robilant and Vanderbilt had invited, Lucherini filled the room with Ekberg, Linda Christian, Elsa Martinelli, Anna Maria Mussolini (yes, *his* daughter), the singer Laura Betti, the Via Margutta painter and scene-stirrer Novella Parigini, and several of the Via Veneto photographers.

He hadn't, however, invited the girl who had so shocked Secchiaroli. She, technically, had tagged along to the party in the company of a Neapolitan journalist who himself barely qualified to get through the door and who was, up until then, the only person present who knew her name. But her anonymity would soon, like that white dress, fall away.

The first people to learn who she was would be the police. Mingling among the celebrants were a couple of plainclothes cops moonlighting as guards at the request of Rugantino's owner, who was anxious about all the jewels and furs that would be in the restaurant. When the girl undressed, these detectives called in policemen who arrested her, questioned the hosts and the restaurateurs, and tried to confiscate the photographers' film. A few of the snappers *were* stopped by the cops, and their film was taken from them. This wasn't the first time Secchiaroli had landed red-hot material in a fevered atmosphere, though, and he had shown foresight: even while the girl was dancing, he passed rolls of exposed film to Lucherini, who had a gofer secret them out of the restaurant to a nearby parked car.

The girl wasn't so lucky. Taken into custody, breaking down in tears of confusion and fear, she revealed her name as Aiche Nana,

her age as twenty-two, her nationality as Lebanese, and her profession as actress and dancer. She had appeared as a belly dancer
in two films, one made in London and one shot in Lebanon starring a young Omar Sharif. She was virtually unknown, but in the
coming weeks, she would become the focus of scrutiny, gossip, and
outrage throughout Rome and beyond.

At first, the police tried to keep it all as quiet as possible, treat-
ing it as a banal case of disturbing the peace and public indecency,
a fracas involving a bar full of overheated partyers and a girl on a
toot. The only visible sign of anything unusual was the indefinite
closing of Rugantino. The party had been so utterly deflated by the
girl's arrest that a bunch of celebrants simply left Trastevere and
carried on making merry on Via Veneto at the Café de Paris, which
never closed before sunrise.

But within hours of Nana's dance, scuttlebutt blazed through
the city, and Secchiaroli's pictures made their way to the editors of
legitimate newspapers and scandal sheets. No one, though, dared
publish them. They were risqué even by the lurid standards of the
cronaca rosa, and there was the matter of liability: a great many of
the faces surrounding the nude girl were not only visible but readily identifiable—artists and movie people and men and women with
titles and money and public positions. It was explosive stuff, and at
least one gossip columnist, Victor Ciuffa of the Milanese paper Corri-
ere d'Informazione, claimed to have been told by police simply to bury
the matter. "'Nothing happened,'" they'd told him when he called
with questions about the legality of publication. "'If you journalists
don't talk about this, nothing happened.'" But that was hardly likely.
Ciuffa and a few other columnists printed stories about the party,
without naming too many names or showing any faces. But mere
reports were enough to set off yet more gossip and indignation.

Almost inevitably, Secchiaroli's remarkable photos found their
way into the pages of several publications, including the reputable

L'Europeo and *L'Espresso* and splashier venues such as *Epoca* and *Lo Specchio*. The accompanying stories were spiced with the names, details, and eyewitness accounts that had been circulating around the city. They bore headlines like "Rome's Turkish Night," "The Sins of Trastevere," "At the End the Turkish Girl Cried," and "This Is How the Upper Crust Undress."

The headlines had to be lurid, because the images were spellbinding. Few of the printed photos showed fully bared breasts, and some used black bars to hide the eyes and identities of spectators, but even in their most chaste form Secchiaroli's photos galvanized and shocked. Nana was pale and smiling, sometimes with her eyes closed dreamily, sometimes staring into space or into the eyes of partygoers, and, in one almost chilling shot, looking straight into the photographer's lens: She *knew* she was being photographed.[3] Around her, a roomful of (almost solely) men stared with calculation, cynicism, appraisal, like the wolves in Ruth Orkin's famous 1951 photo *American Girl in Italy*, in which a fearful young woman walked, breath held, gaze down, through a gauntlet of no less than fifteen sets of men's eyes, amid laughs and catcalls and at least one vulgar gesture. The Rugantino crowd wasn't quite so crude as that street-corner pack, but the air they bore in these images was arguably worse: entitled, haughty, cynical. The spectacle of a jaded mob looking on with such dispassion on such a scene was chilling: it brought to mind the Rome of the later caesars, the nastier Borgias, the most frightening Fascists.

Now the murmurs and whispers about the party turned into denunciatory shouts, echoed in the opinion pages of the legitimate press and in the halls of power, both secular and papal. Stacks of

3 There could have been no secret about the photographers' presence. They took shots throughout the night, many of them posed. Secchiaroli said that Ekberg scolded him for shooting Nana's dance, but photos of the girl taken from more than one angle would eventually be published, so he wasn't alone.

newspapers and magazines containing the scandalous photos vanished from newsstands, confiscated by censors or by moral crusaders. The band that was entertaining at the party was briefly barred from performing. The most eye-opening response to the events appeared in *L'Osservatore Romano*, where Count Giuseppe Dalla Torre, the editor and a longtime friend of the newly enthroned Pope John XXIII, lashed out at Rome's partygoing set, decrying them as "lice of society who, like all parasites, live outside the life they exploit," and explicitly urging Roman police to crack down on their licentious behavior. The night at Rugantino wasn't mentioned, but everyone in Rome knew the context, virtually assuring that gossip would increase and more details would emerge. What was more, given the unusual fervor and titillating theme of Dalla Torre's editorial, the episode wound up being reported all around the world; even *The New York Times* shared details of the "wild carousal" in Trastevere that had occasioned it.

Nana's prosecution proceeded, and she tried to temper her disastrous publicity with interviews in which she accused the hosts of getting her drunk and dosing her with marijuana before goading her into stripping.[4] In the aftermath of her night at Rugantino,

---

4 Italian authorities (and, really, the culture at large) had a complex relationship with striptease, which was seen as a foreign import and an affront to morality yet thrived after the war, inspired, in part, by the popularity of beauty pageants, which similarly took no pains to hide the fact that they were designed to profit off of the exploitation of female bodies. At various times during the decade after the war, burlesque shows featuring nudity were shut down with force by authorities; at others, they were openly tolerated. Simultaneously, inspired by the advocacy of Lina Merlin, a Socialist parliamentarian from the Veneto region of the North, the country was moving to shut down its licensed brothels, which had thrived for decades as a sexual outlet for men who found little satisfaction in their marriages (which, of course, could not be ended legally). The number of brothels and girls declined steadily from 800 and 6000, respectively, in 1950 to 550 and 2600 in 1958. The final legislation ordering the permanent closing of the nation's hundreds of licensed brothels was passed only a few months before the sensational episode at Rugantino.

she would retire from performing, convert to Catholicism, marry, and become a mother—despite all of which she was sentenced, in 1960, to two months in jail. Olga di Robilant, now laden with more fame than she had bargained for, convened with her family lawyers to strategize a defense against any possible charges.[5] Vanderbilt, twice burned by the press, was whisked out of Italy with the help of the American consulate (di Robilant and Lucherini invited the press to a farewell scene at Stazione Termini). Novella Parigini, as was her wont, confirmed all over town that she was among the partyers at Rugantino and got several published profiles (and, presumably, some sales and commissions) out of the affair. A few of the young aristocrats who had proffered their jackets for the striptease were denounced in court and faced fines and (suspended) jail sentences. Anita Ekberg, who, in fact, kept her clothes on throughout the evening, became the international face of the incident, showing up on the cover of *Whisper* magazine beside a headline about "The Wild Party That Shook Rome."

And Tazio Secchiaroli got invited out to dinner with Federico Fellini.

---

5 She would forever claim that the press had sensationalized the goings-on at Rugantino and may even have staged them. She would further claim that it was she and not Anita Ekberg who first dove into the Trevi Fountain at night, and she denounced Federico Fellini as "a maid looking through the keyhole." Her memoirs were published in Milan in 2007 under the title *Snob*.

23 Babylon, 2000 Years After Christ

Almost as much as he loved movies, food, cartoons, cars, scarves, and the circus, Federico Fellini loved women. He had a wife whom, by all accounts, he adored. But his imagination, as evidenced by his movies and his dream diaries, was populated with voluptuous *maggiorate*, curvy temptresses, buxom sirens, and seminude goddesses who made mincemeat of the men who, stupefied, were helplessly drawn to them. By all accounts, he could be a shameless hound in chasing after them, ogling them, whispering to them, trying to make them laugh, giving them parts in his films.

Even before he was world-famous, he had a reputation in Rome as a flirt and satyr. "The eye of Fellini, round and pasty, resembles that of many Romans," wrote a Milanese journalist in early 1960. "His gaze is slow and heavy and sticks itself, like a leech, on the inviting target of other men's wives. But it returns, immediately, meekly and hypocritically, to the graces of his well-known and boring wife. . . . Fellini, in short, is not there to drink."

It wasn't clear that Fellini was an adulterer—although it was very likely. He certainly *talked* as if he was. As Giulietta Masina admitted, "He is an Italian man, and they *have* to talk about their sexual exploits in order to have the respect of other Italian men." But she was sanguine that he was hers, that he always came home, that along with his Latin lover's wandering eye he had a Catholic schoolboy's need to confess himself. The truth, she mused, could never be known: "If I asked him questions about whether there were other women in his life, he told me approximately what I wanted to hear. If I accused him of lying, he agreed with me."

Whatever it was that he got up to, he had friends in the press who protected him from scandal. Whether it was because they had worked with him, or wanted to follow him into the movies, or relied on their connection to him for access to his sets or stars, the editors of even the trashiest tabloids never ran pictures of Fellini with other women. And when they *did* try to catch him up to no good, they were almost always wrong, accusing him of affairs with Anita Ekberg and Anouk Aimée, neither of whom ever got close to him in that way. (Tellingly, when he was accused of hypocrisy for his jaded portrait of Roman sexual liberty, he replied in an article entitled *"Sono un Peccatore anch'Io"* ["I, Too, Am a Sinner"]).

From the point of view of his biographer and friend Tullio Kezich, Fellini "had a lot of fun with women, but it was never anything serious. . . . [He] had masses of little affairs. They were diversions. . . . He talked a lot and did little. . . . After a while, he would get weary and irritated when the object of his infatuation imagined that this was her great love." And then he would, inevitably, run back to Giulietta.

There was one exception, and it was so exceptional that Fellini never spoke of it. According to Kezich, "It was only after his death that we got to know that he had a lifelong friendship with a certain Anna [Giovannini], whom he had been in love with in his youth. For forty years, while he was still seeing her, he never talked about her to me, nor did he to Marcello [Mastroianni], who was furious when he learned about this secret love through the newspapers: 'And to think that I told him everything, all my adventures, all my *pasticci*!'" (Mastroianni was referring to his "little messes.")

Despite his roving eye, Fellini didn't visit Via Veneto much. He preferred to frequent Canova in the Piazza del Popolo, just down the hill from his home on Via Archimede,[1] and his favorite restaurant was Cesarina, near the Piazza di Spagna, though he also favored Giuseppe, an Emilian joint not far from his home, and Bruni, near the Vatican. But he had plenty of friends among the writers and intellectuals who spent their days on Via Veneto, in Rossetti's bookshop and at the Caffè Strega, and he had been obliged more than once to meet a producer or an agent at Doney or the Café de Paris.

So he knew the street, and he knew a lot of the people who were regulars there. What he didn't know was what was going on with these photographers: their backgrounds and daily lives, their equipment and techniques, their ruses, their hearts and minds. He was fascinated with the new way of life that was exploding all

1 Soon he would move to Via Margutta, and he'd live there the rest of his life—proof positive that he was a bona fide bohemian and *never* an arriviste.

around Rome, with the souls of the people who inhabited it and, on a human scale, closer to his own soul, with the way an artist's ambitions could be scuttled by the glitter of earthly delights. Nobody knew more about that alluring world than these crazy young photographers who had an uncanny—and very cinematic—ability to capture people and gobble them up in the stark light of a flashbulb. He began to conceive a movie about them and their milieu, as he called it, "a conflagration in the culminating moment of its splendor, just before its disintegration." He even shared with a few people a title he was playing with for the thing: *Babylon, 2,000 Years After Christ.* . . .

Fellini was also cagey about his relationships with his films, claiming that his creative impulse wasn't one of joy but loathing, agony, struggle. "I make a film as if I were escaping," he once said, "as if I had to avoid an illness. . . . when I am overcome by hatred, when I am full of bitterness." And when it was over, he continued, his feelings about the finished work were rarely positive: "With each one of my films . . . our relationship is one of mutual dislike. I feel like a criminal. I want to leave no traces of what a film has cost me. I destroy everything."

Worse, still was his attitude toward the film business. "The movie business is macabre," he would often say. "Grotesque. It is a combination of a football game and a brothel."

And worse yet, worst of all, were producers. Fellini would tell anyone who would listen to him—dinner guests, journalists, waiters, psychotherapists—about the wars he fought against producers over film subjects, casting, budgets, salaries, sets, props, music, editing, publicity: everything. He loved to share pointed anecdotes about producers and damning jokes, like this one about seeking financing for *Le Notti di Cabiria*: "The producer says, 'We have to talk about this. You made pictures about homosexuals, you had a script about an insane asylum, and now you have prostitutes. Whatever will your next film be about?' . . . I respond angrily, 'My next film will be about producers!'"[2]

But being an independent director who had to seek funding and support from scratch for each new project meant that he had to dance anew with a variety of producers every time he wanted to make another film, and he hated it: "It's always the same story. . . . The fatigue of finding money—meetings after meetings, talks upon talks, endless telephone calls, fights and threats galore. . . . Today everything is settled, tomorrow everything is up in the air." But the single thing he hated most of all was the sheer, predictable obstinacy of producers who, time after time, thought the best idea for the next Fellini movie was the *last* Fellini movie. After the success of *I Vitelloni*, he griped, the producers he spoke with wanted him to make *The Friends of i Vitelloni* or *The Relatives of i Vitelloni*. After *La Strada*, they all wanted more stories about Gelsomina: "*Gelsomina on a Bicycle,* or anything with Gelsomina in the title," he groused. "I could have earned a fortune selling her name to doll manufacturers, to sweets firms; even Walt Disney wanted to make a film about her. I could have lived on Gelsomina for twenty years!"

And yet there was a character in his oeuvre who haunted him, who kept suggesting himself for a new look, who virtually demanded to be revisited, restored, reshaped on screen: Moraldo, the wistful youngest member of the *Vitelloni* who fatefully boarded the train to Rome and exchanged his provincial life for a stab at life in the larger world. For several years, Fellini nurtured the seed of

2 Self-confessed liar that he was, Fellini disputed the anecdote, but added a caveat: "I can't imagine how that story got started, unless I started it myself."

an idea that he called *Moraldo in Città—Moraldo in the City*—musing about what might have happened to the hopeful dreamer as he explored his new hometown. An autobiographical impulse suggested the subject: "As a youthful provincial," Fellini confessed, "I kept a chronicle of my experiences and observations and was determined one day to document them one way or another." As the high tide of *Notte di Cabiria* buoyed him, he thought again of that young man and his experiences and even conceived of a sexy new title for the material: *Moraldo '58*. But, he explained, "When I pulled the bundle of notes out of my desk drawer, the adventures of that young man of twenty years ago, I found myself reading with less and less enthusiasm. It was speaking of the Rome of another time. . . . The charming bohemian life and the community of artists who lived from day to day no longer existed."

Disappointed, he turned his attention from Moraldo to another idea, *Viaggio con Anita*, a story about a married man, his lover, and his dying father. (Fellini's own father, Urbano, had died in 1955, within hours of a deathbed reunion with his son.) Early talks were promising, with that great icon of Rome, Gregory Peck, agreeing to appear as the central character and Sophia Loren as the mistress. But when Sophia's struggle to marry Carlo Ponti made it virtually impossible for her to commit to a film production in Italy, the project was abandoned.[3]

And so Fellini and his team of creative collaborators—Ennio Flaiano, Tullio Pinelli, Pier Paolo Pasolini, and Brunello Rondi, a new member of the team—took another look at the Moraldo story and had a creative breakthrough. "Today is the day of the journalist, the cameraman, mechanization, and of café society," Fellini

3 Rewritten, it was made in 1979 with Giancarlo Giannini and Goldie Hawn starring for Mario Monicelli and released in English-speaking countries as *Lovers and Liars*.

Roman romance, posh style: Irma Capece Minutolo and King Farouk.

Roman romance, the people's style: Sophia Loren and Marcello Mastroianni in *Peccato che Sia una Canaglia* (*Too Bad She's Bad*, 1954).

Valentino in his atelier, 1959.

Before the crash: Fon de Portago and Linda Christian.

Walter Chiari chases Tazio Secchiaroli.

Anthony Steel ready for
action on the infamous
night of *Ferragosto*, 1958

William Wyler (left) and Federico Fellini toast their simultaneous 1959 productions of *Ben Hur* and *La Dolce Vita*.

Fellini meets the as-yet-unlabeled paparazzi, including Pierluigi Praturlon (hand on chin) and Tazio Secchiaroli (with camera).

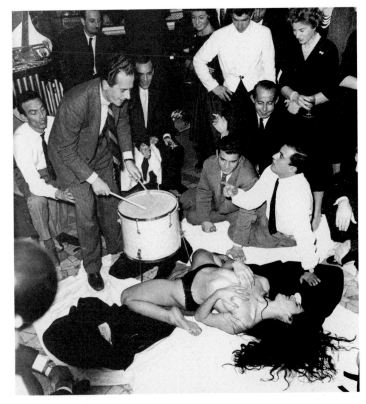

"The most sinful, transgressive thing that I had ever photographed": Aiche Nana shot by Tazio Secchiaroli at the infamous Rugantino party, November 1958.

The prince and the showgirl: Belinda Lee and Filippo Orsini.

The birth of Venus: Anita Ekberg stirs the waters while Federico Fellini (kneeling) directs.

The kiss: Marcello Mastroianni and Anita Ekberg in *La Dolce Vita* (1960).

A body on a beach: Marcello Mastroianni in *La Dolce Vita* (1960).

Diana on the hunt: Anita Ekberg, tired of being hounded by paparazzi, shoots back.

The triumph of Sofia Toothpick: Carlo Ponti (left) and Vittorio De Sica celebrate Sophia Loren's 1962 Oscar victory with the star they created.

Telephoto tell-all: one of Marcello Geppetti's sensational shots of Richard Burton and Elizabeth Taylor kissing in Ischia.

explained. "A different world. I then decided to keep the pattern and write a script about the turbulent times of today."

What they had in mind was a story about a young man who, like Moraldo, came to Rome with the dreams of living a big life and creating something important, only to find himself slipping, incrementally, into the fallen world around him, chasing and steeping himself in materialism, sensationalism, professional exigency, and moral relativism. Flaiano, the gimlet-eyed stepuncle of the enterprise, noted that the hero "is one of those journalists a civilization of sensationalism has produced, that is, he reports scandals, the damned fool behavior of others. He allows himself to be adopted by the same society he despises."

This jaded character didn't have a name or, really, a story. But Fellini and his cohorts started recognizing his spoor all over Rome, particularly on Via Veneto, and in a variety of stories that were emerging in the very media that they were so keen to hold up as a symptom, an illness, even an evil. Through the summer of 1958, as printed accounts of incidents between photographers and celebrities became more lurid and more common, Fellini was increasingly taken with the thought of capturing the overheated atmosphere of the city. And, somewhat to his surprise, more than one producer saw the point (and the appeal) of what he had in mind.

The first of these was Dino De Laurentiis who, as the producer of *Notti di Cabiria*, had right of first refusal on Fellini's next film, as well as a buyout price should someone else want to take it off his hands. When he heard that Fellini wanted to depict the carousel of modern Roman society, he was immediately receptive. But he had in mind something bigger, gaudier, and more obviously salable than the director had in mind. He wanted Fellini to find a way to use big international stars: Maurice Chevalier as the leading character's father; Barbara Stanwyck and Silvana Mangano (Mrs. De Laurentiis, yes, but an altogether worthy and popular actress) as some of the women in his life; Henry Fonda as his intellectual mentor and friend; and, in the central role, the rising American leading man Paul Newman, whose representatives had indicated that he was at least interested in hearing more about the film.

At most of these suggestions, Fellini balked. Casting was always, for him, a very specific craft and one of his favorite parts of the moviemaking process. He had vast files of photographs of faces and bodies and would sift through them tirelessly looking for the right performer—professional or amateur—to fill a role, or even, in many cases, to build the role to fit. Some of De Laurentiis's ideas struck him as worthwhile: Fonda, for instance, was possessed of just the right air of majesty and iciness for the part, and as he had only the previous year married an Italian heiress, he might even be planning to be around town. But Fonda balked because of the way in which the character's story ended. Newman, however, was a complete nonstarter for the director. For one thing, it was still early enough in his career (Newman's first screen credit had come just four years earlier) that it wasn't clear that he could master a role so alien to his own experience and personality. Moreover, Fellini later explained, the film was about a nobody, a hack writer from the provinces: "I could not cast a great star to play this role." [4]

At an impasse with each other, De Laurentiis and Fellini agreed that the director should seek another source of funding for the film. There were a few lowball offers, and they almost always came with the producer's ideas about casting, which Fellini nearly always found inappropriate. And then, walking by the Hotel Excelsior on

---

4 Newman's name would be dropped in the finished film in a joke about a publicist prone to exaggerating the popularity of one of his actor clients.

Via Veneto, Fellini ran into Peppino Amato, a colorful Neapolitan producer and *rimediatore*, who suggested that Fellini consider working with Angelo Rizzoli, the Milanese publishing magnate who had begun producing films before the war and had a hand in such significant pictures as Roberto Rossellini's *The Flowers of St. Francis*, Vittorio De Sica's *Umberto D*, the Hollywood on the Tiber products *Beat the Devil* and *The Barefoot Contessa*, and the massively popular *Don Camillo* comedy series about a kind and wily village priest.

After much back-and-forth, Rizzoli was disposed to funding the film, to the tune of $1.6 million, but with some stipulations. For one, he wanted the film to be entitled *Via Veneto* (which, as Flaiano could have told him, Fellini would never allow).[5] For another, he wanted to pay a onetime flat fee for Fellini's services, insisting that the director forgo the stipulation in his contract with De Laurentiis that he earn a percentage of the profits of the film as his salary, with, as was traditional, a higher percentage accruing to international profits. Fellini agreed. "I had to do what was good for my film," he later said. "Without a second's hesitation, I surrendered all future rights to any monetary benefits. . . . I received $50,000 to make the film. That was it."[6]

Even with his director willingly sacrificing his own interests to get financing, Flaiano was sure that the film was an impossibility. Fellini was pushing his cowriters (and, with them, his producer)

5 According to one account, the work in progress had a title that Fellini was threatening producers with: *Although Life Is Brutal and Terrible, You Can Always Find a Few Wonderful Moments of Sensuality and Sweetness*.

6 Rizzoli may have had his occasional doubts about the movie biz, but he was a showman with more than a touch of classic show biz vulgarity to him. Once he told a group of journalists that "Fellini is great, like that mountain . . . ," only able to come up with the name "Everest" when an assistant stage-whispered it to him. A few days later, he repeated his praise thus: "Fellini is great, like that mountain . . . that my assistant knows."

into a narrative that would make even *I Vitelloni* and *La Strada* look conventional: "We have to make a Picasso sculpture, smash it, then put it back together the way we want it," Flaiano recalled.

In many cases, the pieces of the sculpture were directly inspired by real-life events. Fellini devoured tabloid newspapers and magazines, which he mischievously liked to purchase at the newsstand on Via Veneto, within eyeshot of the locations where so many of the lurid events had taken place, and he plastered the walls of his office with evocative images clipped from their pages. "They amounted to a window onto the film," wrote a journalist who visited the director at work. "Everywhere there were beautiful women in dresses made by the greatest clothiers; monstrous, custom-built cars of unbridled luxury; Anita Ekberg and Anthony Steel holding hands; Walter Chiari nearly engaged in a bullfight with photographers; a series of pictures of Via Veneto, with the tables lit and people strolling on a summer night." The result of being surrounded by this inspiration, Fellini explained, would be visible in the look and feel of the finished movie: "If you're looking for a precedent for this film, you'll find it in the tabloids."

There were news headlines that he had in mind and which would find their way into the script: the puzzling and haunting 1950 suicide of the author Cesare Pavese; the 1956 delivery of a statue of Jesus Christ by helicopter to Vatican City; the dubious miracle of the Madonna at the dairy farm that Tazio Secchiaroli photographed in 1958. But the most intriguing for him were the explosive episodes on Via Veneto and thereabouts during the summer of 1958, in particular the wild night of *Ferragosto*. As he told the English journalist John Francis Lane (who would appear in a cameo in the finished film . . . as an English journalist), the movie would be "a portrait of Rome at a certain moment in its eternal history, the Summer of 1958 . . . as if it were a film in period costume."

In a quest to learn more about the incidents that were firing his imagination, Fellini had his assistants reach out to several of the Via Veneto photographers with an invitation to dinner. One night in early November 1958, Fellini hosted a gathering at Da Gigetto er Pescatore, a seafood restaurant in the northern stretch of the Flaminio neighborhood, at which Guglielmo Coluzzi, Pierluigi Praturlon, Tazio Secchiaroli, Ezio Vitale, and Sandro Vespasiani were his guests. As Secchiaroli recalled, Fellini "was carrying some pictures under his arm and asked who had taken them. In those days, we did not sign our pictures ... we were all anonymous. But those were photographs that I had taken ... and, I'm not saying this to brag ... he told his press manager to stand up and let me sit beside him."

Throughout the long, liquid evening, Fellini picked the brains of the photographers, learning essential details of their trade, their personal lives, their adventures: "How they fixed on their victim, how they behaved to make him nervous, how they prepared their pieces, exactly as required, for the various papers," as Fellini recalled. "They had amusing tales to tell: waiting in ambush for hours, thrilling escapes, dramatic chases." The photographers were eager to make a good impression on the director, if only to countervail the widening impression that they were hooligans, and in no small part because they thought they could get work or money from him for their most sensational yarns. After a while, though, the born liar Fellini could tell that some of these tales were too much to be believed. "They thought up all kinds of tall stories for my benefit," Fellini remembered. "In the end, Secchiaroli said, 'Stop inventing, you idiots, you're talking to an old hand at the game,' and I didn't know whether to take it as a compliment or an insult."

From that evening on, though, Fellini made a kind of expert

witness of Secchiaroli, extracting stories from him and, more important, using him to train the actors hired to play the mob of photographers in the subtleties of handling cameras, lenses, and flashes and jostling one another for the best angle for a shot. At one point, press accounts of the production said that Secchiaroli was in talks to play a photographer in the film (Fellini liked to cast the actual players in Rome's various subcultures whenever possible), but that wasn't to be. He did eventually get a couple of days of work on the film, shooting portraits of the principal cast—glamour shots taken with, at Fellini's assistance, the same lighting technique that he used on the street: stark, flat, high-contrast.

With new sensations turning up in the papers virtually every day, and a direct line to the fellows who were reporting (if not instigating) them, Fellini's film in progress was never short of inspiration. But a serious question remained as to whether it would all add up to a script, let alone a film. Ennio Flaiano, for one, couldn't see how anyone could manage the trick: "It seems certain that his film will never be made," he wrote of Fellini in his diary. "Even so, Fellini never wearies of thinking about it and spends all his time talking to actors, choosing types, sending out telegrams, acquainting himself with the equivocal underbrush of Via Veneto and its surroundings. He wants to portray an unreal Rome, to reconstruct everything."

Some unrealities, though, would have to be discovered, like a lost city. And in the case of one crucial element of the film, Fellini made the discovery himself when, turning a page of an American magazine, he caught an eyeful of a curvy blonde in a photograph. "I thought, 'My God, please don't let me meet her!'" he remembered. And when the time came for him to meet her, he was even more addled.

He beheld her in the flesh for the first time in the garden of the Hotel de la Ville, just above the Spanish Steps, and even though he had by then studied her image in photographs and knew a great deal about her life, at least by reputation, he was staggered: "I was experiencing again that sense of rapt wonder, astonishment, disbelief which one feels at the sight of extraordinary creations such as the giraffe, the elephant, or the baobab."

They spoke about the movie and her role—she had lots of questions, but all he could do was stare at her body, not ogling her so much as calming himself with the thought that she was no different from anyone else: "Ah, so those are her earlobes, those are her gums, this is the skin of a human being."

In his little bit of English, the one language they shared, he found a way to speak words.

"You are my imagination come to life," he told her.

"I do not go to bed with you," she replied.

She was, of course, Anita Ekberg, and he simply *had* to have her in his movie.

In many ways, the Swedish starlet was the one person in all of Rome in 1958 who embodied the various themes and contours Fellini had in mind for the movie. She was born in 1931 in the city of Malmö, where her father was a harbormaster. At twenty, she won a hometown beauty pageant. She represented her nation in similar competitions in the United States and, on the strength of those appearances (and, to be fair, her 39-22-37 physique), she was offered a contract with Universal, which immediately set her to work on such noteworthy assignments as *Abbott and Costello Go to Mars*, *The Golden Blade* (with Rock Hudson as an Arab prince), and the short-lived TV version of *Casablanca*. Better opportunities followed, including two of the last pictures by the comedy team of

Dean Martin and Jerry Lewis, *Artists and Models* (1954) and *Hollywood or Bust* (1956).[7]

In 1956, she worked in Rome for the first time, with a small part in *War and Peace*, after which she won a Golden Globe as Most Promising Newcomer. That was also the year that she married Anthony Steel, in Italy, where, like her, he found that there were slightly more opportunities for performers of his finite gifts than back home or in Hollywood.

For the next few years, Ekberg and Steel worked steadily, if never spectacularly, on pictures that would be forgotten soon after being released. The spectacular they saved for their private life, which was of the liquor- and fury-fueled, plate-throwing, foot-stomping, scene-making sort. As the tabloid-reading world came to know, they could burst into a row at a restaurant or a party or, especially, at a late-night spot on, inevitably, Via Veneto. Images of Steel falling prey to his fondness for drink and quickness to temper were balanced by images of Ekberg alongside him, often beautifully dressed in the latest Roman fashions. (Like so many actresses visiting the city, she favored the Fontana sisters and Schuberth and often wore their clothes to premieres and press events). Her aloof air—a mere façade—led publicists to saddle her with the nickname the Iceberg.

Ekberg was the very type of woman that Fellini was always drawn toward with an almost infantile eroticism: big-bosomed, blonde, glamorous, unattainable. She was, as he said, a creature from his imagination or from a movie screen, descended to Rome in mortal form: "healthy as a shark," Fellini said of her, "emanating the heat of a summer day."

---

7 The title of the latter was a schoolboyish allusion to her bosom; as the object of Jerry's sex fantasies, Ekberg played herself.

"Oh my God," concurred Tullio Kezich, Fellini's friend and biographer, who had permission to witness firsthand the gestation of the new movie, from the script stage through production and editing to the release, "her splendor was incredible, her outsized, totally exaggerated beauty!" To marshal a bona fide sex goddess into the film—with all the personal trappings and implications she bore—was, in many ways, the very point, as Kezich would later say, of what Fellini was doing: "The idea for the film is inseparable from the idea of Anita Ekberg."

And yet, at some deeper level, the film was unimaginable without Marcello Mastroianni in the central role.[8]

Mastroianni had been a front-row spectator as his frequent costar Sophia Loren launched a Hollywood career right when the two were devloping a truly delicious on-screen rapport. The actor would recall his costar going home to study English every night after shooting, a habit that he, inveterate lazybones, took to be an enormous waste of time. "They wanted me to go, too," he recalled. "But I couldn't imagine for what. What was I supposed to do there, play a Hollywood cabdriver?" (He understood, too, that Loren was always going to be a bigger draw at the box office and, thus, earn more than he. "It's only fair," he told *Time*. "Bosoms are bosoms.")

Still, while working in Rome was fine with him, a future of earnest cabbie roles most decidedly was not. He returned briefly to the stage, at first thinking of starting his own troupe but then, almost inevitably, made his way back to Luchino Visconti. Together, Mastroianni and Visconti agreed to pursue a film that suited the director's style and would afford the actor a chance to show himself as

8 Surely the changing of the character's name from Moraldo to Marcello signaled this, if nothing else.

something other than an affable bumpkin. *Le Notti Bianche* (*White Nights*) was adapted by Visconti and Suso Cecchi d'Amico from the story of that title by Fyodor Dostoyevsky. A timorous clerk in St. Petersburg meets a despondent girl mourning the absence of her lover and slowly opens himself up to wooing her, unaware that it is doomed to end badly. Mastroianni was willing to throw his own money into it, even as the project grew in Visconti's mind from a small art film into something grander. The setting was shifted to the Italian port city of Livorno, the canals of which were expensively reconstructed at Cinecittà, and two well-known actors, Maria Schell and Jean Marais, were cast as the girl and her absent lover, also at great expense. The risks, Mastroianni explained, were calculated. Visconti, he said, "was brilliant with actors and very artistic for the festivals." And when the film came out, it was, just as he predicted, "very arty," and it was received well, winning a Silver Lion prize at the Venice Film Festival and adulatory reviews for its star, who received a Nastro d'Argento for his performance.

What it didn't win was an audience. "It didn't make a cent," Mastroianni moaned. Despite the positive reviews and festival buzz, *Le Notti Bianche* opened in September 1957 to anemic ticket sales and wasn't picked up for distribution in the United States until another four years had passed. Speaking to the Italian press in the midst of this disappointment, Mastroianni confessed, "I have no more hope. I am resigned. I'll be playing taxi drivers until the end of my days." He had another notable turn the following year, as a soft-hearted con artist who joins in with of a gang of inept robbers in Mario Monicelli's charming caper comedy *I Soliti Ignoti* (*Big Deal on Madonna Street*), and a less notable one in Jules Dassin's *La Loi* (*The Law*). But he was foundering—working, pushing, hoping, but foundering.

And then he got a call to go meet with Fellini, who was spending time at the seaside resort of Fregene. The director was familiar with his work, Mastroianni was told, and was interested in him for his next picture. It was an enticing prospect—until they met.

Fellini was encamped on the beach when Mastroianni arrived, and the first thing he told the actor was, "I need an ordinary face." Feeling belittled but holding on to his professionalism, Mastroianni asked to see a script. Fellini turned to Ennio Flaiano, who was seated under a nearby umbrella, and told him to go inside and get "the script." Flaiano returned with a batch of papers and handed them to the actor. "He handed me a folder," Mastroianni recalled,

> and I opened it. There was not the least bit of a script in it. Instead, there was one of his cartoons (Fellini made them constantly) in which a man was drawn swimming in the sea, with a long prick that reached the ocean floor, and all around it, like in an Esther Williams film, was a ballet of mermaids. I naturally blushed—no, I know, I became yellow, green, all the colors. I felt truly teased. I realized that I had demanded too much in calling for a script. What could I do? I said, "Oh, sure: it seems very interesting. Where do I sign?"

Mastroianni, like Marcello Rubini, as the fictional journalist was named, bore the world-weary, nearly defeated, cynical, opportunistic air of a modern Roman almost like an aroma. You couldn't see where the guise ended and the man began. Hired by Fellini at a moment when he wasn't sure if he would ever be anything more than a middling leading man in domestic comedies (and, so often, a taxi driver's cap), he gave off an air of being on the edge of throwing it all in for another line of work altogether, a capitulation that was, inevitably, forestalled by the advent of some new titillation or curiosity or opportunity. In many ways, the actor, like his character, was at once too weak to beat the game and too weak to quit it.

As Mastroianni himself confessed, "I am very much like Marcello. . . . We have the same hypocrisy, the same sentimental instability, the same sudden enthusiasms that always end up being drowned in boredom, the same sense of fatality. It's that way in everything, whether it be art, an interest in fast racing cars,[9] or in love. . . . We don't believe in it any more, we know the mechanism, we know exactly what is going to happen before we even start."

Fellini saw these qualities in Mastroianni right away, and he knew that the actor was perfect for a film that he described, somewhat modestly but, also, accurately, as "the adventures, by day and by night, of a hack journalist." As he would in every film that he'd make with Mastroianni, the director took steps to make the actor look less like a matinee idol than a hollowed-out wreck: "I made him lose ten kilos in weight," he confessed, "and tried everything to get him to look more sinister, to give him a more mean and menacing expression."

Not only did Mastroianni not mind being reshaped, he would positively come to relish the experience of working under Fellini's ringmaster filmmaking process:

The way he moved around the set like a friend who wasn't going to be distracted by small things was stunning. . . . The man *enjoyed* what he was doing, and that feeling was communicated to everybody. . . . Visconti had always stood to the side, like the Maestro watching his pupils recite the les-

9 In their initial conversations, Fellini and Mastroianni discovered that they both loved to drive sports cars and were constantly replacing their current rides with sexy new ones; they began a lifelong game of oneupmanship, each eagerly racing over to the other's house to show off his newest set of wheels.

sons he had taught them. Fellini was in the middle of every-thing. . . . I thought, "This is great! It's all a game as far as he's concerned!"

But one playmate left Mastroianni cold: Anita Ekberg. After Fellini had met her, he had a meeting with Mastroianni during which the director couldn't stop crowing about the goddess whom he had hired for the film, and, as Fellini recalled, the actor took a typically cynical attitude toward his rhapsodizing: "Get away with you! Really? You're not serious." When they met, Ekberg lived up to her "Iceberg" reputation, offering a hand for Mastroianni to kiss but looking away from him while he did it, then saying almost noth-ing to him over the course of a dinner. Mastroianni groused about her to Fellini, who naturally presumed that the actor felt slighted sexually by his prospective costar. Only later did he learn the real reason that Mastroianni felt an aversion to Ekberg: "She reminded him very much of a German soldier in the Wehrmacht who had once tried to make him jump up onto a lorry during a round-up." There would come a thaw between them, but it would take some weeks—and no little volume of running water—to achieve.

Other important roles—Marcello's women, his father, his intel-lectual mentor—were cast in traditional Italian fashion, which meant that the performers were chosen for their appearances and not their voices (which would be dubbed later, often by other actors, so that nuances of the dialogue could be teased out without the actors' having the burden of being photographed while speak-ing it). The most important women's parts went to Anouk Aimée, Yvonne Furneaux, Magali Noël, and Nadia Gray, who were French, French, Turkish, and Romanian, respectively, while the role of the mentor, for which Henry Fonda had been considered, was filled by the French actor Alain Cuny. For the role of Marcello's father, Fellini had a particular actor in mind and then stumbled on Annibale Ninchi, a film veteran who had almost stopped acting entirely but who bore an astonishing resemblance to Fellini's own recently deceased father.[10]

There was one big coup: For the role of a wealthy noblewoman whom Marcello served as a kind of amanuensis/boy toy, Fellini was able to persuade the actress Luise Rainer out of retirement. Rainer had won back-to-back Best Actress Oscars for *The Great Ziegfeld* (1936) and *The Good Earth* (1937), her second and third Hollywood films, before letting her career slip away with puzzling indifference and returning to Europe, where she acted only occasionally, usually on TV. She had strong opinions about the role Fellini had offered her, and she was increasingly insistent on writing her own dialogue and adding complications and nuances to her character (she *had* once been married to the playwright Clifford Odets). "She was so full of ideas," Fellini recalled, "it reminded me of me." Perturbed but respectful, he listened to her suggestions for rewrites—which eventually spread beyond her own role into the entire film. In the end, it was too much: he took advantage of the fact that the episode involving her character could be removed from the narrative and did just that, erasing the entire sequence from the script and bidding her adieu not very long after sitting beside her at a publicity function announcing her arrival in his cast. "I cannot say," Fellini confessed, "that I was exactly heartbroken."

Otherwise, he had his pick of performers. Applying a combination of his neorealist taste for nonactors and his love of the infinite variety of human faces, he seemed to, in Kezich's words, "have promised a part to half of Rome." He found a variety of players in

---

10 Ninchi would play the father of the protagonist in Fellini's next feature as well.

the demimondes that the film would depict. From the Via Margutta art scene he plucked two comely young painters, Anna Salvator and the headline-making gadabout Novella Parigini. From the louche worlds he'd traveled with Pier Paolo Pasolini during the research for *Le Notti di Cabiria* and the new film, he selected Gio Stajano, one of the first openly gay semicelebrities (and, later, transsexuals) in Rome. He heard about a young Italian singer who had something of the air of Elvis Presley, and he hired him—a fellow by the name of Adriano Celentano.[11] He found journalists from the Roman and international press to fill out the scenes of press conferences. He cast Lex Barker, a B-movie actor best known as a late-in-the-game Tarzan and more recently the star of some low-budget Hollywood on the Tiber action pictures, as the semi-washed-up Hollywood muscleman engaged to Ekberg's screen goddess. The great Italian clown Polidor performed in a nightclub scene. The Italian pop star Laura Betti appeared at a party. The German chanteuse Nico (who would in a few years be selected by Andy Warhol to front The Velvet Underground) had a largish role as a model with an aristocratic boyfriend. And about fifteen or twenty people with noble titles or ancient family names (including Ruspoli, Orsini, Hohenlohe, Paolozzi, and Aligheri) swelled the ranks of partyers in nightclubs, café terraces, a castle, an orgy. For a key small role, a waitress in a seaside restaurant who would come to represent innocence in the increasingly foggy mind of the protagonist, he chose a fourteen-year-old newcomer, Valeria Ciangottini. In some important ways, the film was shaping up as a documentary. Fellini would later grouse that the outside world thought that his fantasy vision of Roman life was factual, but in his casting, especially, the

11 Who would go on to be one of Italy's all-time biggest-selling recording artists and, almost incidentally, a popular film comedian.

line he drew between the dream world and the real world was, at the very least, perforated by his own hand.

Surely the greatest instance of life-imitating-art-imitating-life that would come out of the movie was a single word: *Paparazzo*. It was simply a name, selected by Fellini and Flaiano for the character of the photographer with whom the journalist Marcello teamed up, a mostly nondescript part to be played by the experienced but unheralded actor Walter Santesso. The origin of the word would be subject, in the decades to come, to all sorts of conjecture: "The term was a contraction of *pappataci* (mosquito) and *ragazzi* (boys or guys)," suggested one such etymological effort. (Throw in *razzo* as well, meaning a burst or flash like that of a camera bulb.)

But the truth was more pedestrian. Flaiano had been reading *By the Ionian Sea*, a travelogue written by the English novelist George Gissing in 1901 and first translated into Italian in the 1950s. In it, Gissing described a hotel, the Albergo Centrale, in Catanzaro, a town in the very sole of the boot of the Italian peninsula. The hotel was operated by a man who bore the name Paparazzo—which may have derived from the Greek word *papasaratsis*, or "saddlemaker," and which was peculiar to the town. Flaiano suggested it to Fellini, who heard in the word the sound of an insect that you couldn't shoo ("buzzing . . . hovering, darting, stinging" as he said), and they selected it. During production, the technicians working on the film would expand the use of the word from the one character to the mass of faux photographers, taking the singular name Paparazzo and pluralizing it to *paparazzi* to refer to the entire corps of player-photographers, who were choreographed by Fellini in a writhing, snapping, shouting mass. The word *paparazzi* was not in the script, not even once, and yet it evolved from a character's name to a backstage nickname to a universal name for the phenomenon of a provocative pack of privacy-invading photographers almost as soon as the film was released.

The news that Fellini was up to something new and that it had something to do with the overheated life that was splashed in all the tabloids was a cause for great excitement and, inevitably, headlines. Speculation about who had been cast, which incidents would be included, and what sort of treatment the Via Veneto set could expect from Fellini and his collaborators became a staple of newspapers and magazines, almost from the week that production began. It reached an absurd apex when a fire struck a hotel off the Via Veneto in June 1959, and rumors circulated that not only was the blaze to be included in Fellini's film but that it might even have been started to fuel interest in the movie, which was madness.[12]

Shooting began on March 16, 1959, on a set at Cinecittà that reproduced the stairway inside the dome of the Basilica of St. Peter. Ekberg, wearing a dress that costume designer Piero Gherardi had cribbed from the scandalous *linea cardinale* of vestment-like dresses that the Fontana sisters had designed for Ava Gardner, was meant to scurry up the stairs with Mastroianni in dogged—and exhausted—pursuit. She was so game and fit for the effort that crew members joked that she should enter the Giro d'Italia bicycle race. As the spring weather softened, production moved on to several outdoor locations in and around the city, including the ancient

12 A handful of other films on similar themes were being made at around the same time: Mauro Bolognini's *La Notte Brava* (*The Big Night*), based on Pier Paolo Pasolini's novel and script about youth-gone-wild; Mario Monicelli's *Risate di Gioia* (*Burst of Joy*, but released in the United States as *The Passionate Thief*), in which Ben Gazzara played a pickpocket on a New Year's Eve spree with Anna Magnani in tow; and Mario Camerini's *Via Margutta* (*Run with the Devil* in the United States), a light melodrama set in the art world. None had any significant resonance before or after their release, however.

Termi di Caracalla baths, just south of the Colosseum, which had been transformed into an outdoor nightclub, complete with a bathhouse theme that included waiters dressed in slaves' tunics.

Given all the publicity accorded the film in progress, location shooting proved a real challenge. Fellini still smarted, years after the fact, from an incident that occurred along Via Veneto during one of the very few times footage was actually shot there. It was a scene of Marcello driving along with the high-born Maddalena, his sometime mistress, played by Anouk Aimée. Even though the production was only permitted to shoot on Via Veneto between two and six a.m., dispensation was given for one night to shoot while the street was alive with scene makers—provided that it was done *once,* and without pause. Fellini and his crew concocted a plan to have a motorcade with Mastroianni (at the wheel, naturally) in the last car and the camera in the one in front of it; they would take *seven* circuits around the block on which the Hotel Excelsior sat, without stopping, to be sure they had enough usable footage.

It was complicated, but not impossible, and, inevitably, it drew a crowd, which wasn't in and of itself a problem. But in front of the Excelsior, Fellini recalled, there was "a bloke with a little beret, and a face as dark-skinned as a Saracen" who, each time the director's car passed, would "shout an absolutely unrepeatable oath at me in Roman dialect." It happened, Fellini recalled, "four, five, six times: The minute I reached the traffic lights, this Saracen eyed me from a distance with a sneer, looking forward to the pleasure of insulting me again. Then, as I drew level with him, bang, every time he unleashed this word, always the same one, but uttered with a crescendo of enthusiasm." Fellini couldn't interrupt the apparatus of the filming to deal with the fellow, so he resigned himself to retorting in kind: "telling him where he could get off, using indecorous expressions and gestures which could only be justified by the impotent rage of that moment." The minute the camera stopped rolling, however, he sought his revenge: "I asked a couple of the burliest stagehands to come with me and ran in the direction of the Excelsior to sort him out." But the fellow had departed. "To this day," Fellini said years later, "I have the image of him imprinted on my memory, little beret, the lot, and I have not given up hope that I shall meet him one of these days."

In late March, the crew set up at the Trevi Fountain for the scene in which Ekberg, repeating her own adventure of the previous year, would wade into the coin-filled waters and beckon Mastroianni to join her. It was, by all accounts, cold, but the actors would do all the work in the nearly freezing fountain themselves (for the close-ups, both Ekberg and Mastroianni were equipped with wading boots, which she, hardy Swede, rejected). In between, they huddled over thermoses of coffee and hot chocolate and flasks of hooch and got rubdowns to keep their muscles loose. And they did it all in front of a throng of onlookers that grew in number steadily even as the night ticked toward dawn.[13]

Ekberg, according to witnesses, was an absolute trouper in the scene that would stand as the very apex of her career. "She was a horse," remembered Tullio Kezich. "She plunged into that cold fountain without hesitation or fuss. She was so Swedish and healthy; she never caught a cold. Mastroianni was terrorized at the idea of getting wet." In fact, Mastroianni was half of the mind that Ekberg was goading him. "As a child she had gotten used to diving into icy water," he recalled. "I think it was meant as sort of a challenge to me, but what the hell did I care about how she had grown up in Sweden?" He made it through in his own fashion: "I was half-drunk with vodka by the time we got finished."

13 Among the mob one night was the poet Giuseppe Ungaretti, who then lived nearby.

One witness to the night's work had an especially close connection to it: Pierluigi Praturlon, who had been hired by Fellini
as the stills photographer for the production and was granted the
extremely unusual privilege of being permitted, after Fellini had
yelled, "Cut!," to ask the actors and crew members to stay within
a scene so that he could shoot it. As Kezich recalled, "As soon as
a sequence was shot, Pierluigi would howl like a drowning man,
'Photograph!' That would start a game that was to continue for
the duration of the film: The technicians would pretend to ignore
him; Martelli, the camera operator, would threaten to turn out the
lights; and Fellini would shout picturesque insults at him." That
night at the Trevi Fountain, though, Pierluigi got his way, as he
almost always did, meaning that he took photos (and immortal
ones) of the making of a movie scene inspired by a real event that
he had captured with his camera not one year prior. Dizzying.[14]

Fortunately for the chill-prone Mastroianni and his excitable
director, little else of the film was shot in public or even outdoors.
Although there would have been some advantages to shooting on
the actual Via Veneto, it wasn't as easy as that might sound. For one
thing, the famed chestnut trees that lined the streets would make
it difficult for Fellini to get the panoramic shots of a typical hectic
night that he envisioned. For another, the production never failed
to draw crowds—including, inevitably, the Via Veneto photogra-

---

14 And if *that* wasn't sufficiently mind-boggling: the finished Trevi Fountain
sequence would become so iconic that even the *shooting* of it grew into a legend. In his
1974 film *C'eravamo Tanto Amati* (*We All Loved Each Other So Much*), Ettore Scola included
a scene in which two of his (fictional) characters would unexpectedly encounter each
other after years of separation on the set of the Trevi Fountain scene in *La Dolce Vita*.
Charmingly, the roles of Mastroianni and Fellini were played in Scola's film by no less
than Mastroianni and Fellini—a stupendous case, if the math was right, of art imitating life making art imitating life.

phers who were, at least in their alter egos, part of the scenes that would be shot there.

During preproduction, Fellini had convinced Rizzoli that the best way to shoot Via Veneto would be to rebuild it at Cinecittà, to construct a fake Via Veneto that could be used under controlled conditions. Piero Gherardi, who served as art director as well as costumier, oversaw construction of the upper end of Via Veneto in Cinecittà's largest soundstage, the 40-by-80-meter Studio 5. The completed set, down to the tiniest detail, which Fellini himself confirmed with sketches and photographs of his own making, was inaugurated with a press event, attended, of course, by the actual Via Veneto photographers. As Fellini explained to reporters, his set offered numerous advantages: there would be no worry about crowds or weather; he could shoot even nighttime scenes during normal working hours; there were no tree limbs to slalom through; and the set was not only *larger* than the actual Via Veneto setting but, crucially, *flatter*. Via Veneto was steeply inclined in its rise from Piazza Barberini to Porta Pinciana. But Fellini's Via Veneto was much easier to stroll along and, in the director's view, superior to the real one. "Working there," he later said, "I got so used to it that my dislike for the real Via Veneto increased still further and will never disappear, I believe. When I pass the Café de Paris nowadays, I cannot help feeling that the real Via Veneto is that other one, long since scrapped in Studio 5, that its proportions were more perfect and its whole outlook more attractive. I am still tempted, when in the real street, to assume the despotic authority I was entitled to in the fictitious one."

Another touch of realism would be the notorious orgy scene, during which the debased Marcello attended a drunken party with a jaded group of nobles that climaxed in a striptease by a woman celebrating the end of her marriage. According to Fellini, when

word got out that he would be, in a sense, restaging the Rugantino scandal of the previous fall, he was overwhelmed by actresses
wanting the part, which was sure to be attention-grabbing. In the
end, he cast Nadia Gray because she possessed an air of propriety:
"It had to be shocking, and it could be shocking only if done by
somebody ladylike."

Initially, Fellini imagined that Gray's character would also be
ridden by Marcello like a donkey, but she refused, and he could see
the point of it. Then he decided that she should be wearing a white
bra and white panties under her black cocktail dress. Once again,
she balked, and, once again, he relented. He won only one point
with her, insisting that she remove her bra from underneath her
blouse. When she claimed it couldn't be done, he demonstrated it
for her and she assented.

Another of the most memorable scenes in the film would be the
climax, filmed on the beach at Fregene and featuring the corpse of
some sort of sea monster washed up on the shore for a debauched
party of Romans, including Marcello, to ponder in the dawn light.[15]
Fellini would always claim that the inspiration came from his boyhood: a huge, deformed fish was pulled out of the sea near Rimini,
and he was galvanized by the images of it that ran in the newspapers. He dreamed of sea monsters his whole life, he explained,
and there was some personal excavation going on in depicting one
on-screen. It would've been natural, then, for him to be particular about the prop that Piero Gherardi's team produced for the
sequence, but that wasn't the case. He'd allowed the crew to create
several possible creatures, a decomposed jellyfish and a partially
devoured whale among them. On shooting day, he decided to leave

15 Just seven years after the fact, the image of that dead beast on the shore couldn't
help but remind Italians of the body of Wilma Montesi, whose presumed murder was
still making headlines and would never be solved, legally or otherwise.

the decision to Gherardi, and he was satisfied with the choice: a large white ray, ten feet or so in diameter, with bright, staring eyes. It was, per Fellini, "the most shocking," and it pleased him.

He didn't always get what he wanted. For one sequence, he hoped to use the song "*Die Moritat von Mackie Messer*" ("Mack the Knife") from *The Threepenny Opera*, but the music publishers insisted on too steep a price, and so he had Nino Rota write a piece "inspired" by the original. He wanted the poet Vincenzo Cardarelli, the long-time fixture of the Via Veneto, to appear as himself sitting in his hat and coat on a café terrace on the set at Cinecittà, but was stunned to learn, just days before the poet would be needed, that he had died; a look-alike Cardarelli can be glimpsed in the finished film. Giulietta Masina might have played a small part—she had appeared in all but one of his feature films to date—but she was abroad for most of the production, shooting a film for director Julien Duvivier in Germany.

And, despite the rumor-churning of the tabloids, he never did sleep with Anita Ekberg (though pestered by a journalist about the matter he said, "Please tell everyone that I have!"). She eventually thawed to him (and to Mastroianni, with whom she also, apparently, did not sleep) and came to appreciate his spirit of playful collaboration. At first, when he dubbed her Anitona and made a great show of doting on her, she was wary. "Federico, you're making a fool of me," she said on the set one day. But he stayed steady for her as she endured private travails (she divorced Anthony Steel in May 1959, just weeks after shooting the Trevi Fountain scene, declaring him "insanely jealous" in her filing). And when her work on the film ended, she sat in her car just off the set, not wanting to go. "She gripped the steering wheel and cried," Fellini remembered. "She did not want it all to be over."

Mastroianni, too, was reluctant to let go of the film. It was clear to him that there was something extraordinary about what he and Fellini were doing. (Not entirely coincidentally, Mastroianni was briefly estranged from his wife, Flora, during the shoot—he actually bunked with Fellini for a time—but moved back in before too much damage had been done.) Toward the end of the filming, even though he was a man without a trace of pretension about art or life or himself, Mastroianni found himself taken by gravitas. "I have the impression," he told Tulio Kezich, "that this film is changing something in my personality as a man. I know it's a little ridiculous to say it, but I feel already that it will be a key episode in my life." As he put it later, "It was like I was being administered a truth serum. Until then I was hiding my true self even from myself. I analyzed myself. I discovered many faults but also some virtues. The sum total was not so bad. I never hid from myself again."

24 — "Poor You"

La Dolce Vita finished shooting in late August 1959, five months or so from the day production had begun. It was a remarkable pace considering the amount of footage that was being shot (one very preliminary cut topped ten hours), the elaborate nature of so many of the sequences, and the loosey-goosey manner in which Fellini tended to treat the pages of the script, which were, in his view, mere outlines for what would eventually be filmed on set. Editing, scoring, and dubbing would take months, in large part because Fellini was still playing with the sequence of the narrative, not to mention the structure of individual scenes. When he delivered a rough cut to his producers, he got his first taste of how deeply divisive a thing he had made. According to Fellini's coscenarist Brunello Rondi, Angelo Rizzoli "understood absolutely nothing of what he had seen," and feared that the film would not only fail commercially but would be accused of defaming the Italian public. Peppino Amato, who'd originally brought the film to Rizzoli's attention, listened to his coproducer's lament and responded, Rondi reported, "screaming at the top of his lungs, 'Angelo, you don't understand shit! Fellini has done a great and magnificent thing!' And for weeks afterward, while Rizzoli refused to see Fellini, Amato would keep telling Federico, 'You've done a great and magnificent thing, absolutely great and magnificent!'"

The film premiered for the press, the movie world, and assorted glitterati at Rome's Cinema Fiamma, just down the hill from the American embassy on Via Veneto, on February 3, 1960.[1] The reception was mixed: a short but vigorous round of applause, peppered with catcalls, and muted reactions from the critics and commentators in the audience, which included Alberto Moravia, Italo Calvino, and Pier Paolo Pasolini. (Sophia Loren, leaving the screening, stopped to commiserate with Fellini: "Poor you: What do you have inside of you?") The following night, Fellini, Ekberg, Mastroianni, Giulietta Masina, and others took a train to Milan to present the film in that far more upright (and uptight) city. By the time they got there, the word of the movie's scandalous content had spread throughout the nation, and the antagonists were wait-

---

1 Late that very same night, after partying at the Rancho Grande nightclub, the popular comic singer Fred Buscaglione, who was at the time all over TV alongside Anita Ekberg in a commercial encouraging Italians to drink more beer, was killed at the wheel of his purple Ford Thunderbird convertible after plowing it into a garbage truck near the Villa Borghese—a *Dolce Vita*–ish death if ever there was one.

ing, knives sharpened. After the screening, the ovation was mixed with shouts of "Coward!," "Vagabond!," "Scoundrel!," "Communist!," "Disgusting!," and "Shame on you!" Fellini had to be led through a wall of angry faces by bodyguards, and he was spit upon by one incensed viewer.

Reviewers and commentators were equally embroiled. The film was picked up as a cudgel by both the left and the right, Communists and Catholics, partisans of neorealism and proponents of a new kind of filmmaking. "*La Dolce Vita* was seismic," said Tullio Kezich. "It ruined old friendships and built new ones." There were public forums about the film in Rome, where a turnaway crowd of more than two thousand showed up for one particular debate, and in Milan, where a small sect of Jesuit monks announced support for it and created a scandal that roiled for weeks in the Catholic press. In the Italian parliament, right-wing politicians denounced the film, the people who made it, the whole of show business: "Projects of this kind should be crushed immediately," went one such tirade, "for they are highly corrosive and worm their way into the lives of young people with their images of easy, materialistic life without ideals"—which was exactly the opposite of what the film intended and, really, achieved. In the Vatican's official *Osservatore Romano*, an article entitled "*Basta!*" ("Enough!") declared the film "an incentive to evil, to sin, to vice" and argued that "it's time that the audience finally shouts 'enough' to the authorities who protect the public well-being and the respect for the good name of the populace." There were explicit pleas to pull the film from theaters, many written by a would-be censor who proudly admitted that he hadn't seen it: "One doesn't need to see filth to condemn it," he boasted.

As Fellini was walking through the Piazza di Spagna one day, a Mercedes-Benz screeched to a halt near him, and an old woman came out of a rear door and shouted, "It would have been better if you'd tied a stone to your throat and thrown yourself into the deepest ocean than give such scandal to people!" In Padua, where he went to attend the local premiere, Fellini was startled to see a sign hanging on the door of a large church near the central train station, "a big white square framed with a black line, like a death announcement. I thought I recognized something about it and went closer. To my surprise, it read, 'We pray for the soul of the public sinner Federico Fellini.'"

At the same time, the left was equally adamant in support of *La Dolce Vita*. Moravia, Calvino, and, especially, Pasolini, wrote about the moral and aesthetic quality of the film, and their knotty thoughts were widely quoted in the tabloids that feasted on the controversy. (Moravia was particularly forceful in his praise; in a review entitled, prophetically, "*Il Satyricon di Fellini*," he declared, "Fellini has made his best film and one of the most important and significant of recent years.") Fellini had been castigated by some Communist critics for moving away from neorealism in *La Strada* and *Le Notti di Cabiria*, but those same voices rallied behind *La Dolce Vita* for what they saw as its unflinching critique of material excess and bourgeois hedonism. Fellini remembered one young partisan passing him in the street and signaling his solidarity with "Bravo! Keep it up!" "Keep *what* up?" he wondered.

Among Italian directors, there were similar divisions. For the older guard, the film was too fantastical, polemical, manipulative, and, worst, gossipy. Luchino Visconti said of Fellini's vision of a bored and licentious upper class, "Those are aristocrats as seen by my valet." Vittorio De Sica, dining in Fellini's favorite restaurant, Cesarina, declared the film "boorish, the dream of a small-towner." But Pasolini ceased writing for one particular magazine when its editors decided that they would come out against the film, and Antonioni, who had reason to be jealous of Fellini as his own breakthrough masterwork, *L'Avventura*, was in release almost simultaneously, spoke for seemingly all filmmakers when he sat still after first seeing *La Dolce Vita* and asked no one in particular, "*Now* what are we going to do?" The debate raged for months. As the weekly newsmagazine *Il Reporter* put it, "One could almost say that Italians don't have anything else to think about."

Fellini was truly appalled by the ruckus his film had occasioned. In an article that appeared under his byline in *L'Europeo,* he said, "I'm sorry. These polemics fill me with sorrow. I'm a storyteller. I've told a fable, a fable of our times. And now I see that this fable has provoked interpretations in Parliament, a painful division among Catholics, the disdain of the guardians of public morals.... They tell me, 'You should be happy: All this fuss means that you've hit the nail on the head.' I respond: 'No. I'm not happy. I didn't want to condemn anyone, nor did I ever wish to pity anyone.'"

And as the war of words carried on and on, he remained a somewhat stunned observer of it all. In a typical statement distancing himself from the insane controversy, he told a journalist:

> What I intended was to show the state of Rome's *soul*, a way of being a people. What it *became* was a scandalous report, a fresco of a street and a society.... The left-wing press played it up as headline reportage on Rome, but it didn't have to be Rome; it could have been Bangkok or a thousand other cities. I intended it as a report on Sodom and Gomorrah, a trip into anguish and despair. I intended for it to be a document, not a documentary.

He revealed to another journalist that the film and the response it incurred were complete mysteries to him: "It's terrifying to realize that I don't have the secret for *La Dolce Vita* any more than anyone else." And he replied to yet another journalist's questions about how he conceived the film with a combination of confession and excuse: "It's like getting me to talk about, I don't know, about secondary school. I did it, of course, but it's not my fault!"

Angelo Rizzoli may have initially feared alienating the public with the explosive depictions of Roman high life in the film. And the polemics surrounding it likely did little to settle his nerves. But the box-office receipts for the film were immense. On the day it opened in Milan, Fellini saw a mob assembled outside the theater, with policemen wrangling it, and he assumed there was some sort of fire or medical emergency. But, no: the crowd was there to see *La Dolce Vita*; show after show was sold out, and tickets were being resold on the street at premium prices.

The response in Rome and the other large cities to which the film made its way was just as feverish. It was so hard to get tickets in the biggest cities, in fact, that eager moviegoers would travel to smaller cities hoping to find provincial cinemas with available seats.[2] At the Fiamma, where it debuted, *La Dolce Vita* was setting box-office records well into the summer. Rizzoli may have been frightened, but he had the consolation of all those ticket sales to soothe him—more than 2 *billion* lire in Italy alone.[3] And the clamor wasn't limited to the film's homeland. Wherever it played throughout 1960 and 1961, *La Dolce Vita* was a smash hit, earning more than $20 million combined in foreign territories other than the United States. And when it arrived in America, in April 1961, it would

2 A sense of the commotion the film caused throughout Italy would be imparted in Pietro Germi's 1961 film *Divorce Italian Style*, in which the men (and only men) of a small Sicilian town turn out to see what all the scandal was about, among them a local nobleman played by . . . Marcello Mastroianni.

3 Nearly $3 million in 1960 dollars, and more than $24 million in 2016.

gross more than $10 million, an astounding sum for a three-hour-long subtitled film.[4]

Whenever asked about this stunning commercial success, Fellini readily reminded the world that he wasn't a beneficiary of it: "It made many people rich, but I wasn't one of them. Angelo Rizzoli gave me a gift—a gold watch."

The initial American reviews were mixed, although the ones that were positive were overwhelmingly so. A photo feature in *Life* promoted the film with the headline "Angry Cry Against a Sinful City," which surely sold a few tickets. In *The New York Times*, Bosley Crowther declared it, "a titanic film. . . . an awesome picture, licentious in content but moral in its attitude. . . . one of the most important and serious works made for the screen." Hollis Alpert, writing in *Saturday Review*, called it "the most brilliant of all the movies that have attempted to portray the modern temper." Even Hollywood insiders acclaimed the film. William Wyler pronounced it "a poignant social document about a phase of modern society. . . . a great, great film."

But there were dissenters, and more than a few of them. Writing in *Showbill*, Andrew Sarris said the film was "as bloated as the fish that terminates the orgy sequence." An unsigned review in *Time* was even sharper, calling it "decadent, an artistic failure" and, after quoting Fellini's assertion that the film held "a thermometer to a sick world," surmised that "he has simply taken his own temperature."

---

4. In both the United States and the United Kingdom, dubbed versions of the film were prepared and released, but they foundered at the box office, where the original was preferred by a wide margin. Distributors in both countries theorized that audiences suspected that the subtitled version was the racier, even though the films were, save for the dubbing, identical.

And then there was the lunatic response of Hedda Hopper, who fetishistically described what she found objectionable in the film in a way that actually made it sound great: "It was made in Rome, features homosexuals, Lesbians, a wealthy nymphomaniac who makes love in the miserable quarters of a Roman prostitute, an arid intellectual who kills his two innocent children and then himself, effete nobles, aimless artists and writers, and repulsive orgies too sordid to write about."

Before its explosive American debut, the film played at the Cannes Film Festival, where there was a crush to get into the premiere—rumors of a black market in tickets spread, and Roberto Rossellini was among those shut out. The film evoked a typically Cannesian chorus of applause mixed with boos. "Why would you applaud your own ruin," asked one French critic. It wasn't clear to some that *La Dolce Vita* was even the best Italian film in the competition: Michelangelo Antonioni's *L'Avventura* was also shown. Rizzoli threw a boozy party after the screening at a nearby villa; Fellini, Mastroianni, and several of the actresses were there, but not Ekberg—another disappointment. Despite the cloudy prospects, the jury, led by novelist Georges Simenon and including novelist Henry Miller, awarded Fellini's film the top prize, the Palme d'Or. *"Viva il cinema!"* he shouted as he accepted. Back in Rome, the movie won the Nastro d'Argento prizes from the press for Mastroianni's performance, Best Original Story, and Best Production Design, and Fellini was named Best Director in the David di Donatello awards, the Italian equivalent of the Oscars. In the United States, the following year, *La Dolce Vita* was named Best Foreign Language Film by the New York Film Critics Circle, and in early 1962 it was nominated for Academy Awards for Best Director, Best Original Screenplay, and, in the

black-and-white categories, Best Art Direction and Best Costume Design, the latter being the only prize it won.[5]

To anyone who didn't have a stake in Italian polemics, it was completely obvious that Fellini had created an absolute masterpiece.

La Dolce Vita was a teeming work, with hundreds of incidents
and characters and costumes and melodies and sequences of dialogue and behavior, and yet it managed to seem as pointed, precise,
and intimate as heart surgery. Fellini's characteristic carnival of
images, sounds, and impressions made it something of a grab bag,
but he had utterly rid the film of anything that he didn't want in it.
It was as thoroughgoing a work of art as the cinema had ever seen.
If one measure of aesthetic greatness is mastery over not what is
included in the finished work but over what is excluded, then *La
Dolce Vita* achieved it.

Inevitably, it would be taken as a portrait—if not an indictment—
of a culture and a time. And the film did range up and down and
through the various strata of Italian society with a gaze of horror,
even when it clearly luxuriated in the extravagance, beauty, and,
yes, vulgarity on display. Fellini was the first important artist to
appreciate every aspect of the hyperactive, gorgeous, superficial
world that had sprung up in Rome in that time. That also meant,
almost inevitably, that he was among the first to condemn it all.

Ultimately, though, he was less interested in the culture than
in one man. The film is an exposé of the soul of Marcello Rubini,
a would-be author turned gossip columnist (and, eventually,

5 Perhaps because the infighting around the film never quite died down, *La Dolce
Vita* had *not* been selected the year before, when it was eligible, as the official Italian
entry for the Best Foreign Language Film prize. That honor went to Gillo Pontecorvo's
Holocaust drama *Kapo*, which lost in the final voting to Ingmar Bergman's *The Virgin
Spring*.

publicist), the owner of a sporty but small car and an apartment under repair in an unfashionable neighborhood, a man with a live-in girlfriend whose complete devotion doesn't keep him from sleeping with other women. His downfall—less a collapse than an erosion—is the spine of the film and, at least in a sense, is a self-indictment on the part of the director and screenwriters who created him.

Marcello begins the film in a helicopter, flying above a Roman aqueduct with a statue of Christ dangling below (a cunning depiction of the three ages of Rome: imperial, Christian, and modern). The film sees him decay and sink from that point, if not always in a straight downward line: a prostitute's basement flat, the dome of St. Peter's Basilica, the nightclubs and sidewalks of Via Veneto, a church organ loft, a lighting tower at a mobile TV broadcast site, a high-rise apartment terrace, the nooks and crannies of an ancient castle high on a crag, and, finally, a beachfront, where he literally drops to his knees, hopeless, defeated, lost.

In his decline, he is completely alone, and yet he is surrounded by a host, indeed, by *hosts*.

There are his women: the chilly yet sensual heiress Maddalena; the frothy sex kitten Sylvia; the suicidally possessive Emma; the American painter Jane, who takes him by the hand in the dark and to whose advances he succumbs because why not; the seaside café waitress Paola, who looks like an angel and may be one; the girls around town whom he knows because it is his job to know them, and he is awfully fond of at least some aspects of his job.

There are his professional colleagues and contacts: the omnipresent Paparazzo, always begging for a leg up; the producers, headwaiters, and night-crawlers on whom he depends for scoops and access; the swells and movie people and cabaret dancers whom he writes about (or, just as often, doesn't) and who are flattered or, more vividly, incensed by his words. There is Steiner, his friend and role model, whose heart he really doesn't know. And there is his father, who, likewise, is a stranger to him.

But no one is more remote to him than himself. As played by Mastroianni, with world-weariness and impeccable style, Marcello is, in the terms of the time, an existential antihero, removed emotionally and intellectually from the goings-on around him, including his own words and deeds, even as he stands smack-dab in the center, steeping in it all and, in the final phase, instigating it.

His self-descriptions, even at high moments, are utterly damning. "I'm making a mistake. We're all making a mistake," he tells Sylvia as he wades into the Trevi Fountain. Later, he confesses to Steiner, "I'm wasting time. I can't manage anything anymore. Once I had ambitions but maybe I'm losing everything. I forgot everything." And, at the last, on his knees on the seashore, meekly, resignedly, in response to Paola's gestures of friendship and purity and hope: "I don't understand. . . . I can't hear."

It would be hard to picture the sweet Moraldo of *I Vitelloni* in such a wretched state—all while surrounded by opulence, decadence, sensuality, sensation, money, opportunity. Marcello was in the unenviable position of the man who got everything he wanted and lost everything he had, which was among the reasons that Fellini and Flaiano always believed *La Dolce Vita* to be a deeply moral film about the fate of humanity in a fallen—and falling faster and faster with each passing moment—world.

On the level of film craft, the thing that Fellini and his crew made was a marvel, a symphony of images, sounds, motion, and, especially, light: the high-contrast black-and-white photography of Otello Martelli, the director's favored cinematographer, bore a frank starkness and an oily sheen, at once capturing Marcello's world as if in newsprint and sheathing it from being fully revealed. The production design of Piero Gherardi was merry and cluttered and, in a way that Fellini favored, not fully finished: gantries and scaffolding and rubble were everywhere, even in the homes of the wealthy. And Gherardi's Oscar-winning costumes captured Italian—and, especially, Roman—fashion at its historic height: not just Ekberg's vestmentlike dress, cribbed from the Fontana sisters' *linea cardinale*, but Mastroianni's suits straight out of the Brioni showroom, as well as a couple of massive sculptural gowns of the sort that Emilio Schuberth and Roberto Capucci favored and which reminded Fellini of swathing or a cocoon.

The most prominent site in the film might have seemed to be Via Veneto, but in fact very little time was spent in either the real street or its Cinecittà doppelganger. The real street could be seen several times, fleetingly: a brief nighttime driving sequence (the fruit of Fellini's run-in with the obstreperous onlooker); the dawn encounter between Sylvia and Marcello, still waterlogged from their moment in the Trevi Fountain, and Robert, her boyfriend, drunk from the night's revels and sufficiently riled to beat them both. Mainly, the faux Via Veneto was on display as a meeting place, a workstation, a traffic jam, a playground, a battlefield. In almost every scene of the film, Marcello was accompanied by or encountered someone he knew from those few small blocks of the city, which spit out a certain stripe of person like an assembly line: movie stars, businessmen, slumming nobles, pretty girls, and those who depended on them for a living.

More than it did the city, the film traversed a variety of layers and classes of Roman society, circa 1959: show folk, intellectuals, fashion models, tycoons, artists, prostitutes, aristocrats, journalists, and ordinary workaday waiters, doctors, priests, and homemakers—plus a helping of countryside peasants cruelly gulled by a phony miracle. It wasn't a complete anatomy of Italian culture, but it was as thoroughgoing as a feature film, even a three-hour one, could hope to be, and the picture it painted wasn't, in sum, very flattering.

The paparazzi (referred to repeatedly in the script as "photo-reporters") could reasonably claim to be the most aggrieved of all Romans depicted in the film—other than the protagonist himself. They were shown as intrusive, maniacal, scheming, greedy, crude, pugnacious, opportunistic, bloodthirsty, and, in the scene in which they accost Steiner's wife, cruel and heartless. "Guys, some compassion please, at least this one time," begs the police commissioner as the woman innocently returns home to a scene that will devastate her. Naturally, they ignore him, dancing around her as if she were just another pretty hopeful arrived in the big city to make her fortune. "Did you mistake me for an actress," she asks, slightly flustered. None has the courage to answer. And for all their pushiness, Paparazzo and his buddies are absent from all the best moments, such as Sylvia's impromptu bath in the Trevi Fountain.

What a thing to have missed. Appropriate to the chilly conditions in which it was filmed, the scene is entirely chaste. Marcello can't bring himself to kiss Sylvia even as she closes her eyes and lifts her chin to him, expectantly. The roaring of the fountain, the marble statuary, the predawn air, the vision of a goddess fallen to earth, the nagging sense of his own insignificance: it all combines to freeze his ardor, his daring, his zeal.

Yet the moment would be recognized immediately and would stand for decades as one of the most erotic scenes ever presented in the cinema—a reverie, a dream come to life, a true coupling of object and subject, divine and mortal, masculine and feminine, fantasy and reality. Ekberg, undulant and ample and alluring, and Mastroianni, bladelike and dashing and (at least to a point) game, were visually perfect—living creatures in a marble tableau with water as their medium of communion, transformation, exchange. In its palpably gorgeous textures, its almost tactile physicality, its luxurious sensuality, and the sense it imparted to viewers of witnessing something profound, elemental, and permanent, it carried echoes of a work of art that stood not a mile away: Michelangelo's *Creation of Adam* on the ceiling of the Sistine Chapel, another immortal depiction of the divine and the human almost but not quite touching.

The other moment that everyone who saw the film would remember would be the final scene: the booze-steeped, sex-bored, holloweyed decadents, led by Marcello in the white suit that replaced his more businesslike reporter's ensemble, staggering onto the beach and beholding the dead sea monster that was a clear metaphor for the state of their collective soul. Bedraggled, insensate, apathetic, Marcello was, himself, beached and moribund. Not even the happy sight of Paola, the young waitress who once appeared to be an agent of salvation to him, could raise his spirit above the miserable mire into which it had sunk. If his near tryst with Sylvia was a moment of divinity almost touching a man, this abortive encounter was proof that he had flung himself out of grace and into a fen from which there was no escape—a self-inflicted damnation, a moral suicide, a living death: the "sweet life" indeed.

The film echoed in popular culture for years. A fashionable Beverly Hills bistro dubbed La Dolce Vita became a favorite of Frank Sinatra and his Rat Pack chums, and their political pal, John F. Kennedy, dined there (it was said that the restaurant's namesake movie was Mrs. Kennedy's favorite). Bob Dylan sang suggestively about Anita Ekberg on his second album, in 1963, and namedropped *La Dolce Vita* outright on his fourth, the following year. In time, even for people who didn't know that it had been the title of a film, the very phrase became synonymous with high living, with a certain fashionable veneer, and, most of all, with Rome. For decades afterward, images of Ekberg and Mastroianni in the Trevi Fountain became as common a staple of touristic souvenirs as beauty shots of the Colosseum. Never mind that the film was condemnatory of sybaritic living or made the Rome from which it arose look like a circle of Dantean torment. It was gorgeous, it was historic, it was evocative. Rome had always had a way of making even the most egregious aspects of its past look romantic and alluring. Why shouldn't it do the same with the moral crises of its midcentury coming-out party?

Among the interpretations to which *La Dolce Vita* was subject was the idea that Marcello and Paparazzo were somehow to be envied for their proximity to the high life. In the wake of the film's release there appeared along Via Veneto more photographers than ever. Not only were there news photographers looking for stories, of which there were plenty, but young chancers and bounders with secondhand cameras (not always loaded with film), their eyes set on money and women and only sometimes, and often as an afterthought, on capturing images of life on the famed boulevard. Just as young men around the world would, after a few more years, declare themselves guitar players, young men, usually Roman, started appearing around Via Veneto like toadstools after a downpour, offering to take pictures of attractive young women and to introduce them to various allegedly important people they allegedly knew.

And it wasn't just phony photographers. There were aspiring starlets and models trying to outdo one another to gain attention and maybe get their names and faces into print: piloting cars down the street by using reins to turn the steering wheel; showing up on actual horses and riding into cafés; walking around in nightgowns with vacant gazes and arms outstretched as if sleepwalking; sitting at a sidewalk table with a leopard on a leash as if every home in Rome had such a pet. Ennio Flaiano came out of a tobacconist's one night in late 1961 and encountered a young woman dressed as a Christmas tree, complete with hanging ornaments and lit candles. Astounded that none of the photographers standing there seemed to take note of her, he asked why not and was told, "I don't know. . . . Maybe if somebody slapped her."

Fellini admitted feeling largely responsible for the circus that had become life on the famous street. "I had invented a nonexistent Via Veneto," he wrote in 1962,

> distorting and remodeling it with the freedom of imagination into the shape of a grand allegorical fresco. In fact, Via Veneto, as if in backlash to *La Dolce Vita*, was transformed. . . . The photographers multiplied on every corner, the fistfights became a daily phenomenon. . . . I opened the newspaper each morning with my heart stopped, with an absurd sense of remorse. I would ask myself, "What happened last night on Via Veneto to satisfy the fans of *La Dolce Vita*?"

Fellini often griped that foreigners traveling to Rome, especially American movie people, would frequently ask him if he could introduce them to a "real" Roman orgy. "And bring Anita Ekberg," they would add, helpfully. As if to provide him with a means of responding to such bumptious requests, a guidebook to the menu of sin and vice available in the city would appear soon after the debut of *La Dolce Vita*. *Rome After Dark* was published under the pseudonym Roberto Orsi, a man (presumably) who, according to his publishers, was "a prominent member of the Italian aristocracy" whose "intimate association with Rome's 'La Dolce Vita' crowd is well known." The book spilled details on orgies, illegal brothels, bars and neighborhoods where homosexuals and lesbians could be found, the drug scene, even the skinny on a black mass. It was modeled on the famed "Confidential" guidebooks to New York and Chicago that had been big sellers for authors Jack Tait and Lee Mortimer just a few years prior. And, like those books, it contained just enough truth—names, addresses, famous stories (like the Rugantino striptease party), knowing little jokes and details—to be credible.

What it didn't contain was cautions. As was to be expected in a big city, especially one experiencing a golden age, there was crime along Via Veneto and environs during its heyday, and not just of the pocket-picking, purse-snatching, tourist-hornswoggling, sex-and/or-drug varieties that might be found in any European capital. Several violent deaths occurred in the Ludovisi district surrounding the famed boulevard at a time when so much of the world was flocking to it or sitting back home enviously imagining life there. None of these incidents captured the Italian imagination quite as electrically as had the death of Wilma Montesi, which was still under investigation and which had knit together so many of the most salient threads of its moment: class, corruption, sex, drugs, celebrity, and tabloid media. But they made ripples in their moments.

The first, and most notorious, incident occurred when Fellini and company were still in production. One June night in 1959, photographer Marcello Geppetti was camped outside of a Via Veneto nightspot hoping for a shot of Princess Soraya, who was said to be out clubbing with Prince Filippo Orsini. If it was true, it would be a brilliant—and lucrative—scoop. Geppetti was having no luck, though, and at about two a.m. he went looking for a coffee to gird himself for the long wait. Finding his usual late-night go-to closed, he wandered, only to hear, as if in a dream, a voice shouting "Help! Call the firemen! Save us!" He looked around, skyward, and he saw a woman leaning out a fifth- or sixth-floor window of the nearby Hotel Ambasciatori, shouting into the night. Soon, two small crowds started forming: onlookers on the sidewalk alongside Geppetti and nightgowned women in the upper windows of the hotel, all hollering that they were so afraid that they would jump.

Geppetti and a patrolman ran to the nearest nightspot that was still open and commandeered the phone, calling the fire department. When they got back to the Ambasciatori, flames were shooting from its upper stories, smoke was pouring into the night, and more figures could be seen at windows, shouting for help. Minutes passed, and no firemen arrived. The policeman, knowing that there were many people inside the hotel still sleeping through the noise, fired his pistol into the air, hoping to wake them. Presently, roused and confounded hotel guests began to tumble into the street, still in their nightclothes, while hotel workers carried out mattresses, intending to create landing areas for those who were trapped above and had no way out save to leap. But that would surely only serve as the most desperate measure.

As word of the fire spread among the various nightspots that were still open, the crowd on the street grew. The flames thickened and soared; the voices of the people in the windows became more frantic. Geppetti and the others on the ground tried to reassure the frightened women that help was on the way, that they should stay calm. But there was no sound of fire trucks approaching. And the situation was clearly reaching a terrible moment.

"Up to that moment," Geppetti recalled, "I had forgotten that I was a photographer." But he had done everything he could. And he was angry that the response of the fire company was so lazy. So he took out his camera to capture the scene . . . and the unthinkable happened: a woman who had been seated on a windowsill high above, with her legs dangling, pushed herself off.

As Geppetti remembered years later, "She fell . . . an interminable flight . . . to the ground." He was pretty certain that he had captured an image of her descent. "I was stunned," he said, "petrified by the spectacle of something I had never, ever wished to see." And yet he kept shooting: the woman, whose fall had been broken by the roof of a convertible car and who had somehow survived, tended by onlookers; the horrified crowd; the smoke and flames pouring out of the hotel windows; the street dotted with gawkers and no rescue vehicles in sight.

The shock was broken by the sound of fire trucks, arriving at last. But none had a ladder long enough to reach the imperiled people above, and none had a canvas that could be used to catch someone who needed to leap from the smoke and flames. As if they sensed the end of all hope, four more women, in rapid sequence, pushed themselves into the night air rather than face the fire behind them. Geppetti continued to photograph them as, night-gowns blooming like parachutes, they plummeted to ground. One survived, but three died on impact. Only then, after five horrific plunges, did the proper rescue vehicles arrive, and firemen began to see to those still trapped inside and to deal with the blaze.

After a while, Geppetti, knowing he had the most unforgettable images conceivable in his camera, left the scene, uncertain what to do with his work. On the one hand, the pictures would be horrifying, even obscene, and probably unprintable. On the other hand, there was real news value and even a public service dimension to revealing just how inadequate the emergency response had been and in demonstrating in the most unforgettable way possible the awful cost of the delay. He decided to offer the images to editors.

No one in Rome would touch them. But after a few weeks, *Der Spiegel* in Germany published several of his photos of the falling bodies, and Roman newspapers followed suit. Geppetti anticipated that there might an outcry against the images, which needed to be published with black bars over the midsections of some of the women, who were rendered seminude by the rush of air through their nightclothes. He didn't count, however, on the moral indignation leveled at him, personally, for taking pictures of the scene rather than doing whatever he could to rescue the women. In the pages of *L'Osservatore Romano* there were even calls for his excommunication. Years later, he could rise to indignation in his self-defense: "I had done, as quickly as possible, everything I could. I had summoned the firemen, the management of the hotel, the police, the people in the nightclubs. . . . But I could see that no one was going to intervene. And I, by myself, couldn't do a thing."

His failure to react heroically became part of controversy brewing around the Via Veneto photographers, while the inept response of rescuers and the lives that were lost and shattered—all four women, it happened, were maids working at the hotel and sleeping in a staff dormitory—apparently mattered less than the thought that Geppetti chose to take photographs rather than risks.[6] And so blurred had the line between reality and art become that, almost as soon as the flames died out, rumors began circulating along Via

---

6 One man *inside* the hotel did act heroically. John "Shipwreck" Kelly, a onetime football star at the University of Kentucky and ex-husband of American debutante and socialite Brenda Frazer, was a guest at the Ambasciatori and was celebrated the next day as "the man in the green bathrobe" who ran through the hotel corridors banging on doors to awake anyone who might have slept through the screaming and tumult of the fire.

Veneto that Fellini's screenplay had been rewritten to include a hotel fire—which was never the case.

*A*fter *La Dolce Vita* had lifted the popular renown of Via Veneto to an acme, three sordid murders of foreign nationals made clear just how dubious a culture it was that Fellini's film had captured. In November 1960, Norman Donges, fifty-six, a former U.S. Army intelligence officer who had been living at Rome's YMCA and studying Italian language and literature on the GI Bill, was found locked inside his Volkswagen, squeezed between the front and rear seats, a newspaper covering his head, dead by strangulation. He had no wallet, although he was known to carry large sums of cash. The diamond ring and platinum watch he liked to show off were missing, and the keys to the car were nowhere to be found.

Donges was known to frequent the areas around Via Veneto and Villa Borghese where young men loitered waiting for older men with money to come around and pay them for their time and, inevitably, for sex. At about 3:15 a.m. on the rainy autumn morning on which he died, he had been seen driving away from a Via Veneto café with a tall blond boy. Within two days, police apprehended seventeen-year-old Orante Cardarelli, a hotel waiter, who confessed to the crime and eventually received a sentence of thirteen years—so light, it was said, because of his age at the time of the incident and his expressions of remorse, but no doubt because the murder of a foreign homosexual, who was depicted in the press as a predator and maybe even a spy, wasn't deemed as serious as a crime as one against a more socially reputable victim.

In the coming years, two other foreigners connected to Via Veneto met violent ends. In May 1963, on Via Emilia, steps from Via Veneto, a twenty-three-year-old German girl named Christa Wanninger was stabbed a dozen times on the doorstep of her friend, another German named Gerda Hoddap, who slept through the commotion outside her apartment even though it had woken her neighbors. The following year, on Via Lazio, in the same neighborhood, a well-to-do Egyptian businessman and cabinet minister's son, twenty-seven-year-old Farouk Chourbagi, was found dead in the offices of his textile firm, where he kept a small apartment separate from his main residence; in addition to four fatal pistol shots, an assassin had attacked the victim with acid, splashing it on his face, leaving a grotesque spectacle.

Although notably violent, these were mean little crimes of passion, and police quickly tied them to romantic entanglements. None of the principals—victims or perpetrators—was, in strict terms, part of the society that had risen around the film or fashion trades, or of the world of tabloid media and paparazzi, or of the high society and louche cliques that mingled on Via Veneto. But they had all, the victims and the killers, been drawn into the sometimes shifting morality of the demimonde that Fellini and company had captured in *La Dolce Vita*. They had come to Rome with dreams of fortune, glory, romance, and they found different fates. It would be ludicrous to suggest that they had died at the hands of the scene that attracted them. But it would also be disingenuous to suggest that the images of Via Veneto high life that had spread throughout the world played no part in luring them to the rocks on which their lives crashed.

25 "I Am Not a Sexy Pot"

Even as the evidence mounted that the Roman scene wasn't all gaiety and glamour, the city kept sprouting new attractions that caught the world's eye and made people want to come there. In the late summer of 1960, as *La Dolce Vita* made its way out into the world, Rome hosted the games of the fifteenth Summer Olympics, a gargatuan spectacle that supported the idea that the city was the global capital of sensation.

Throughout 1959 and well into the summer of 1960, Rome underwent significant physical transformations. New stadia and an Olympic Village to house the world's athletes were built north of the Flaminio district on the east bank of the Tiber and across the river in the Della Vittoria neighborhood. More facilities were built south of the city in the already modernistic EUR district. Several roads were straightened out, rerouted, or just plain made from scratch. A brand-new airport, Leonardo da Vinci International, was built just north of coastal Ostia in the town of Fiumicino, by which name it would also be commonly known. And a highway was constructed spanning the twenty or so miles from the new airport to the center of the city. The total cost of all these public works was estimated at $250 million (more than $2 billion in 2016 terms), and the result would be a number of permanent changes to the cityscape: the Stadio Olimpico and Palazzetto dello Sport in the north, a larger Palazzo dello Sport and a velodrome in the south,[1] and the Olympic Village, which was, after the games, used as a housing project for a city where residents still had to wait months for places in which to live. The Summer Olympics proved that Rome (and, beyond it, Italy) didn't just mean affordable fashion, tiny cars and scooters, epic costume films, and churches and ruins: the games were a spectacle worthy of the Colosseum *and* proof of Italy's crescent modernity—real first-world stuff.[2] They were telecast as close to live as possible in North America. They were rife with political tensions, some involving the Cold War, others focused on South Africa, which would be banned from the Olympics until 1992, after it had finally abolished apartheid, and Taiwan, which competed as the Republic of China and caused the Communist Peo-

---

1 These latter buildings would appear in the backgrounds of both *La Dolce Vita* and Michelangelo Antonioni's *L'Eclisse*.

2 Italy, like many host nations, performed brilliantly in the actual competition, finishing fourth in the overall medal count with 36, behind the United States (103), the USSR (71), and West Germany (42)—and third overall in golds, with 13.

ple's Republic of China to sit the games out for another twenty years. They featured the first appearance of sponsored athletic wear, shoes from rival German companies Adidas and Puma, *both* worn by the German track star Armin Hary, who had Pumas on his feet when he won the 100-meter sprint and Adidas when he accepted the gold medal. There were doping scandals, also a first, in weightlifting and in cycling, in which a Danish rider collapsed during a race and died of complications arising from a combination of heat and amphetamine use.

The most impressive firsts, though, involved black athletes. The United States team was led in the opening ceremonies by Rafer Johnson, the first African-American to carry the flag in front of a U.S. squad and the eventual gold medalist in a furiously contested decathlon. Behind him in the pack of young hopefuls was Wilma Rudolph, a onetime polio patient who would win gold medals in three sprint events, and a lean and hungry eighteen-year-old light-heavyweight boxer from Louisville, Kentucky, named, with an appropriately Roman flourish, Cassius Clay, who would also take home gold.

Most inspiring of all, though, was an unknown runner on the twelve-man Ethiopian team, a member of Emperor Haile Selassie's palace guard named Abebe Bikila. He was twenty-eight years old, which meant he had been a toddler when Mussolini's troops invaded his country in 1935, and he and his teammates almost didn't travel to Rome at all, lacking means until the government was embarrassed into paying for their transportation and upkeep. On the day of the marathon, Bikila reported to the starting area hopeful of getting a pair of the running shoes with which Adidas was outfitting the competitors. But there weren't any in his size, so he ran the 26.2 miles in the same way he had trained back home: barefoot. All he did was win, in 2 hours, 15 minutes, and 16.2 seconds—8/10ths of a second faster than the previous world record and a full 25 seconds ahead of his nearest competitor.

At the outset of the Olympic games, Bikila and his eleven Ethiopian teammates had marched, almost defiantly, through the Foro Italico, a public monument built, in part, to commemorate the conquest of their homeland by Mussolini's forces. When the closing ceremonies were held, he repeated that walk with the gold medal of a marquee event hanging around his neck, a living—and speedy—symbol of his people, his nation, and his times: a curtain scene that Fellini himself might have deemed too fantastical to believe.

*B*y the time the Olympic flame was extinguished, another young hopeful could claim that she, too, had conquered the world. Based partly on her successes in Italian films (including a couple of well-received imports), partly on her sheer beauty, and partly on the machinations of Carlo Ponti, Sophia Loren, still only twenty-five years old, had become a Hollywood star.

As before, she was preceded by Gina Lollobrigida, who had resumed her pursuit of an international career with a string of productions in France, where she starred in Carol Reed's circus film *Trapeze* (alongside Burt Lancaster and Tony Curtis), Jean Delannoy's *The Hunchback of Notre Dame* (with Anthony Quinn), and Jules Dassin's *La Loi* (which was shot in rural Southern Italy and a Parisian studio and also starred Marcello Mastroianni and Yves Montand). None of these films conquered the world, but Gina's beauty, accentuated by trapeze costumes in the Reed film and by a display of feral sexuality in the others, was evident, and Hollywood summoned her again (the Howard Hughes contract and its noncompete clauses had expired). This time, the terms were more favorably spelled out and her English was better, and she appeared in several visible but only modestly successful films:

King Vidor's *Solomon and Sheba* (with Yul Brynner, a late replacement for Tyrone Power, who died of a heart attack halfway through
production), John Sturges's *Never So Few* (with Frank Sinatra and
Peter Lawford), and Robert Mulligan's *Come September* (with Rock
Hudson). Her charms were still evident, but so were her limits.
And she wound up back in Italian films, almost exclusively, for
what would remain of her career.[3]

Following Lollo, Sophia's first step on the path to Hollywood
was familiar: an approach to a pretty girl by an American producer. But *this* pretty girl had a man who protected her interests
and knew how the movie business worked and understood what
her name, looks, and talent were truly worth. The American caller
was writer-director Stanley Kramer, then working for United Artists on *The Pride and the Passion*, an epic about the Napoleonic Wars
being shot in Spain.[4] The film was to have starred Cary Grant,
Marlon Brando, and Ava Gardner. But Brando dropped out and
was replaced by Frank Sinatra, whose divorce from Gardner was
still such a raw matter that there was no question of their working together. When Kramer inquired whether Sophia was available, Ponti knew he had the upper hand, but even he was surprised
by the size of the offer that ensued: $200,000 firm—*if* her costars
approved, and *if* her English was up to snuff.

For the latter stipulation, Sophia embarked on a rigorous crash

3 And though she would keep busy in increasingly frivolous films in the 1960s,
Lollo had lost her zest for the work, frankly. Since girlhood she had wanted to make
art, and she became an adept photographer, traveling the world to shoot current events
and contemporary life, a pursuit that would lead her, in 1974, to sit with Cuban dictator Fidel Castro and obtain an exclusive interview that was published, along with her
photos of the meeting, all over the world. By then she had also begun to paint and sculpt
and publish books of her work, acting only occasionally and then mainly on TV.

4 Noting Italy's success in luring Hollywood films (and money), Spain's government had begun offering itself as an even less expensive alternative.

course under an English teacher named Sarah Spain, whom she adored but described as a "persecutor." As for the former, she simply showed up at a publicity event in Madrid—a cocktail party/press conference featuring Kramer and his stars—and, predictably, won them over, particularly Grant, then married to his third wife, actress Betsy Drake, but smitten like a schoolboy by his young costar. Grant sent Sophia flowers daily, wooed her over romantic dinners at picturesque inns, told her repeatedly that his marriage was all over but for the paperwork. She was tempted, she would later admit, but despite her public persona, on-screen and off-, and despite her ongoing relationship with Ponti, Sophia was an old-style respectable girl. She was admittedly overwhelmed by Grant's attentions—and consquently watchful of her own words, behavior, and feelings. She wanted to honor her bond, both personal and professional, with Ponti. But it was a genuine challenge.

Drake got wind of her husband's activities and came to Spain to confront him, without taming his ardor one bit. She sailed home on, of all ships, the *Andrea Doria*, surviving its sinking off the coast of Massachusetts in July 1956 without the succor of her husband, who used the excuse of the film production to avoid returning home to ease her back from her brush with death. Ponti, too, hovered about the set, aware that Sophia was being lured but patient in his own way, which proved the right choice. When location shooting ended—early, because Sinatra had become restless in rural Spain, which he derided as "Windmillville"—Grant returned to Hollywood without Sophia.

She, however, had made her entrée into Hollywood productions, and after signing a contract with Paramount, found herself cast opposite a dizzying array of famous costars in what looked like a willy-nilly selection of films. She worked in Greece with Alan Ladd in *Boy on a Dolphin* (and caused a global sensation in a diving costume that clung to her like a layer of body paint), in Tunisia and Rome with John Wayne in *Legend of the Lost*, in London with William Holden and Trevor Howard in *The Key*, and in Hollywood and New York in a series of films that did almost no business: *Desire Under the Elms* with Anthony Perkins and Burl Ives; *The Black Orchid* with Anthony Quinn; *That Kind of Woman* with Tab Hunter and George Sanders; and *Heller in Pink Tights*, a western, of all things, directed by George Cukor. Only one of her films during this time was truly a hit either critically or commercially: *Houseboat*, again opposite Cary Grant, who was still pursuing her. Or, at least he was until he learned, in a newspaper, that she had chosen Carlo Ponti over him.

The romance of Romilda Villani and Ricardo Scicolone, which had produced baby Sophia, was protracted, torturous, mean, sordid—and an entirely private matter. But the romance of Sophia Loren and Carlo Ponti played out in the newspapers, bureaucracies, judicial chambers, and pulpits of at least five nations on two continents for a solid decade in a perverse, large-scale echo of the private scandal of her birth. By 1955, Ponti had formally separated from his wife and determined that he would throw his lot together with Sophia's. But divorce didn't exist in Italy (and wouldn't until 1970), and it didn't matter anyway, since the incumbent Mrs. Ponti had no thought of surrendering her station. Despite the fact that he had almost no hope that he could make an end of his first marriage and live with a second wife in his homeland, Ponti had his lawyers persist in trying to find a way. At the time, it was easiest for them to seek a divorce for their client in Mexico, where the laws about dissolving a marriage were relatively lax and a quick second marriage could also subsequently be arranged; the couple in question need not even be present if the paperwork was in order.

As a result, one morning in 1957, Sophia and Ponti woke to

a startling newspaper account under the byline of the Hollywood gossip columnist Louella Parsons: the day before, they had been married, if only on paper, in Mexico, where Ponti had been granted a divorce. All of this was news to them. And none of it meant a thing in Italy, where both the government and the church refused to recognize the dissolution of the first Ponti marriage and would thus count Ponti as a bigamist and Sophia as—well, suffice it to say that the word *cortigiana* ("courtesan") got a healthy workout in the press. The couple could live together as man and wife in the United States, in Great Britain, in France, in Mexico—but not in Italy, where they owned a villa that they weren't able to visit together. When two more years had passed and Sophia had an opportunity to work again at home, she and Ponti were threatened with legal action. Their lawyers suggested they have their Mexican marriage annulled, and they agreed. That didn't stop the assaults or the inquests, though, and they were hauled before investigators who insisted on knowing various details of their lives.

There was a bitter irony to all of this: although she was now considered around the globe to be the living embodiment of the spirit of Italy, she was more or less persona non grata there—particularly in comparison to the so-called good star, Gina Lollobrigida, who had managed to forge an international career *and* enjoy what looked like a regular family life with husband and child. As a result, Sophia avoided working in Italy for several years, because it would have meant separation from the man whom she considered her husband. The only thing that got her back onto Italian soundstages during this period of tumult was the opportunity to work on a new film produced by Ponti and directed by Vittorio De Sica, *La Ciociara*, a story of the wartime desperation and trauma suffered by a mother and her daughter and based on a novel by Alberto Moravia. The project was originally intended as a George Cukor film starring Anna Magnani, but Magnani backed out in part because it was suggested that she play Sophia's mother (which, by the way, she was old enough to, being twenty-six years the elder), Cukor left, and Ponti refashioned the project.

La Ciociara is a painful drama about a woman, Cesira, forced by the tumult of the war to flee her comfortable life in Rome and seek refuge in her hometown in the Ciociara region of central Italy (incidentally, the home region of Marcello Mastroianni). With her prepubescent daughter, Rosetta, she makes an arduous trek to her village, which is also war-battered and filled with refugees, including a young intellectual, Michele, who grows close to the new arrivals.[5] As the Germans retreat and the Allies arrive, the small village becomes more dangerous than ever, climaxing in the death of Michele at the hands of Nazis and the gang rape of Cesira and Rosetta by a platoon of Moroccans who are fighting along with the Allies.[6]

The role was a stretch for Loren, who was still only twenty-five at the time of filming and known for light comedy and glamour, not the searing drama of Moravia's story. But no director would ever have a stronger connection with Loren as an actress than De Sica, and he knew how to get her best work out of her. As before, he precisely acted out for her what she should do—often while she was performing before a rolling camera. In one of the film's most harrowing sequences, when Cesira broke down in tears while

5 The role of Michele would be played by Jean-Paul Belmondo, newly minted as a star after Jean-Luc Godard's *Breathless*. He spoke no Italian, but a considerable portion of the budget was put up by a French company, which demanded a French actor in a key role, so . . .

6 The story had a real-life precedence: after the battle of Monte Cassino, Moroccan Goumier troops conducted a rampage of rapes throughout the area. Their victims, who numbered in the thousands, were known as *marocchinate*, or, "the Moroccan-ized."

telling Rosetta of Michele's fate, De Sica wept alongside his star: "Each time I played the scene," Loren remembered, "I would see him crying, and each time he was crying in a different way." Buoyed by this support, Loren gave a superb performance: sexy, knowing, funny, and potent when Cesira seemed to be in control of her own fate; skittery, shattered, desperate, and lost when the world crashed viciously down on her. It was far beyond anything she had ever attempted and successful in ways that maybe only Ponti and De Sica could have predicted. Her raw beauty and saucy bearing were, for once, *aspects* of the character she played, rather than the pith of it; it was a real job of acting.

Her work was received with kudos in Italy when the film premiered in December 1960. In the United States, where Loren's Hollywood films had almost completely disappointed, it was the focus of an ingenious publicity campaign by the veteran film distributor Joseph E. Levine, whose Embassy Pictures had made its name with such imports as *Godzilla* and the made-in-Rome *Hercules* in previous years. He acquired the rights to *La Ciociara*, renamed it *Two Women*, and had Loren herself do the English-language dubbing of her role. But, as with *La Dolce Vita*, that work wasn't necessary. Levine had chosen to gamble that audiences who were favorably disposed to Loren based on the likes of *Houseboat* would want to see her acting in Italian—the real thing, as it were—and he released *Two Women* nationally in the original Italian with subtitles; it was a huge hit, earning more than $5 million in ticket sales.[7] And what was more, Loren was acknowledged, even by those who had mocked her previously, as having delivered a staggering performance.

Levine then took the next step and aimed at the ultimate movie

7 Eventually, the dubbed version would be released and bring in another $12 million (more than $95 million in 2016 terms): a massive haul.

prize: an Oscar. Loren had already taken home the top acting award from the Cannes Film Festival. As 1961 wound down, she won both the Nastro d'Argento from the Italian film press and the Donatello from the Italian film academy. Levine pushed in the United States, getting Loren booked on national TV variety and interview shows and even talking NBC into creating a special around her, *The Life of Sophia Loren*. ("I said before I am not a sexy pot," she told one interviewer during this press binge. "Now I can prove it.") She went on to win the New York Film Critics Circle award and then, some weeks later, to be nominated for an Oscar as Best Actress.

The competition was stiff: Audrey Hepburn for *Breakfast at Tiffany's*, Piper Laurie for *The Hustler*, Geraldine Page for *Summer and Smoke*, and Natalie Wood for *Splendor in the Grass*. Levine pulled every publicity trick that there was at the time, buying ads in trade newspapers and holding private screenings for voters—and not just in L.A. but in New York, Chicago, London, Paris, even Rome. But he couldn't persuade his star to attend the Oscar ceremony itself.

For one thing, there was a tragic incident to recover from. In March, Sophia's sister, Maria, married Romano Mussolini, a jazz musician and another offspring of the Fascist dictator. At the end of the reception, the groom's mother insisted that the wedding party stop at his father's grave to lay a wreath. Returning to Rome from the cemetery, the rented Rolls-Royce that was chauffeuring Loren and her mother collided with a motor scooter, killing the driver instantly.

But even without that, she was simply too nervous to attend. She put a humble spin on her decision: "If I lost, I might faint from disappointment; if I won, I would also very likely faint with joy. Instead of spreading my fainting all over the world, I decided it was better that I faint at home."

As it turned out, she really was a nervous wreck, drinking and smoking into the wee hours and then going to bed—at approximately six a.m. Rome time—before Burt Lancaster stepped on stage to announce the Best Actress winner. "Somebody else got it and no one has the courage to call me," she told Ponti as she went off to try to get some sleep.

Not one hour later, the phone rang. It was Cary Grant.

"Darling, do you know?"

"Know what?" she asked.

"Oh, darling. I'm so glad I'm the first to tell you. You won!"

She marked the occasion with the most curious but selfless of gestures: giving a pint of blood at a Roman office of the Red Cross. Some in the conservative Catholic press managed to take affront even at this gesture—"concubine's blood," sneered one—but those voices increasingly represented the bleatings of a rump guard. The dark, skinny girl with the big nose from Pozzuoli, Sophia Stuzzicadente, daughter of an unwed mother, unschooled refugee, beauty pageant perennial, star of *fumetti* and racy comedies, accused bigamist, sexpot import whose Hollywood movies had nearly all flopped, was, in the eyes of the film world, the best actress of 1961. She had well and truly conquered the world.

26 "You've Done It, You've Won"

Sophia Loren and Cassius Clay weren't the only world beaters.

"The last nine years have passed like nine days," Emilio Pucci told a reporter when asked about his successes, and you could sympathize with his sense of having rushed through a landscape like a passenger on a high-speed train.

From the unlikely conjunction of a ski slope in Oregon and a palazzo in Florence, he had created a fashion empire that was growing bigger and more influential with each year. His signature designs were appearing on ever expanding lines of sportswear, ready-to-wear, and household items. He was making—or at least sketching out and approving the manufacture of—scarves and neckties and coats and shoes and men's sport shirts and household linens and glassware and silverware and home decorations; soon he'd produce yacht interiors, seat covers for commercial airliners, and stewardesses' uniforms. He was working toward his first line of true couture formal wear (it would debut in 1962) and toward opening a shop in Paris (likewise). His work had been honored with a Neiman Marcus Fashion Oscar and a Sporting Look Award from *Sports Illustrated.* In 1960, he obtained a patent on an elastic nylon-based fabric called Emilioform, infused with shantung silk, and he had the exclusive right to use it in his still immensely popular lines of skiwear. He was dressing noblewomen and sportswomen and the wives of politicians and magnates and such icons of style as Jacqueline Kennedy, Audrey Hepburn, Elizabeth Taylor, and Marilyn Monroe, who would be buried in 1962 in a green Pucci sheath dress she favored. The Pucci brand (he no longer used the label Emilio, although he still signed his designs and some finished products that way) was a worldwide sensation.

So he did what any self-respecting Florentine nobleman with a global name would do: he ran for office. In April 1963, Pucci put his name up for a position in the Italian Chamber of Deputies, running on the Liberal party ticket (in the European way of these things, this was a conservative slate; Pucci had renounced Mussolini's fascism but not his ideal of strong government control of the economy). "The reason I am going into politics is because of my American education," he told *The New York Times.* "I learned here that when something goes wrong, you're supposed to pitch in and do something about it." His understanding of Yankee politics didn't translate into votes in Florence, though; fewer than

3000 ballots were cast in his name. But that summer, a Liberal deputy died suddenly and Pucci, as the highest Liberal vote earner who hadn't actually won a seat, was appointed by his party to the chamber.

He would eventually serve two terms, the latter of which found him in office in November 1966, when the Arno River swelled past its banks and flooded central Florence. It was estimated that more damage was done to the city's priceless art and antiquities by the inundation than by all of the destruction, thievery, and tumult of World War II. The days and weeks that followed the disaster saw the birth of the first truly grassroots youth movement in Italy in the 1960s: the *Angeli di Firenze*, angels of Florence, hundreds of young people from all over Italy and beyond who came to the city to help rescue whatever could be saved.

Pucci himself lost upward of $1 million in fabrics (some 150,000 yards) and finished clothes (two entire collections of one-of-a-kind originals)—though he would, he reassured the fashion press, be able to get a new season's designs out. And he did, working from memory, as many of his sketches and papers were lost, and by candlelight, as electricity, along with running water and telephone service, was spotty or nonexistent throughout the city for weeks. Moreover, as a politician *and* a star of international fashion, he was in a unique position to help his city recover from the disaster. He went to New York to plead to retailers and bankers for recovery assistance for Florentine craftspeople and manufacturers, and he got guarantees of low-interest loans and other forms of investment—an archangel of Florence, as it were, with seemingly divine powers in whatever he touched.

As loyal to Rome as Pucci was to Florence, the Fontana sisters would never leave the city, but that was appropriate given the institutions they and their work became. Their ascent appeared unstoppable. Not long after they were given their grand day at the Vatican, they moved into a larger atelier on Via di San Sebastianello, just a few steps off the Piazza di Spagna, with a retail space on the ground floor and a couture salon and workshops upstairs. By the 1960s, they had lines of boutique clothes, ready-to-wear, sportswear, shoes, perfume, leather goods, household linens, umbrellas, and suitcases.[1] Their couture work was still handmade in the atelier, but they had factories outside of Rome with hundreds of employees producing items for mass sale, particularly in Italy and the United States, but also in Great Britain, the rest of the Continent, and, eventually, Japan. They operated retail boutiques in various Italian cities and a couture showroom in New York. They designed work uniforms for the stewardesses of several airlines and contributed costumes to several more films, including Ursula Andress's outfits for *The Tenth Victim*, Elio Petri's 1966 science fiction drama. They were *importing* American accessories and knitwear into Italy to sell. Even their onetime model, Princess Irene Galitzine, was touched by their magic wand; she went into business as a designer herself in 1959, and the following year she introduced what she called "palazzo pajamas," a combination of loungewear and couture that swept the world immediately.

The sisters even appeared, briefly, as themselves in a film, *Gidget Goes to Rome*. Three ordinary girls from Traversetolo in a Hollywood movie: the Cinderella story fully realized.

If the marriage of Simonetta and Fabiani had made headlines, the news they announced in the spring of 1962 practically

---

1 These, too, were often family businesses: the sisters' uncle was their shoe designer, and one of Zoe's daughters was one of the firm's principal creators of sportswear.

demanded special editions: the pair would work jointly, for the first time, but not in Rome or even Florence. They would move their base of operations to Paris, where their friend and colleague Roberto Capucci had broken ground by exhibiting a new collection, to critical and commercial success, just a few months prior. Under the label Simonetta et Fabiani, they would work and exhibit together, and Simonetta would close her Roman atelier the following year. (Fabiani would keep his Via dei Condotti headquarters, but he would use it only to service select private clients.)

In fashion houses and newsrooms in Rome, Florence, Paris, and New York, this was a thunderbolt. *The New York Times*, describing the couple as "the best known couturiers in Italy," declared that their move "would inflict serious damage on the Italian fashion market." An unnamed department store buyer said, "It will be practically the end of the Pitti Palace showings," and claimed already to have scrapped plans to attend that summer's Italian shows altogether. In Florence, Giovanni Battista Giorgini put on a brave face, saying that the news was something he'd expected—"they have been talking about it for the last two years"—and even tried to spin it as a sign of the vigor of Italian fashion, that it was good enough "to go to Paris." But he was rattled, assuring the press that no other important names would follow.

In May, ahead of a summer debut of their first French collections, Simonetta and Fabiani held a cocktail party for Parisian clothiers, buyers, and press, the new kids on the block extending a show of courtesy and respect to the local establishment. It had to be played just right: on the one hand, they might be seen as interlopers or provincials trying to compete with a creative industry that was, at least in the French view, always ahead of them; on the other hand, their very presence, along with that of Capucci, brought a new energy and attention to Paris, underscoring its long-standing status as world capital of fashion.

They held their Paris debut in late July at their atelier on Rue François 1er, and it was, despite some reluctance evinced in the partisan French press, well received. "They are extremely well made," said an American buyer of the designs. "They give a lift to Paris. They are really couture clothes, with flair and shape. They don't look like ready-to-wear, as many of the clothes in Paris do." As ever, Fabiani's pieces were singled out for their technical quality and sense of flow and design, and Simonetta's for their vivacity and, yes, joie de vivre. It was as if they were back home, still, standing above the fray, combining their individual talents into something greater than the estimable results that either could achieve alone.

And it barely lasted two years. In 1964, Fabiani returned to Rome and Simonetta stayed in Paris, putting an end to their joint business venture. He went straight back to Via dei Condotti and picked up where he'd left off, as if he'd merely stepped out for a coffee, designing for private clients and exhibiting in Florence and/or Rome, as the political winds that buffeted the business of Italian fashion dictated. And she began to think beyond sketchbooks and catwalks altogether.

There seemed to be only one place where Italian fashion hadn't completely triumphed, and that was, ironically, on the shoulders of the nation's two most famous screen divas.

Sophia Loren and Gina Lollobrigida may have become the world's idea of the spirit of Italy and its women, but they were almost never seen out and about in Rome, and certainly not among the throng on Via Veneto, partly because they were simply mobbed by the paparazzi whenever they stepped out somewhere in the capital.[2] When they did appear in public, moreover, they preferred French clothes to Italian, or, at least, to Italian clothes that didn't look French. They were always stylish, and they wore the creations of many designers, many of whom were Italian and many of whom were the stars or rising stars of the day. But among Roman couturiers, their favorite for special-occasion-wear was Emilio Schuberth, whose impeccable gowns tended toward a French classicism and elegance far more than did the work of, say, Pucci or Simonetta. Far more often, they would be seen in Dior, Givenchy, Chanel. It was almost as if they were asserting the international status of their names and careers in their choice of clothiers, rather than being seen as local girls who got lucky and still clung to familiar ways. In a sense, by using Italian design as but one source of their wardrobes, they painted their stardom with a more international color.

But then an Italian designer emerged who combined the elegance and worldliness of the Parisian school with the sensuality, ingenuity, and high craft of the Italian, an artist whose work was Rome's last trump card against competition from Florence and France (and, for that matter, in later decades, Milan) and whose career began in the most Roman of ways, even if, over the years, the principals involved couldn't agree where it actually began. One insisted it was at Caffè Doney, the other that it was Caffè Strega. In the end, they settled, for the sake of not quarreling, and maybe because it was more chic, on the Café de Paris.

But there was no confusion about the impact: When the designer

2 Sophia, always canny with the press, would pose for a shot or two, and they would keep the hounding to a respectful minimum. So thorough was her wish to manage her photographic image that eventually she hired Pierluigi Praturlon as her personal photographer, a gig he would hold for several years before being replaced by Tazio Secchiaroli.

Valentino Clemente Ludovico Garavani met the architecture student Giancarlo Giammetti on Via Veneto one afternoon in early 1960, the last truly great name in Roman fashion—arguably, indeed, the greatest—was born.

It wasn't an overnight thing. Valentino, as he would become known in the world of fashion and beyond, had a Parisian pedigree and had been working in Rome for about three years in an atelier on Via dei Condotti. His first full collection had debuted to little note the previous summer ("nothing not on view for the last four days," sniffed *The New York Times* in its first gander at his work). He was but one more aspirant, however impeccably groomed, amid a throng of many such. He never lacked confidence—he had been aiming for a great career since boyhood—but he hadn't yet found a way to channel his gifts, his vision, his flair. In Giammetti, though, he met his counterpart, his conduit, his champion, his mate. Their casual meeting would not only change their lives and make their fortunes, it would ensure that Rome would be considered an important site on the map of world fashion for decades.

Valentino was born in 1932 in Voghera, a small city in southern Lombardy, almost as far from Milan as from Turin and as far from the aeries of haute couture as from the moon. As a boy, he was allowed to play in the back room of the passementerie shop of his aunt, and he so delighted in the cloth and lace and beads and ornaments he found there that she encouraged him to design an outfit for her. The promise of that first effort, and the fierce support of his family, stayed with and encouraged him. At seventeen, he left home for an apprenticeship in Paris under designer Jean Dessès, where he singled himself out for the speed and beauty of his sketchwork and for a burgeoning love of a certain hue: cardinal or blood or crimson or something between them all—which he would someday make so thoroughly his own that it would become known as "Valentino red." In 1955, he took a job with Guy Laroche (during which time he befriended a young German designer named Karl Lagerfeld). In 1957, he returned to Italy—to Rome, using a loan from his family to set up a workshop near the Piazza di Spagna, where his reputation as a whiz kid just back from Paris attracted enough customers for him to earn a living.

By the summer of 1959, he was ready to make his full debut for the press, which resulted, so the legend goes, in zero sales. And then came the encounter with Giammetti, six years the younger, who remembered, "Valentino was incredibly seductive, with his deep tan, blue eyes and soft but intense way of speaking." They met again in Capri, where they became lovers. (The two were born of a generation which could barely admit to homosexuality; still, they dressed and comported themselves rather like twin brothers and were so inseparable that, decades later, they estimated that the days they had spent apart from each other amounted to less than two months—even if, as they admitted, their physical relationship had ended in their thirties.) Even more important, they became business partners. Valentino designed; Giammatti managed the financial and practical affairs, from contracts to balance sheets to personnel management to publicity. The fantasist had discovered the rock from which he could leap into flight; the bean counter had discovered the angel who could lift him into the sky. "I always felt," Giammetti was fond of saying, "that my life began when I met Valentino." And Valentino, too, would someday reach an age and a station from which he could admit that everything that he'd achieved he'd achieved alongside Giammatti.

They aimed themselves at a place atop the hierarchy of Italian fashion and it didn't take long for them to stake their claim. In the spring of 1962, Valentino was selected as the final designer to show at the Sala Bianca in Florence, and the throng of journalists and buyers received his work ecstatically. As the crowd roared, Valentino remembered, "My mother said to me, 'You hear them? They want you because you've done it, you've won.' Less than an hour later, I had sold my entire collection and I was swamped with orders."

From there, Valentino's star rose perpetually. The influential twin sisters Consuelo Crespi and Gloria Schiff—who at various times each edited some or another edition of *Vogue*—began wearing his work, followed by such noted socialites and clothes horses as Magnella Agnelli, Babe Paley, Charlotte Niarchos, and Jacqueline Kennedy, who would wear Valentino when she married Aristotle Onassis. Elizabeth Taylor was said to have been wearing Valentino when she met Richard Burton (she certainly patronized his atelier during one particularly long spell of work in Rome in 1962), and Farah Diba Pahlavi, the wife of the shah, was wearing Valentino when she fled Iran forever. One of the designer's gowns once received a ten-minute ovation upon its debut; hundreds of others appeared on red carpets, Oscarcasts, ballroom floors, and wedding altars. He was the grandest of fashion grandees, standing on the shoulders of Giorgini, the Fontanas, Simonetta, and the rest to lift Italian haute couture to a height that even the haughtiest of Parisians had to crane to see. And, in a sense, though he might never concede it, he had a Via Veneto café terrace to thank for it, at least in part.

27 "A Ravenous Wolf Pack"

Thanks to Fellini and Flaiano, the Via Veneto photographers had a new name—*paparazzi*. And thanks, as ever, to their own antics and ethics, they had a global reputation. And they weren't happy with either.

They had already established themselves as a nuisance to visiting stars and Italian VIPs who wished to avoid the spotlight. But after *La Dolce Vita* they were increasingly seen, and written about, as a downright pestilence and a genuine threat.

In April 1962, an American film publicist, Jack

Brodsky, wrote to a colleague in New York who would soon be en route to Rome:

> I have come to learn who the *paparazzi* are. Remember that horde of photographers who followed Ekberg everywhere in *La Dolce Vita*? Well, they're for real. They are as numerous as termites and they multiply the same way. . . . [A movie star] told me that they've been following him, trying to provoke him into a fight, so that he'd take a poke at one of them and someone would get a shot worth thousands of lire. You'll enjoy them.

His boss, Walter Wanger, the producer of an epic Hollywood on the Tiber film they were in Italy to make, referred in his diary to "Rome's jackal-like photographers" and recounted the efforts of one, the self-proclaimed "king" of the paparazzi, to bribe him—with the princely sum of about $160 U.S.—for a negative of that movie star and a woman not his wife together. "It doesn't have to be salacious," the photographer assured him, "as long as I can say it's a shot that was stolen from the picture."

The antipathy toward the paparazzi had been gestating for some time. Take Anita Ekberg, who had played a friendly game of leapfrog with the photographers in their simultaneous rise to fame and fortune. She had always sat quietly when they caught her ex-husband Anthony Steel in his cups and ready to rumble. She had no qualms of demureness when, as on that infamous night at Rugantino, she would throw aside her shoes and ignite an explosion on the dance floor. And she had cavorted gladly for Pierluigi Praturlon's lens in the Trevi Fountain in real life and then, again, on the set of *La Dolce Vita*. But one night in October 1960, she demonstrated that she, too, was no longer willing to let herself be prey to the photographers' interminable intrusions.

She had been out on the town and been photographed, without incident, by a group of photographers, including Felice Quinto and Marcello Geppetti. It must have been a slow night, because the paparazzi decided to follow her home in the very early hours to a villa on Viale Cortina d'Ampezzo, northwest of the city center. She went inside without incident and they loitered outside her gate, only to find themselves under fire a few minutes later: an arrow—that is, *an actual archer's arrow*—whizzed through the air, brushing against someone's hand and smashing with a thud into a car door. Anita herself presently appeared, barefoot, still in her black evening attire, armed with a full-sized bow and four or five more arrows and a look of determination and purpose. There was a little bit of a scuffle as someone tried to disarm her, and then they all dutifully scattered, but not before Geppetti got several amazing shots of the scene: the Venus of the Trevi Fountain turned into a vengeful Diana and meaning business.

In April 1961, *Time* magazine ran a feature on the paparazzi and used particularly sharp language, calling them "a ravenous wolf pack . . . who stalk big names . . . with flash guns at point-blank range" and with "lips leaking cigarettes, cameras drawn like automatics." The sneering report continued, "No one is safe, not even royalty. . . . Legitimate news photographers scorn the paparazzi as streetwalkers of Roman journalism. But like streetwalkers, they cling to their place in society."

It was one thing to be scorned and smeared by the people whom they were hunting down for photos and profits. But to be assailed like this from within their own profession felt like a real affront. The Via Veneto photographers had dubbed themselves "action photographers" and "photojournalists" and, with admirable self-awareness, "assault photographers," and for some they were known as "teddy-photographers," after teddy boys, a British subculture of the moment that was noted for the dandyish clothes and iconoclastic attitudes of its adherents. But none of those names ever stuck. Now, thanks to *La Dolce Vita*, not only did they have a name that the whole world had picked up, but it was indisputably disparaging and used almost invariably as an epithet.[1]

They kicked back at the word, but good luck with that. "What annoys me is the word *paparazzo*," lamented Sergio Spinelli decades later. "We . . . invented things. All of us action photographers invented that period." Not alone among his peers, Spinelli blamed a great deal of the negative changes in Rome and in the culture of street photography on Fellini's film:

> It irritates me to hear someone talking about the Rome of the *Dolce Vita*, because the moment the film was released, everything ended. Via Veneto was over, everything was over. The Rome of Via Veneto was the Rome of the photographers, it was created and made by the photographers. I dislike the word *paparazzo* because we were photo-reporters, we created reportages [*sic*]. . . . The movie *La Dolce Vita* was born out of the published reportages. Fellini, Flaiano and all the others simply copied from them, they looked at those pictures and from them got the idea for the movie. In other words, we are the real authors of *La Dolce Vita*, not them.

It didn't help Spinelli's case, though, that the most visible face of the Via Veneto photographers was no longer the discreet Tazio Secchiaroli or the chummy Pierluigi Praturlon but a rougher,

---

1 It was also quickly adopted by the press and the public alike. Whereas *Time* had to define the word in the April 1961 piece quoted here, the term appeared in an interview with Marcello Mastroianni published in another American magazine some twenty months later without any explanation: "It is very difficult to have an affair in Italy these days," he told a reporter. "With all the paparazzi around, one must go to the moon."

younger sort of fellow who boasted about his thick skin and thirst for blood sport and who avowedly saw his celebrity targets as the enemy, a type personified by the Russian Ivan Kroscenko (the only foreign-born photographer among the regular paparazzi crowd) and the young Calabrian Rino Barillari. Each had been, or would soon be, the center of serial fracases with bold-faced names, each had a pugnacious and even confrontational attitude about his work, and each wished to be known—at least for a time, whether through his own hubris or in the wake of the semiserious anointment of chums in some afterhours revelry—as "the king of the paparazzi."

The paparazzi had always used laddish nicknames among themselves as part of their show of esprit de corps. It was the stuff of a locker room or barracks, infused with affection, free of pretense. But to call yourself "the king," as Kroscenko was apparently first to do, and to call a gathering of the tribe together and pass the title on to someone else, to *abdicate*, as he did a few years later, that was another level of self-seriousness and conceit. Even at their most incendiary, audacious, and scheming, the first wave of Via Veneto photographers, the first paparazzi anywhere, understood that in the algebra of work, opportunity, money, and fame that tied them to their famous photographic subjects, *they* were the smaller factor, and that it was the luster of the people whom they shot which imparted meaning, newsworthiness, glamour, sensation, and monetary value to their work, not the other way around. But for the newer breed of paparazzi, who were larger in number than ever by the time the new term for them took hold, there was another attitude: "I make the Via Veneto," Kroscenko told *Time*, without any hint of irony, "and it makes me."

*W*as it any wonder that somebody with the temperament and professional ethos of Tazio Secchiaroli had tired of the game?

He was still fast, still cunning, still able to deliver scoops, still a boss. But he had lost his taste for the sort of skullduggery, hustle, and cheek that had been, of necessity, his stock in trade for so long. Soon after the release of *La Dolce Vita*, he quietly slipped into another role, joining Pierluigi Praturlon as an official portraitist and set photographer for Sophia Loren, Federico Fellini, Marcello Mastroianni, and a handful of others, jobs he held for two-plus decades. He would always be remembered for his pioneering work among the paparazzi. But he aspired to something more genteel, reliable, respectable. And he achieved and earned it.

Besides, the game had changed. In the early 1960s, as Secchiaroli was making his career shift, new technologies were emerging that would make the sort of in-your-face work he did on Via Veneto and around the Montesi case seem quaint. To inflame Farouk and Tony Franciosa, to shoot the secret meeting of Ugo Montagna and Piero Piccioni and get recognizable images of their faces, he had physically stood in front of them, even when bodyguards were on hand or a car was aimed at him with intent. But there were new cameras that would allow paparazzi to nail their prey from distances. The SLR cameras that had come into use in the past few years could now be equipped with interchangeable lenses, including lightweight zoom lenses which would allow photographers to get close-up shots from far away, without necessitating the sort of brushes with danger that had so electrified Via Veneto.

Among those who favored the new equipment was Marcello Geppetti, and in the spring of 1962 he put it to a use that echoed in newspapers, magazines, and electronic media all over the world. Once again it involved a woman lying prone by the sea: a movie star, in Italy to work on probably the biggest movie ever made, behaving intimately with a man. From a comfortable distance, with his new telephoto lens, Geppetti got several eye-popping shots of the pair sunning and smooching on the deck of a yacht, providing the world's gossip columnists with tangible proof of an affair between the two that had been rumored but not yet proved.

  Hot wasn't the word for it. . . .

28 "Everybody Becomes a Roman Within Three Days"

Despite nearly a decade of generating moneymaking films in Italy, Hollywood studios were still beset by an unprecedented series of pressures: competing with television for the public's entertainment time and money; bidding against one another for the services of actors, directors, and writers, very few of whom worked under the sorts of long-term contracts that once made the studio system viable; and figuring out what constituted mass entertainment in an epoch during which young people had begun to gravitate toward material geared specifically to them and adults were increasingly demanding grand spectacle or grown-up themes.

There was a time when a big Hollywood movie could be a unifying event, something that pleased the whole family, respected the intelligence and emotions of an audience, earned the esteem of other filmmakers, and made the people who produced it a nice return on their investment. The Cadillac of that business, the brand that meant more quality, more stars, and more money than any of the others, was Metro-Goldwyn-Mayer. But of the classic studios, MGM was the one most unsettled by the new climate of the entertainment industry. Its ledger books were spattered with red ink—bankruptcy was a legitimate fear—and its glories were all in the past.

That past was where some at the studio believed salvation could be found. MGM had distinguished itself with blockbusters throughout the decades; why shouldn't it do so again? More specifically, why shouldn't it repeat the trick it had pulled off almost a decade prior and turn its locked funds into an investment? And even more specifically, why shouldn't it gamble its future on a project of a scale that made people forget even so massive an undertaking as *Quo Vadis*?

And so MGM staffers looked through the studio library for a blockbuster that would benefit from the full Hollywood on the Tiber treatment, and somebody remembered *Ben-Hur: A Tale of the Christ*, the silent epic based on Lew Wallace's novel about a Jewish nobleman, thrown into slavery by an enemy, who witnesses the trial and crucifixion of Jesus and loses his taste for revenge. It had been filmed in 1925 with Ramon Novarro in the lead and had been a massive undertaking: a $4 million budget, two years of production (including location work in Italy), and as many as five directors. And it was a hit, greeted as an epic masterwork and grossing more than six times what it cost to make.

In 1957, MGM decided to remake it, with a budget four times that of the previous version. William Wyler, who had served as an uncredited assistant on the original, would direct, and Charlton Heston, riding the wave of popularity that had accrued to his performance as Moses in Cecil B. De Mille's *The Ten Commandments* just the year before, would play Ben-Hur.[1] The film would take the better part of a year to shoot, and MGM leased out the bulk of Cinecittà for almost all of 1958, occupying an army of craftspeople in building sets, props (including slave galleys and racing chariots), and costumes (for upward of fifteen thousand extras).

From MGM's standpoint, it was a gamble, but for Rome's film community and the businesses and individuals that supported themselves on the economic spillover from moviemaking, it was a bonanza. For the paparazzi, there was a new haul of flesh to snap away at: Heston, Stephen Boyd, Jack Hawkins, and Martha Scott (cast, as in *The Ten Commandments*, as Heston's mother—even though she was only nine years older than him). For those who escorted tourists around town, there was the five-week production of the film's remarkable chariot race sequence, during which tour buses were permitted to stop and observe the filming in hourly intervals. Italian actors may not have had many speaking parts (as often, Hollywood preferred British actors for biblical roles), but Italian nobles were afforded the unique experience of swelling the crowd in nonspeaking roles as aristocrats in a number of sequences: a variety of princes, princesses, counts, duchesses, Ruspolis, Medicis, and Hohenlohes were on hand. Roman nobility always did, after all, have a thick vein of show biz running through it.

Like *Quo Vadis* before it, *Ben-Hur* was a gamble for MGM, which

---

1 Paul Newman was the studio's first choice. He passed because of the critical drubbing suffered by his first feature, *The Silver Chalice*, a stylized biblical epic with a plot not unlike that of *Ben-Hur*. Had Newman said yes, the part of his nemesis would've been offered to Heston.

might have collapsed under the weight of its $16 million budget had it flopped. But it did anything but. Released in November 1959, it was one of the biggest hits Hollywood had ever produced, grossing a minimum of $70 million during several domestic releases and more than doubling that overseas. It was nominated for a dozen Oscars and won a record eleven.[2] It was, by every meaningful measure, a big picture.

And yet, just when Hollywood on the Tiber seemed to have reached a commercial and artistic apex, Italian *and* American films were making the case that the scene on Via Veneto and surroundings was rotting from the inside and had always been rotting. Yes, *La Dolce Vita* itself had critiqued the epoch, but it was widely seen, and not unfairly, as a celebration of it as well. The new films about modern Rome weren't so ambivalent.

Some took the form of parody, such as 1961's *Totò, Peppino e . . . la Dolce Vita*, in which the famed Neapolitan comedian found himself involved with actresses, cocaine, and orgies on Via Veneto—or, specifically, the set of Via Veneto that Fellini had built at Cinecittà. Others were reminders of how Italians—and Italian movies—had once treated the social and economic conditions facing them, such as *Rocco e I Suoi Fratelli* (*Rocco and His Brothers*), Luchino Visconti's epic-scale neorealist film about a family of southerners who move to Milan to find work and endure emotional traumas, including a murder.

And then there was a series of elliptical films made by the one figure in Italian culture who had, like Fellini, risen from the ranks

2 That total prize haul has never been surpassed even more than fifty years later, though it was equaled twice, by *Titanic* and *The Lord of the Rings: The Return of the King*, each of which won prizes in technical categories that didn't exist at the time *Ben-Hur* was made.

of neorealists and cooperative writers and directors and forged an idiosyncratic style, a characteristic worldview, and an international reputation. Since 1957, Michelangelo Antonioni had made a string of films that succeeded in every way he could have hoped: as works of art; as intellectual inquiries; as portraits of an age; as financial ventures; and as entries in the dizzying world of, as it were, competitive international auteurist cinema.

After portraying a nearly neorealist vision of human confusion and suffering in *Il Grido*, Antonioni returned to the more familiar company of educated, urban, monied, reserved, uptight, unhappy bourgeoisie that he'd depicted in *Le Amiche* and earlier films. But he was returning home, in effect, with his ability to manipulate and create images and sequences at a higher level of mastery than ever. And the films that he made in just three years' time formed a trilogy equal to any the cinema would ever see.

In *L'Avventura* (1960), a woman disappears from a boating party and is sought throughout Southern Italy by her fiancé and her best friend. In *La Notte* (1961), a celebrated author and his wife face the inevitable decay of their marriage against a backdrop of parties, strange encounters, and even a death in modern Milan. In *L'Eclisse* (1962), a Roman translator ends an unhappy engagement and becomes involved, almost accidentally, with her mother's stockbroker, a superficial go-getter.

The surfaces and textures of these films were remarkable. Antonioni had command of everything in the frames, which were often modern and austere and pitched from unusual angles. He used striking music and edited at a deliberate pace, sometimes juxtaposing nearly abstract images to create subliminal effects of uneasiness or tension. Like Fellini, he made films that looked, sounded, and felt like no one else's.

They weren't quite as delightful, though. Antonioni's characters were broody, enervated, introverted, angsty. They lived in lovely homes; had soft, well-paying jobs; dressed beautifully; drove nice cars; knew lots of people; had access to sex—and were completely miserable. His movies examined the people who appeared to have won *Il Boom*, were the beneficiaries of the economic and cultural miracle of postwar Italy, embodied the height of the moment (and, by the by, looked great doing it). In this they resembled the novels of Alberto Moravia, which dissected the well-to-do and the comfortable and found great veins of fear, doubt, anxiety, and self-loathing. That worldview, coupled with the extreme rigor of their technique, meant that the films would have a finite appeal. It would be one thing for cinematically and culturally educated audiences to confront long, slow, abstract meditations on the empty lives of the *nouveau riche* intelligentsia; it would be another to ask the mass audiences who'd made *Ben-Hur* or even *La Dolce Vita* into huge hits to appreciate them.

Unlike Fellini, Antonioni offered no bread or circuses with which to offset his piercing, acrid vision of modern life. He rather served up his vision with angularity, acuity, and absolute control. But his essential position was absolutely right: the happy dance of progress for which his fellow Italians and his fellow human beings were so merrily congratulating themselves also revealed how bitter, lost, and cloudy their souls had become. Modernity and humanity almost couldn't coexist, and it took works of art that were at once beautiful and painful to show this sorry truth. It wasn't exactly a recipe for the commercial cinema. But it made for great art.

Other of the most scathing attacks on the economic boom and the hedonistic Via Veneto culture came from Pier Paolo Pasolini, who had helped Fellini wrap his mind around the goings-on in the Roman underground of *Le Notti di Cabiria* and *La Dolce Vita*. "A young man with a dark reputation," as Fellini's assistant Dominique Delouche recalled him, Pasolini had escorted Fellini from one shadowy spot to another, showing the director where prostitutes and pimps and drug dealers and addicts huddled and met and schemed. He knew these worlds—he had drifted in and out of them and written about them for years, and he began to capture them in films of his own, films that showed a Rome far different from the one of Via Veneto, Brioni suits, and fisticuffs with photographers.

In 1960, he filmed a script of his own set almost entirely in this netherworld of exurban shantytowns and housing projects. For him, the people who lived there were far more realistic (indeed, *neo*realistic) than anything in the films of Fellini, which were steeped in the director's idiosyncratic fantasies, or those of Antonioni, with their bourgeois protagonists struggling with their precious first-world problems.

The film was called *Accattone* (Romanesco slang for, roughly, "beggar" or "scrounger"), and it took its title from the nickname of a pimp and thief in the Pigneto neighborhood, east of the city center but close enough to the heart of town that the protagonist and his chums would visit cafés along the Tiber. Through the course of the film, Accattone spiraled ever downward, mirroring the decline of Marcello Rubini in *La Dolce Vita* but without any polish, veneer, or finery. Life in the exurban slums, the *borgate*, was a daily battle for food, shelter, liberty, dignity. Nothing there was easy or sweet, even ironically, and life's dramas almost inevitably ended painfully—and without inspiring any trends in fashion, music, nightlife, or tourism.

Accattone was respected but not a hit, its squalid setting and instances of human meanness and desperation a far cry from the image of Rome in the popular mind, its sympathetic portrait of an often heartless and ignorant criminal too dark for mass consumption. Pasolini followed it with *Mamma Roma*, another tale of life in a city "ringed by its Hell of suburbs," in his phrase, a slightly more conventionally built picture of workaday poverty, struggle, and despair, built around the title character, a former prostitute who saved enough money to buy a decent home and open a fruit stand. The film starred Anna Magnani, which, in theory, made it significantly more appealing abroad. But there was no mistaking the Rome of this particular mamma for that which had drawn international attention through, in part, the work of Fellini, Antonioni, and others, especially foreigners, who saw the city as a theme park of ancient wonders and modern liberties. Pasolini's films may not have been expressly intended as counterarguments but that was their impact: if you could ride a bike from the Trevi Fountain to the destitute quarter where Accattone and Mamma Roma lived—as Pasolini often did—you really couldn't say you were in a paradise, even a fallen one.

Another filmmaker who was intent on puncturing myths of Roman high life and bounty, even as his career benefited from what was real and what was make-believe about them, was Dino Risi. He was best known for romantic comedies about young people of scanty means aspiring to more (the more including, naturally, love), which marked him as a pioneer of the genre known as *commedia all'Italiana*—"comedy Italian-style"—films that focused on the travails of ordinary folk, often involving romance, rarely with the heavy hand associated with neorealism.

The crowning achievement of this stage of Risi's career was 1962's *Il Sorpasso* (literally, *The Overtaking*—as in one car passing another—but released in English-speaking countries as *The Easy Life*, in obvious reference to *La Dolce Vita*). It concerns Roberto, an introverted law student (Jean-Louis Trintignant) drawn away from his books one *Ferragosto* by Bruno, a hypermanic thrill seeker (Vittorio Gassman) who takes him for a joy ride (his crazed motoring style informs the film's title). Precious little of the action takes place in Rome, which, appropriately, was depicted as deserted. But Bruno is clearly one of the types who'd swell the mob at a café on Via Veneto, an embodiment of Roman excess, indulgence, and vanity.

Late in the film, the pair encounter a stolid businessman from the North who responds to Bruno's boasting about his life in Rome thus: "I never like going to Rome. It is sad and damp and the people there don't want to work. Sorry that's my opinion. In every other city people stay who they are: A Genoese stays a Genoese, a Florentine a Florentine. But in Rome everybody becomes a Roman within three days." For Bruno, this speech marks the man as a provincial prig. But it fairly summarized the effect of Rome's great moment on the people of the city—both natives and visitors—and on the waning of the appeal of Rome and its Dolce Vita elsewhere in Italy. Bruno and his playmates might have thought the world of themselves, but their allure in the larger world was on the decline.

An even starker vision of the end of the high times was afforded in *Il Boom*, a 1963 film by Vittorio De Sica, from a script by Cesare Zavattini. The story concerns Giovanni Alberti (Alberto Sordi, once the mythological *American in Rome*), a small-time businessman and speculator who experiences the economic boom of the era by living beyond his means to meet the high standard of comfort and elegance that his wife, born to wealth, expects. When a land deal that could grow into a bonanza falls his way, he tries to borrow beyond his already considerable debt, but nobody will take a chance on him. Finally, he gets an offer of financing: in exchange for the money, a wealthy woman asks for his *left eye*—to replace the one that is failing her husband. Sordi was brilliant: desperate, haughty, boisterous, horrified, scheming, and cowering in turns. And the situation was entirely credible: an economic upturn, an overconfident middle class, excessive reliance on credit, and ruthless capitalism that would actually devour a man, starting with his eyeball.

Even foreign filmmakers were apparently starting to feel that Italy—and, specifically, Rome, and, even more specifically, Hollywood on the Tiber—had become overripe. The most explicit evidence would be Vincente Minnelli's 1962 potboiler *Two Weeks in Another Town*, a backstage moviemaking story based on a novel by Irwin Shaw concerning Jack Andrus (Kirk Douglas), a past-his-moment Hollywood actor visiting Rome to do the vocal dubbing for a melodrama only to find himself directing the film after its original director (Edward G. Robinson) suffers a heart attack. Andrus has to contend with an ex-wife (Cyd Charisse) running amok on Via Veneto (right out there in the street) and an undisciplined leading man (George Hamilton, in the most cack-handed depiction of a moody method actor ever filmed). The strains would bring him close to cracking up.

The film rehashed material covered by Minnelli and Douglas in *The Bad and the Beautiful* a full decade previously, but without quite imparting the same sense that Hollywood was telling scandalous tales on itself. Everyone in *Two Weeks* was damaged by the time they arrived on-screen, and the film that they were making looked unwatchably stilted and hokey. Runaway productions made in Rome had already gotten a reputation as the last refuge of has-beens, a source not of innovation but of make-work. And Minnelli's film was no exception. Slapping it down in *The New York Times*, Bosley Crowther expressly commented on Rome's increasingly lackluster reputation: "It is well known that a class of trashy movies of a certain lush, synthetic sort is made in Rome. . . . But when a group of top American filmmakers goes all the way to Rome to make a picture about the sort of Hollywood rejects who sometimes get involved in this sort of trash and then make it as trashy as the worst stuff, it is time for a loud and pained complaint."

But these were all art movies, in some regard. While certain gimlet-eyed filmmakers, pundits, and critics were sounding an alarm at the extravagance and decadence being valorized in the global affection for the Dolce Vita, they were drowned out by a chorus of voices still singing of Rome as a no-holds-barred adventure, a place for wantonness without price, for romance without commitment, for leaving behind workaday scruples and morals and indulging in sensation—sex, wine, food, shopping, whatever your vice of choice. The year 1960 brought *It Started in Naples*, one of Clark Gable's last roles; 1961 brought *The Roman Spring of Mrs. Stone*, with Warren Beatty as an Italian gigolo seducing Vivien Leigh, and *Come September*, with Rock Hudson wooing Gina Lollobrigida; and 1962 saw *Rome Adventure* with Troy Donahue and Suzanne Pleshette as vacationing lovers. In 1963, that most all-American of girls came to town in *Gidget Goes to Rome*. To a certain way of thinking, it was clear that the arrival of Gidget (and not even the *real* Gidget, Sandra Dee, but demi-Gidget Cindy Carol) signaled that the place was no longer truly chic. With its young people in suits and evening gowns talking about their hopes and hearts in tourist locales, its sloe-eyed Latin lovers, its jokes about hard-to-manage plates of spaghetti and bitter aperitifs, the film was just as stiff and unconvincing as *Three Coins in the Fountain* had been a decade before, tone-deaf filmic bookends to an epoch of American Italophilia.

And just as steadily as these travelogue-type movies emerged, so too, as if from an assembly line, did megasized movies of the sort in which Cinecittà specialized: *Barabbas* (1961), *Francis of Assisi* (1961), *The Cardinal* (1963), *Jason and the Argonauts* (1963), and dozens of cheap and quick and lousy sword-and-sandal pictures that independent Italian studios still made—and made money on.

Ironically, it continued to be worthwhile for Italian filmmakers to work on costume pictures because the success of *Ben-Hur* had encouraged Hollywood to embark on its own biggest costume epic ever, a production so grandiose that it spilled money and equipment into the very Italian film industry it might, at first blush, seemed to have been threatening. Not only did it help fund and outfit scores of smaller movies, but it would take years to film—such a long and a volatile gestation that the forces which conceived it all but died off while it was still in utero.

29 "There's No Erotic Charge in Me"

"Exhaustion, crisis, burnout. . . ."

In the years since the global triumph of *La Dolce Vita*, Federico Fellini found himself enervated and apathetic, as if the success of the film had sucked from him the very life force that made its creation possible in the first place, as if having made one of the most celebrated, emblematic, iconic, and profitable works of art of the era had somehow diminished him.

His name had become a household word: It always tickled him to note that along with the phrase *la dolce vita* and the noun *paparazzi*, the word *Felliniesque* would become common usage and even appear in dictionaries.[1] He was presented with the opportunity to do whatever he wished (although, as he was always quick to remind journalists, friends, and even waiters, not the financial means). But instead of being on top of the world, he was spent, flailing, anguished.

Back when *La Dolce Vita* was still rolling out around the world, Fellini began an intensive course of Jungian analysis, which eventually led him to keep drawing pads and colored pencils on a bedside table so that he could describe and—gifted cartoonist that he was—illustrate the contents of his dreams to share with his therapist, Dr. Ernst Bernhard. Under Bernhard's guidance, Fellini started slowly to steer his artistic energies toward more self-reflective, dreamlike, fantastical themes, ideas, and images—the inimitable work that he would produce for the next three decades of his career.

But before any of that could happen, he had to overcome the torpor in which the making, release, and reception of *La Dolce Vita* had left him. And to do that, in part, he went into business. Along with Angelo Rizzoli, he started a production company, Federiz, which was intended to make his movies and those of some friends and collaborators whom he wished to shepherd through the obstacle course of independent financing. Among the slate of films announced by Federiz at its launch were the debut of Pier Paolo Pasolini, *Accattone*, and the second film by Milanese writer-director Ermanno Olmi, *Il Posto*. Both films would eventually be made and widely lauded, but neither would be produced by Federiz, which barely existed after that party and which did little more in its few years of existence than open some nice offices near Piazza di Spagna, get its name on a few

[1] "I always wanted to be an adjective when I grew up," he liked to joke, though not really joking.

films (which were, in reality, funded by other entities), and drive wedges between Fellini and several of the directors whom he had hoped to champion, including, sadly, Pasolini.

Instead of producing, Fellini dove back into directing, not a feature but an episode—a quite long one—in one of those anthology films that Italian directors so happily worked on. This one, *Boccaccio '70*, was meant explicitly to thumb a nose at Italy's censors, official and otherwise, who had helped make Fellini's life hell after the release of *La Dolce Vita*. Alongside episodes by Vittorio De Sica, Mario Monicelli, and Luchino Visconti, Fellini would present a thick and heavy satire of the moralizing Italian bourgeois gentleman of his day, a religious, bureaucratic prig who one day found his inner peace ruined by the placement of a billboard in the environs of his apartment. The trouble? The billboard, advertising the healthful benefits of drinking milk, was illustrated with the image of a smiling woman with generous décolletage: none other than Anita Ekberg herself.

In the course of the story, *Le Tentazioni del Dottor Antonio* (*The Temptation of Dr. Antonio*), the title character would be subjected to a truly Felliniesque nightmare, horrifying to him but comical to the audience, in which Ekberg, a gigantic dream figure of sexual bounty, would come alive, step out of the frame of the billboard, and stomp around his neighborhood (Fellini had the modernist EUR district of southern Rome re-created at Cinecittà in miniature), taunting the prudish *dottore* with her libidinous freedom and well-being. It was good fun—and, as the film also featured episodes starring Sophia Loren and Romy Schneider and was released while *La Dolce Vita* was still being talked about, it resulted in good box-office receipts.[2] But

2 The American release, in June 1962, was notable in that *Boccaccio '70* was the inaugural feature at Cinema I *and* Cinema II, a pair of theaters on New York's Upper East Side that would for decades be among the most deluxe venues for art-house films and prestige American studio pictures.

it wasn't a true follow-up to *La Dolce Vita*. That film, whatever it might be, was still gestating in Fellini's tired head.

*A*t first, Fellini blamed moneymen for his inability to move forward: "The producers didn't want to make a Fellini film," he groused, "they only wanted a film done by Fellini." But he had no idea, not really, what his next movie might be. He traveled throughout Italy, claiming to be scouting locations, and he ended up taking the waters at a thermal spa near the border of Tuscany and Umbria. There he had an epiphany: he would make a film about a man in his early forties (Fellini was then forty-one) visiting a thermal spa in the grips of a crisis concerning his work, his marriage (and, yes, his love affairs), his hopes, his regrets, his intellectual capacity, his wobbly morality, his tenuous relationship to religion—the whole of his inner life. It would, he imagined, have an episodic quality like *La Dolce Vita*, but the episodes would encompass not the events of the world as a journalist would experience them, but a blending of the character's internal and external lives. He really didn't know much more about it than that: not who would play the lead, not how it ended, and not, least of all, what it might mean. He wanted Angelo Rizzoli to fund it to the tune of, he estimated, $6 million. Oh, and he did have a title, if only a tentative one: *Otto e Mezzo*—8½—it being, by his own count, not quite his ninth feature film.[3]

As far as a leading man went, he was ambitious: he spoke of hiring a forty-year-old Charlie Chaplin, who didn't exist, and he met with Laurence Olivier, almost out of obligation to Rizzoli, who, like every Italian producer, saw more upside in foreign than domestic actors. But really, there was only ever one person who could play the part: Marcello Mastroianni.

3 At one stage of its gestation, the film may have been called *Il Labirinto* (*The Labyrinth*), but its eventual title was selected and publicized quite early on.

* * *

*I*n the wake of the international success of *La Dolce Vita*, Mastroianni was catapulted to the forefront of European actors, in demand as a box-office draw and as a new kind of leading man. Amazingly, a large swath of the ranks of moviemakers and audiences saw Fellini's film and thought they were looking at the screen's next Latin lover, the man who could do what, say, Rosanno Brazzi couldn't—namely, bring the legacy of Rudolph Valentino and Ramon Novarro back to life in a contemporary idiom. Mastroianni didn't have an old-fashioned air, like Brazzi; rather, he ranked alongside Alain Delon and Jean-Paul Belmondo: new faces who distilled the allure of the past into modern packages, sex symbols of a bold and frank and confused new age.

Mastroianni, though, wouldn't have any of such talk. In interview after interview, he rejected suggestions that he was somehow a sex symbol or an icon of romance. He talked of his ugly body (he hated his skinny legs), of his marriage (then entering its second decade), of how preposterous the very ideal of the Latin lover was in the modern era, of his own aversion to romance and seduction. "I am not a lover type," he declared in the pages of *Playboy*, "not in the conventional sense, anyway. There's no erotic charge in me."

Yes, *on-screen* he got about with the ladies and was steeped in sexual opportunity, atmosphere, and urges. But Mastroianni didn't strive, as, say, Brazzi might have, to be seen as a smoldering Lothario. He appeared, rather, careworn and uncertain and even sad. He wasn't a confident he-man in the vein of Valentino or Clark Gable, who would win the girl with devastating charm or drag her away with sheer brawn. He appeared frightened of his own urges, cynical as to his chances, bemused by each setback or tangent. In 1962, *Time* magazine described him as, "a mantis who has lost

faith in the efficacy of prayer . . . painfully aware of nearly everything, truly able at nothing. His spine seems to be a stack of plastic
napkin rings," and concluded, despite all that, "he is relentlessly
attractive."

The talk of his sexual magnetism, the trotting out of the Latin
lover clichés, the comparisons to Gable: it all drove him daffy.
"Latin lover! What madness!" he said bemusedly late in life. "I was
thirty-five when I made *La Dolce Vita* and the Americans decided
that I was a Latin Lover. But how? I've never frequented night
clubs, I never combed Via Veneto, even though I made a film on Via
Veneto. Yeah, a coffee now and then."

At other times, the topic rankled him. "If anything," Mastroianni complained to an interviewer, "I am the *anti*-Gable." Riffing
on that thought with another journalist, he said,

> Something has happened in the thirty years that separate
> Gable and me. The women who wanted to be slapped and
> kissed found that they were dealing with men who were either
> too lazy or too disenchanted to play the hero. Even posing as
> one was a bore. So, poor dears, they had to adapt themselves
> to the new circumstances. In their perennial thirst for love
> and romantic idealism they developed a new type of man they
> could worship. It wasn't Clark Gable any more—hard, violent,
> a lion—but Mastroianni—inconstant, distracted, a house cat.
> . . . They have come to grips with reality and have transferred
> their affections to someone like me, someone who is lost,
> ready to compromise, without backbone.

He continually swore to his own ineffectuality: "I'm a flash in the
pan," he told Oriana Fallaci, "a spark that goes right out if someone doesn't throw some gasoline on it." He even coined a phrase to

describe his characteristic mood: "I'm like a flag without pride. . . . I don't think it makes any sense. It's just the way I feel."

As if to flaunt his aversion to being labeled a he-man or a lady-killer, he chose for his first film after *La Dolce Vita* Mauro Bolognini's *Il Bell'Antonio*, in which he plays a staggeringly handsome young man who returns to his Sicilian home from Rome, where he is rumored to have bedded the wives of men of power and influence. Nothing could be further from the truth. As is suggested frequently and indelicately, Antonio *may* be gay; he *certainly*, however, is impotent, a fact that emerges only after he has been married to a beautiful local girl for more than a year.

It was another well-received performance, and Mastroianni followed with a similarly sexless work, Antonioni's *La Notte*. Despite sharing the screen with Jeanne Moreau and Monica Vitti, despite Antonioni's growing reputation as one of Italy's—if not the world's—most important directors, it wasn't a happy experience for Mastroianni. After working with Fellini, Mastroianni found Antonioni as sterile as his movies: "He hates actors," he complained to a reporter. "For the kind of films he makes, he doesn't need actors." To another journalist he compared his most famous directors thus: "Visconti was the Maestro, the professor. Fellini is like a classmate. Antonioni is like a surgeon: He can save your life, but you're better off not getting sick to begin with." Unpleasant or no, Antonioni's movie was greeted with great fervor (and no little puzzlement—which might, in fact, have *increased* its reputation), and Mastroianni once again benefited. *La Notte* played around the world, and the actor's position as a pillar of the new Italian cinema solidified.

It would reach an acme with Pietro Germi's 1961 *Divorzio all'Italiana* (*Divorce Italian Style*), a stunningly frank and dark comedy in which Mastroianni plays a Sicilian nobleman in an unhappy marriage who falls in love with his wife's young cousin and contrives to get his wife to cuckold him and thereby afford him a reason to kill her and free himself (divorce still being unavailable in Italy). With his hair slicked down like a lounge lizard's, a pencil mustache hovering over his mouth like a scar, a dainty cigarette holder, and a nagging facial tic (borrowed, mischievously, from Germi, in whom it was a genuine mark of stress and tension), Mastroianni was subtle, broad, cunning, childish, repulsive, and altogether brilliant. The film became a sensation everywhere it played, grossing more than $2 million in the United States alone. Mastroianni said that for the rest of his life strangers would greet him by imitating the tic he'd stolen from Germi. Even more, it earned him an Oscar nomination as Best Actor, the first time a male performer had been cited for a role performed other than in English. Facing the competition of Burt Lancaster (*Birdman of Alcatraz*), Jack Lemmon (*Days of Wine and Roses*), Peter O'Toole (*Lawrence of Arabia*) and the ultimate winner, Gregory Peck (*To Kill a Mockingbird*), Mastroianni stayed home.[4] But there was no doubt that he was on Hollywood's most wanted list.

But he still wouldn't be lured to the United States to act, and he still didn't want to learn English. (When he did learn it, near the end of the 1960s, he discovered a favorite word: *fuck.* "It's the first word I learned in English," he told *The New York Times*, which wouldn't print it. "It's a good one. It covers just about everything."[5])

4 Impressively, *Divorce Italian Style* won the Oscar for Original Screenplay.

5 He would cause a scandal in 1977 when he used the word *fucker* during a live TV interview with Sophia Loren and Dick Cavett. Inevitably, he was responding to the question of whether or not he was a Latin lover: "To be a Latin lover you must first of all be a great fucker," he said, adding, "You have to be infallible. I'm not infallible. I often fall into *fallo*"—meaning "flaw" or "error," but also "phallus," a pun lost on Cavett, his audience, and the American press and public, the latter two of which went into predictably hysterical paroxysms over this dastardly assault on decency.

More pertinent, he said, there was no reason to make movies anywhere but home. "What is being done here in Italy," he said in *Time*, "is far better and much more mature and advanced than anything cinematic being done elsewhere." He visited the United States occasionally to promote a movie, inevitably meeting movie stars, including Greta Garbo, who had asked to see him, Anne Bancroft, who spoke with him in Italian and for whom he had great admiration, and Jack Lemmon, his first conversation with whom consisted of a single spoken word—"scotch" —and a pantomime of pouring and drinking whiskey.[6]

In Rome, he explained, he knew where to go for a coffee, where to get his hair cut, where to test-drive the sports cars in which he'd begun to indulge himself once he started commanding substantial salaries. And he had a friendly relationship with a press corps that granted him a remarkable degree of discretion as he indulged in what had become a habit of wandering from the steadfast marriage he bragged about in interviews. During *La Notte*, for instance, he had an affair with Moreau ("She's one of the few women I know who would be worth falling in love with," he told a reporter, adding, appreciatively, "Have you seen the bags under her eyes?"); and during the production of Louis Malle's *La Vie Privée* (*A Very Private Affair*), he managed, quite publicly, to escape the clutches of Brigitte Bardot, who, quite publicly, pursued him. In the coming years, he would enjoy dalliances with costars Ursula Andress and Faye Dunaway, and in the 1970s he would have a rela-

---

6 He lamented that he never got to meet Marilyn Monroe, for whom he had concocted a film story: *Quo Vadis, Marilyn?*, in which he hoped for her to play a Hollywood star on location in Rome opposite his ordinary Italian chap hired as an extra—a Roman soldier—on her film. It was a great idea, as was the one he had late in life to make a film about Tarzan as an aged, forgotten figure: "a comedy with a melancholy undertone," as he described it.

tionship of several years' duration with Catherine Deneuve that produced a daughter, the actress Chiara Mastroianni. But he never divorced Flora. (And, for that matter, he never had an affair with Sophia Loren, even as they would go on to make another eight feature films together in the next thirty years, one of the international cinema's greatest screen pairings.)

Mastroianni's other great creative relationship was the one with his cinematic pal, Federico Fellini, who finally selected the subject for the full-length follow-up to *La Dolce Vita*. Even before there was a script, Mastroianni had no hesistations about accepting the director's invitation to appear in *8½*: "It was like playing one of those childhood games with a friend," he said, "where one of you says, 'Okay, you're the cop, and I'm the robber. Let's go!'"

$\mathcal{F}$ellini was equally happy to reunite with his former star, but he had some issues to address. He didn't want any of Mastroianni's reputation as a sex symbol to permeate the new film. He did everything he could to make his star *less* attractive, having him lose weight (again), shave his body, add gray streaks to his hair, wear thick spectacles, sport dark bags under his eyes, and reveal the skinny legs of which Mastroianni was always embarrassed. "The role was of a man being eaten alive by his neuroses," Fellini explained, "so I thought that called for somebody who didn't look like he had just gotten up from the table after a sumptuous lunch." Mastroianni recalled the director telling him, "I want my intellectual to be very fragile, very delicate."

Working with most of the writing team from *La Dolce Vita*, Fellini settled on a name for his protagonist, Guido Anselmi, and an occupation: he would be a filmmaker, inevitably, whose inability to overcome his crisis threatened the big-budget science fiction movie he was slated to make. He cast the key roles, once again, with a combination of beautiful women (Anouk Aimée as the neglected wife, Sandra Milo as the frivolous mistress,[7] Claudia Cardinale as the ingénue whom Guido hopes can rescue his film and his soul) and nonactors playing roles very like their real-world personalities: the liquor magnate Guido Alberti as a movie producer, the journalist Jean Rougeul as a film critic, the playwright and mystic Ian Dallas as a telepath. He had a huge set representing a rocket gantry built at Cinecittà, and he planned to re-create Guido's childhood village, the thermal spa, and other elaborate sets on locations all around Rome and its environs.

But at some level Fellini didn't want to do it. He joked that it would be his "Unfinished," but beneath his apparent levity were real doubts that he could follow through. Virtually on the eve of production, in late April 1962, he sat in his office beside his beloved Studio 5 at Cinecittà, drafting a letter to Rizzoli explaining that he was going to have to abandon the production, revealing the depth of his personal crisis and his regrets for having concealed his predicament for so long. He had, he felt, no idea what he was doing or how to carry the burden of the money and the man-hours that had been invested in the film: "I feel like a train conductor who's sold all the tickets," he had been telling people, "lined up the passengers, tucked the bags away. . . . But where is the track?" He broke down and began writing his letter of resignation: "Dear Angelo," it began, "I am aware that what I am about to tell you will irreparably undermine our professional relationship. Our friendship will also be jeopardized by it. I ought to have written this letter to you three months ago, but up until last night I had hoped that. . . ."

And then, a knock at his door: a stagehand inviting him to have

---

7 This bit of casting—and the continued absence of Giulietta Masina from her husband's films—fueled widespread rumors of an affair between Fellini and Milo, gossip that the actress encouraged with zest.

a drink and a piece of cake in celebration of the birthday of another member of the crew. The assembled workers were delighted to see him, and the honoree himself raised a glass to toast the boss: "This is going to be a great film, *dottore*! Here's to it! Long live *Otto e Mezzo*!" Ashamed at his cowardice, Fellini joined the toast, went back to his office, tore up the unfinished letter, and got on with the job.

Production began on May 9, and fate continually provided difficulties beyond the considerable ones that Fellini had created for himself. Because workers in the photo lab went on strike, he would have to film for several weeks without the benefit of seeing the previous day's rushes; he chose to abandon the practice altogether and work by instinct. He printed only seven copies of the entire script—an outline, really—and he kept them locked in a safe every night so that nobody else would know how tenuous a hold he had on the material. He still didn't have an ending, so he shot a place-holder, in which Guido was surrounded by all the characters in the film—both the "real" ones and the ones who lived in his head—in the dining car of a train. And he taped a note to the camera so that he could see it before every single shot of the film: "Ricordati *che é un film* comico"—"*Remember* this is a *comedy*."

In October, near the completion of production, he was inspired with a new vision of the ending. Instead of being railroaded to his fate, Guido would scurry away from it. Instead of the people in his life staring him down accusingly, they would celebrate his liberty with him. Instead of abandoning the expensive set, it would become the centerpiece of a party: Guido and all the characters in the film, "real" or no, would dance around in a circle, affirming life and happiness and possibility—a long cry from the dark endings of the films Fellini had made since *I Vitelloni*. There was such a feeling of joy upon this inspiration that Fellini shot the sequence in color, even though the rest of the film (and the final version of the finale) was photographed in (glorious) black-and-white by cinematographer Gianni Di Venanzo. Remarkably, by *making* the film, Fellini had solved the puzzle of exactly what film it was he was trying to make. A recipe for catastrophe had catalyzed into a formula for what might be his greatest achievement.

Where *La Dolce Vita* seemed desperate to gobble up an entire outside world, *8½* was pitched inward, diving into the psyche of its protagonist in such fever and frenzy that the impulse could only have been autobiographical. Guido Anselmi had all of Fellini's self-professed flaws and foibles and problems and gifts and attachments and tics and desires and dreams—plus some new ones that Fellini and his cowriters had thrown onto his beleaguered shoulders almost as if for the fun of watching him try to balance one more thing.

Any number of markers declared the kinship of character and creator: his age; his career; his marital crisis; his colleagues; his Borsalino hats and colored scarves;[8] his reputation as an artistic apostate; his reputation as a poor businessman; his vexed relationship with religion; his interest in the occult; his interest in women; the ticking clock of a film production sounding off his doom to a steady beat; the scrutiny of a dunderheaded press, from all over the world, who, like his producer, never ceased asking him just what exactly it was that he was doing; his own inner voice, asking that very same question and many, many more.

The film mixed dream and nightmare and fantasy and real life willy-nilly, or so it could appear at first sight. In fact, Fellini always made it evident what layer or type of "reality" you were watching:

8 In his decades of work at Cinecittà, Fellini had given rise to a gambling pool among his longtime crews, who bet on what color scarf he would choose on a given day from his vast wardrobe of them.

Guido's now, his then, his what-if. Like Wagner or Rothko, Fellini could morph from one dimension of abstract expression into another almost without the audience knowing exactly when or how it had happened. You simply found yourself in another psychological, emotional, and cinematic world as if by magic.

Mastroianni was amazing—broken and lost and distractable and cynical and blithe, a gorgeous catastrophe who always had the right and the wrong thing to say, often at the same moment. He was deeply attractive and shattered at once, as fashionable as he'd been in *La Dolce Vita* and convincingly suffering a nervous breakdown.

And the filmmaking was extraordinary in every way: as narrative; as psychodrama; as confession; as act of artistic audacity in the face of hysterical enmities and quarrels and polemics; as a demonstration of postwar Italian filmcraft at its absolute zenith; in its gorgeous cinematography, décor, wardrobe, makeup, and music; in the bottomless toy chest of human bodies, faces, fashions, and behaviors in which Fellini so loved to play. Nobody had ever made a movie like it, and nobody ever would again. In its time and place, in its making and its thought, *8½* was, in all meaningful senses, a masterpiece.

Despite the film's opacity and elusiveness, despite Fellini's lingering reputation as an apostate and an obscurantist and an upstart, despite some voices that castigated the film for solipsism and incoherence, *8½* was a success with critics and audiences in Italy. As with *La Dolce Vita*, an air of scandal surrounded the release and encouraged ticket sales, and the artfulness (and artiness) of the film somehow appealed even to some viewers who were hopelessly puzzled by it. Abroad, it was more celebrated. Fellini and Mastroianni brought it to the Moscow Film Festival, where it played to an audience of more than eight thousand and was a surprise winner of the top prize. The following spring, the film was nominated for five Oscars, including Best Director, Original Screenplay, Black-and-White Art Direction, and it won two: Best Black-and-White Costume Design and Foreign Language Film—the third victory for Fellini in the latter category in a remarkable run of five films spanning nine years.

Fellini accepted his statuette from Julie Andrews and, visibly moved, thanked the audience in heavily accented English: "I am particularly happy to receive this fabulous award because it comes to me on the eve of my next picture. I don't think a director about to start a job could wish for anything more stimulating and auspicious as this. *Arrivederci!*"

30 "We Are on Stage All the Time"

Once again, a scandal that radiated out of Via Veneto and Rome and reverberated around the world began with a woman in her twenties lying beside the sea.

But unlike Wilma Montesi, this young woman wasn't anonymous, wasn't alone, wasn't linked to some beguiling mystery—and, in fact, was very much alive.

She lay not on a beach but on the sunning deck of a yacht (a converted submarine chaser, as it happened, but absolutely deluxe), and not at dawn but at midday, sometimes on her stomach with her top lowered down her back so that her tan would be even, more often on her back, so that she could gaze at her companion, who, like her, wore only a swimsuit. Their rapport was unrehearsed, natural, real; they kissed, whispered, shared laughs.

The photographer was hundreds of yards away, hidden, patient, quick to react; he'd likely been in his spot for hours, maybe days.

It was a tender and intimate scene and completely ordinary.

And yet a half dozen images of it would soon circulate throughout Italy, the rest of Europe, and, especially, the United States, creating a scandal that would enliven news headlines for months, drawing attention in the American Congress and the halls of the Vatican, playing a part in the dismantling of a major American entertainment corporation, and turning two people sharing a moment of peace, sunshine, and new love into household names, spoken of equally in tones of condemnation and envy.

At least one of them, the woman, was already world famous. Not yet thirty, Elizabeth Taylor had been a movie star for two decades, a child actress who had transformed into a major movie star and a sex symbol. She was in Italy—Rome, mostly, but the Tyrrhenian island of Ischia on the day of the photos—making a film that would become the biggest, gaudiest and most notorious of all the Hollywood on the Tiber productions. It was a gargantuan epic that was already several years (and nations and screenwriters and directors and stars) in the making, and it was stacking up expenses and enduring overruns and interruptions so regularly that it would soon become, by a sizable margin, the costliest film yet made. It had brought the company producing it, 20th Century Fox, to its knees, with the board of directors and top executives under constant scrutiny and attack and bankruptcy a real possibility. It wouldn't come to the world's screens for almost a year, yet it was being talked about almost daily in newspapers and magazines simply on the basis of those photos.

The main point of interest was this: that man beside Taylor, rubbing sunscreen onto her bare shoulders and hovering above her to indulge in kisses and whispers? That wasn't her husband, Eddie Fisher (her fourth, it happened), but rather her costar in the colossal film in question, the actor Richard Burton, himself thirty-six and still wed, for more than thirteen years, to the former Sybil Williams, an actress from his native Wales.

The photographs taken that day by the tireless Marcello Geppetti were the clearest evidence yet that the rumors roaring up and down Via Veneto concerning an affair between the two stars were true. There had been scuttlebutt and jokes and tales from servants and movie extras and mysterious comings and goings at airports and hospitals and restaurants, and even a few photos of the pair that could be explained away. But actual proof of something truly steamy had up to that moment been lacking. Now the world could see it—and would pay again and again at the newsstand to do so. Elizabeth Taylor—fickle, brazen, wanton, insatiable as she was deemed at the time—had once again seduced another woman's husband. And the story of this affair was even more of a doozy than any of her previous.

Burton was in Italy because he had been cast in the role of a Roman general and politician in the film, replacing Stephen Boyd, who had filled the part opposite Taylor in a production of *the very same movie* that had been aborted two years earlier in London. That first attempt by Fox and producer Walter Wanger to make an epic film of a historical novel by Carlo Maria Franzero (purchased for a mere $15,000), was a complete waste of time and money—millions of dollars of it. The director, Rouben Mamoulian, produced no footage that the studio wanted to use, the London locations were unconvincing, and the star herself was eventually incapacitated by illness, delaying the production beyond the point at which it was economically feasible to keep it on hold. Nearly everyone involved in the film was let go, and the studio chose to start over with a new writer-director, Joseph L. Mankiewicz, and two new stars, Rex Harrison (replacing Peter Finch) and Burton. Only Taylor remained. In fact, she was, by the admission of a flustered Wanger, who had been making movies since buying the property that turned Rudolph Valentino into *The Sheik*, the one essential ingredient in the whole mammoth exercise. "Elizabeth Taylor," he wrote soon after the ordeal had played itself entirely out, "*is* the picture."

And the picture, *Cleopatra*, would be the end of an era—of several eras—both in Hollywood and in Rome.

Cleopatra dwarfed *Ben-Hur* in size, in cost, in ambition, in length, and, almost especially, in notoriety. The scale of the thing was staggering. Under the guidance of Mankiewicz and Wanger, *Cleopatra* occupied nearly the whole of Cinecittà, where a twelve-acre reproduction of the Roman Forum was built (larger than the real thing). A seaside reproduction of the ancient harbor of Ostia was constructed (again, larger than the original and fully operational). As many as 7,000 extras appeared on *many* filming days. Upward of 26,000 costumes were designed and created (the wardrobe for Elizabeth Taylor accounted for only 58 of them, but one of those was made of gold and cost $6,500).[1] The sets were built and decorated with 6,000 tons of cement and 26,000 gallons of paint. The archers in the film's battle scenes were equipped with 150,000 prop arrows. Elephants for several processionals were shipped in from England (the Italian elephant trainer whose animals were

---

1 Approximately $52,000 in 2016.

deemed inadequate by the production sued for defamation of his brood). An entire building on the back lot was reconfigured into a dressing room and private office for the leading lady. And there were the salaries: Taylor's, most notably, averaged out to approximately $10,000 *per day*, with an additional $3,000 per week for expenses. When the production began in Rome in September 1961, the total cost of the film was estimated at being somewhere in the $15 to $20 million range; it rose steadily in the following months, passing the $30 million mark in May 1962, and settled somewhere around $37 or $40 million by the time the film debuted in the spring of 1963.[2]

That right there would have been headache enough for any producer. But *Cleopatra* was absolutely hobbled by other difficulties, some self-imposed, such as the lack of a completed script when filming began, but others external and uncontrollable: cold and rainy weather in Rome; illnesses striking Taylor, Mankiewicz, and several key actors; damage done to exposed film during the ungainly procedure of shipping it from Rome to Los Angeles for processing; sheer bad luck such as discovering that a beach near Anzio that had been rented as a location (for $150,000) was still peppered with land mines left behind after the war; interference from 20th Century Fox executives who were panicked, appropriately, by the company's massive financial losses of the previous two years and its new slate of poorly received releases (including *Tender Is the Night, Hemingway's Adventures of a Young Man, Satan Never Sleeps*, and a remake of *State Fair* starring Pat Boone and Bobby Darin); and, then, the scandal that turned *Cleopatra* into the most ardently discussed film in production ever.

2 Approximately $290 to $310 million in 2016—almost five times, after adjusting for inflation, what MGM had spent to make *Gone With the Wind* almost a quarter century previously.

Mankiewicz joked darkly about his fate as the director of the enterprise, calling *Cleopatra* "the hardest three pictures I ever made . . . conceived in emergency, shot in hysteria, and wound up in blind panic." In Wanger's view, the trouble surrounding the film may well have been self-inflicted:

> Our company on location was like an invading army. We disturbed the Roman economy by hiring so many artisans and extras. We monopolized the Roman press because of the excitement generated by our picture. We were lionized by sophisticated and blasé Roman society because we had the glamour of Hollywood and big money. . . . The *pièce de résistance* of a VIP visit to Rome was no longer an audience with the Pope—it was an invitation to visit our set. . . . Here in Rome we are on stage all the time—it's easy to feel the whole world revolves around us.

Some of these claims could have been made about previous Hollywood productions in Rome. But the response of the world's press—and its readers, viewers, and listeners—to the romance that was going on behind the scenes of *Cleopatra* was unprecedented. Little wonder that the publicists sent to Rome by the studio to, in effect, fight a raging inferno with a water pistol took to referring to the film in their correspondence as "*It*."

The possibility of an affair between Taylor and Burton came to public notice on New Year's Eve 1961, when Burton and his wife, Sybil, threw a party at Bricktop's on Via Veneto and hosted Taylor and Eddie Fisher as guests of honor. It was a long, boozy, wild evening, and at least one photographer who'd managed to sneak into the event got a glimpse—but not a picture—of the two stars with their hands clasped together under a table. In the coming weeks, as gossip on the streets and in the newspapers became louder with the charge that Taylor—already condemned in many quarters as what was then termed a "home wrecker"—would dump the husband she'd stolen from Debbie Reynolds for a new man, who, again, belonged to still another woman. The film's publicists dismissed the rumors, and Fisher, in particular, tried to put a brave face on things, talking to the press about his blissful marriage, taking his wife to Paris on a shopping spree, and even joining in her quest to adopt a child.

But the talk persisted and intensified, in no small part because it was completely true. At the end of March, a single, grainy photograph of Burton and Taylor seeming to share a kiss had found its way into *Lo Specchio*, courtesy of Elio Sorci and his new telephoto lens, but it could've been a moment of collegial warmth between a pair of show biz luvvies. A few weeks later, the pair went out for a night on the town, to Via Veneto and Bricktop's, once again, where they even permitted one photographer, Gilberto Petrucci, whom Burton had not long before attacked drunkenly with a brass pole, to take pictures—but, again, no indisputable signs of romance. They were, as Mankiewicz lamented over drinks at his hotel one night, "two actors who don't know to get offstage." As if to underscore the point, Taylor went out once again on Via Veneto with Burton not long after, this time sporting the elaborate Egyptian-style eye makeup that she and her stylist had devised for the film: the part she was playing had, in a sense, taken over her life and even her appearance.

And then came Marcello Geppetti's shots from Ischia, which put all doubts to rest. The stars of the biggest movie ever made were engaged in an affair in the world capital of sex and glamour and high living: no doubt; full stop; print it.

That so much tumult, excess, chatter, and drama should be

emerging from Rome surprised no one. It had been going on for years. But even in that context, this revelation landed like a bombshell. Taylor and Burton and the culture that sparked their romance were reviled by Hollywood gossip columnists, American congressmen, and in news reports from the Vatican. On its official radio station, the Vatican referred scornfully to the "caprices of adult children," while its newspaper published a searing open letter about the sanctity of marriage, recounting Taylor's romantic history in a sneering, prosecutorial tone.

When the production in Rome finally wrapped, in late July 1962, months behind schedule, Taylor and Burton went off to London to perform in a less volatile production, *The V.I.P.s*, and Mankiewicz went on to edit the gigantic thing he'd filmed and to fight for his version of it, which began in rough cut at six hours.[3]

And after all that, *Cleopatra* was a hit. No doubt fueled by all the talk and gossip and curiosity, the world's moviegoers made it the number one box-office draw of 1963, with more than $57 million in ticket sales—still, technically, not enough to cover the expense of making and releasing it. In New York, it played for fifteen months, and when it became available for television in 1966, it commanded a price of $5 million from the ABC network, which put it into the black. It was nominated for nine Academy Awards, including Best Picture and Actor (Harrison, not Burton) and wound up winning four: Best Special Effects, Color Art Direction, Color Cinematography, and Color Costume Design.[4]

---

3 The initial release of the film clocked in at four hours, and the most commonly screened version was a little longer than three.

4 This prize dovetailed nicely with the Oscar for Black-and-White Costumes, which went to *8½*, another example of the great art and craft of Italian costumiers and clothiers and, by coincidence, a movie that was being made at Cinecittà at exactly the same time as *Cleopatra*.

But all of that was too late to save 20th Century Fox. The extra-curricular turmoil in the press, the obvious excesses of the production, the studio's unfortunate streak of big, poorly attended movies, the clamor among stockholders, and the political machinations of executives seeking to improve their positions: it all proved fatal. A huge chunk of the studio's back lot was carved off and sold—180 acres. By the end of 1963, when *Cleopatra* was still rolling out around the world, the first building of what would be the new neighborhood of Century City opened for occupancy on what was once the Fox lot. And unlike the venerable practice in Rome, where the past was always left visible, the builders of this new layer of western Los Angeles left no traces of the old.

In a way, that was the fate of everything about *Cleopatra*, including the very culture that inspired and nourished it. There would only be one or two subsequent films of any ambitious scale that bore the Hollywood on the Tiber stamp—but they weren't really made by Hollywood or shot along the Tiber. Anthony Mann's 1964 epic *The Fall of the Roman Empire*, which starred Sophia Loren and, again, Stephen Boyd, was filmed almost entirely in Spain, and John Huston's 1966 *The Bible: In the Beginning . . .* , which was conceived as an American production, wound up being produced, principally but not entirely in Rome, by Dino De Laurentiis.

Neither of those last epics had anything like the impact—in production or at the box office—of *Cleopatra*. In part that was explicable by the absence of drama and scandal to encourage public interest. In part, though, it was simply changing times. The scale of *Cleopatra* indicated how big and how far a certain type of movie could go, and although there were still instances of it, the era of the megamovie was over, even if the emperors and strivers of Hollywood and moviemaking Rome hadn't realized it yet.

31 "Please Stop Crying!"

The one bit of popular culture that hadn't blossomed in Rome in all this time was music. When they first became popular, the nightclubs of Via Veneto featured prewar jazz music: Dixieland, swing. After a few years, they mixed in the Latin American sounds that were popular in that era of cocktails and cigarettes: mambos, rumbas, cha-chas. In time, there was a hint of American influence, an uptempo beat that suggested rock 'n 'roll but wasn't remotely the real thing.

There were a few local stars: Claudio Villa, Fred Buscaglione, Renato Carosone. But nobody anywhere else ever heard of them. In fact, other than Neapolitan ballads, Italian pop music didn't have a very strong identity. There was a breakout song late in the decade, "*Arrivederci, Roma*," written for the 1958 film *The Seven Hills of Rome* (where it was introduced by Mario Lanza) and later used as the unofficial anthem of the Rome Olympics. That same year gave the world Domenico Modugno, a sometime actor, sometime show biz manager who triumphed spectacularly at the Sanremo Music Festival with the presentation of "*Nel Blu Dipinto di Blu*," aka "Volare." Modugno's record of the tune hit number one all over the world, and the song was almost immediately covered by artists throughout Europe and the Americas. Modugno, unusually at the time, wrote and sang all his own material. But he was hardly Chuck Berry or Buddy Holly, and "Volare" hardly presaged the coming tsunami of popular music that would transform global culture in subsequent decades. In Italy, in truth, there really was no sign that it was coming.

So perhaps it's understandable that when Federico Fellini accepted the Oscar for *8½* he had no idea that the world had changed beneath his feet in the preceding weeks and was getting ready to change even more. On the very day of Fellini's triumph, Richard Lester, an American filmmaker who lived and worked in London, was directing a movie starring four musicians from Liverpool who had only recently debuted on TV in the United States and ignited an energy that would sweep away almost everything that Fellini and his Roman chums had created in the previous decade and a half. *A Hard Day's Night*, starring, of course, the Beatles, would debut later that summer and make its way around the world accompanied by a clamor of electric guitars, pounding beats, and the shrieks of young girls, shifting the focus of the global popular culture forever from the mores and manners and moral crises of adults to the thirsts and passions and energies of their kids.

Fellini had no real feel for contemporary youth culture. *La Dolce Vita* had featured the Italian Elvis, Adriano Celentano, singing a slightly garbled but undeniably energetic version of Little Richard's "Ready Teddy," but the director staged it to look more like the fellow was having a drug fit or an epileptic seizure. The scene displayed rock 'n' roll as another symptom of the despair and decay the film anatomized. When it came to music, Fellini preferred the circuslike melodies of Nino Rota or the old standards he might have tried to Lindy Hop to after the war, tunes such as "Mama (He's Making Eyes at Me)," which is performed in a Via Veneto nightclub early in the film.

In fact, outside of Pasolini, no major Italian cultural figure of the moment—cinematic, literary, journalistic, artistic—had a grasp on what was then evolving as teen culture. In Italy, the primary social unit was the family, and it wasn't uncommon at all for adults to live in their parents' homes until they were wed and even after. No matter that the government and the church were patriarchal institutions of the most hidebound sort or that all kinds of modern novelties had been emerging for more than a decade from Italy's movie studios, fashion ateliers, newsrooms, nightclubs, and factories: the cult of Mama and her apron strings was incontestably the dominant social force in the nation. Elsewhere—in Britain and, especially, the United States—the primary social unit was the individual, and the desire to kick out, break away, and self-define was almost primal. In Italy that was an almost insane thought: Mama, everyone's Mama, was the best cook, housekeeper, nurse, protector, comforter, and advocate in the world. Why on earth would anyone want to leave her or reject her gifts and influence?

It's the nature of every cultural scene or moment or phenomenon that captured the mass imagination to be finite: that, in a sense, is the essence of popular culture. But that Rome's reign over the pop world should come at such a time and be scuttled in such a way was particularly capricious of the fates. You could see the very moments where the old and new met: when the Beatles showed up on *The Ed Sullivan Show* in February 1964, the crowd, though largely young, looked like they were at a Dwight Eisenhower campaign rally (or, for that matter, on Via Veneto): girls in Pucciesque print dresses and blouses, boys in neat, tailored jackets and ties. True, the Beatles wore suits, and they bowed like vaudevillians after their songs, but those were show biz suits, and that hair, those Cuban-heel boots, those wailing harmonies, that beat: this was not your dad's—or even your cool uncle's—way of looking sharp.

Rome tried to keep up: there was a moment of rock 'n' roll in *8½* that wasn't nearly as stilted or arch as the Adriano Celentano scene in *La Dolce Vita*. But nobody would have confused Fellini's movie with Richard Lester's (even if Lester was, as his filmcraft showed, an aficionado of Fellini's work and metier). Existential angst was, almost overnight, old hat. The new gods of culture came soaring in on the backs of two-and-a-half-minute pop songs, with goofy personalities, doe-eyed sexuality, and a fresh energy that made the gilded decadents of Fellini and Antonioni seem like figures in frescoes and tapestries from a bygone era.

*I*ronically, one of the Italians most associated with the Roman moment, however inaptly, was also one of the youngest—though not quite young enough to be among the shrieking mob at a Beatles concert.

Sophia Loren had still not reached thirty when she was reunited with Marcello Mastroianni and Vittorio De Sica for a pair of films that would earn lots of money, win piles of prizes (including an Oscar and a pair of Oscar nominations), and underscore the international celebrity of both stars.

In *Ieri, Oggi, Domani* (*Yesterday, Today and Tomorrow*), Loren and Mastroianni appeared in three stories as three different couples—Neapolitan, Milanese, Roman—defined by distinct social, economic, sexual, and legal relationships. The Neapolitan section was earthy, recollecting *L'Oro di Napoli*: Sophia plays a life-battered, vigorous woman convicted of selling black market cigarettes but allowed to stay out of prison so long as she was pregnant and/or nursing; Marcello is the haggard husband who has to keep her that way. The Milanese portion, based on an Alberto Moravia story, could have been made by Michelangelo Antonioni: a bourgeois couple on the verge of estrangement deals with the aftermath of an automobile accident. The Roman piece would become the most famous: Sophia plays the prostitute Mara, whose Piazza Navona penthouse is adjacent to the home of a seminarian who stares at her longingly across the rooftop, falling in love; Marcello is Mara's client from Bologna, in town for a good time but frustrated by her decision to repent for distracting the seminarian by abstaining from sex for a week. In the most celebrated scene, Mara strips for her customer, who sits in her bed howling, clapping, biting the corner of a pillow, in all ways reminiscent of a wolf in a Tex Avery cartoon.[1] The film was released in Italy at the end of 1963, and after a year and a half of success at the international box office, won an Oscar as Best Foreign Language Film of 1964.

By then, De Sica had directed the stars in another breakout hit, *Matrimonio all'Italiana* (*Marriage Italian Style*), an adaptation of Eduardo De Filippo's play about the decades-long relationship between a wealthy Neapolitan businessman and his lifelong concubine (it

---

1 The pair would repeat the scene thirty-one years later in Robert Altman's *Ready to Wear*.

really was the right word) who begged him for what looked like a deathbed marriage, only to reveal that she was 1) perfectly healthy and 2) hiding a stunning secret from him. This time, along with the massive ticket sales, there were two Oscar nominations—Best Foreign Language Film and Best Actress.

Both films would be remembered fondly, particularly for Loren's performances, which were varied, full, sexy, and emotional. But they hardly represented the best of De Sica's work, or the best of Italian cinema of the moment. They were commercial films—agreeable, entertaining, profitable, but not the stuff from Italy that had so excited the world's film connoisseurs a decade before. Italian cinema, in fact, had, with the exceptions of a handful of auteurs, become less fashionable than the French and the British.

By then it didn't really matter if Loren was seen as Italian. She was the biggest star to have emerged from Europe since the end of the war. In 1965, she was estimated to have the third highest personal income in all of Rome. Mastroianni was launched internationally as well, with a string of hits dating back to *Big Deal on Madonna Street*, but with his apparently intractable bias against learning English, he would always seem a more parochial figure.[2] Still, they were global stars, not a decade after their first pairing in a goofy romantic comedy—not bad at all for a girl who couldn't be photographed and an inveterate lazybones.

And yet there was something missing. Although Sophia was the queen of all she surveyed, there was one thing that she couldn't have—a normal family life with the man she had chosen as her partner, Carlo Ponti—and it mattered more to her, she would regularly declare, than all of her professional successes combined. In 1966,

2 He had a real yen for working with the most artistically ambitious directors and for the theater, which he still loved and occasionally dabbled in; one of his great unrealized inspirations was to stage *The Taming of the Shrew* with himself and Loren.

more than fifteen years after they met and nearly a decade after their first abortive attempt at getting married in Mexico, the legal and political hurdles were at last cleared and they wed—in France, pointedly denying their nemeses in Italy the chance to look on or in any way claim credit for or denigrate it. During their years together, she and Ponti wanted a family, but she had suffered a string of miscarriages. At the very end of 1968, though, she brought Carlo Ponti Jr. into the world, and, in early 1973, not long before her thirty-ninth birthday, his brother, Edoardo. It would be an irony, given how quickly she had risen in her career and at how young an age, that motherhood, the role she wanted most to play, eluded her for so long.

Little else, though, ever did. In time, Sophia Loren would come to be the greatest living vessel of any number of traits associated with Italy: sensuality, practicality, endurance, glamour, an ironic sense of humor, a zest for the simple pleasures of life. Her film roles could vary, she would eventually make her home in Switzerland, she would lose Ponti (but not until 2007, when he was ninety-four), and she would become a grandmother. But she was never not a sex symbol, never not a star, never not somebody who could make men sit upright and women look on admiringly. In her early films, she had often played tough girls from hard backgrounds who fought and scratched their way toward decent lives; she had been that in reality as well. But few of her films followed their protagonists for decades, to see if they ever achieved anything more than human-scale glory, whereas the real-life woman, who started that unlikely trajectory as a mere teen, would rise and rise and rise almost without end, as glorious in her eighties as she was when, as Sophia Lazzaro, she made her first uncertain steps toward a career in front of a camera more than half a century prior.

Federico Fellini felt revived—as a man and as an artist—by the experience of making 8½. "I have a feeling that this picture has set me free," he told a reporter, "that from now on I'll be able to make a dozen different kinds of pictures, or a hundred. I'm not clear yet what my next picture will be. Nevertheless, I'm full of confidence about it."

As it happened, what he chose to do was, like Odysseus, return home to his patient wife after an extended period of (artistic) separation. In 1965, after almost eight full years without a credit together, Fellini and Giulietta Masina were reunited in the fantastical, poignant, sexually frank *Giulietta degli Spiriti* (*Juliet of the Spirits*), a love letter to a mouselike woman whose suburban equilibrium would be shattered by the discovery of her husband's womanizing. It was Fellini's first film in color, and it was glorious. He followed with a string of films with equally bold and dreamlike visuals and increasingly shaggy structures: the anthology piece *Toby Dammit* (based on a story by Edgar Allan Poe), and the features *Satyricon, I Clowns, Fellini Roma, Amarcord* (for which he equaled Vittorio De Sica's remarkable feat of winning four Best Foreign Language Film Oscars), *Il Casanova di Federico Fellini, Prova d'Orchestra* (*Orchestra Rehearsal*), and, in 1980, a reunion with Marcello Mastroianni on the unfortunately misogynistic and confused *La Città delle Donne* (*City of Women*), a last hurrah for the autobiographical selves they had concocted in *La Dolce Vita* and *8½* (Mastroianni's character would be named Snaporaz, one of Fellini's private nicknames for the actor). By then, the director had become like Picasso, Stravinsky, Proust—an artist whose oeuvre and sensibility were synonymous with the modern world and could be evoked with just a single word: Fellini.

*B*esides Fellini, there was another bona fide original whose magnificent work could be summoned with the mere mention of his surname: Pucci. His vision of color, pattern, cut, and flow was seen everywhere in the 1960s, echoed in the work of his fellow designers and, more frequently, in blatant knockoffs that sold at fractions of the prices he charged for the originals. But it didn't matter: the wider the taste for his work spread, the hungrier people seemed to be for the genuine thing. In an article entitled "Everything's Coming Up Pucci," a reporter for *The New York Times* noted, "The growing number of Pucci-influenced items has apparently done nothing to dampen the ardor of true aficionados. Sales of the originals have never been better, stores report."

Of all the designers who had joined Giovanni Battista Giorgini in putting Italian fashion on the map in the early 1950s, Pucci was the only one whose creations remained vital through the 1960s. In part this was because his vision of leisure wear was in harmony with the increasingly casual tenor of the times. The youthquake that had upended the popular arts had cognates in fashion: Londoners like Mary Quant and Vidal Sassoon had challenged traditional hemlines and hairdos, respectively, and international buyers and designers, particularly Americans, were swept up in the exciting energy of these new looks. The other famed couturiers of postwar Italy—the Fontanas, Simonetta, Fabiani, Capucci, Schuberth—still had the attention of grown-up buyers, but the energy of teens was clearly more compelling. Among that storied generation of pioneers, only Pucci regularly produced work that felt youthful. Couture wasn't going away, but its ability to influence daily wear was lessening as fashion trends more and more often rose from the street rather than descending from the catwalk. And that shift suited Pucci's work and style just fine.

By the end of the decade, he had triumphed in fashion, business, politics, education, sport. He had a beautiful wife and children. He had a name that the whole world knew. All that was left was outer space. And, miraculously, he went even *there*, designing the official insignia of the Apollo 15 space mission, meaning that in July 1971, there were literally people walking on the moon wearing Pucci, something that none of his fabled ancestors could have possibly imagined.

"*I*'m an actor because I couldn't exist otherwise. So I act."

In time, acting took Marcello Mastroianni all over the world: to Russia and Greece and Portugal and the Roman stage (where he performed as Rudolph Valentino in the musical *Ciao, Rudy*) and, twice again, to the Academy Awards, where he would become the only performer ever nominated three times for acting in a language other than English, and four more times to the fantasy world of Federico Fellini: the aborted *Il Viaggio di G. Mastorna,* a film that Fellini abandoned after a lengthy gestation, including costume tests for Mastroianni shot by Tazio Secchiaroli; *City of Women*; *Ginger e Fred* (*Ginger and Fred*; 1985); and *Intervista* (*Interview*; 1987). In the last, he took a brief turn as a tuxedoed, caped and top-hatted magician, the famed comic book hero Mandrake, a character whom he and Fellini had always dreamt of capturing on film.

By then, he had worked with a pantheon of Europe's best directors: Roman Polanski, Jacques Demy, Ettore Scola, the Taviani brothers, Lina Wertmüller, Marco Ferreri, Theo Angelopoulos, Marco Bellocchio, and John Boorman. In 1991, he finally agreed to make an actual Hollywood movie, Beeban Kidran's *Used People*, with costars Shirley MacLaine and Jessica Tandy. In 1995, he went to Portugal to make a film with the octogenarian director Manoel de Oliveira, and during that time he sat for a filmed interview with the woman who was then his partner, Anna Maria

Tatò, a conversation that was released, as a documentary at three-plus hours' length, as *Io Ricordo, Si, Io Mi Ricordo* (*I Remember, Yes, I Remember*). At the end of that year, he returned to the stage in *Le Ultime Lune* (*The Last Moons*), about a widowed poet whose family wish to put him in a care facility. He toured Italy in the role for almost the whole of 1996, even though he had been diagnosed with pancreatic cancer.

In December, he left the play in Naples and went to Paris, where he had made his home for more than twenty years. And on the nineteenth, with Tatò, Catherine Deneuve, and his daughters Barbara and Chiara by his bedside, he died (Flora, *still* officially his wife, was absent). There was a funeral in Paris at Saint-Suplice and another in the Piazza del Campidoglio in Rome, attended by the elite of Italy's film world.

The most fitting tribute, however, took place on the site of his most famous screen moment. In a solemn ceremony at the Trevi Fountain, two massive black drapes were lowered slowly as a loudspeaker played a melody from Nino Rota's score for *Otto e Mezzo*. When the curtains were fully unfurled, the flow of the fountain was stopped and two spotlights danced on the shimmering surface of the water, just as Mastroianni and Ekberg, and Marcello and Sylvia, and the hearts of everyone who had ever dreamt of romance in the Eternal City, had been doing for forty years.

Starting with *Roma*, which included sections depicting the arrival of a young provincial journalist in the big city that could well have been part of the abandoned *Moraldo in Città*, a thick vein of nostalgia coursed through Federico Fellini's work, his chatter, his being. In 1987, he fantastically reimagined his own first excursions into the world of movies in *Intervista*, a surreal love poem to Cinecittà.

In his seventies, Fellini was beset with nagging health issues and, perhaps not coincidentally, he found it hard to get financiers to take his ideas for new films seriously. He and Giulietta lived relative modestly, partly by choice and disposition, partly because he'd never received his financial due for his most successful films and because he had long battled the Italian tax authorities. Neither of them was very good, in the end, with money. There was the house on Via Margutta, there was a seaside home in Fregene, and there was always talk of new movies—though, increasingly, talk was all it was.

In 1993, he was invited to Los Angeles to be presented with an honorary Oscar for his life's work. On March 29, he took the stage of the Dorothy Chandler Pavilion, accepted a statuette from Sophia Loren and Marcello Mastroianni, and spoke in heavily accented English:

> I come from a country, and I belong to a generation, for which America and the movies were almost the same thing. . . . I would like, naturally, first of all, to thank all the people that have worked with me. I cannot name everyone, only one name, of an actress, who is also my wife. Thank you, dearest Giulietta. And please stop crying!

The camera cut to a smiling, sobbing Masina.

It would be the last time the world would see them together.

When they returned to Rome, both husband and wife were hit with health crises, causing them to be hospitalized, separately, leaving them longing for each other. She fared better than him, but only slightly. In early October, Fellini persuaded his doctors to let him out of the hospital for a day to share a Sunday lunch with Giulietta. When they finished, she returned to their apartment and he went to look at a potential new production office: he had in mind a film about illness, doctors, human mortality.

That night, back in the hospital, he suffered a stroke and went into a coma. Giulietta visited him in the intensive care unit, but he showed no sign that he knew she was there. Weeks passed; paparazzi camped outside the hospital; Giulietta stayed at home. On October 30, she marked their fiftieth wedding anniversary on her own.

And the following day, he died.

The Italian public grieved as they would never have over a politician or sportsman or even most popes. When a paparazzo managed to sneak into the hospital and get a shot of Fellini's body, it ran *once* on television before a massive outcry caused it to be pulled from *all* media. No newspaper or magazine anywhere dared stoop to print it.

At Cinecittà, a viewing of his body—dressed in the tuxedo he wore to the Oscars—was arranged in, of course, Studio 5; some seventy thousand mourners filed slowly by to pay their respects. There was a funeral mass in Rome and then a burial in Rimini.

Giulietta went on through the winter without him, but her health was increasingly frail. In late March, she was clearly failing, weakened by cancer treatment, brokenhearted at the loss of her partner. On Wednesday of Holy Week, she declared, "I am going to spend Easter with Federico."

Those were her last words. Days later, she was put to rest beside him.

As for the place that Fellini thought of as his spiritual home, the fantastical world known as Cinecittà—time was indifferent to it. Hollywood studios pulled out of Italy for cheaper locations in

Spain and elsewhere; Italy's great directors were offered opportunities to make films throughout Europe and in the United States; the fads for costume epics and films about jet travel to Europe died away. Television, which required less robust facilities, became the engine of the entertainment industry—and advertising wasn't far behind it. The gigantic studio became less and less busy, and in the mid-1990s the Italian government sold it to private hands.

Now and again, Cinecittà still hosted a grand production—in a gesture Fellini would have appreciated, Martin Scorsese built the Lower Manhattan of the 1860s there for 2002's *Gangs of New York*. But TV shows like HBO's *Rome*, for which a permanent Roman Forum set was created, were the new owners' bread and butter. In 2014, they opened an amusement park, Cinecittà World, with roller coasters and attractions designed around classic movie themes, at a cost of $338 million and not at Cinecittà but on the nearby site of Dinocittà, aka the Stabilimenti Cinematografici Pontini, a studio that Dino De Laurentiis had built in 1964.

That hadn't been the best business decision the great Neapolitan producer ever made. A leftist government had been elected in 1963, and in 1965 it changed the laws regulating filmmaking in such a way that big international coproductions such as De Laurentiis's *The Bible* were denied their accustomed financial advantages for having committed the crime of using foreign talent and funding. Italian films by Italian artists would be the new way. Hollywood on the Tiber was effectively legislated out of existence.

*R*ome may have held domain over the global movie and fashion businesses for only a decade or so, but the one thing it truly invented in the wake of World War II grew bigger and spread throughout the world, reaching a point at which more than half the people on the planet, their mobile phones equipped with cameras, could, in some sense, be thought of as potential paparazzi, constantly prepared to snap a photo of a celebrity—or even just an ordinary person—engaged in the criminal, the provocative, the embarrassing, the outré.

Those ambitious, fearless, ready young photographers on Via Veneto had grabbed a variety of the cultural elements that were bubbling up around them and concocted an elixir that the world had never tasted before, a blend of the documentary eye of neorealism, the impeccable chic of the Sala Bianca, the monetary excesses of Hollywood on the Tiber, the sensual carnival of the Roman night, and the timeless backdrops of the Eternal City—and they turned them into vivid images, hair-raising stories, and, incidentally, a modestly comfortable living. The world ate it up. The exciting but mostly trivial and harmless incidents of the late 1950s became more common and more heated in later decades and spread to any place where bold-faced names could be found by undaunted photographers. In turn, celebrities struck back with increasing fire—oaths, fists, dinnerware, lawyers—as the number, frequency, and professional belligerence of the paparazzi increased, which it did, steadily.

"Anyone in Rome with a camera went to Via Veneto to look like a paparazzo," lamented Tazio Secchiaroli. "There was a mob of photographers." Gone were the gentlemanly days of suits and polished shoes. The new breed of photographers began to dress like the younger men they were: in denim and training jackets and tennis shoes, as if they were going to a football match or a neighborhood bar. They didn't need the excuse of a slow news day to feel that they had to get a rise out of a celebrity; they took provocation and confrontation as baselines, and they seemed to work around the clock, making no distinctions between stars' private lives, public lives, and working lives. As one of the young paparazzi put it, "A furious star is news. One quietly having his espresso with a lady friend at a café? Not so much." They did, therefore, what they could to make a situation—*any* situation—into a profitable opportunity. By the time *The Bible* was shot in Rome, the paparazzi had become so obnoxious and so ubiquitous that John Huston told the American press that productions would avoid Italy altogether if something weren't done about them.

In the coming decades, as the phenomenon spread to New York, Los Angeles, London, Paris, and Tokyo, the reputation of the paparazzi sank lower and lower. Out of the throng, one or two might emerge as a notable name in his (for it was always a he) own right, such as Ron Galella, the pugnacious New York paparazzo who got a court order against Marlon Brando for striking him and took the most beautiful candid photo of Jacqueline Kennedy Onassis's life, the famous wind-tousled Mona Jackie crossing a New York street in sweater and jeans. But most of them were anonymous— the arms, legs, mouths, eyes, lenses, and flashes of a single huge, throbbing monster.

Over time, someone from among the lot who ran around Via Veneto in the early days (and, more commonly, from the younger bunch who emerged after Fellini's film), would find himself talking to the press or opening an exhibition of photos or releasing a book of his work and refer to himself as the King of the Paparazzi or take credit for having inspired Fellini. But the two photographers whose works and deeds ran most deeply through the DNA of Fellini's film and the Rome that inspired it weren't terribly keen on such boasts, and, in fact, they had leapt from the business just before it got truly ugly.

Pierluigi Praturlon, virtually the first photographer to be assaulted by a celebrity for taking a picture, hadn't ever, really, been a paparazzo, at least not full-time. He ran with the boys now and again—he was on the scene (indeed, behind the wheel) on the infamous *Ferragosto* night of 1958—but he found a better livelihood as an official photographer for Sophia Loren and the on-set stills photographer for a host of Italian and international productions. The first of the paparazzi to transcend his calling (before it was even identifiable as a calling), he shot stills for Bond films and huge costume dramas and virtually every film Federico Fellini made after 1970. He took the images of Sophia Loren crumpled on a dirt road that helped publicize *Two Women*; he helped Frank Sinatra decorate his private jet (Old Blue Eyes was partial to orange); and Kim Novak once changed the date of her wedding so that Praturlon would be available to photograph it. In 1986, at age sixty-two, he exuded such vitality and confidence in his work on the set of Fellini's *Ginger and Fred* that the director lit and choreographed several scenes by following Pierluigi's lead.

Tazio Secchiaroli had also risen above the mob of paparazzi into a rarefied realm of official photographer to the stars, replacing Pierluigi as Loren's anointed portraitist in 1963, on the set of *Matrimonio all'Italiana*. He caught her attention, he remembered, by arriving after she did, a breach of her personal code of etiquette. She looked at him coolly. "I detest people who arrive after I do," she said. "But you may come when you like. You are an artist." He shot her on film sets and with her family for the next twenty years. As Pierluigi had been given free rein on the set of *La Dolce Vita*, Fellini invited Secchiaroli to do as he wished on the set of *8½*, and the collaboration proved fruitful enough that he was welcome again on the ill-fated *Il Viaggio di G. Mastorna* and such subsequent films as *Amarcord* and *City of Women*. He shot Brigitte Bardot for Jean-Luc Godard during the making of *Le Mépris* (*Contempt*), he went to London with Antonioni to shoot stills on the set of *Blow-Up*, and he worked for and with Marcello Mastroianni, Pietro Germi, Sergio

Leone, Sidney Lumet, Pier Paolo Pasolini. He told amusing stories about his wild past, but he was prouder of what he achieved later: respectability, steady work, acclaim for his eye and his work. He had risen, on the strength of his craft and personality, to become an icon of a star-struck era, and he had built a lasting legacy on that foundation.

And the street that Secchiaroli help make famous, the luxurious boulevard lined with posh hotels and overpriced cafés? It, too, let leave its moment of glory. Fellini, perhaps disingenuously, claimed that he never understood how *La Dolce Vita* made anyone want to take part of the Via Veneto scene: "Someone makes a bitter film," he said, "and what happens? He increases tourism!" And, in fact, Via Veneto, which had only a small local reputation before Fellini's film, became a destination of a sort, if not for very long. The street came to life, ironically, only a few times in the late 1960s, when left-wing students from around Rome protested the Vietnam War outside the American embassy. Otherwise, it simply quieted down until it became a label, a marker of a bygone era, a name people recognized without really knowing why.

In 1959, Fellini had rebuilt the upper end of the street at Studio 5 of Cinecittà, where it would only rouse itself for a few working hours each day and sit eerily still and silent otherwise. Fifty years on, the real street could often be like that. The hotels hosted business travelers, not movie stars, gray figures who would step outside only to be whisked away to meetings, and maybe some shopping or sightseeing, in chauffeured sedans. There were no paparazzi for them to evade.

In the mid-2000s, the Café de Paris shut its doors for a combination of reasons, mostly to do with the shady characters who were allowed access to its bank accounts and ledgers. There was a fire, small, of indeterminate origin, and authorities and lenders stepped in. The café remained closed for years after, a taxidermied carcass that had once hosted royalty of both the aristocratic and cinematic sorts but now stared blankly at the muted, empty space between its front door and the street.

In a way, that made it very Roman. Standing in front of the shuttered premises, one could look uphill at a chunk of the Aurelian Wall that stood between Rome and the outside world from about AD 275 on. It was perfectly situated, within eyeshot of the front door of the Excelsior: an eternal reminder to even the most high-flown of visitors that he or she was in Rome and subject to Roman customs and rules. Often that was a glorious thing to recall, that one had arrived in grand style in one of the greatest cities on earth—indeed, in the *history* of earth. But at the same time, it meant that you were subject to the ways of the Romans, their cynicism, their ennui, their bluntness, their cutthroat commercialism, their indifference to gentilesse, their fashionable whims, their thousands of years of being certain that history may or may not remember *you* but it would surely remember *them*.

*O*n the night of March 2, 2014, very nearly fifty-five years to the day when Federico Fellini·began photography on *La Dolce Vita*, an Italian writer-director stood on a stage in Hollywood and accepted an Oscar for an episodic film about a jaded journalist in Rome whose youthful ambition to do meaningful work had been stunted by his pursuit of pleasure, money, celebrity, and a life of ease. The hero of Paolo Sorrentino's film *La Grande Bellezza* (*The Great Beauty*) wasn't, however, a man coming into what ought to have been the flush of his career; Jep Gambardella was his name, and he was marking his sixty-fifth birthday with a wild party. The story of his work, dalliances, parties, and regrets could have been, in many ways, a sequel to Fellini's exposé of the soul of Marcello Rubini and, indeed, of an age. But, really, in the era of Silvio Berlusconi, after the death of Princess Diana, forty-five years after Fellini had anatomized the Dolce Vita and two decades after he had passed on, did anyone need such a reminder, such an indictment? Surely everyone who saw Sorrentino's sumptuous, dreamy film was already beyond the sort of shock that Fellini's bold and frank movie had ignited.

No, *La Grande Bellezza*, most of all, served as a delicious, poignant, bittersweet reminder of the special place that Rome had in all the culture, imagination, and heart of the world.

The clichés were true: all roads did lead there, it wasn't built in a day, and one should do as the natives did—live beautifully, live richly, live sensationally, live as if your photograph would appear on breakfast tables around the world, live as if you would soon be discovered as a movie star, a fashion icon, a great lover, a great connoisseur of life.

That would be the lesson of Dolce Vita Rome: life really is sweet, even when it seems bitter at first taste, and you should gobble it up.

At their worst, those years revealed humanity at its most base: superficial, competitive, gluttonous, scornful, lustful, callous, crude, even murderous. But at their best they compiled the most transporting of human impulses: to dream of beauty, of luxury, of romance, of glory, of pleasure, of fluency, of ease, of self-fulfillment, of self-transcendence.

The princess and the journalist on the motor scooter; the sex kitten and the gossip columnist in the bubbling fountain; the startled audience of jaded connoisseurs at a fashion show; the tireless photographers chasing down a hypocrite or snob; the visionary filmmakers and actors and writers and clothiers and high-fliers:

who wouldn't want to be among them, to witness the birth of a modern way of living and seeing, to make history in places where the very idea of making history was practically invented?

In the seventeenth century, the Spanish poet and courtier Francisco de Quevedo visited the city and wrote, *"O Roma, en tu grandeza, en tu hermosura, huyó lo que era firme y solamente lo fugitivo permanece y dura!"*: "Oh Rome, in your grandeur, in your beauty, that which was solid has melted away and only that which is fleeting remains and endures!"

The physical Rome through which Quevedo walked, the Rome of classical ruins and papal monuments and baroque fantasias and ordinary neighborhoods unchanged, essentially, for centuries, would persist through empires and invasions and recoveries and innovations that he could never have comprehended: It never, truly, melted away.

And yet he hit on the thing exactly: Rome's great gift to the world has always been—before the caesars, before the popes—not a collection of ruins or holy sites or museums or quaint piazzas or picturesque boulevards, but a way of seeing the world and representing it and living in it: a taste, a posture, a signature, a style.

There have, for millennia, been many Romes and many ways of being Roman in the world, and only a relatively small portion of them have ever required that one actually be in Rome to experience them.

No matter if you've never seen the Colosseum or *La Dolce Vita*, no matter if you can't afford Brioni or Valentino, no matter if you've never ridden a Vespa or thumbed through a tabloid magazine in a supermarket. In our clothes, in our leisure, in our fascinations, in our art, in our society with one another, in our dreams, we are, all of us, everywhere, today, as if St. Ambrose had been warning us, in Rome.

Acknowledgments

W riting this book fulfilled a long held dream to explore a certain cultural epoch, to celebrate a set of personal heroes and favorite works of art, to identify the moment when various elements of the modern world first came together, and, I admit, to spend time in Rome learning the stories, walking the streets, imagining the past, and, yes, eating the food. I can't express how fortunate I feel that my many years of gathering string on these subjects have now been braided into these pages—or that I was able to travel to Italy after failing to do so for three decades.

In Rome, I was granted access to several deeply useful resources: the Biblioteca Nazionale Centrale di Roma and the Centro Sperimentale di Cinematografia, where I used both the Biblioteca Luigi Chiarini and the archives of the Cineteca Nazionale (*grazie tanti a* Emiliano Morreale *e* Alessandro Andreini). I was graciously granted a tour of Cinecittà by Cristina Giubbetti, who provided me with some very helpful materials and insights. Likewise at the

Fondazione Micol Fontana, I was greeted warmly by Maria Cristina Giusti and introduced to some of the remarkable history of the sisters and their work. At the Museo Nazionale delle Arti del XXI Secolo (aka MAXXI), I was invited to the press preview of the fabulous "*Belissima*" exhibit, where I saw many important pieces of Dolce Vita–era fashion. And I filled a suitcase with books on film, fashion, and popular culture that were recommended to me by the staffs of three fabulous bookshops specializing in those subjects: Altroquando, Fahrenheit 451, and Maximum Fax.

In Manhattan, I worked, as ever, at the New York Public Library for the Performing Arts at Lincoln Center, and in Beverly Hills, as ever, at the Margaret Herrick Library of the Academy of Motion Picture Arts and Sciences. Both of those facilities have been instrumental in every book I've written, and I greatly appreciate their staffs and the founders and donors who have built and supported them.

In my hometown of Portland, three of the institutions that make the city so glorious proved, reliably, indispensable: the Multnomah County Library (and its remarkable Interlibrary Loan office) and Powell's City of Books and Movie Madness, which are the best bookstore and video store on earth, respectively—and, in the words of Elvis Presley, I'll lick the guy that says it isn't so. Additionally, the Portland Art Museum did me the particular service of hosting the glorious exhibition "Italian Style: Fashion Since 1945" not long after I began my work. Not only did Brian Ferriso and his staff provide me advance access to the collection, but they introduced me to Sonnet Stanfill, who originally curated the show at the Victoria and Albert Museum in London (and who granted me an illuminating interview), and they invited me to lecture on the Dolce Vita years as part of the educational component of the show. As if that weren't enough, a pair of Portland editors (and longtime chums) asked me to weigh in on the exhibition in their pages: Zach Dundas of *Portland Monthly* and Barry Johnson of *Oregon Arts Watch*; much obliged, guys.

I am extremely grateful to John Glusman, editor-in-chief of W. W. Norton, who had worked with me on a pair of biographies and agreed that it was time that I moved away from big lives to explore a moment of big living. And thanks as well to the whole Norton team, particularly Alexa Pugh for her work as shepherd and Trent Duffy for a superb job of copy editing.

Richard Pine of Inkwell Management remains the ideal agent and one of my most trusted friends and confidants. I can't express how much his partnership and support have meant over the decades.

Closer still are the family and friends who have perennially indulged my (often noisy and sometimes even noisome) interests, my work habits, my travels, and my various and sundry idiosyncrasies. Words like *gratitude* and *thanks* don't begin to express my debt to my children, Paula, Anthony, and Vincent; their mother, Mary Bartholemy (and her partner, Nick Otting); their grandmother, Lu Thornton; their aunt Jennifer Levy (and her beautiful brood); and my blood kin on two coasts. They have never failed me, and I love them all.

In this particular case, though, nobody has offered me more in the way of support, encouragement, commiseration, enthusiasm, warmth, distraction, wisdom, play, hope, love, and happiness than Shannon Brazil.

Baby, in the words of the song, this book, like my heart and me, is dedicated to you.

Notes

INTRODUCTION

xvii   "How many Romes": H. V. Morton, *A Traveller in Rome* (New York: Da Capo Press, 2002), 76.

CHAPTER 2: "An Old River Among the Great Hotels"

10   "Everything is chaste": Ugo Moretti, *Artists in Rome*, trans. William Weaver (New York: Macmillan, 1958), 39.

13   "frequented by high-class": Ibid., xii.

13   "The Baretto was so famous": Ibid., vii.

18   "'To do cinema'": Ennio Flaiano, *The Via Veneto Papers*, trans. John Satriano (Marlboro, Vt.: The Marlboro Press, 1992), 117.

20   "He's not growing": Ibid., 15.

21   "In Rome there is only one street": Tennessee Williams, "A Writer's Quest for Parnassus," in *New Selected Essays: Where I Live* , ed. John S. Bak (New York: New Directions, 2009).

CHAPTER 3: Made in Italy

26   "[His] profile is reminiscent": Guido Vergani, *Fashion Dictionary* (New York: Baldini Castoldi Dalai Editore, 2006), 540.

32   "Since the United States is": Ibid., 548.

CHAPTER 4: "The Three-Sided Mirror"

36   "The dressmaker's was run": Bonizza Giordani Aragno, *Sorelle Fontana* (Rome: Promograph, 2005), 15.

37   "[Zoe] left Traversetolo": Ibid., 16.

37   "We could hear": Virginia Pope, "75-Year-Old Matriarch and 3 Daughters Thrust Casa Fontana in Fashion Spotlight," *The New York Times*, July 17, 1954.

38   "They had the knowledge": Guido Vergani, *Fashion Dictionary* (New York: Baldini Castoldi Dalai Editore, 2006), 1173.

39   "We were hesitant": Courtney Colavita, "Italy's Golden Moment," *Women's Wear Daily*, March 2, 2001.

40   "I would always say": Ibid.

42   "outlined his plan": Vergani, *Fashion Dictionary*, 550.

CHAPTER 5: "Paris Didn't Move Us Like This"

45   "Fashion is the essence": Barbara W. Wyden, "Seven Philosophers of Fashion," *The New York Times*, July 19, 1964.

46   "How did I get to my work": "Emilio Pucci MA '37 Talk on Design at Reed College," October, 10, 1962; available online at https://soundcloud.com/reedcollege/pucci-emilio-talk-on-design-at-reed-college-1962.

47   "Some women were just delighted": Raymond Rendleman, "Thinker. Tailor. Soldier. Spy," *Reed*, March 2014.

50   "Be my doctor": Guido Vergani, *Fashion Dictionary* (New York: Baldini Castoldi Dalai Editore, 2006), 551.

51   "He was a gentleman": Nicola White, *Reconstructing Italian Fashion* (Oxford, Eng.: Berg, 2000), 160.

52   "The boutique was innovative": Ibid., 101.

52   "in line with the taste": Ibid.

54   "Had we known what": Sonnet Stanfill, *The Glamour of Italian Fashion Since 1945* (London: Victoria and Albert Museum, 2014), 15.

54   "Italian fabrics are superlative": "Italian Is Praised for High Fashions," *The New York Times*, January 29, 1952.

CHAPTER 6: "Motion Pictures Are the Most Powerful Weapon"

63   "I had exactly the same strange sensation": Charlotte Chandler, *I, Fellini* (New York: Random House, 1995), 313.

63   "All of a sudden": Federico Fellini, *Cinecittà*, trans. Graham Fawecett (London: Studio Vista, 1989), 16.

63   "cardinals": Ibid., 44.

CHAPTER 7: "Hollywood on the Tiber"

73   "The crowds of job-hunting Romans": Mervyn LeRoy and Dick Kleiner, *Mervyn LeRoy: Take One* (New York: Hawthorn Books, 1974), 178.

CHAPTER 9: A Girl on a Beach

96   "Do not believe any other letter": Wayland Young, *The Montesi Scandal* (Garden City, N.Y.: Doubleday, 1958), 51.

CHAPTER 10: A Nose for *the* Shot

101   "The city streets were empty": Diego Mormorio, *Tazio Secchiaroli*, trans. Alexandra Bonfante-Warren (New York: Harry N. Abrams, 1999), 17.

CHAPTER 12: "She Will Be a Sensation"

112   "no arse, no tits": Pauline Small, *Sophia Loren* (Bristol, Eng.: Intellect, 2009), 96.

116   "He was full of himself": Giannino Malossi, ed., *Latin Lover* (Milan: Charta, 1995), 108.

CHAPTER 13: "She's Impossible to Photograph"

124   "She was at the height": Warren G. Harris, *Sophia Loren* (New York: Simon & Schuster, 1998), 18.

125   "Hunger . . . was the major theme": Sophia Loren, *Yesterday, Today, Tomorrow* (New York: Atria, 2014), 14.

127   "the most stupid job imaginable": Pauline Small, *Sophia Loren* (Bristol, Eng.: Intellect, 2009), 25.

131   "She's impossible to photograph": Loren, *Yesterday, Today, Tomorrow*, 48.

133   "The supervisor of direction": Small, *Sophia Loren*, 68.

CHAPTER 14: "I'm a Peasant"

135   "They come for you": Rex Reed, "Marcello Makes a Big Scandalo," *The New York Times*, June 21, 1970.

135   "He never really knew": Donald Dewey, *Marcello Mastroianni* (New York: Birch Lane, 1993), 23.

136   "I have an absolute need": Michael Stern, "Mastronianni: The Latin Who Put Laughter Back into Love," *Pageant*, January 1965.

136   "Probably a million": Marcello Mastroianni, *Mi Ricordo, Sì Io Mi Ricordo* (Milan: Baldini & Castoldi), 7.

137   "We are an indolent": Marika Aba, "Marcello Mastroianni Takes Life Easy in a Busy World," *The Los Angeles Times*, January 8, 1967.

137   "Until I was twenty-five": Reed, "Marcello Makes a Big Scandalo."

139   "How many years": Mastroianni, *Mi Ricordo*, 29.

139   "I was one man": Henry Gris, "Marcello Mastroianni: A Married Star Talks About His Love Affairs," *Coronet*, July 1971.

140   "I was told you are talented": Francesco Tatò, *The Stuff That Dreams Are Made Of* (Rome: Cinecittà International, 1998), 18.

141   "I saw Marcello being born": Eugene Archer, "Marcello Mastroianni: After *La Dolce Vita*," *The New York Times*, February 28, 1965.

141   "He had the great gift": Tatò, *Stuff That Dreams Are Made Of*, 84.

CHAPTER 15: *Signor Sigarone*

148   "movie producers . . . were just as common": "Hollywood on the Tiber," *Time*, August 16, 1954.

CHAPTER 16: "Sit Down, If You Dare"

155   "If we'd smoked those American cigarettes": Charlotte Chandler, *I, Fellini* (New York: Random House, 1995), 55.

CHAPTER 17: "Florence Is a Lost Cause"

162 "We Italians have been very much": Gloria Emerson, "U.S. Shaped Italy's Styles, Pucci Feels," *The New York Times*, March 31, 1959.

163 "Countess Visconti": Virginia Pope, "Versatility Marks Foreign Fashions," *The New York Times*, November 14, 1951.

165 "Our workroom employees": Nan Robertson, "Happily Wed Pair Compete for Rome's Fashion Trade," *The New York Times*, October 19, 1955.

165 "Of course we discuss": "Happily Married Couple Success in Fashion, Too," *The New York Times*, October 26, 1960.

165 "Fabiani was depressed": Agnes Ash, "Simonetta Stunned to Find Fashion Trends Ignored," *The New York Times*, October 19, 1957.

166 "They wanted the movie stars": Nicola White, *Reconstructing Italian Fashion* (Oxford, Eng.: Berg, 2000), 138.

168 "When you dress people": Ibid., 139.

169 "cavorted hoydenishly": Lee Server, *Ava Gardner* (New York: St. Martin's Griffin, 2006), 287.

169 "The artfully wicked": Quoted in Bonizza Giordani Aragno, *Sorelle Fontana* (Rome: Promograph, 2005), 58.

170 "We are glad": Paul Hoffman, "Pope Blesses Fashion Workers; Urges 'Modest, Healthy' Styles," *The New York Times*, July 5, 1957.

173 "People love to grumble": Gloria Emerson, "Couturier 'Feud' in Italy Minimized by Simonetta," *The New York Times*, May 6, 1959.

173 "are trying to kill": Gloria Emerson, "Italy Begins Fall Shows with Feud," *The New York Times*, July 17, 1965.

176 "More Americans are visiting": Quoted in White, *Reconstructing Italian Fashion*, 54. The statistics in this paragraph come from ibid., 61.

CHAPTER 18: "A Fine Race Horse and a Goat"

181 "She has been involved": "Hollywood on the Tiber," *Time*, August 16, 1954.

CHAPTER 19: "A Charnel House Under a Green Marquee"

198 "swarms of gnats": "Hollywood on the Tiber," *Time*, August 16, 1954.

199 "At the top of Via Vittorio Veneto": H. V. Morton, *A Traveller in Rome* (New York: Da Capo Press, 2002), 71–72, 76.

199   "Only in modern Italy": Melton Davis, *All Rome Trembled* (New York: G. Putnam's Sons, 1957), 162.

200   "[T]his 'café society'": Ennio Flaiano, *The Via Veneto Papers*, trans. John Satriano (Marlboro, Vt.: The Marlboro Press, 1992), 3.

200   "This is no longer a street": Ibid., 4.

200   "So tonight it's Via Veneto": Quoted in Ennio Flaiano, *La Solitudine del Satiro* (Milan: Adelphi, 2013), 274.

202   "topographically protected from the assaults": Flaiano, *Via Veneto Papers*, 13.

204   "an effeminate, strange sort of chap": Roberto Orsi, *Rome After Dark* (New York: Macfadden, 1962), 83.

211   "Why can't you eat": Cleveland Amory, *Who Killed Society?* (New York: Harper & Brothers, 1960), 76.

211   "Are you seriously turning down": Linda Christian, *Linda: My Own Story* (New York: Dell, 1962), 195.

212   "Every time he comes in": Robert Daley, "Marquis at the Wheel," *The New York Times*, March 17, 1957.

213   "Racing is a vice": Alfonso de Portago, "Racing Is a Vice," *Sports Illustrated*, May 13, 1957.

213   "He's a dictator": *The Marquis de Portago: The Story of Racing's Most Colorful Driver* (London: Ace Records, 1997).

214   "I'm not interested in cars": John Christy, *Of Men and Cars* (New York: Ziff-Davis, 1960), 124.

214   "I want to live to be 105": Ibid., 130.

215   "If you have a conscience": Ibid., 134.

215   "As you know": Ibid., 135.

216   "I had a strange sensation": Christian, *Linda*, 220.

CHAPTER 21: "We Take Their Pictures and They Beat Us Up"

240   "The rumor had it": Francesca Taroni, *Paparazzi* (Paris: Assouline, 1998), 5.

240   "I felt myself being lifted": Ibid.

241   "Among the people we hunt": Aurelio Magistà, *Dolce Vita Gossip* (Milan: Bruno Mondadori, 2007), 19.

243   "I started shouting": Taroni, *Paparazzi*, 8.

244   "Now, there's our target": Tazio Secchiaroli, *"Li Fotografiamo e Loro ci Picchiano,"* *Settimo Giorno*, September 1958.

245   "I went up very close": Diego Mormorio, *Tazio Secchiaroli*, trans. Alexandra Bonfante-Warren (New York: Harry N. Abrams, 1999), 26.

CHAPTER 22: "The Most Sinful, Transgressive Thing"

248   "The first sign of Anitona": Roberto Orsi, *Rome After Dark* (New York: Macfadden, 1962), 71.

251   "What was happening before my very eyes": Diego Mormorio, *Tazio Secchiaroli*, trans. Alexandra Bonfante-Warren (New York: Harry N. Abrams, 1999), 32.

253   "'Nothing happened'": Victor Ciuffa, *La Dolce Vita Minuto per Minuto* (Rome: Ciuffa Editore, 2010), 100.

255   "lice of society": Quoted in Paul Hofmann, "Vatican Assails Rome Night Life," *The New York Times*, November 9, 1958.

CHAPTER 23: *Babylon, 2000 Years After Christ*

258   "The eye of Fellini": Gianna Preda, *Il 'Chi É' del Borghese* (Milan: Il Borghese, 1961), 201.

258   "He is an Italian man": Charlotte Chandler, *I, Fellini* (New York: Random House, 1995), 343.

258   "had a lot of fun": Quoted in Jean-Pierre Diufreigne, *Dolce Vita Style* (Paris: Assouline, 2005), 118.

259   "It was only after his death": Ibid.

260   "a conflagration in the culminating moment": Hollis Alpert, *Fellini* (New York: Atheneum, 1986), 141.

260   "I make a film": Federico Fellini, *Fellini on Fellini*, trans. Isabel Quigley (New York: Delta, 1977), 165.

260   "The movie business is macabre": Ibid., 159.

261   "The producer says": Chandler, *I, Fellini*, 113.

261   "It's always the same story": Robert Neville, "Poet-Director of the Sweet Life," *The New York Times*, May 14, 1961.

261   "*Gelsomina on a Bicycle*, or anything": Fellini, *Fellini on Fellini*, 88.

263   "is one of those journalists": Ennio Flaiano, *The Via Veneto Papers*, trans. John Satriano (Marlboro, Vt.: The Marlboro Press, 1992), 8.

264   "I could not cast a great star": Chandler, *I, Fellini*, 118.

265   "I had to do what was good": Ibid., 131.

266 "We have to make": Tullio Kezich, *Federico Fellini* (New York: Faber & Faber, 2006), 196.

266 "If you're looking for a precedent": Aurelio Magistà, *Dolce Vita Gossip* (Milan: Bruno Mondadori, 2007), 16.

266 "a portrait of Rome": John Francis Lane, *To Each His Own Dolce Vita* (Cambridge: Bear Claw Books, 2013 [ebook]).

267 "was carrying some pictures": Achille Bonito Oliva, *A Flash of Art* (Milan: Photology, 2004), 86.

267 "How they fixed": Fellini, *Fellini on Fellini*, 79.

268 "It seems certain that his film": Flaiano, *Via Veneto Papers*, 19.

268 "I thought, 'My God'": Federico Fellini, *Cinecittà*, trans. Graham Fawecett (London: Studio Vista, 1989), 113.

269 "I was experiencing again": Ibid.

271 "her splendor was incredible": Alessandra Stanley, "Still a Blond Bombshell, but of a Certain Age," *The New York Times*, June 13, 1999.

271 "They wanted me to go": Donald Dewey, *Marcello Mastroianni* (New York: Birch Lane, 1993), 74.

271 "It's only fair": "Everymantis," *Time*, October 5, 1962.

272 "was brilliant with actors": Eugene Archer, "Marcello Mastroianni: After *La Dolce Vita*," *The New York Times*, February 28, 1965.

273 "I need an ordinary face": Marcello Mastroianni, *Mi Ricordo, Sì Io Mi Ricordo* (Milan: Baldini & Castoldi, 1997), 65.

274 "I am very much like Marcello": Michael Stern, "Mastroianni: The Latin Who Put Laughter Back into Love," *Pageant*, January 1965.

274 "the adventures, by day": Fellini, *Cinecittà*, 39.

274 "The way he moved around the set": Dewey, *Marcello Mastroianni*, 100.

275 "She reminded him": Fellini, *Cinecittà*, 115.

276 "She was so full of ideas": Chandler, *I, Fellini*, 144.

278 "The term was a contraction": Elizabeth Day, "Paparazzi! How an Unloved Profession Has Shaped Us," *The Guardian*, March 1, 2014.

278 "buzzing . . . hovering, darting, singing": "Paparazzi on the Prowl," *Time*, April 14, 1961.

280 "a bloke with a little beret": Fellini, *Cinecittà*, 121.

281 "She was a horse": Stanley, "Still a Blond Bombshell."

281 "As a child": Dewey, *Marcello Mastroianni*, 101.

282 "As soon as a sequence was shot": Quoted in Diego Mormorio, *Tazio*

Secchiaroli, trans. Alexandra Bonfante-Warren (New York: Harry N. Abrams, 1999), 37.

283   "I got so used to it that my dislike": Federico Fellini, "End of the Sweet Parade," *Esquire*, January 1963.

284   "It had to be shocking": Chandler, *I, Fellini*, 126

285   "Please tell everyone that I have": Tullio Kezich, *Federico Fellini* (New York: Faber & Faber, 2006), 164.

285   "Federico, you're making a fool": Neville, "Poet-Director of the Sweet Life."

285   "She gripped the steering wheel": Fellini, *Cinecittà*, 115.

286   "It was like I was being administered": Henry Gris, "Marcello Mastroianni: A Married Star Talks About His Love Affairs," *Coronet*, July 1971.

CHAPTER 24: "Poor You"

288   "understood absolutely nothing": Quoted in Donald Dewey, *Marcello Mastroianni* (New York: Birch Lane, 1993), 101–2.

288   "Poor you": Tullio Kezich, *Federico Fellini* (New York: Faber & Faber, 2006), 215.

289   "*La Dolce Vita* was seismic": Ibid.

289   "Projects of this kind": Matilde Hochkofler, *Marcello Mastroianni* (Rome: Gremese, 2001), 45.

289   "an incentive to evil": Quoted in Domenico Monetti and Giuseppe Ricci, "*La Dolce Vita*" (Rome: Centro Sperimentale di Cinematografia, 2010), 247.

289   "One doesn't need": Kezich, *Federico Fellini*, 209.

289   "It would have been better": Aurelio Magistà, *Dolce Vita Gossip* (Milan: Bruno Mondadori, 2007), 171.

290   "a big white square": Kezich, *Federico Fellini*, 212.

290   "Fellini has made his best film": Quoted in Monetti and Ricci, "*La Dolce Vita*," 406.

290   "Those are aristocrats": Vittorio Boarini and Tullio Kezich, *Mezzo Secolo di Dolce Vita* (Rimini: Fondazione Federico Fellini, 2009), 19.

290   "boorish, the dream of a small-towner": Ibid.

291   "*Now* what are we going to do": Ibid, p. 31.

291   "One could almost say": Quoted in Eileen Lanouette Hughes, "*La Dolce Vita* of Federico Fellini," *Esquire*, August 1960.

291   "I'm sorry. These polemics": Federico Fellini, "*Sono un Peccatore anch'Io*," *L'Europeo*, February 21, 1960.

291   "What I intended was to show": "*Playboy* Interview: Federico Fellini," *Playboy*, February 1966.

291   "It's terryifying to realize": Charlotte Chandler, *I, Fellini* (New York: Random House, 1995), 253.

292   "It's like getting me to talk": Boarini and Kezich, *Mezzo Secola*, 30.

293   "It made many people rich": Chandler, *I, Fellini*, 132.

293   "a poignant social document": Murray Schumach, "Wyler Is Critical of Foreign Films," *The New York Times*, April 27, 1964

294   "Why would you applaud": Jean-Pierre Diufreigne, *Dolce Vita Style* (Paris: Assouline, 2005), 71.

302   "Maybe if somebody slapped her": Magistà, *Dolce Vita Gossip*, 5.

302   "I had invented": Federico Fellini, "*La Storia di Via Veneto*," *L'Europeo*, July 8, 1962.

304   "Up to that moment": Quoted in Andrea Nemiz, *La Ricosturzione* (Rome: Editori Riuniti, 1998), 69.

CHAPTER 25: "I Am Not a Sexy Pot"

318   "Each time I played": Warren G. Harris, *Sophia Loren* (New York: Simon & Schuster, 1998), 157.

319   "I am not a sexy pot": Mason Wiley and Damien Bona, *Inside Oscar*, 332.

319   "If I lost, I might faint": Harris, *Sophia Loren*, 176.

320   "Somebody else got it": A. E. Hotchner, *Sophia Loren* (New York: Bantam, 1979), 140.

CHAPTER 26: "You've Done It, You've Won"

321   "The last nine years": Gloria Emerson, "U.S. Shaped Italy's Styles, Pucci Feels," *The New York Times*, March 31, 1959.

322   "The reason I am going": Charlotte Curtis, "Skiwear Shows Only One of Pucci's Many Talents," *The New York Times*, April 26, 1963.

325   "the best known couturiers": "Simonetta and Fabiani Plan Joint Paris Salon," *The New York Times*, April 4, 1962.

326   "They are extemely well made": "Simonetta-Fabiani Team a Success," *The New York Times*, July 28, 1962.

328 "nothing not on view": Patricia Peterson, "Fashion Trends Abroad; Rome: Two Collections Outstanding," *The New York Times*, July 20, 1959.

329 "Valentino was incredibly seductive": Suzy Menkes, "Of Yachts, Chateaus, and a Special Tribe," *The New York Times*, December 16, 2013.

329 "I always felt": Ibid.

330 "My mother said": Guido Vergani, *Fashion Dictionary* (New York: Baldini Castoldi Dalai Editore, 2006), 1275.

CHAPTER 27: "A Ravenous Wolf Pack"

332 "I have come to learn who": Jack Brodsky and Nathan Weiss, *The Cleopatra Papers* (New York: Simon & Schuster), 69.

332 "It doesn't have to be salacious": Walter Wanger and Joe Hyams, *My Life with Cleopatra* (New York: Vintage, 2013), 151.

333 "a ravenous wolf pack": "Paparazzi on the Prowl," *Time*, April 14, 1961.

334 "It is very difficult to have an affair": Lyn Tornabene, "Lunch Date with Marcello Mastroianni," *Cosmopolitan*, December 1962.

334 "What annoys me": Achille Bonito Oliva, *A Flash of Art* (Milan, Photology, 2004), 332.

334 "It irritates me": Ibid., 314-15, 322.

335 "I make the Via Veneto": "Paparazzi on the Prowl."

CHAPTER 29: "There's No Erotic Charge in Me"

353 "The producers didn't want": Charlotte Chandler, *I, Fellini* (New York: Random House, 1995), 133.

354 "I am not a lover type": "*Playboy* Interview: Marcello Mastroianni," *Playboy*, July 1965.

354 "a mantis who has lost faith": "Everymantis," *Time*, October 5, 1962.

355 "Latin lover!": Marcello Mastroianni, *Mi Ricordo, Sì Io Mi Ricordo* (Milan: Baldini & Castoldi), 41.

355 "I am the *anti*-Gable": "*Playboy* Interview: Marcello Mastroianni."

355 "Something has happened": Michael Stern, "Mastroianni: The Latin Who Put Laughter Back into Love," *Pageant*, January 1965.

356 "He hates actors": Donald Dewey, *Marcello Mastroianni* (New York: Birch Lane, 1993), 116.

356 "Visconti was the Maestro": Ibid.

357   "It's the first word": Rex Reed, "Marcello Makes a Big Scandalo," *The New York Times*, June 21, 1970.

358   "What is being done": "Everymantis."

358   "She's one of the few women": "Playboy Interview: Marcello Mastroianni."

359   "It was like playing": Dewey, *Marcello Mastroianni*, 149.

360   "I feel like a train conductor": Quoted in Tullio Kezich, *Federico Fellini* (New York: Faber & Faber, 2006), 244.

CHAPTER 30: "We Are on Stage All the Time"

368   "Elizabeth Taylor . . . *is* the picture": Walter Wanger and Joe Hyams, *My Life with Cleopatra* (New York: Vintage, 2013), 1.

370   "the hardest three pictures": Quoted in ibid., 222.

370   "Our company on location": Ibid., 157.

371   "two actors who don't know": Jack Brodsky and Nathan Weiss, *The Cleopatra Papers* (New York: Simon & Schuster, 1963), 151.

CHAPTER 31: "Please Stop Crying!"

379   "I have a feeling": "The Talk of the Town," *The New Yorker*, July 6, 1963.

382   "The growing number": Enid Nemy, "Everything's Coming Up Pucci," *The New York Times*, February 23, 1966.

388   "Anyone in Rome": Diego Mormorio, *Tazio Secchiaroli*, trans. Alexandra Bonfante-Warren (New York: Harry N. Abrams, 1999), 39.

388   "A furious star": Marta Cattaneo, Elena Bajetta, and Timothy Stroud, *Fellini!* (Milan: Skira, 2003), 55.

390   "I detest people who arrive": Mormorio, *Tazio Secchiaroli*, 42.

391   "Someone makes a bitter film": Jean-Pierre Diufreigne, *Dolce Vita Style* (Paris: Assouline, 2005), 47.

Bibliography

HISTORY AND SETTING

Augias, Corrado. *The Secrets of Rome: Love and Death in the Eternal City.* New York: Rizzoli Ex Libris, 2007.

Barzini, Luigi. *The Italians.* New York: Penguin, 1968.

Bondanella, Peter. *The Eternal City: Roman Images in the Modern World.* Chapel Hill: University of North Carolina Press, 1987.

Calabrese, Omar. *War, Postwar, Reconstruction, Take-off.* Vol. 3 of *Modern Italy: Images and History of a National Identity.* Milan: Electra, 1984.

Calvenzi, Giovanna. *Italia: Portrait of a Country Throughout Sixty Years of Photography.* Rome: Contrasto, 2003.

Celant, Germano. *The Italian Metamorphosis: 1943–1968.* New York: Guggenheim Museum, 1994.

Chamberlin, Mary. *Dear Friends and Darling Romans.* Philadelphia: J. B. Lippincott, 1959.

Clark, Eleanor. *Rome and a Villa.* New York: Pantheon, 1974.

Duggan, Christopher. *The Force of Destiny: A History of Italy Since 1879.* Boston: Houghton Mifflin, 2008.

Fagiolo dell'Arco, Maurizio, and Claudia Terenzi. *Roma, 1948–1959: Arte, Cronaca e Cultura dal Neorealismo alla Dolce Vita.* Milan: Skira, 2002.

Ginsborg, Paul. *A History of Contemporary Italy: Society and Politics, 1943–1988.* London: Penguin, 1990.

Holmes, George. *The Oxford History of Italy.* Oxford: Oxford University Press, 1997.

Hughes, Robert. *Rome: A Cultural, Visual, and Personal History.* New York: Vintage, 2012.

Levi, Carlo. *Fleeting Rome: In Seach of La Dolce Vita.* Chichester: John Wiley & Sons, 2005.

Levine, Irving R. *Main Street, Italy.* New York: Doubleday, 1963.

Lewis, Norman. *Naples '44: A World War II Diary of Occupied Italy.* New York: Carroll & Graf, 2005.

Maraniss, David. *Rome 1960: The Olympics That Changed the World.* New York: Simon & Schuster, 2008.

Montanelli, Indro. *Romans Without Laurels: A New Perspective on Their Rise and Fall.* London: Pantheon, 1962.

Morton, H. V. *A Traveller in Rome.* New York: Da Capo Press, 2002.

Nemiz, Andrea. *La Ricosturzione, 1945–1953.* Rome: Editori Riuniti, 1998.

Olmoti, Giorgio. *Il Boom, 1954–1967.* Rome: Editori Riuniti, 1998.

Packard, Reynolds. *Rome Was My Beat.* Secaucus, N.J.: Lyle Stuart, 1975.

Salwa, Ursula, and Attilio Wanderlingh. *Roma Nella "Dolce Vita."* Naples: Edizione Intra Moenia, 2011.

Sheridan, Michael. *Romans: Their Lives and Times.* London: Phoenix, 1995.

Stern, Michael. *An American in Rome.* New York: Bernard Geis, 1964.

PAPARAZZI AND JOURNALISM

Ciuffa, Victor. *La Dolce Vita Minuto per Minuto: Tutta la Verità su un Fenomeno Falsato.* Rome: Ciuffa Eidtore, 2010.

Costantini, Paolo, Silvio Fuso, Sandro Mescola, and Italo Zannier. *Paparazzi.* Florence: Fratelli Alinari, 1988.

Howe, Peter. *Paparazzi.* New York: Artisan, 2005.

Jay, Bill. "The Photographer as Aggressor." In *Observations: Essays on Documentary Photography,* edited by David Featherstone. Carmel, Calif.: The Friends of Photography, 1984.

Magistà, Aurelio. *Dolce Vita Gossip: Star, Amori, Mondanità e Kolossal Negli Anni d'Oro di Cinecittà.* Milan: Bruno Mondadori, 2007.

Mormorio, Diego. *Tazio Secchiaroli: Greatest of the Paparazzi.* Translated by Alexandra Bonfante-Warren. New York: Harry N. Abrams, 1999.

Nemiz, Andrea. *Vita da Paparazzo Rino Barillari, Il "King."* Rome: Nuova Arnica Editrice, 1997.

——. *Vita, Dolce Vita.* Rome: Network Edizione, 1983.

Oliva, Achille Bonito. *A Flash of Art: Action Photography in Rome, 1953–1973.* Milan: Photology, 2004.

Russo, Giovanni. *Con Flaiano e Fellini a Via Veneto: Dalla "Dolce Vita" alla Roma di Oggi.* Soveria Mannelli, Italy: Rubbettino, 2005.

Scalfari, Eugenio. *La Sera Andavamo in Via Veneto: Storia di un Gruppo dal "Mondo" alla "Repubblica."* Turin: Einaudi, 2009.

Squires, Carol. "Original Sin: The Birth of the Paparazzo." In *Exposed: Voyeurism, Surveillance, and the Camera Since 1870,* edited by Sandra S. Phillips. San Francisco: San Francisco Museum of Modern Art, 2010.

Taroni, Francesca. *Paparazzi: The Early Years.* Paris: Assouline, 1998.

FASHION AND STYLE

Adinolfi, Francesco. *Mondo Exotica: Sounds, Visions, Obsessions of the Cocktail Generation.* Translated by Karen Pinkus with Jason Vivrette. Durham, N.C.: Duke University Press, 2008.

Bender, Marilyn. *The Beautiful People.* New York, Coward-McCann, 1967.

Börnsen-Holtman, Nina. *Italian Design.* Cologne: Taschen, 1994.

Carter, Ernestine. *Magic Names of Fashion.* Englewood Cliffs, N.J.: Prentice Hall, 1980.

Cawthorne, Nigel. *Sixties Source Book: A Visual Guide to the Style of a Decade.* Rochester, Eng.: Grange, 1998.

Diufreigne, Jean-Pierre. *Dolce Vita Style.* Paris: Assouline, 2005.

Giordani Aragno, Bonizza. *Sorelle Fontana: Lo Stile dell'Alta Moda Italiana.* Rome: Promograph, 2005.

Gnoli, Sofia. *Fernanda Gattinoni: Moda e Stelle ai Tempi della Hollywood sul Tevere.* Milan: Silvana Editoriale, 2011.

Gundle, Stephen. *Bellissima: Feminine Beauty and the Idea of Italy.* New Haven: Yale University Press, 2007.

Jackson, Lesley. *The Sixties: Decade of Design Revolution*. London: Phaidon, 1998.

Malossi, Giannino. *Volare: The Icon of Italy in Global Pop Culture*. New York: Monacelli Press, 1999.

Paulicelli, Eugenia. *Fashion Under Fascism: Beyond the Black Shirt*. Oxford, Eng.: Berg, 2004.

Stanfill, Sonnet. *The Glamour of Italian Fashion Since 1945*. London: Victoria and Albert Museum, 2014.

Steele, Valerie. *Fashion, Italian Style*. New Haven: Yale University Press, 2003.

Vergani, Guido. *Fashion Dictionary*. New York: Baldini Castoldi Dalai Editore, 2006.

White, Nicola. *Reconstructing Italian Fashion: America and the Development of the Italian Fashion Industry*. Oxford, Eng.: Berg, 2000.

MOVIES AND MOVIE PEOPLE

Affron, Charles, ed. *8½*. New Brunswick, N.J.: Rutgers University Press, 1987.

Alpert, Hollis. *Fellini: A Life*. New York: Atheneum, 1986.

Bertelli, Giovanna. *Divi e Paparazzi: La Dolce Vita di Fellini*. Genoa: Le Mani, 2009.

——. *Marcello Mastroianni Nelle Fotografie di Tazio Secchiaroli*. Azzano San Paolo, Italy: Bolis, 2006.

Bondanella, Peter. *Italian Cinema from Neorealism to the Present*. Rev. ed. New York: Continuum, 1990.

Boarini, Vittorio, and Tullio Kezich. *Fellini: Mezzo Secolo di Dolce Vita*. Rimini: Fondazione Federico Fellini, 2009.

Brodsky, Jack, and Nathan Weiss. *The Cleopatra Papers: A Private Correspondence (1963)*. New York: Simon & Schuster, 1963.

Buford, Kate. *Burt Lancaster: An American Life*. New York: Alfred A. Knopf, 2000.

Caldiron, Orio. *C'Era una Volta il '48: La Grande Stagione del Cinema Italiano*. Rome: Minimum Fax, 2008.

Cattaneo, Marco. *Cinecittà: The Magic Never Ends*. Rome: National Geographic Italia, 2013.

Cattaneo, Marta, Elena Bajetta, and Timothy Stroud. *Fellini!* Milan: Skira, 2003.

Chandler, Charlotte. *I, Fellini*. New York: Random House, 1995.

Chrissochiodis, Ilias. *The Cleopatra Files: Selected Documents from the Spyros P. Skouras Archive*. Stanford, Calif.: Brave World, 2013.

Christian, Linda. *Linda: My Own Story*. New York: Dell, 1962.

D'Avino, Mauro. *Roma, Si Gira! Gli Scorci Ritrovati del Cinema di Ieri*. Rome: Gremese, 2012.

Della Casa, Stefano. *Capitani Coraggiosi: Produttori Italiani, 1945–1975*. Milan: Mondadori Electa, 2003.

Della Casa, Stefano, and Dario E. Viganò. *Hollywood sul Tevere: Anatomia di un Fenomeno*. Milan: Mondadori Electa, 2010.

Dewey, Donald. *Marcello Mastroianni: His Life and Times*. New York: Birch Lane, 1993.

Di Biagi, Flaminio. *Il Cinema a Roma: Guida alla Storia e ai Luoghi del Cinema Nella Capitale*. Rome: Palombi Editori, 2003.

———. *La Roma di Fellini*. Genoa: Le Mani, 2008.

Evans, Peter, and Ava Gardner. *Ava Gardner: The Secret Conversations*. New York: Simon & Schuster, 2013.

Fallaci, Oriana. *I Sette Peccati di Hollywood*. Milan: BUR, 2009.

Fellini, Federico. *The Book of Dreams*. Milan: Rizzoli, 2007.

———. *Cinecittà*. Translated by Graham Fawecett. London: Studio Vista, 1989.

———. *La Dolce Vita*. Translated by Oscar DeLiso and Bernard Shir-Cliff. New York: Ballantine, 1961.

———. *Fare un Film*. Turin: Einaudi, 1993.

———. *Fellini on Fellini*. Translated by Isabel Quigley, New York: Delta, 1977.

———. *Il Viaggio di G. Mastorna*. Macerata, Italy: Quodlibet, 2008.

Flaiano, Ennio. *La Solitudine del Satiro*. Milan: Adelphi, 2013.

———. *The Via Veneto Papers*. Translated by John Satriano. Marlboro, Vt.: Marlboro Press, 1992.

García Márquez, Gabriel. "El Papa Dio Audiencia a Sofia Loren; Se Pohibieron las Fotos," "Sin Dispapar un Tiro, Gina Gana a Sofia Loren su Primera Batalla," "Gina, un Simbolo Nacional," and "La Batalla la Decidera el Publico." In *Crónicas y Reportajes*. Bogotá: Oveja Negra, 1985.

Gardner, Ava. *My Story*. New York: Bantam, 1990.

Harris, Warren G. *Sophia Loren*. New York: Simon & Schuster, 1998.

Hochkofler, Matilde. *Marcello Mastroianni: The Fun of Cinema*. Rome: Gremese, 2001.

Hotchner, A. E. *Sophia: Living and Loving, Her Own Story*. New York: Bantam, 1979.

Iarussi, Oscar. *C'Era una Volta il Futuro: L'Italia della Dolce Vita*. Bologna: Il Mulino, 2007.

Kaufman, Hank, and Gene Lerner. *Hollywood sul Tevere*. Milan: Sperling & Kupfer, 1980.

Kezich, Tullio. *"La Dolce Vita" di Federico Fellini*. Bologna: Cappelli Editori, 1960.

———. *Federico Fellini: His Life and Work*. New York: Faber & Faber, 2006.

———. *Primavera a Cinecittà: Il Cinema Italiano alla Svolta della "Dolce Vita."* Rome: Bulzoni, 1999.

———. *Su La Dolce Vita con Federico Fellini*. Venice: Marsilio, 1996.

Knox, Mickey. *The Good, the Bad and the Dolce Vita: The Adventures of an Actor in Hollywood, Paris, and Rome*. New York: Nation Books, 2004.

LeRoy, Mervyn, and Dick Kleiner. *Mervyn LeRoy: Take One*. New York: Hawthorn Books, 1974.

Levy, Alan. *Forever, Sophia*. New York: Tempo Star, 1979.

Liehm, Mira. *Passion and Defiance: Film in Italy from 1942 to the Present*. Berkeley: University of California Press, 1984.

Lo Duca. *Sweet Life*. Translated by Mervyn Savill. London: World Distributors, 1960.

Loren, Sophia. *Yesterday, Today, Tomorrow: My Life*. New York: Atria, 2014.

Malerba, Luigi, and Carmine Siniscalco. *Fifty Years of Italian Cinema*. Rome: Carlo Bestetti, 1954.

Mann, William J. *How to Be a Movie Star: Elizabeth Taylor in Hollywood*. Boston: Houghton Mifflin Harcourt, 2009.

Mastroianni, Marcello. *Mi Ricordo, Sì Io Mi Ricordo*. Milan: Baldini & Castoldi, 1997.

Monetti, Domenico, and Giuseppe Ricci. *"La Dolce Vita": Raccontato Dagli Archivi Rizzoli*. Rome: Centro Sperimentale di Cinematografia, 2010.

———. *"8½": Raccontato Dagli Archivi Rizzoli*. Rome: Centro Sperimentale di Cinematografia, 2008.

Pasolini, Pier Paolo. *Stories from the City of God: Sketches and Chronicles of Rome, 1950–1966*. Edited by Walter Siti; translated by Marina Hass. New York: Handsel Books, 2003.

Pettigrew, Damian. *I'm a Born Liar: A Fellini Lexicon*. New York: Harry N. Abrams, 2003.

Reich, Jacqueline. *Beyond the Latin Lover: Marcello Mastroianni, Masculinity, and Italian Cinema*. Bloomington: Indiana University Press, 2004.

Rhodes, John David. *Stupendous, Miserable City: Pasolini's Rome*. Minneapolis: University of Minnesota Press, 2007.

Rohdie, Sam. *Fellini Lexicon*. London: BFI, 2002.

Rondi, Gian Luigi. *Italian Cinema Today: 1952–1965*. New York: Hill & Wang, 1966.

Secchiaroli, Tazio. *Fellini 8½*. Milan: Federico Motta Editore, 1999.

——. *G. Mastorna, Opera Incompiuta*. Palermo: Sellerio, 2000.

Server, Lee. *Ava Gardner: "Love Is Nothing."* New York: St. Martin's Griffin, 2006.

Small, Pauline. *Sophia Loren: Moulding the Star*. Bristol, Eng.: Intellect, 2009.

Solmi, Angelo. *Fellini*. New York: Humanities Press, 1967.

Stritch, Christian. *Fellini's Faces*. Zurich: Diogenes, 1981.

Tatò, Francesco. *The Stuff That Dreams Are Made Of: The Films of Marcello Mastroianni*. Rome: Cinecittà International, 1998.

Tornabuoni, Lietta. *Federico Fellini*. New York: Rizzoli, 1995.

Verdone, Mario. *Il Cinema a Roma*. Rome: Edilazio, 2003.

Vermilye, Jerry. *Great Italian Films*. New York: Citadel Press, 1994.

Wanger, Walter, and Joe Hyams. *My Life with Cleopatra: The Making of a Hollywood Classic*. New York: Vintage, 2013.

Wiley, Mason, and Damien Bona. *Inside Oscar: The Unofficial History of the Academy Awards*. New York: Ballantine, 1987.

NAMES AND FACES

Albertini, Andrea, Silvia Pesci, and Giuseppe Villirillo. *Caffè and Stars*. Bologna: Damiani, 2004.

Altomonte, Antonio. *Roma: Diario a Piú Voci*. Milan: Bietti, 1974.

Amory, Cleveland. *Who Killed Society?* New York: Harper & Brothers, 1960.

Barrow, Andrew. *Gossip, 1920–1970*. New York: Coward, McCann & Geoghegan, 1979.

Bayley, Stephen. *La Dolce Vita: The Golden Age of Italian Style and Celebrity*. London: Fiell, 2011.

Christy, John. *Of Men and Cars*. New York: Ziff-Davis, 1960.

Delli Carri, Luca. *Gli Indisciplinati: Vivere e Morire su una Ferrari: Cinque Storie di Giovani Piloti*. Milan: Fucina, 2001.

Dolcini, Carlo. *Mille Miglia 1957: L'Ultimo Atto di una Corsa Leggendaria*. Milan: Giorgrio Nada Editore, 2011.

Fallaci, Oriani. *Gli Antipatici*. Milan: BUR, 2009.

Gasparini, Marco. *La Dolce Vita: '60s Lifestyle in Rome*. Florence: Scala, 2011.

Lanza di Trabia, Raimonda, and Ottavia Casagrande. *Mi Toccherà Ballare: L'Ultimo Principe di Trabia*. Milan: Feltrinelli, 2014.

Leigh, Dorian, with Laura Hobe. *The Girl Who Had Everything*. New York: Bantam, 1980.

Malossi, Giannino, ed. *Latin Lover: The Passionate South*. Milan, Charta, 1995.

McDonough, Ed. *Marquis de Portago: The Legend*. Coventry, Eng.: Mercian Manuals, 2006.

McLeave, Hugh. *The Last Pharaoh: Farouk of Egypt*. New York: McCall, 1969.

Moats, Alice-Leone. *The Million Dollar Studs*. New York: Delacorte Press, 1977.

Montagner, Lorenzo. *De Portago: Il Pianto del Drake*. Mantua: Editorial Sometti, 2007.

Moretti, Ugo. *Artists in Rome: Tales of the Babuino*. Translated by William Weaver. New York: Macmillan, 1958.

Napolitano, Gian Gaspare. *Un Tavolo a Via Veneto*. Rome: Rendina, 2000.

Nolan, William F., and Charles Beaumont. *When Engines Roar*. New York: Bantam, 1964.

Preda, Gianna. *Il 'Chi È' del Borghese: Vecchi Fusti e Nuovi Fusti*. Milan: Il Borghese, 1961.

Stadiem, William. *Too Rich: The High Life and Tragic Death of King Farouk*. New York: Carroll & Graf, 1991.

Stern, Michael, *Farouk*. New York: Bantam, 1965.

Yates, Brock. *Enzo Ferrari: The Man and the Machines*. New York: Bantam, 1992.

CRIME AND VICE

Costantini, Costanzo. *Sangue Sulla Dolce Vita*. Rome: L'Airone Editrice, 2006.

Davis, Melton. *All Rome Trembled: The Strange Affair of Wilma Montesi*. New York: G. P. Putnam's Sons, 1957.

Gundel, Stephen. *Death and the Dolce Vita: The Dark Side of Rome in the 1950s*. Edinburgh: Canongate, 2011.

Orsi, Roberto. *Rome After Dark*. New York: Macfadden, 1962.

Pinkus, Karen. *The Montesi Scandal: The Death of Wilma Montesi and the Birth of the Paparazzi in Fellini's Rome*. Chicago: University of Chicago Press, 2003.

Sanvitale, Fabio, and Armano Palmegiani. *Morte a Via Veneto: Storie di Assassissini, Tradimenti e Dolce Vita*. Rome: Sovera Edizioni, 2012.

Stern, Michael. *No Innocence Abroad*. New York: Random House, 1953.

Young, Wayland. *The Montesi Scandal*. Garden City, N.Y.: Doubleday, 1958.

INSTRUCTIVE DIVERSIONS

Bartolini, Luigi. *Ladri di Biciclette*. Florence: Vallecchi Editore, 1954.

Gadda, Carlo Emilio. *That Awful Mess on the Via Merulana*. Translated by William Weaver. New York: New York Review of Books, 2007.

Horace. *Satires and Epistles*. Translated by Niall Rudd. London: Penguin, 1979.

Juvenal. *The Satires of Juvenal*. Translated by Rolfe Humphries. Bloomington: Indiana University Press, 1958.

Moravia, Alberto. *Boredom*. Translated by Angus Davidson. New York: New York Review of Books, 1999.

———. *Contempt*. Translated by Angus Davidson. London: Prion, 1999.

———. *Racconti Romani*. Milan: Bompiani, 2014.

Pasolini, Pier Paolo. *Poesie*. Milan: Garzanti, 1999.

———. *The Ragazzi*. Translated by Emile Capouya. London: Paladin, 1989.

———. *Roman Poems*. Translated by Lawrence Ferlinghetti and Francesca Valenti. San Francisco: City Lights, 1986.

Pavese, Cesare. "The Beach." In *The Selected Works of Cesare Pavese*, translated by R. W. Flint. New York: Farrar, Straus & Giroux, 1968.

Petronius. *The Satyricon*. Translated by William Arrowsmith. New York: Meridian, 1994.

Rachman, Tom. *The Imperfectionists*. New York: Dial Press, 2010.

Shaw, Irwin. *Two Weeks in Another Town*. New York: Random House, 1960.

Spark, Muriel. *The Public Image*. New York: Alfred A. Knopf, 1968.

Walter, Jess. *Beautiful Ruins*. New York: HarperCollins, 2012.

FILMS WATCHED

NOTE: Titles are given in Italian unless a film has a commonly used English title. After the director's name, the release date listed for each film is that in the country of origin.

Accattone (Pier Paolo Pasolini, 1961).

Adua e le Compagne (Antonio Pietrangeli, 1960).

Alina (Giorgio Pastina, 1950).

Amarcord (Federico Fellini, 1973).

An American in Rome (Steno, 1954).

Amore (Roberto Rossellini, 1948).

L'Avventura (Michelangelo Antonioni, 1960).

The Barefoot Contessa (Joseph L. Mankiewicz, 1954).

Beat the Devil (John Huston, 1953).

Bell'Antonio (Mauro Bolognini, 1960).

Bellissima (Luchino Visconti, 1952).

Ben-Hur (William Wyler, 1959).

The Bicycle Thief (Vittorio De Sica, 1948).

Il Bidone (Federico Fellini, 1955).

Big Deal on Madonna Street (Mario Monicelli, 1958).

Bitter Rice (Giuseppe De Santis, 1949).

Boccaccio '70 (Vittorio De Sica, Federico Fellini, Mario Monicelli, and Luchino Visconti, 1962).

Il Boom (Vittorio De Sica, 1963).

City of Women (Federico Fellini, 1980).

Cleopatra (Joseph L. Mankiewicz, 1963).

The Clowns (Federico Fellini, 1970).

La Commare Secca (Bernardo Bertolucci, 1962).

Contempt (Jean-Luc Godard, 1963).

Divorce Italian Style (Pietro Germi, 1961).

La Dolce Vita (Federico Fellini, 1960).

L'Eclisse (Michelangelo Antonioni, 1962).

8½ (Federico Fellini, 1963).

Europa '51 (Roberto Rossellini, 1952).

The Facts of Murder (Pietro Germi, 1959).

Fanfan la Tulipe (Christian-Jaque, 1952).

Fellini's Casanova (Federico Fellini, 1976).

Fellini's Roma (Federico Fellini, 1972).

Four Ways Out (Pietro Germi, 1951).

Gidget Goes to Rome (Paul Wendkos, 1963).

Ginger and Fred (Federico Fellini, 1986).

Il Grido (Michelangelo Antonioni, 1957).

The Gold of Naples (Vittorio De Sica, 1954).

The Great Beauty (Paolo Sorrentino, 2013).

Hands over the City (Francesco Rosi, 1963).

Intervista (Federico Fellini, 1987).

Juliet of the Spirits (Federico Fellini, 1965).

La Loi (Jules Dassin, 1959).

Love in the City (Michelangelo Antonioni, Federico Fellini, Alberto Lattuada, Carlo Lizzani, Francesco Maselli, Dino Risi, and Cesare Zavattini, 1953).

Mamma Roma (Pier Paolo Pasolini, 1962).

Marcello Mastroianni: Mi Ricordo, Si, Io Mi Ricordo (Anna Maria Tatò, 1997).

Marriage Italian Style (Vittorio De Sica, 1964).

La Notte (Michelangelo Antonioni, 1961).

La Notte Brava (Mauro Bolognini, 1959).

Le Notti Bianche (Luchino Visconti, 1957).

The Organizer (Mario Monicelli, 1963).

Paisan (Roberto Rossellini, 1946).

Rocco and His Brothers (Luchino Visconti, 1960).

Ro.Go.Pa.G. (Jean-Luc Godard, Ugo Gregoretti, Pier Paolo Pasolini, and Roberto Rossellini, 1963).

Roman Holiday (William Wyler, 1953).

Rome: Open City (Roberto Rossellini, 1945).

The Rose Tattoo (Daniel Mann, 1955).

Shoeshine (Vittorio De Sica, 1946).

Il Sorpasso (Dino Risi, 1962).

Stazione Termini (Vittorio De Sica, 1953).

Story of a Love Affair (Michelangelo Antonioni, 1950).

La Strada (Federico Fellini, 1954).

Stromboli (Roberto Rossellini, 1950).

Three Coins in the Fountain (Jean Negulesco, 1954).

Too Bad She's Bad (Alessandro Blasetti, 1954).

Two Nights with Cleopatra (Mario Mattoli, 1954).

Two Weeks in Another Town (Vincente Minnelli, 1962).

Two Women (Vittorio De Sica, 1960).

Umberto D (Vittorio De Sica, 1952).

Valentino: The Last Emperor (Matt Tyrnauer, 2008).

Variety Lights (Federico Fellini and Alberto Lattuada, 1950).

I Vinti (Michelangelo Antonioni, 1953).

I Vitelloni (Federico Fellini, 1953).

Voyage in Italy (Roberto Rossellini, 1954).

We All Loved Each Other So Much (Ettore Scola, 1974).

What a Woman! (Alessandro Blasetti, 1956).

The White Sheik (Federico Fellini, 1952).

Yesterday, Today and Tomorrow (Vittorio De Sica, 1963).

Illustration Credits

INSERT 2

King Farouk and Irma Capece Minutolo (Photofest).

Sophia Loren and Marcello Mastroianni in *Too Bad She's Bad* (Photofest).

Valentino (Reporters Associati & Archivi/Mondadori Portfolio/Bridgeman Images).

Fon de Portago and Linda Christian (Interfoto).

Walter Chiari and Tazio Secchiaroli (Courtesy of David Secchiaroli).

Anthony Steel (Courtesy of David Secchiaroli).

William Wyler and Federico Fellini (©age footstock).

Federico Fellini and paparazzi (Courtesy of David Secchiaroli).

Aiche Nana striptease (Courtesy of David Secchiaroli).

Belinda Lee and Filippo Orsini (Photofest).

Anita Ekberg during the production of *La Dolce Vita* (Publicity Still Courtesy of Astor Pictures).

The Kiss (*La Dolce Vita*) (Publicity Still Courtesy of Astor Pictures).

The Fish (*La Dolce Vita*) (Publicity Still Courtesy of Astor Pictures).

Anita Ekberg attacks paparazzi (Photofest).

Sophia Loren, Carlo Ponti, and Vittorio De Sica celebrate her Oscar (Photofest).

Elizabeth Taylor and Richard Burton (ImageCollect).

Index